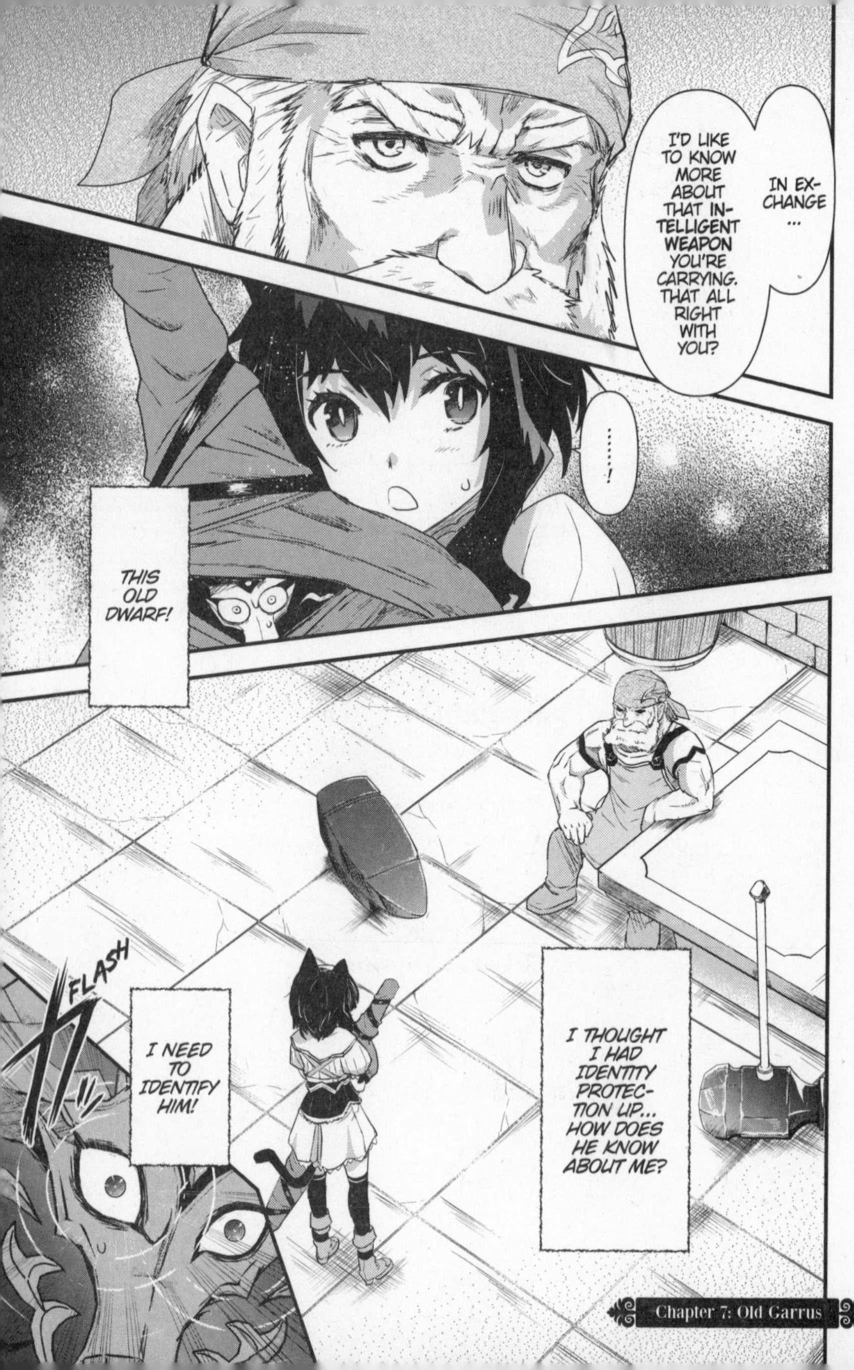
IN EX-CHANGE...
I'D LIKE TO KNOW MORE ABOUT THAT INTELLIGENT WEAPON YOU'RE CARRYING. THAT ALL RIGHT WITH YOU?
......!
THIS OLD DWARF!
I THOUGHT I HAD IDENTITY PROTECTION UP... HOW DOES HE KNOW ABOUT ME?
I NEED TO IDENTIFY HIM!
FLASH
Chapter 7: Old Garrus

Chapter 7: Old Garrus

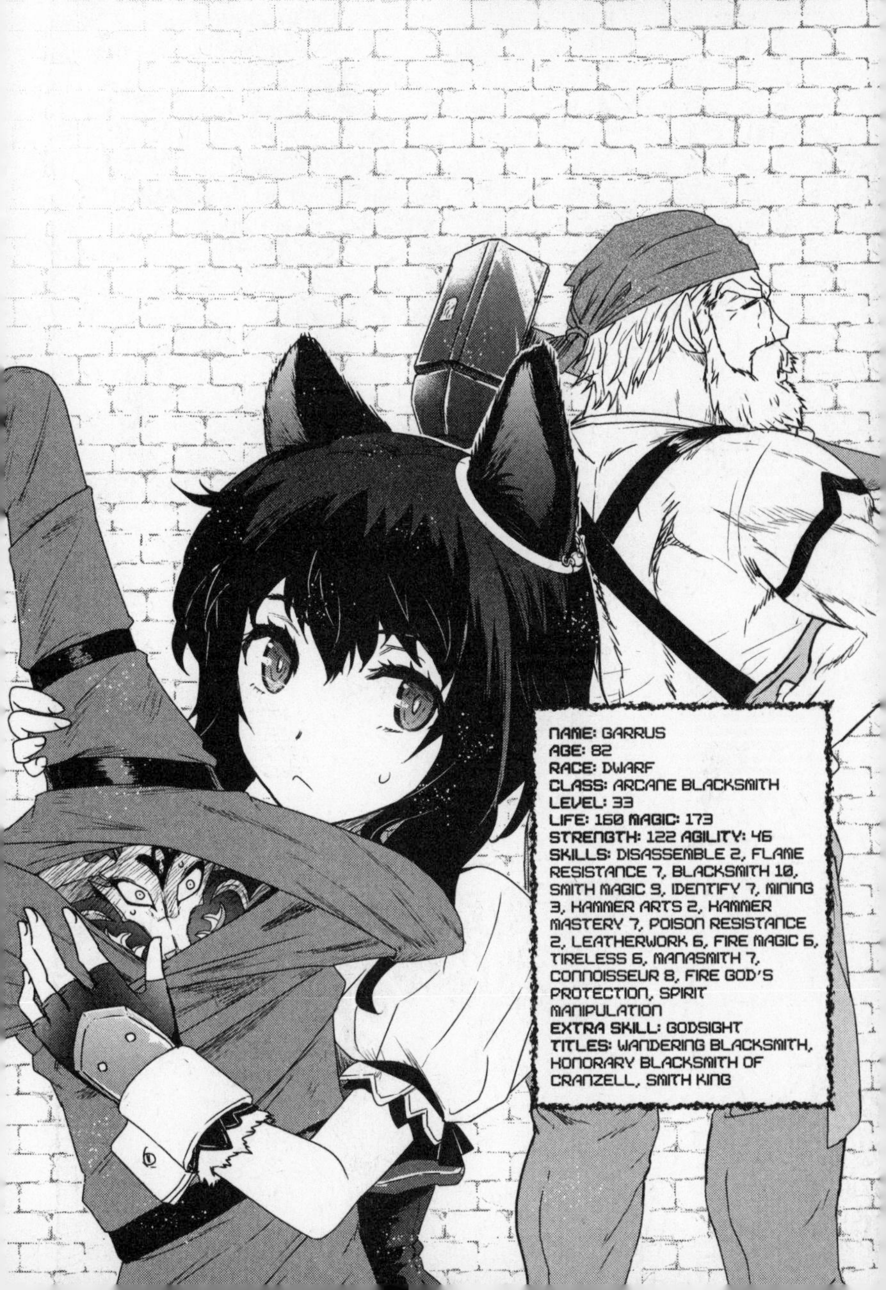
NAME: GARRUS
AGE: 82
RACE: DWARF
CLASS: ARCANE BLACKSMITH
LEVEL: 33
LIFE: 160 MAGIC: 173
STRENGTH: 122 AGILITY: 46
SKILLS: DISASSEMBLE 2, FLAME RESISTANCE 7, BLACKSMITH 10, SMITH MAGIC 9, IDENTIFY 7, MINING 3, HAMMER ARTS 2, HAMMER MASTERY 7, POISON RESISTANCE 2, LEATHERWORK 6, FIRE MAGIC 6, TIRELESS 6, MANASMITH 7, CONNOISSEUR 8, FIRE GOD'S PROTECTION, SPIRIT MANIPULATION
EXTRA SKILL: GODSIGHT
TITLES: WANDERING BLACKSMITH, HONORARY BLACKSMITH OF CRANZELL, SMITH KING

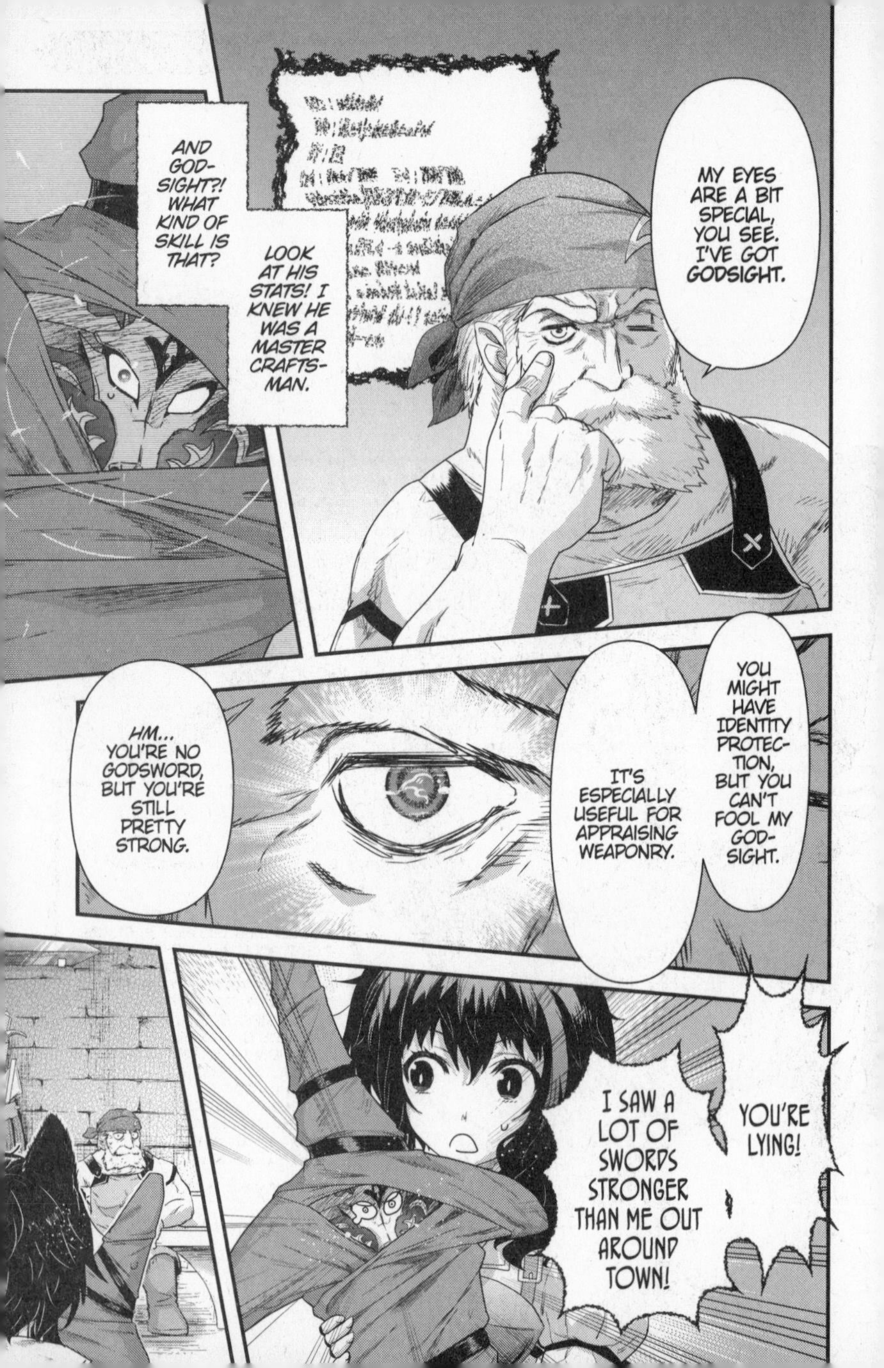
MY EYES ARE A BIT SPECIAL, YOU SEE. I'VE GOT GODSIGHT.
LOOK AT HIS STATS! I KNEW HE WAS A MASTER CRAFTSMAN.
AND GODSIGHT?! WHAT KIND OF SKILL IS THAT?
YOU MIGHT HAVE IDENTITY PROTECTION, BUT YOU CAN'T FOOL MY GODSIGHT.
IT'S ESPECIALLY USEFUL FOR APPRAISING WEAPONRY.
HM... YOU'RE NO GODSWORD, BUT YOU'RE STILL PRETTY STRONG.
YOU'RE LYING!
I SAW A LOT OF SWORDS STRONGER THAN ME OUT AROUND TOWN!

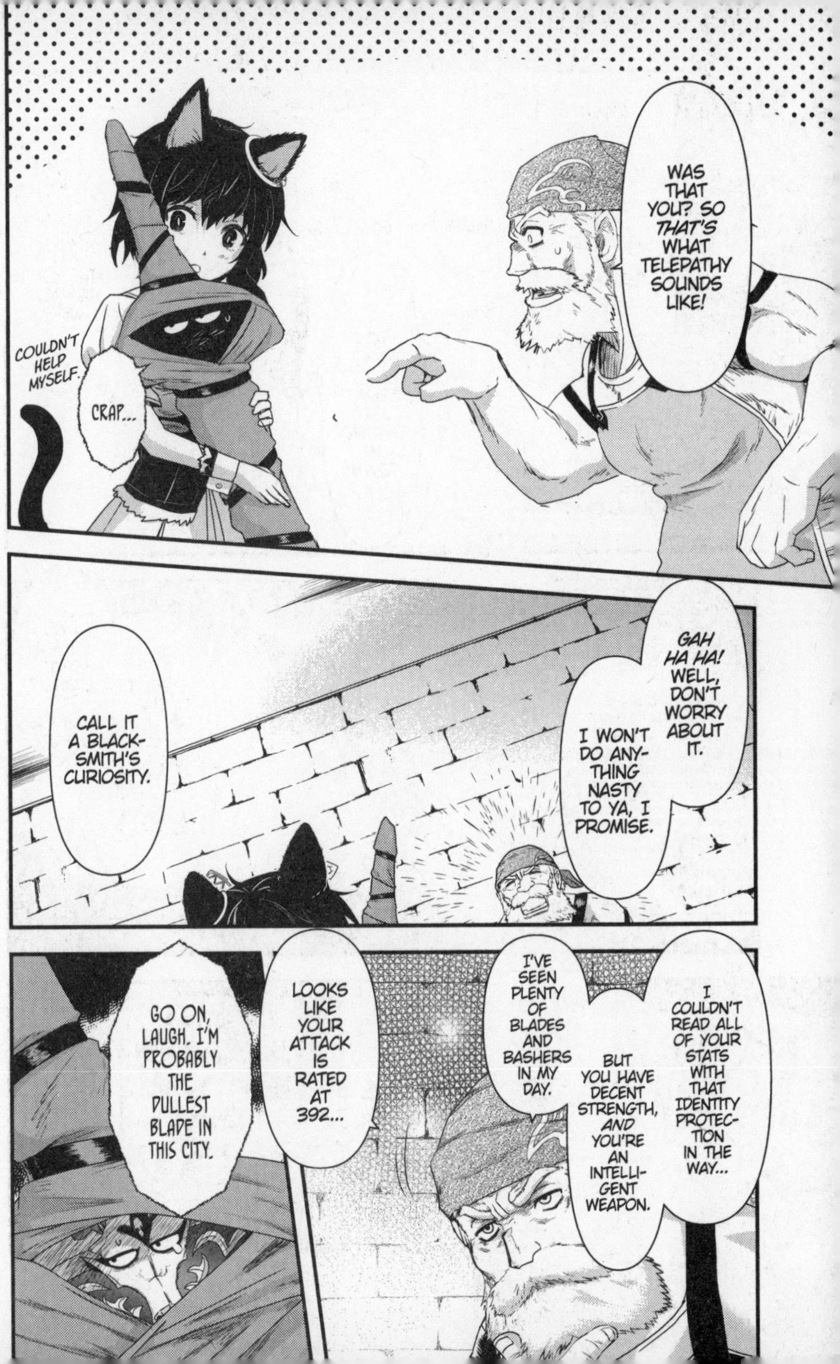
WAS THAT YOU? SO *THAT'S* WHAT TELEPATHY SOUNDS LIKE!
COULDN'T HELP MYSELF.
CRAP...
GAH HA HA! WELL, DON'T WORRY ABOUT IT.
I WON'T DO ANYTHING NASTY TO YA, I PROMISE.
CALL IT A BLACKSMITH'S CURIOSITY.
I COULDN'T READ ALL OF YOUR STATS WITH THAT IDENTITY PROTECTION IN THE WAY...
I'VE SEEN PLENTY OF BLADES AND BASHERS IN MY DAY.
BUT YOU HAVE DECENT STRENGTH, *AND* YOU'RE AN INTELLIGENT WEAPON.
LOOKS LIKE YOUR ATTACK IS RATED AT 392...
GO ON, LAUGH. I'M PROBABLY THE DULLEST BLADE IN THIS CITY.

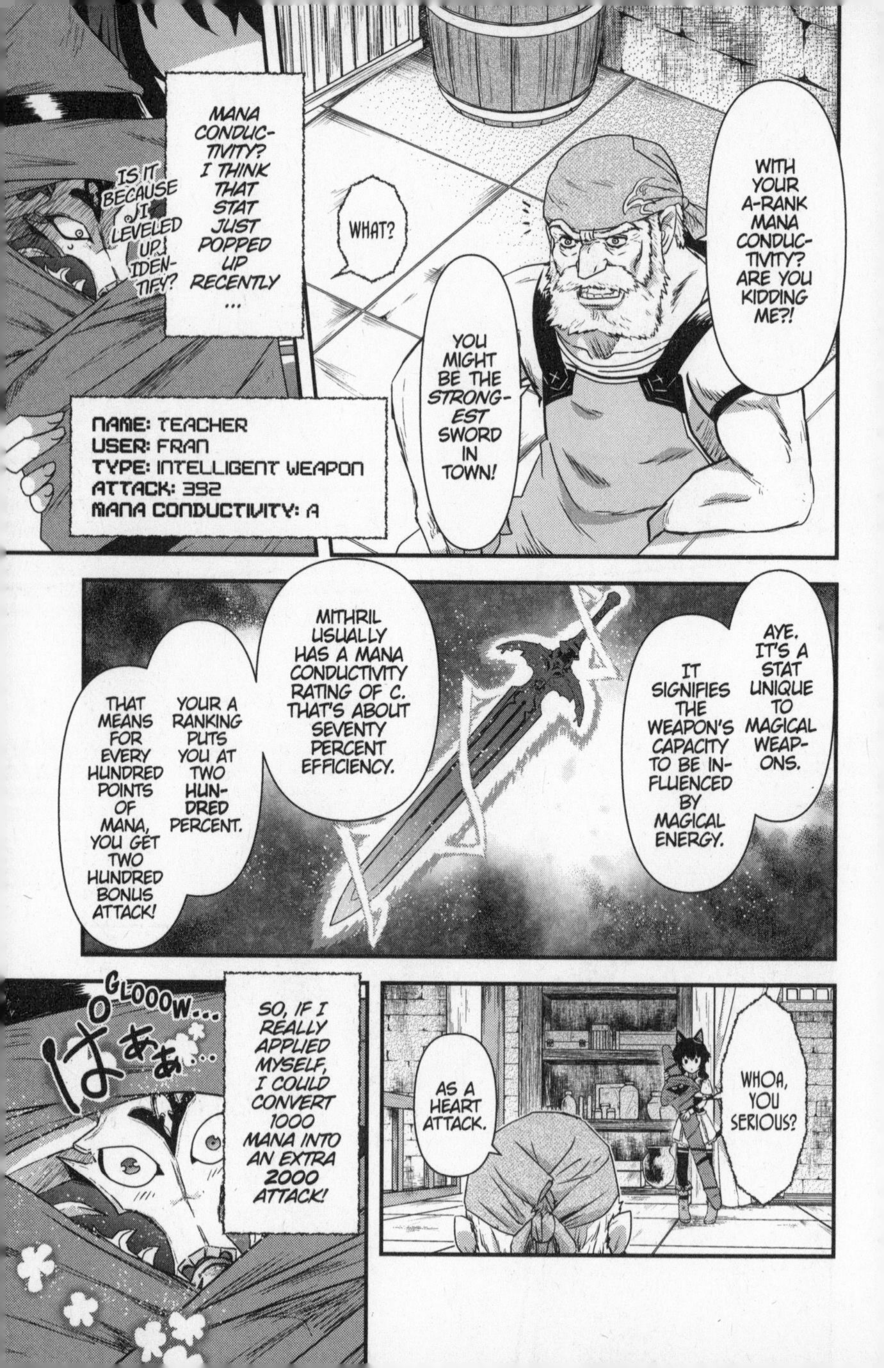
WITH YOUR A-RANK MANA CONDUCTIVITY? ARE YOU KIDDING ME?!
YOU MIGHT BE THE STRONGEST SWORD IN TOWN!
WHAT?
MANA CONDUCTIVITY? I THINK THAT STAT JUST POPPED UP RECENTLY...
IS IT BECAUSE I LEVELED UP IDENTIFY?
NAME: TEACHER
USER: FRAN
TYPE: INTELLIGENT WEAPON
ATTACK: 392
MANA CONDUCTIVITY: A
AYE. IT'S A STAT UNIQUE TO MAGICAL WEAPONS.
IT SIGNIFIES THE WEAPON'S CAPACITY TO BE INFLUENCED BY MAGICAL ENERGY.
MITHRIL USUALLY HAS A MANA CONDUCTIVITY RATING OF C. THAT'S ABOUT SEVENTY PERCENT EFFICIENCY.
YOUR A RANKING PUTS YOU AT TWO HUNDRED PERCENT.
THAT MEANS FOR EVERY HUNDRED POINTS OF MANA, YOU GET TWO HUNDRED BONUS ATTACK!
WHOA, YOU SERIOUS?
AS A HEART ATTACK.
SO, IF I REALLY APPLIED MYSELF, I COULD CONVERT 1000 MANA INTO AN EXTRA 2000 ATTACK!
OGLOOOW...
はあ...

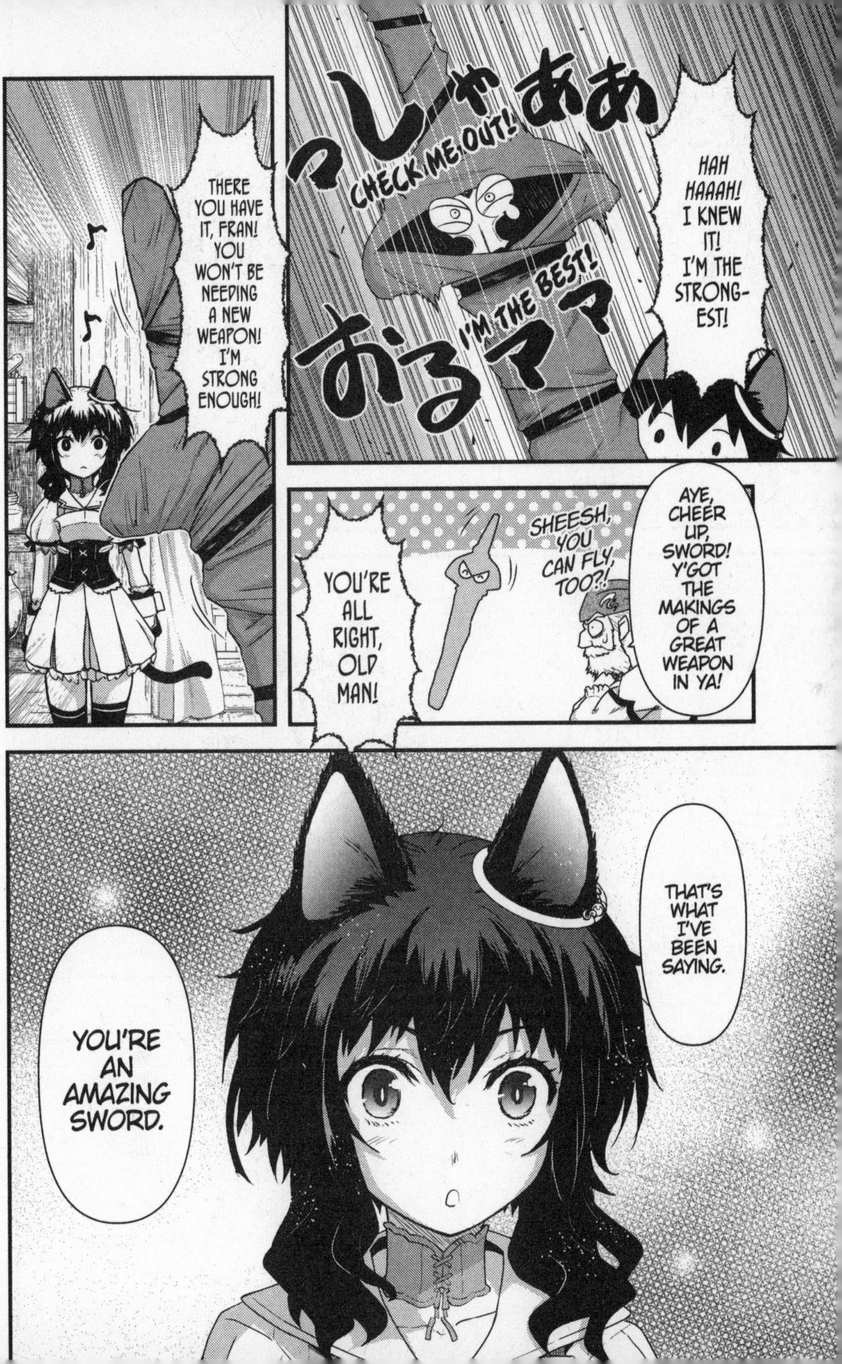
HAH HAAAH! I KNEW IT! I'M THE STRONGEST!
っしゃああ
CHECK ME OUT!
おるァァ
I'M THE BEST!
AYE, CHEER UP, SWORD! Y'GOT THE MAKINGS OF A GREAT WEAPON IN YA!
SHEESH, YOU CAN FLY, TOO?!
YOU'RE ALL RIGHT, OLD MAN!
THERE YOU HAVE IT, FRAN! YOU WON'T BE NEEDING A NEW WEAPON! I'M STRONG ENOUGH!
THAT'S WHAT I'VE BEEN SAYING.
YOU'RE AN AMAZING SWORD.

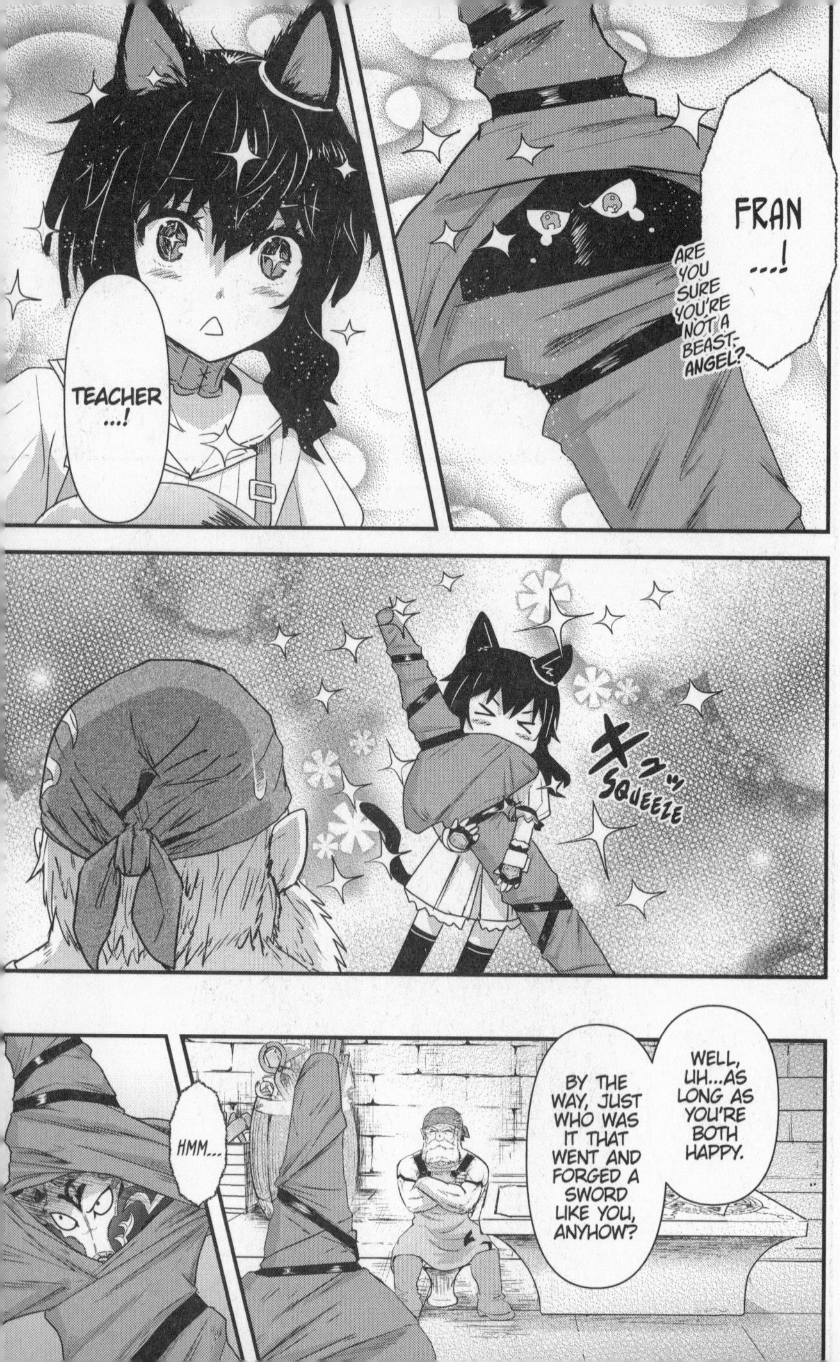
FRAN ...!
ARE YOU SURE YOU'RE NOT A BEAST-ANGEL?
TEACHER ...!
SQUEEZE
WELL, UH...AS LONG AS YOU'RE BOTH HAPPY.
BY THE WAY, JUST WHO WAS IT THAT WENT AND FORGED A SWORD LIKE YOU, ANYHOW?
HMM...

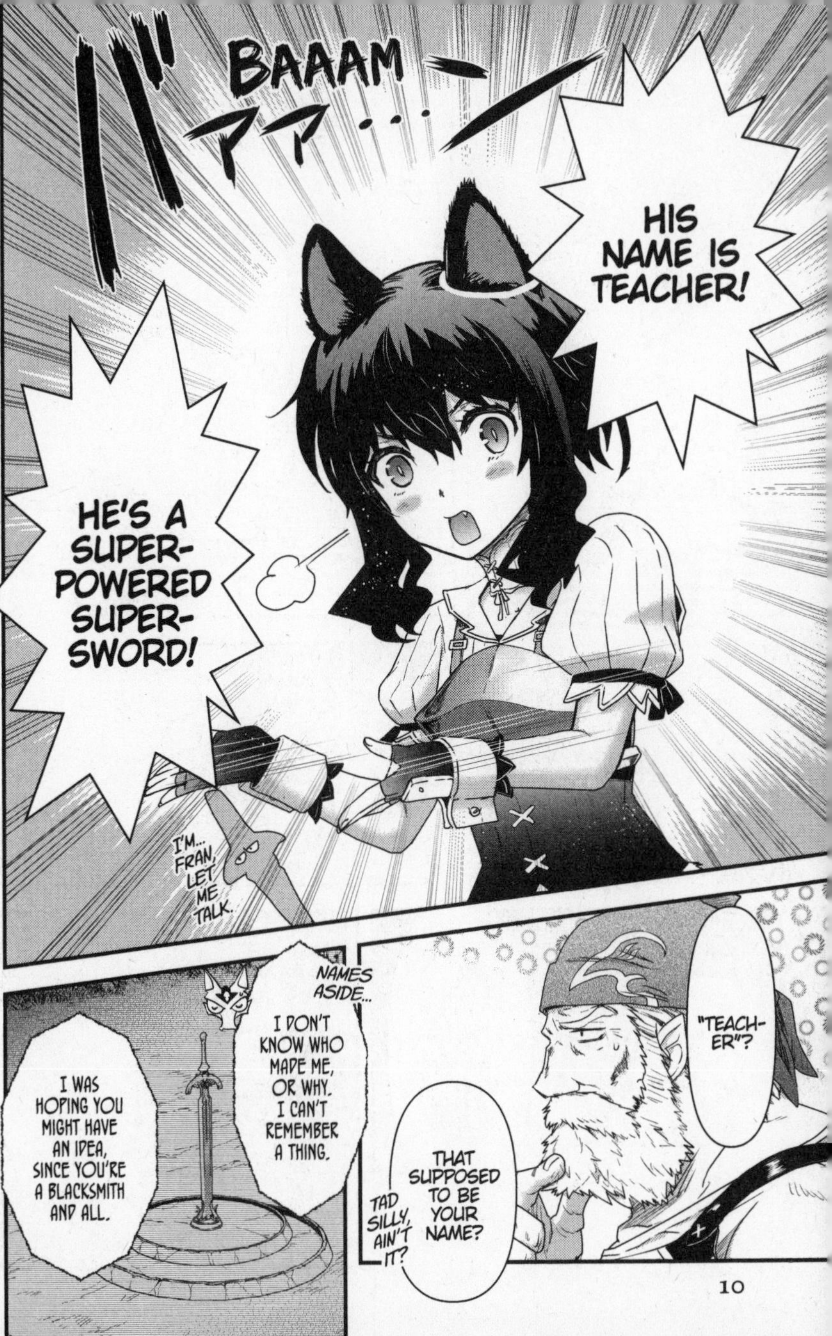
BAAAM
バァァ…
HIS NAME IS TEACHER!
HE'S A SUPER-POWERED SUPER-SWORD!
I'M... FRAN, LET ME TALK.
"TEACHER"?
THAT SUPPOSED TO BE YOUR NAME?
TAD SILLY, AIN'T IT?
NAMES ASIDE...
I DON'T KNOW WHO MADE ME, OR WHY. I CAN'T REMEMBER A THING.
I WAS HOPING YOU MIGHT HAVE AN IDEA, SINCE YOU'RE A BLACKSMITH AND ALL.

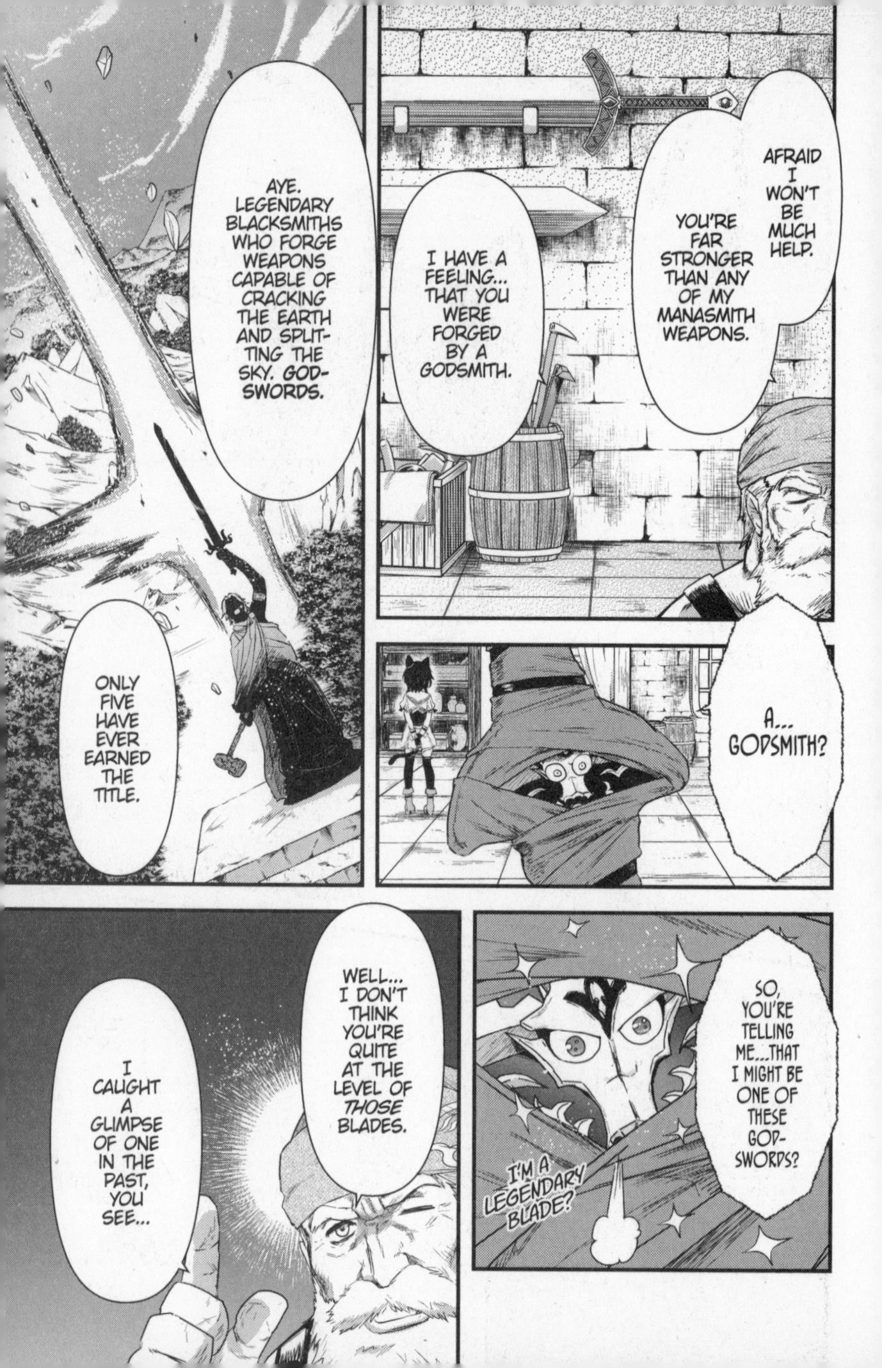
AFRAID I WON'T BE MUCH HELP.
YOU'RE FAR STRONGER THAN ANY OF MY MANASMITH WEAPONS.
I HAVE A FEELING... THAT YOU WERE FORGED BY A GODSMITH.
A... GODSMITH?
AYE. LEGENDARY BLACKSMITHS WHO FORGE WEAPONS CAPABLE OF CRACKING THE EARTH AND SPLIT-TING THE SKY. GOD-SWORDS.
ONLY FIVE HAVE EVER EARNED THE TITLE.
SO, YOU'RE TELLING ME...THAT I MIGHT BE ONE OF THESE GOD-SWORDS?
I'M A LEGENDARY BLADE?
WELL... I DON'T THINK YOU'RE QUITE AT THE LEVEL OF *THOSE* BLADES.
I CAUGHT A GLIMPSE OF ONE IN THE PAST, YOU SEE...

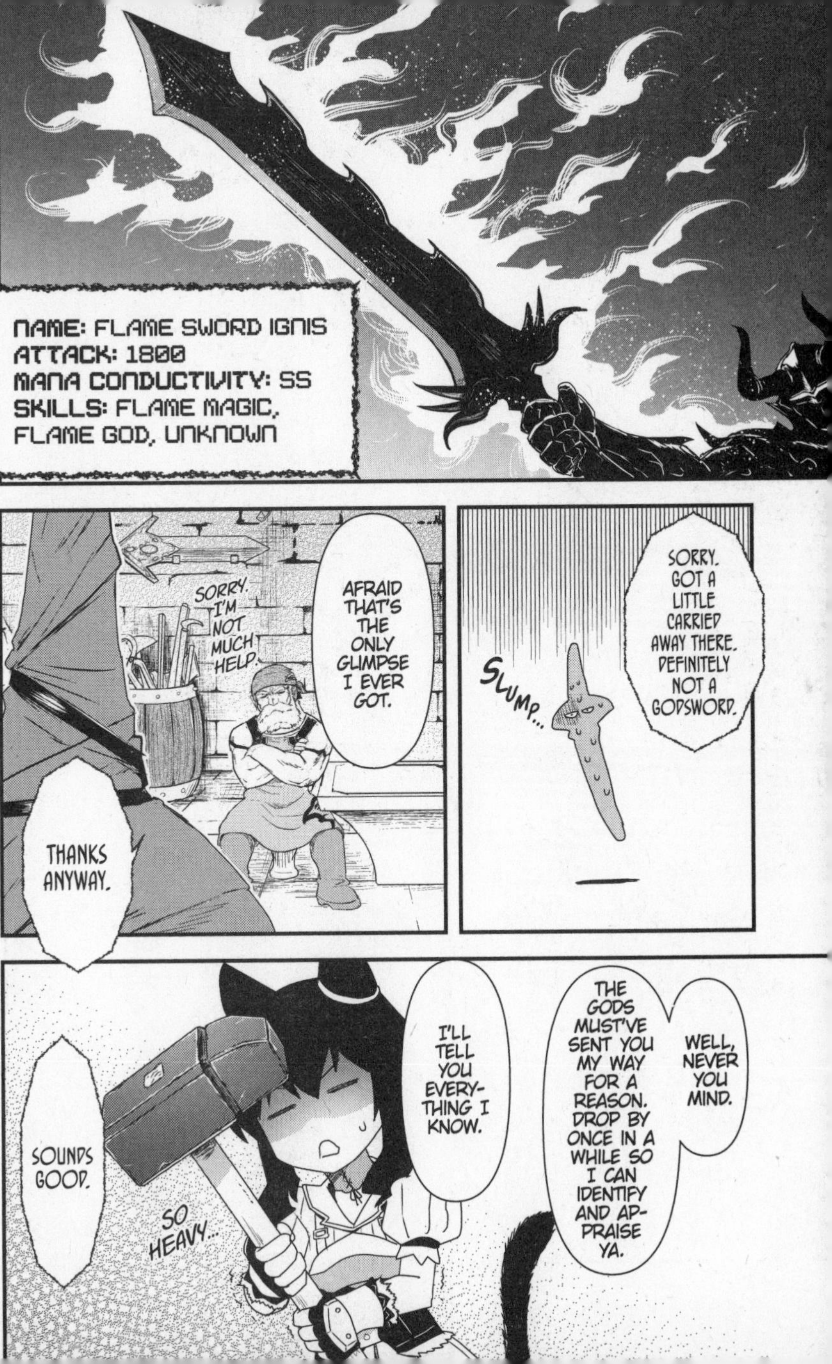
NAME: FLAME SWORD IGNIS
ATTACK: 1800
MANA CONDUCTIVITY: SS
SKILLS: FLAME MAGIC, FLAME GOD, UNKNOWN
SORRY. GOT A LITTLE CARRIED AWAY THERE. DEFINITELY NOT A GODSWORD.
SLUMP...
AFRAID THAT'S THE ONLY GLIMPSE I EVER GOT.
SORRY. I'M NOT MUCH HELP.
THANKS ANYWAY.
WELL, NEVER YOU MIND.
THE GODS MUST'VE SENT YOU MY WAY FOR A REASON. DROP BY ONCE IN A WHILE SO I CAN IDENTIFY AND AP-PRAISE YA.
I'LL TELL YOU EVERY-THING I KNOW.
SOUNDS GOOD.
SO HEAVY...

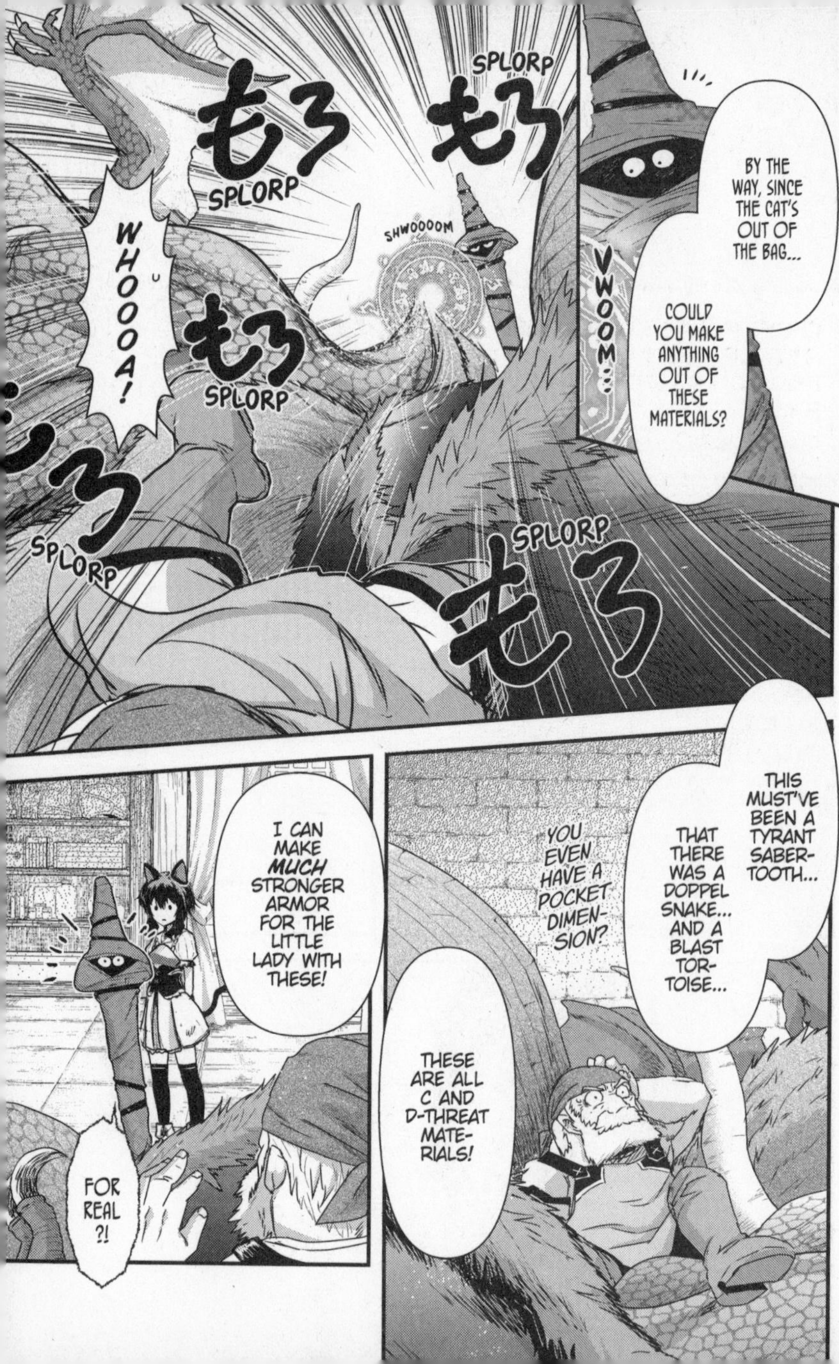
BY THE WAY, SINCE THE CAT'S OUT OF THE BAG...
COULD YOU MAKE ANYTHING OUT OF THESE MATERIALS?
VWOOOM...
SPLORP
もろ
SPLORP
もろ
SHWOOOOM
WHOOOOA!
もろ
SPLORP
SPLORP
SPLORP
もろ
THIS MUST'VE BEEN A TYRANT SABER-TOOTH...
THAT THERE WAS A DOPPEL SNAKE... AND A BLAST TOR-TOISE...
YOU EVEN HAVE A POCKET DIMEN-SION?
THESE ARE ALL C AND D-THREAT MATE-RIALS!
I CAN MAKE *MUCH* STRONGER ARMOR FOR THE LITTLE LADY WITH THESE!
FOR REAL?!

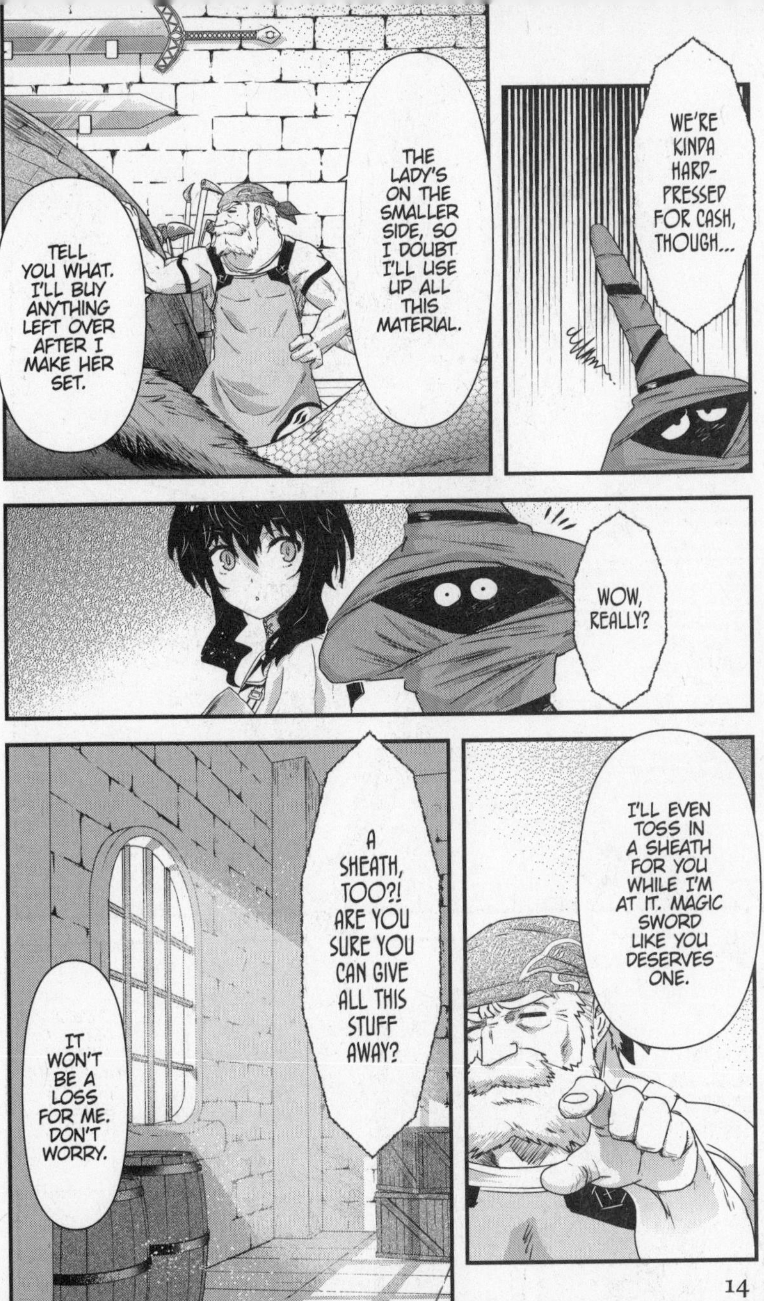
WE'RE KINDA HARD-PRESSED FOR CASH, THOUGH...
THE LADY'S ON THE SMALLER SIDE, SO I DOUBT I'LL USE UP ALL THIS MATERIAL.
TELL YOU WHAT. I'LL BUY ANYTHING LEFT OVER AFTER I MAKE HER SET.
WOW, REALLY?
I'LL EVEN TOSS IN A SHEATH FOR YOU WHILE I'M AT IT. MAGIC SWORD LIKE YOU DESERVES ONE.
A SHEATH, TOO?! ARE YOU SURE YOU CAN GIVE ALL THIS STUFF AWAY?
IT WON'T BE A LOSS FOR ME. DON'T WORRY.

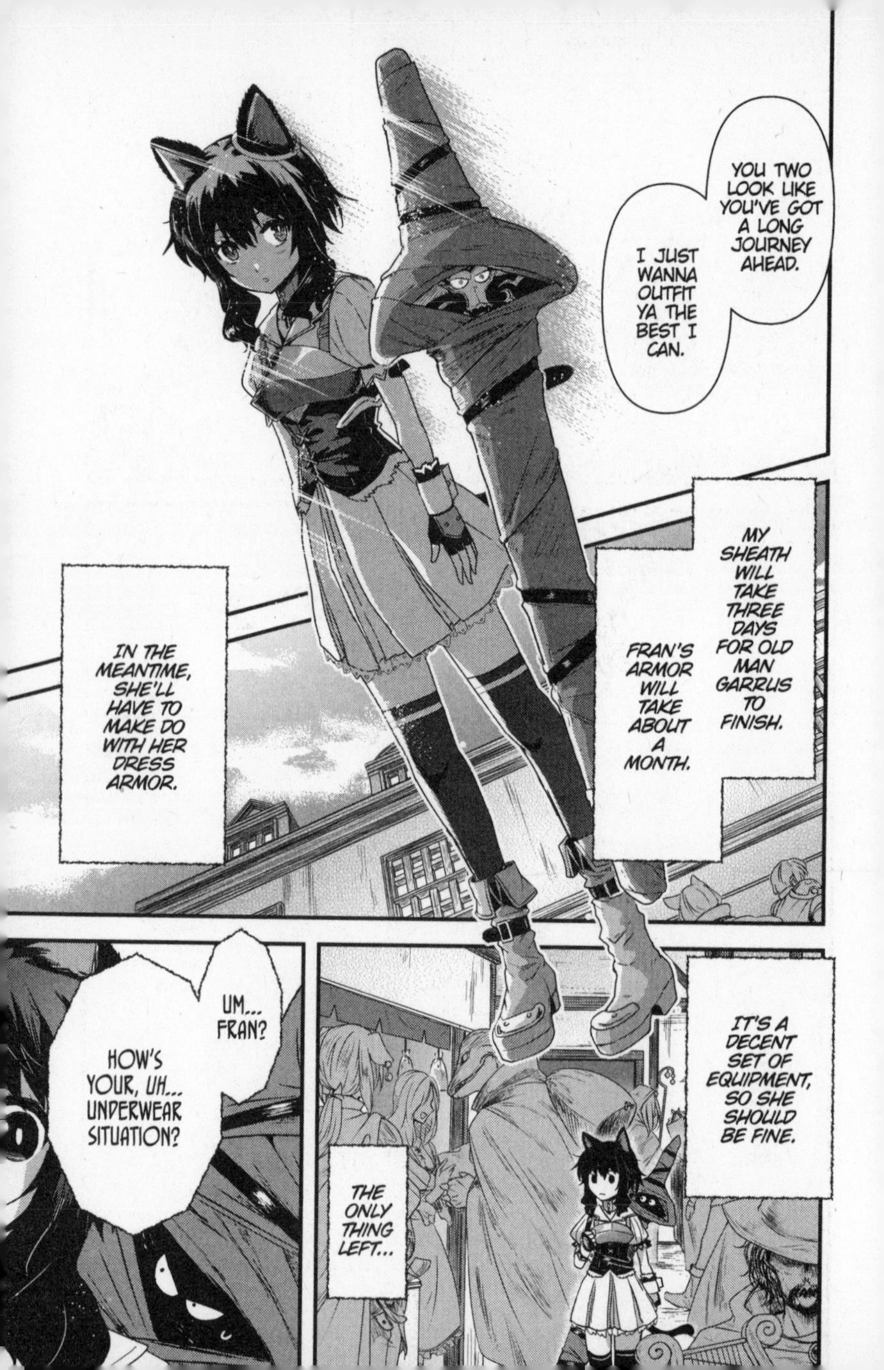
YOU TWO LOOK LIKE YOU'VE GOT A LONG JOURNEY AHEAD.
I JUST WANNA OUTFIT YA THE BEST I CAN.
MY SHEATH WILL TAKE THREE DAYS FOR OLD MAN GARRUS TO FINISH.
FRAN'S ARMOR WILL TAKE ABOUT A MONTH.
IN THE MEANTIME, SHE'LL HAVE TO MAKE DO WITH HER DRESS ARMOR.
IT'S A DECENT SET OF EQUIPMENT, SO SHE SHOULD BE FINE.
THE ONLY THING LEFT...
UM... FRAN?
HOW'S YOUR, UH... UNDERWEAR SITUATION?

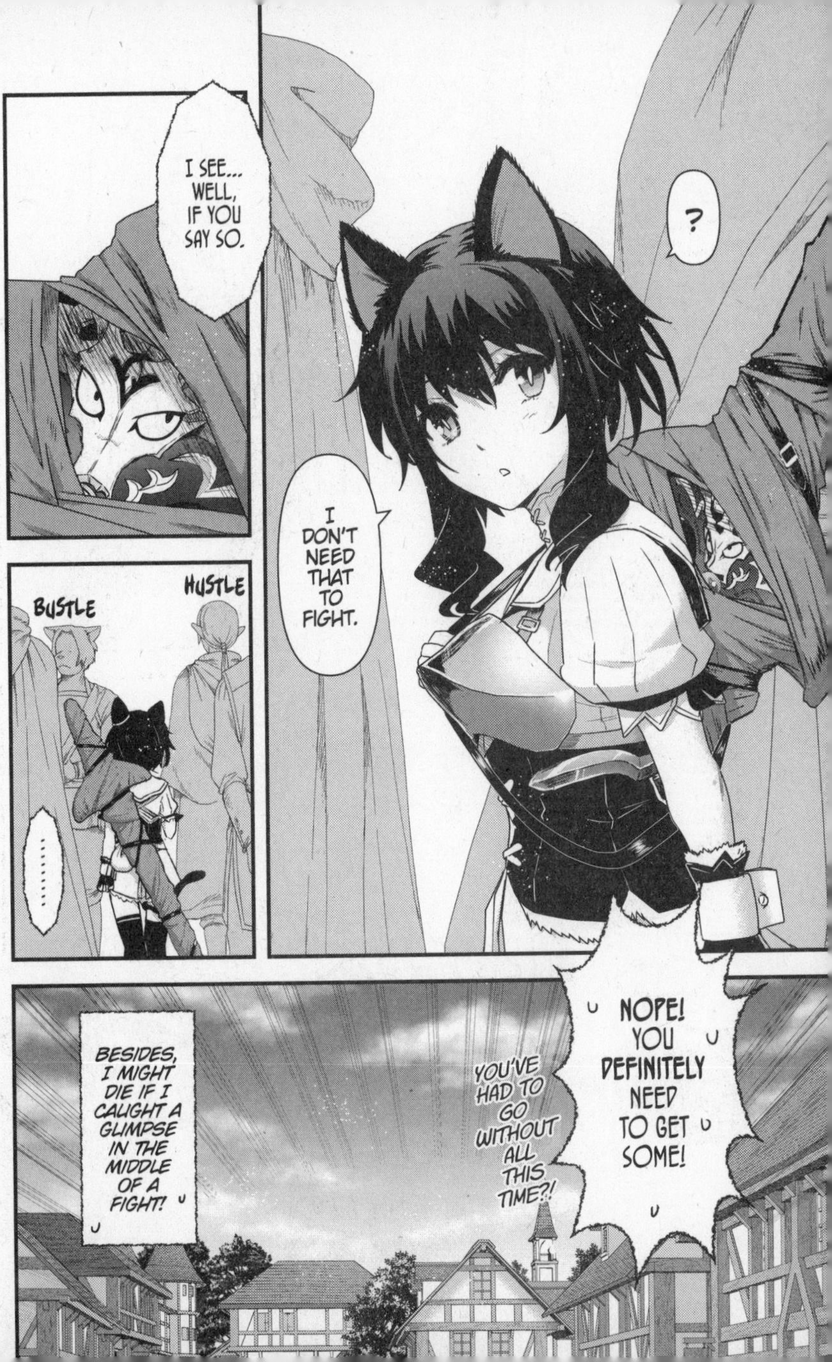
?
I DON'T NEED THAT TO FIGHT.
I SEE... WELL, IF YOU SAY SO.
HUSTLE
BUSTLE
......
NOPE! YOU DEFINITELY NEED TO GET SOME!
YOU'VE HAD TO GO WITHOUT ALL THIS TIME?!
BESIDES, I MIGHT DIE IF I CAUGHT A GLIMPSE IN THE MIDDLE OF A FIGHT!

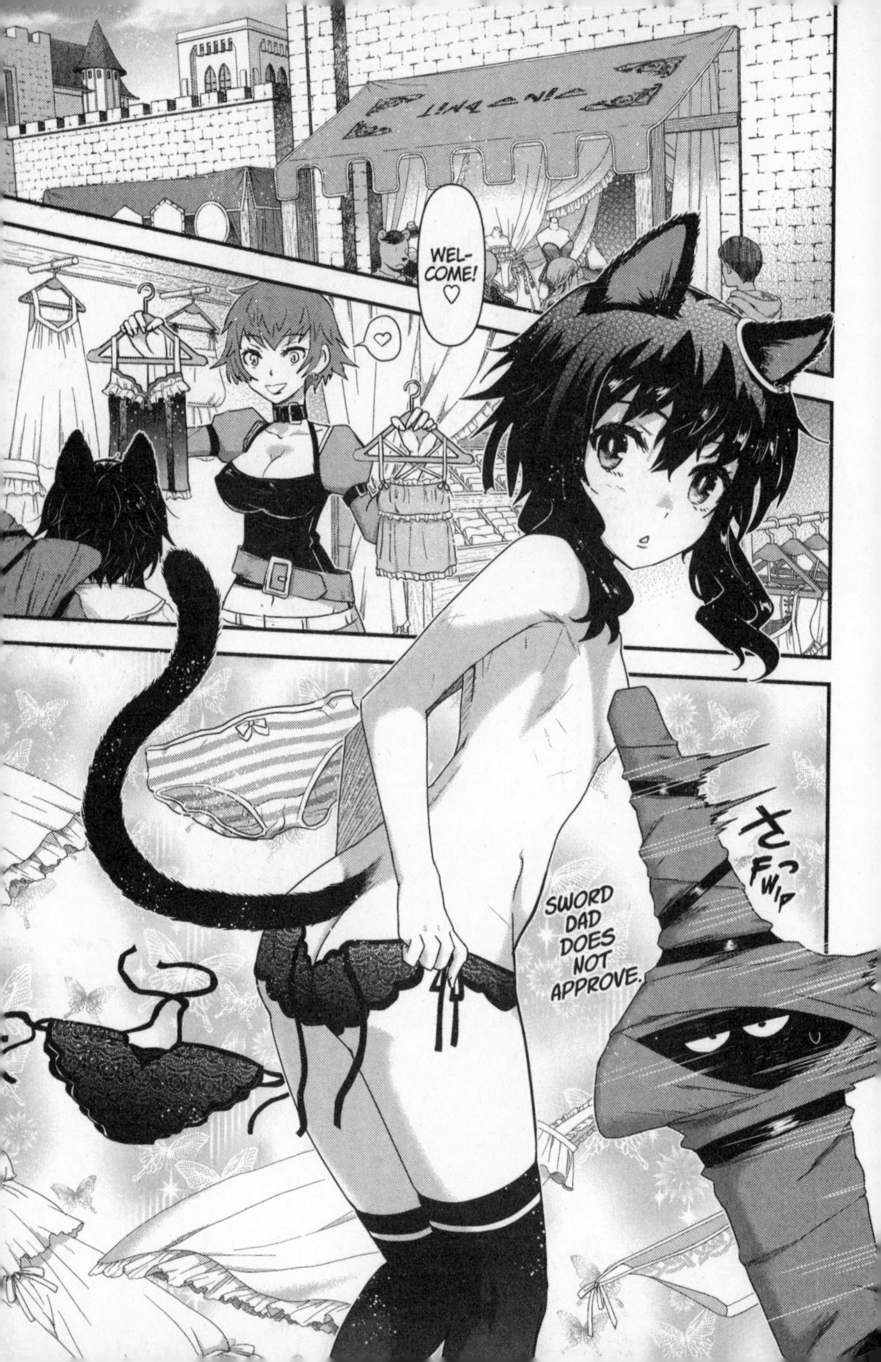
WEL-
COME!
♡
♡
さっ
FWIP
SWORD DAD DOES NOT APPROVE.

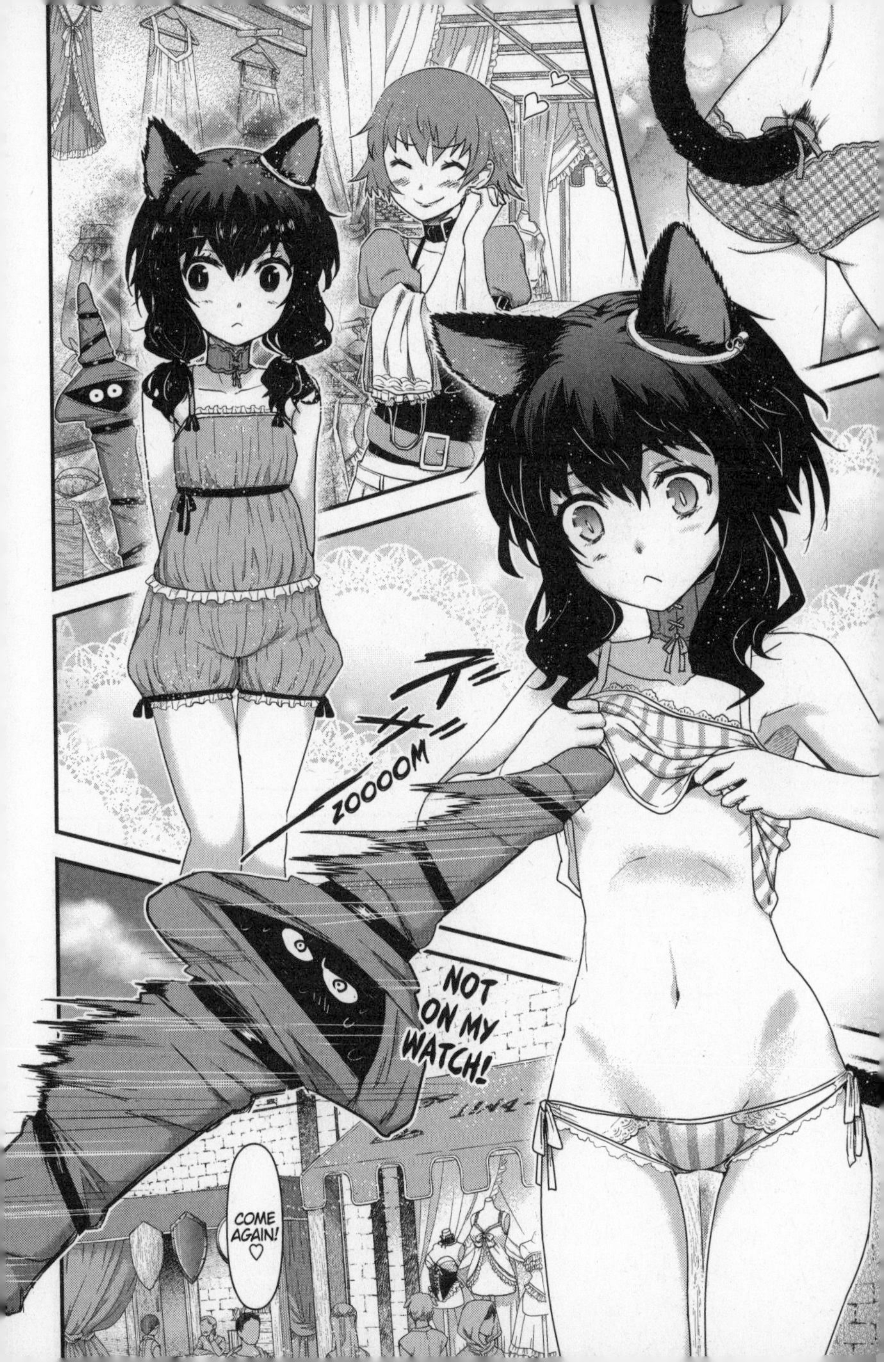
ZOOOOM
NOT ON MY WATCH!
COME AGAIN! ♡

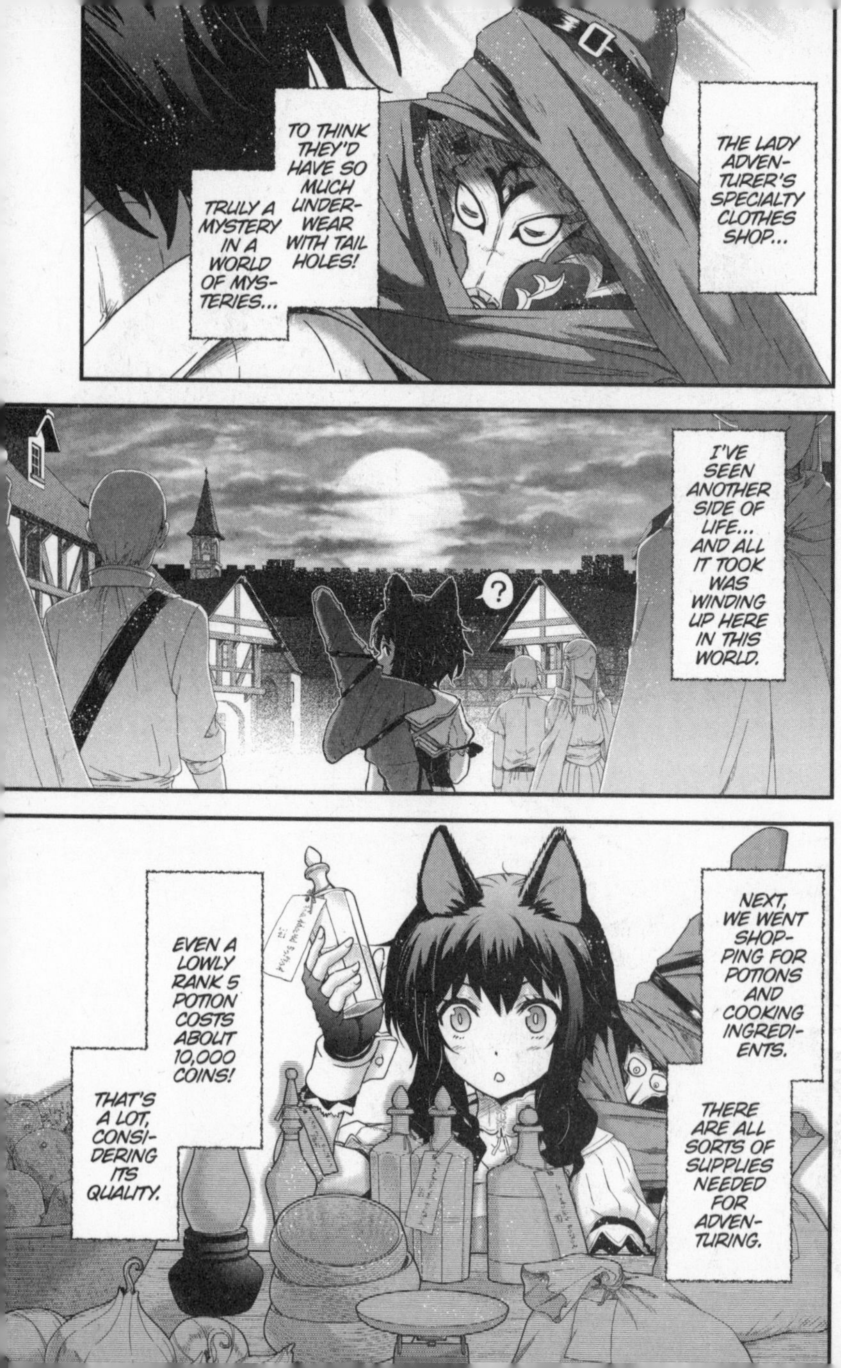
THE LADY ADVENTURER'S SPECIALTY CLOTHES SHOP...
TO THINK THEY'D HAVE SO MUCH UNDERWEAR WITH TAIL HOLES!
TRULY A MYSTERY IN A WORLD OF MYSTERIES...
I'VE SEEN ANOTHER SIDE OF LIFE... AND ALL IT TOOK WAS WINDING UP HERE IN THIS WORLD.
?
NEXT, WE WENT SHOPPING FOR POTIONS AND COOKING INGREDIENTS.
THERE ARE ALL SORTS OF SUPPLIES NEEDED FOR ADVENTURING.
EVEN A LOWLY RANK 5 POTION COSTS ABOUT 10,000 COINS!
THAT'S A LOT, CONSIDERING ITS QUALITY.

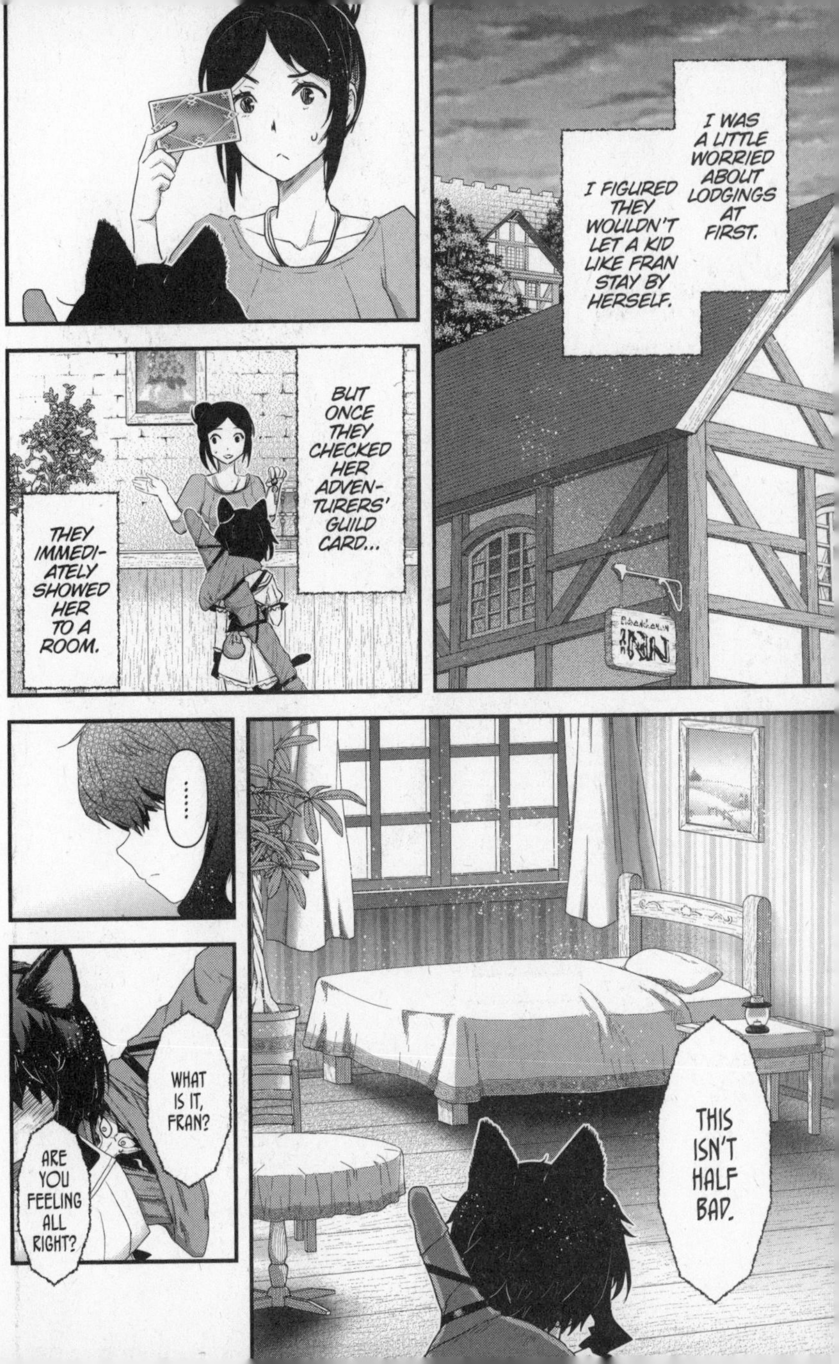

I WAS A LITTLE WORRIED ABOUT LODGINGS AT FIRST.
I FIGURED THEY WOULDN'T LET A KID LIKE FRAN STAY BY HERSELF.
INN
BUT ONCE THEY CHECKED HER ADVEN-TURERS' GUILD CARD...
THEY IMMEDI-ATELY SHOWED HER TO A ROOM.
THIS ISN'T HALF BAD.
......
WHAT IS IT, FRAN?
ARE YOU FEELING ALL RIGHT?

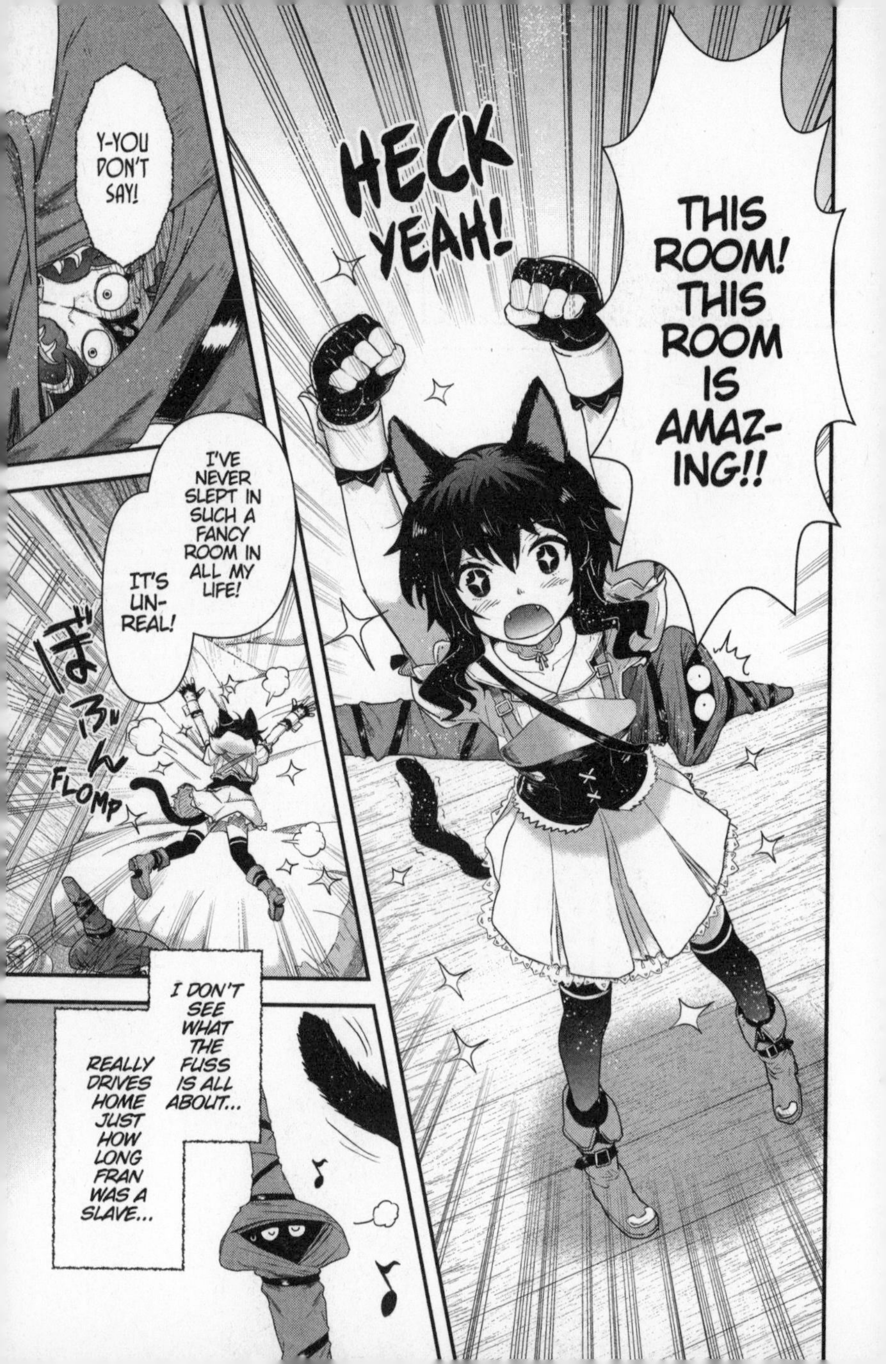
THIS ROOM! THIS ROOM IS AMAZ-ING!!
HECK YEAH!
Y-YOU DON'T SAY!
I'VE NEVER SLEPT IN SUCH A FANCY ROOM IN ALL MY LIFE!
IT'S UN-REAL!
FLOMP
I DON'T SEE WHAT THE FUSS IS ALL ABOUT...
REALLY DRIVES HOME JUST HOW LONG FRAN WAS A SLAVE...

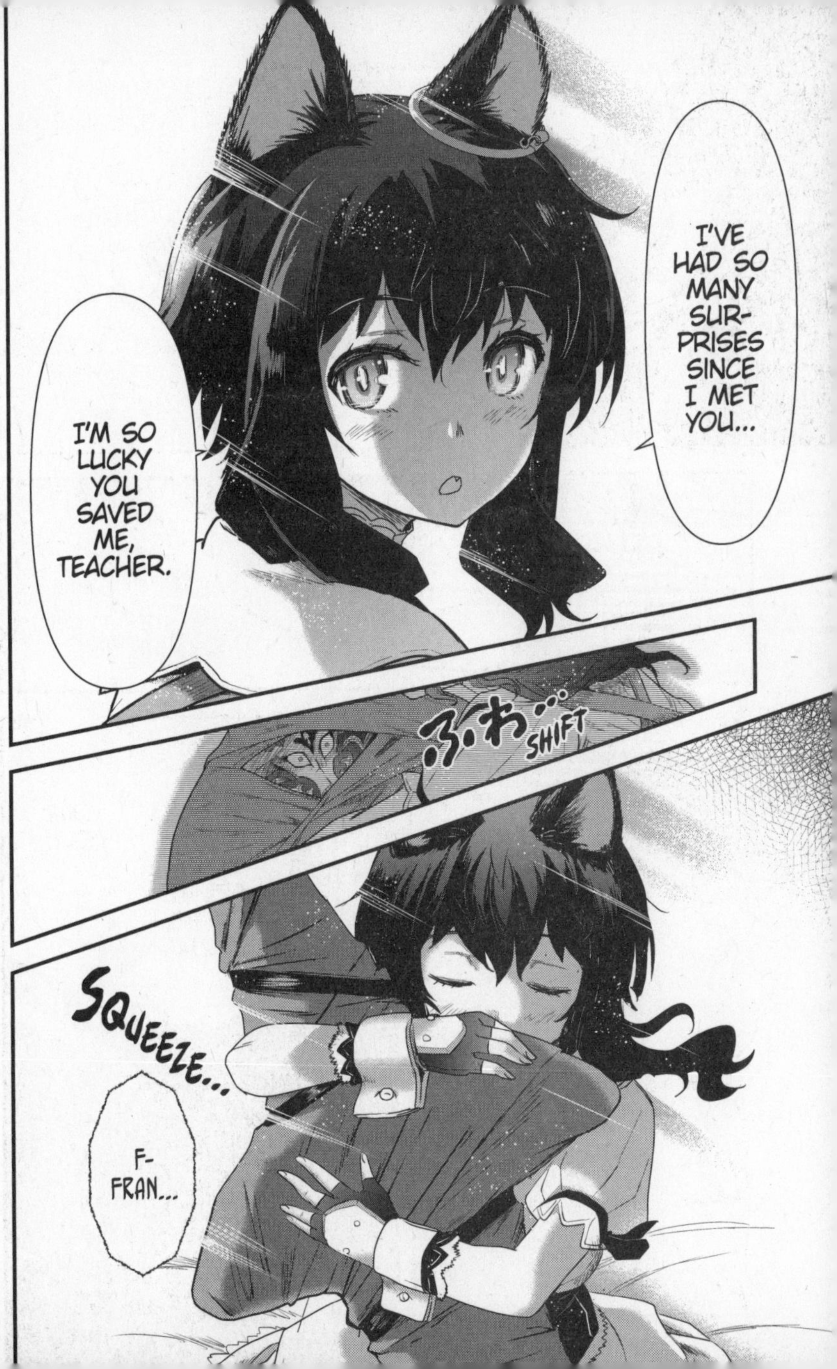
I'VE HAD SO MANY SUR-PRISES SINCE I MET YOU...
I'M SO LUCKY YOU SAVED ME, TEACHER.
ふわ…
SHIFT
SQUEEZE...
F-FRAN...

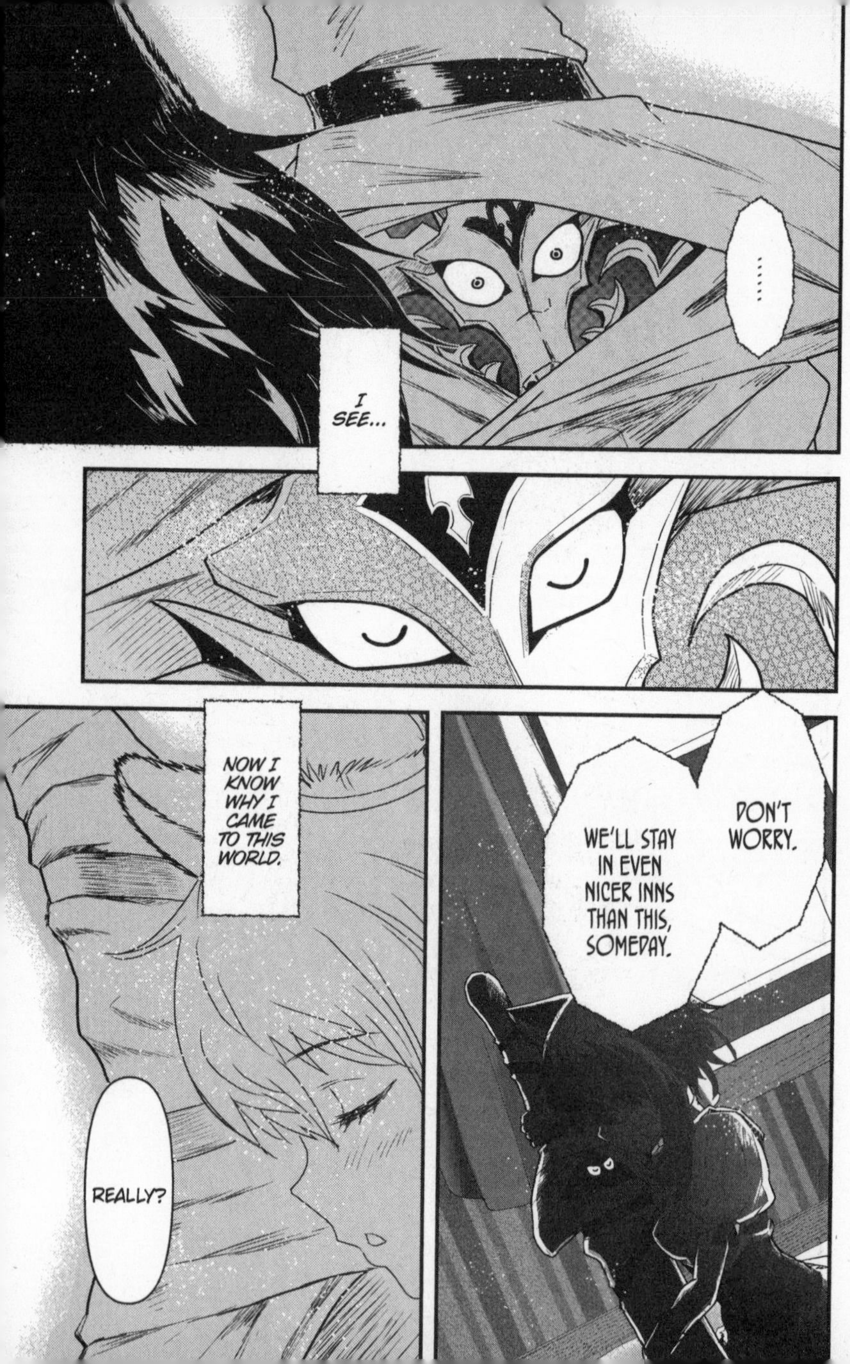
......
I SEE...
DON'T WORRY.
WE'LL STAY IN EVEN NICER INNS THAN THIS, SOMEDAY.
NOW I KNOW WHY I CAME TO THIS WORLD.
REALLY?

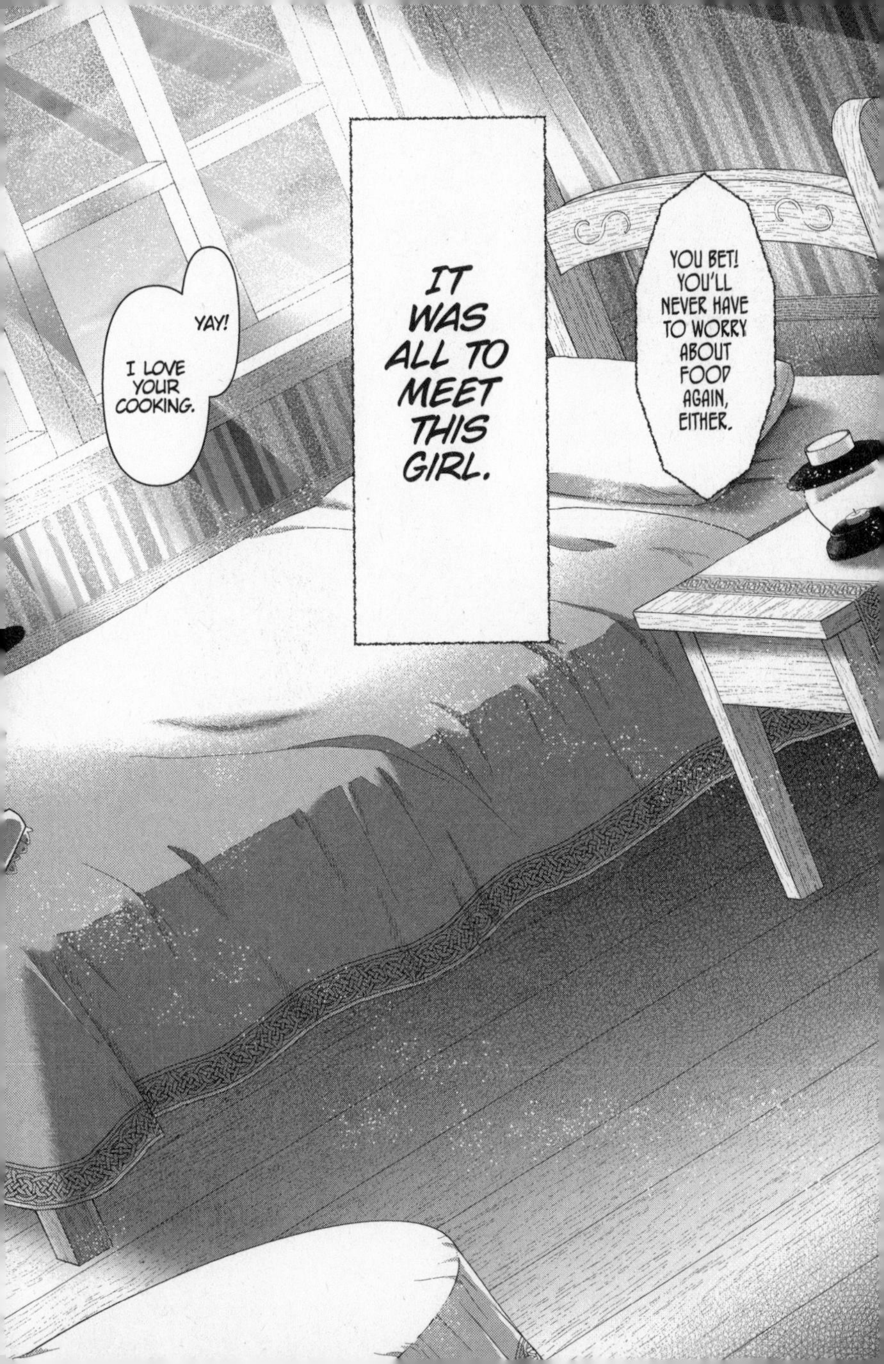
YOU BET! YOU'LL NEVER HAVE TO WORRY ABOUT FOOD AGAIN, EITHER.
IT WAS ALL TO MEET THIS GIRL.
YAY!
I LOVE YOUR COOKING.

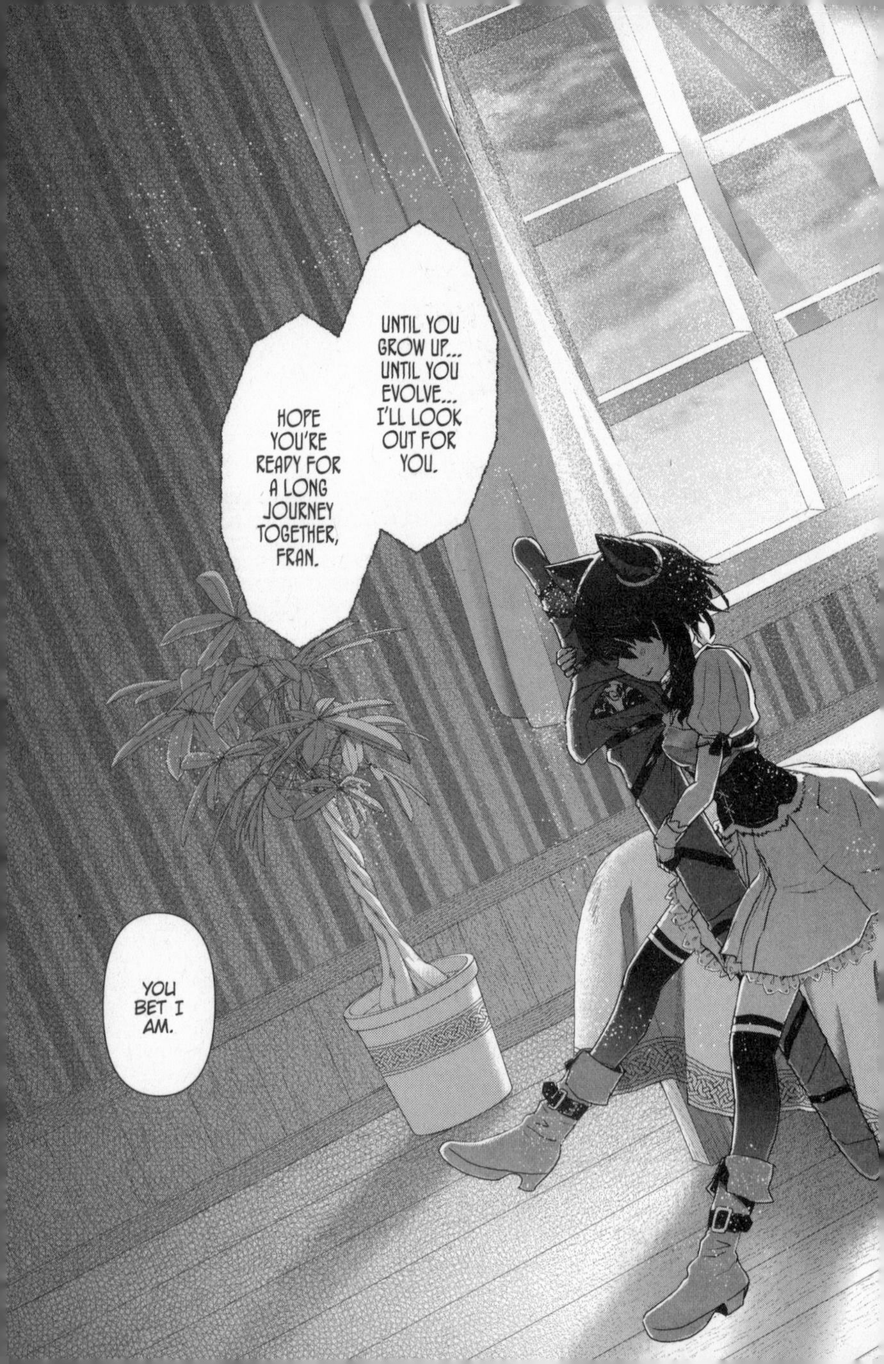
UNTIL YOU GROW UP... UNTIL YOU EVOLVE... I'LL LOOK OUT FOR YOU.
HOPE YOU'RE READY FOR A LONG JOURNEY TOGETHER, FRAN.
YOU BET I AM.

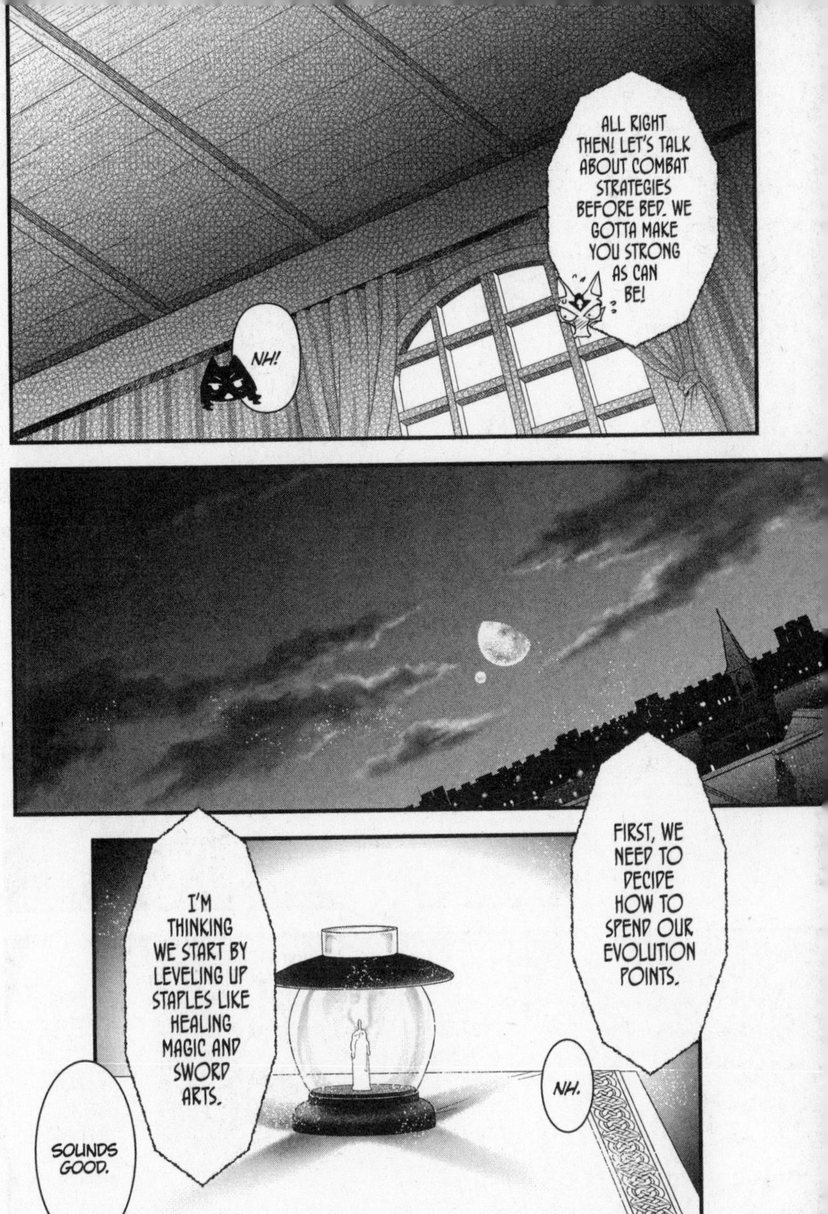
ALL RIGHT THEN! LET'S TALK ABOUT COMBAT STRATEGIES BEFORE BED. WE GOTTA MAKE YOU STRONG AS CAN BE!
NH!
FIRST, WE NEED TO DECIDE HOW TO SPEND OUR EVOLUTION POINTS.
NH.
I'M THINKING WE START BY LEVELING UP STAPLES LIKE HEALING MAGIC AND SWORD ARTS.
SOUNDS GOOD.

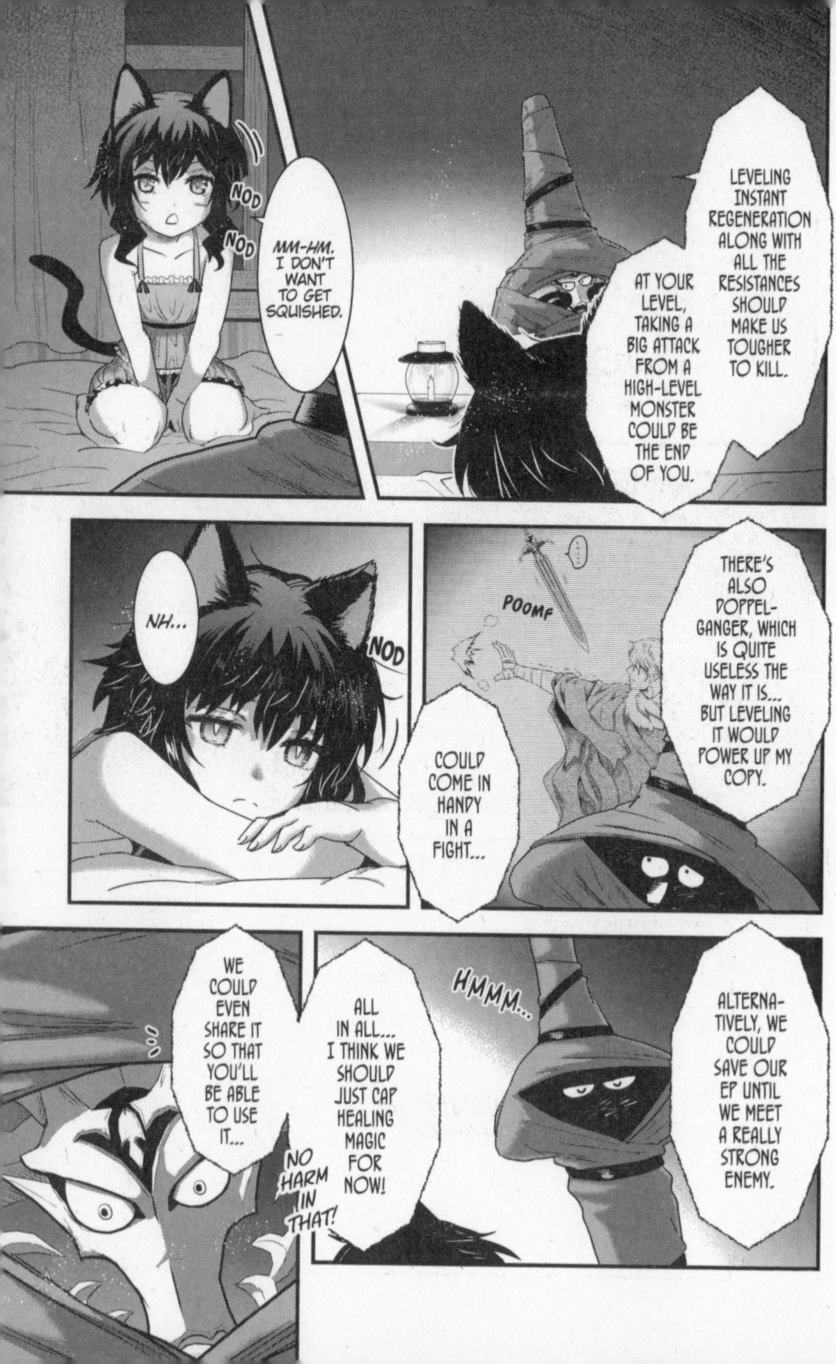
LEVELING INSTANT REGENERATION ALONG WITH ALL THE RESISTANCES SHOULD MAKE US TOUGHER TO KILL.
AT YOUR LEVEL, TAKING A BIG ATTACK FROM A HIGH-LEVEL MONSTER COULD BE THE END OF YOU.
NOD
NOD
MM-HM. I DON'T WANT TO GET SQUISHED.
THERE'S ALSO DOPPEL-GANGER, WHICH IS QUITE USELESS THE WAY IT IS... BUT LEVELING IT WOULD POWER UP MY COPY.
...
POOMF
COULD COME IN HANDY IN A FIGHT...
NH...
NOD
ALTERNA-TIVELY, WE COULD SAVE OUR EP UNTIL WE MEET A REALLY STRONG ENEMY.
HMMM...
ALL IN ALL... I THINK WE SHOULD JUST CAP HEALING MAGIC FOR NOW!
WE COULD EVEN SHARE IT SO THAT YOU'LL BE ABLE TO USE IT...
NO HARM IN THAT!

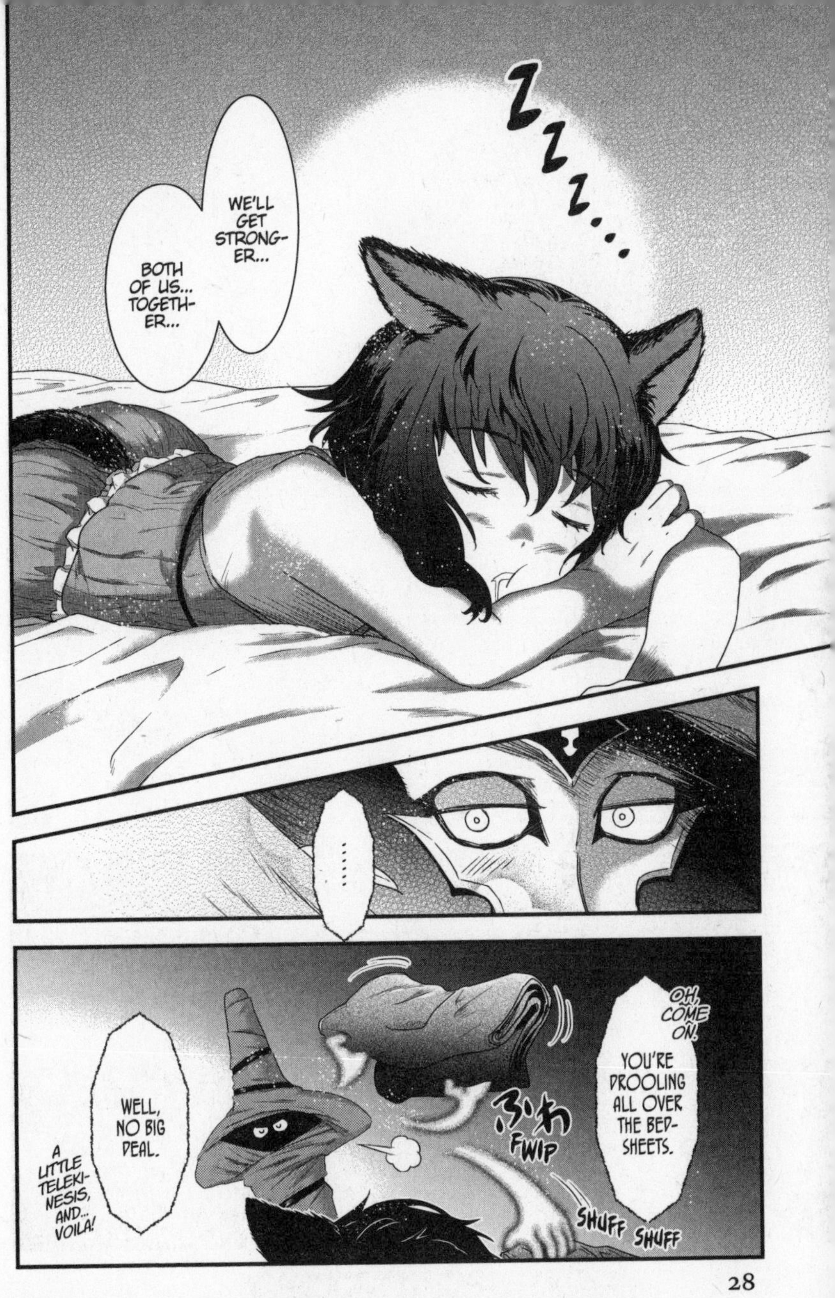
ZZZ...
WE'LL GET STRONGER...
BOTH OF US... TOGETHER...
......
OH, COME ON.
YOU'RE DROOLING ALL OVER THE BED-SHEETS.
ふわ
FWIP
SHUFF SHUFF
WELL, NO BIG DEAL.
A LITTLE TELEKINESIS, AND... VOILA!

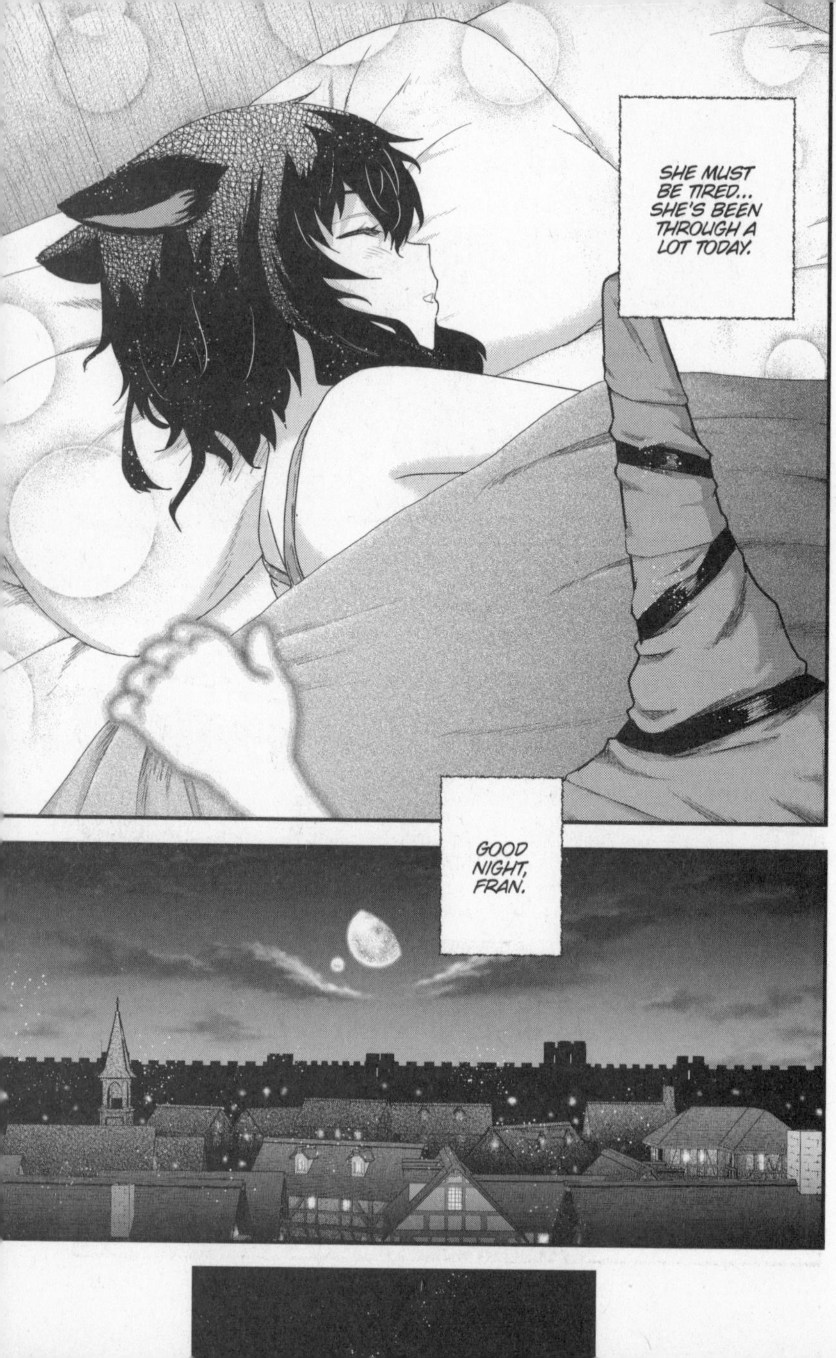
SHE MUST BE TIRED... SHE'S BEEN THROUGH A LOT TODAY.
GOOD NIGHT, FRAN.

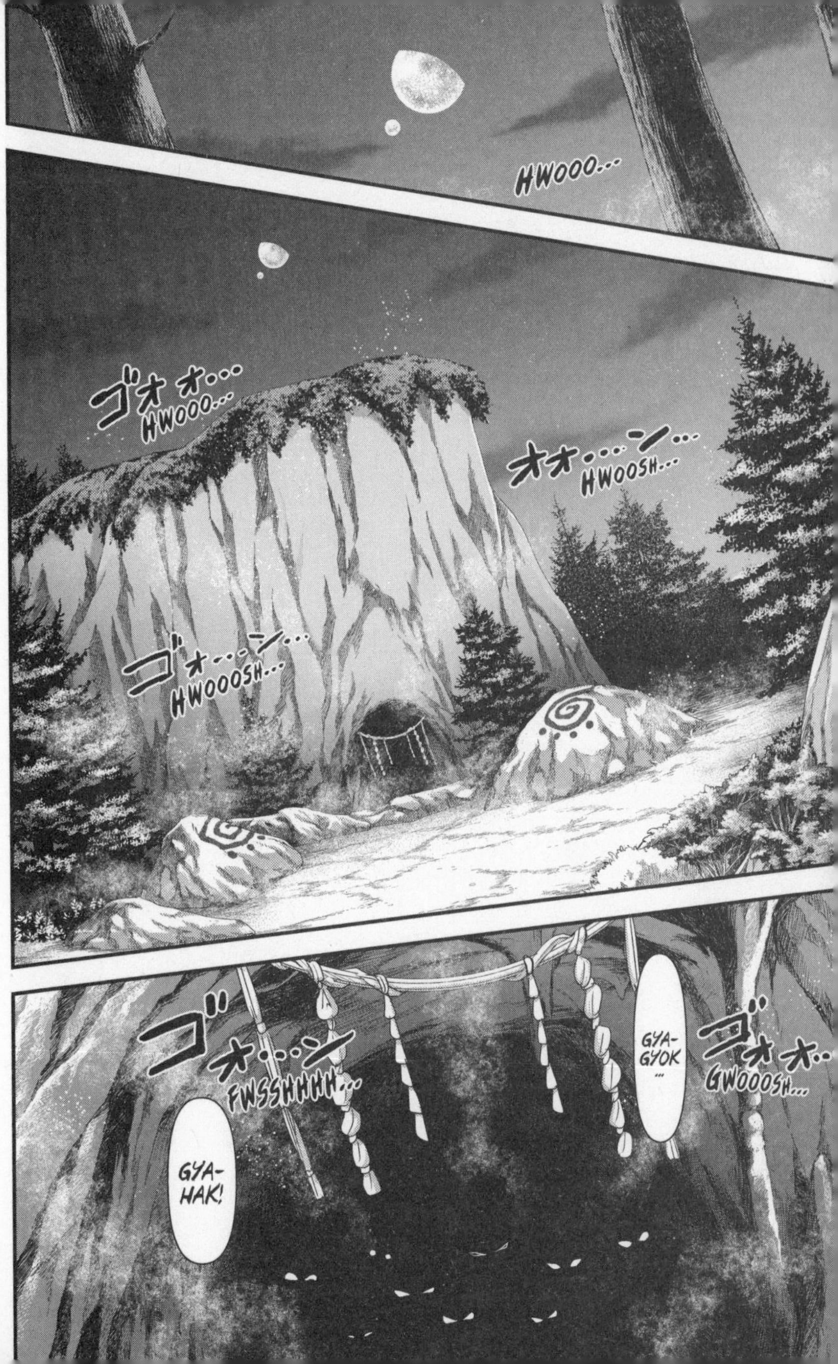
HWOOO...
ゴオオ...
HWOOO...
オオ...ン...
HWOOSH...
ゴオ...ン...
HWOOOSH...
ゴオオ...
GWOOOSH...
GYA-GYOK...
ゴオ...ン
FWSSHHHH...
GYA-HAK!

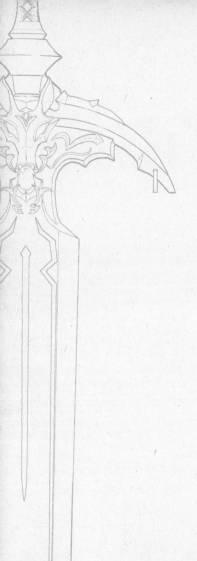

Reincarnated
as a Sword

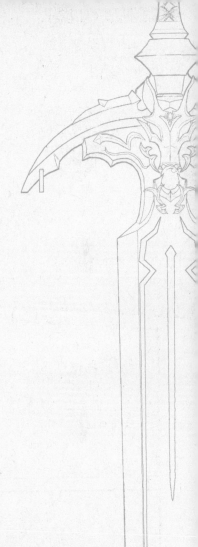

Reincarnated as a sword

Chapter 8: Hundred Slayer

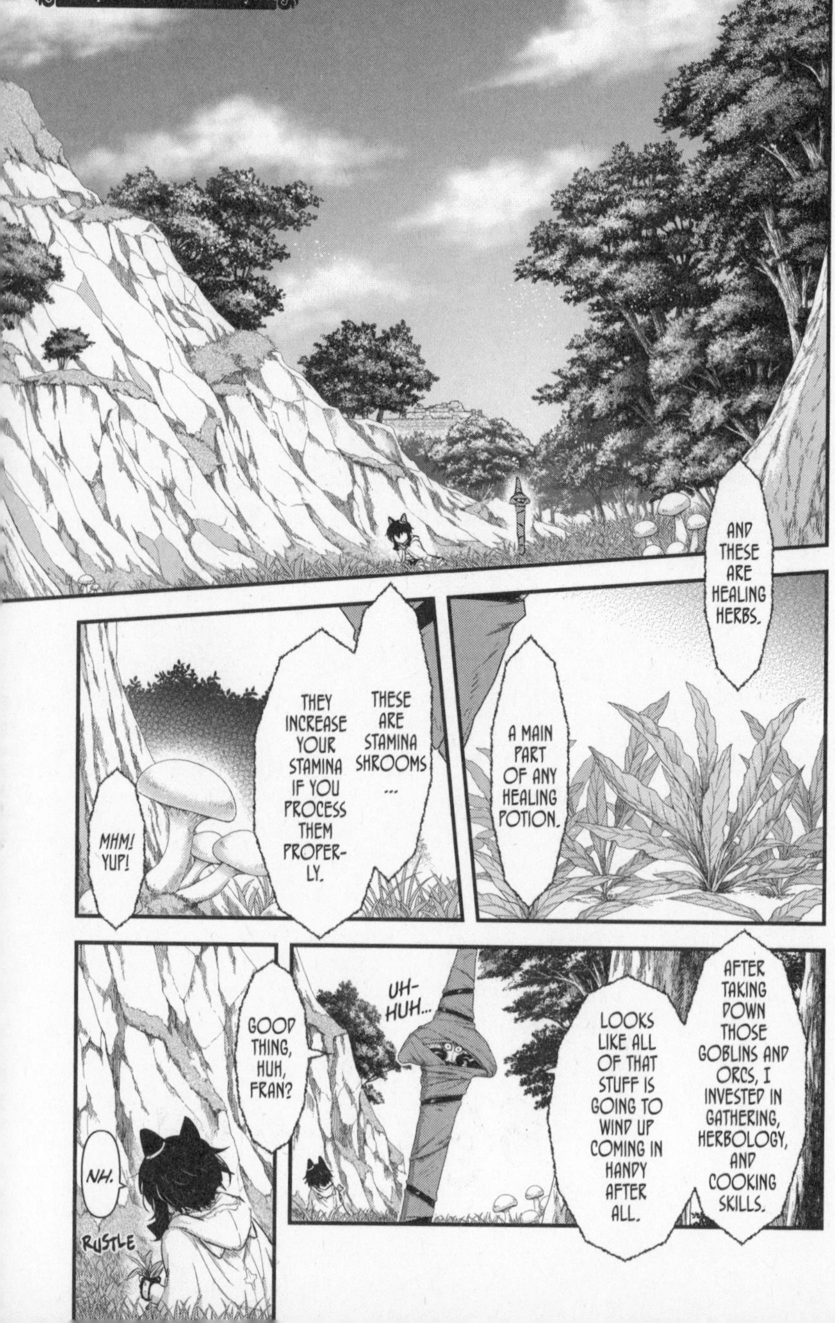
AND THESE ARE HEALING HERBS.
A MAIN PART OF ANY HEALING POTION.
THESE ARE STAMINA SHROOMS...
THEY INCREASE YOUR STAMINA IF YOU PROCESS THEM PROPER-LY.
MHM! YUP!
AFTER TAKING DOWN THOSE GOBLINS AND ORCS, I INVESTED IN GATHERING, HERBOLOGY, AND COOKING SKILLS.
LOOKS LIKE ALL OF THAT STUFF IS GOING TO WIND UP COMING IN HANDY AFTER ALL.
UH-HUH...
GOOD THING, HUH, FRAN?
NH.
RUSTLE

Chapter 8: Hundred Slayer

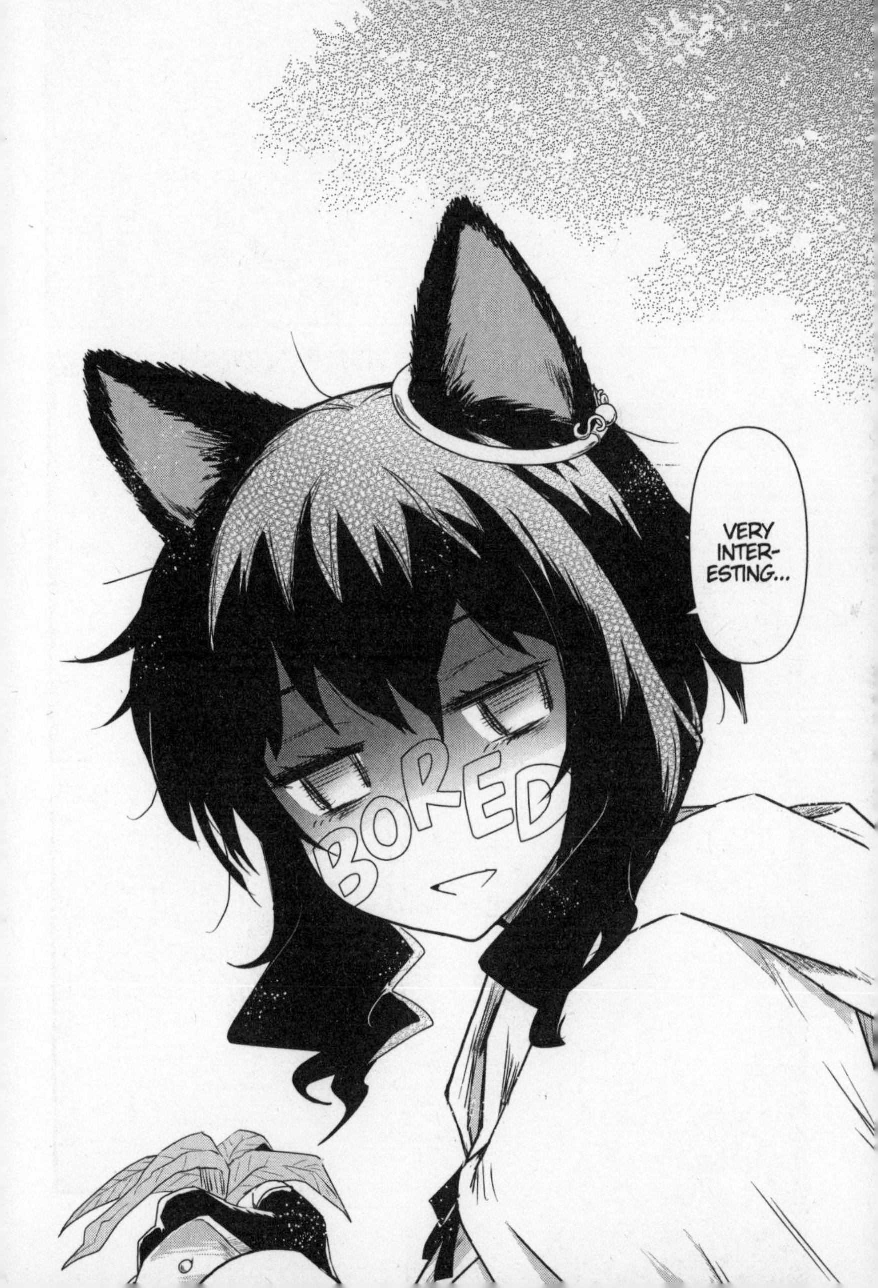
VERY INTER-ESTING...
BORED

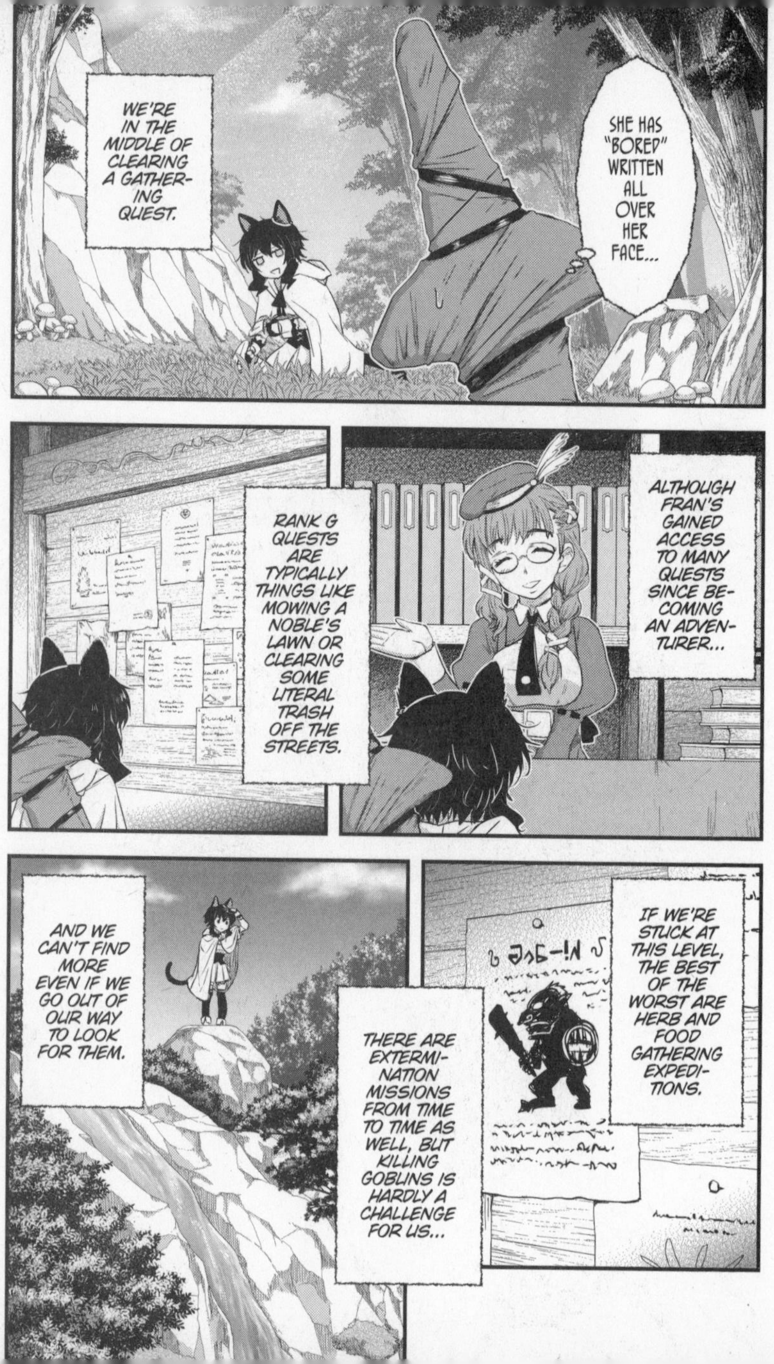
SHE HAS "BORED" WRITTEN ALL OVER HER FACE...
WE'RE IN THE MIDDLE OF CLEARING A GATHER-ING QUEST.
ALTHOUGH FRAN'S GAINED ACCESS TO MANY QUESTS SINCE BE-COMING AN ADVEN-TURER...
RANK G QUESTS ARE TYPICALLY THINGS LIKE MOWING A NOBLE'S LAWN OR CLEARING SOME LITERAL TRASH OFF THE STREETS.
IF WE'RE STUCK AT THIS LEVEL, THE BEST OF THE WORST ARE HERB AND FOOD GATHERING EXPEDI-TIONS.
THERE ARE EXTERMI-NATION MISSIONS FROM TIME TO TIME AS WELL, BUT KILLING GOBLINS IS HARDLY A CHALLENGE FOR US...
AND WE CAN'T FIND MORE EVEN IF WE GO OUT OF OUR WAY TO LOOK FOR THEM.

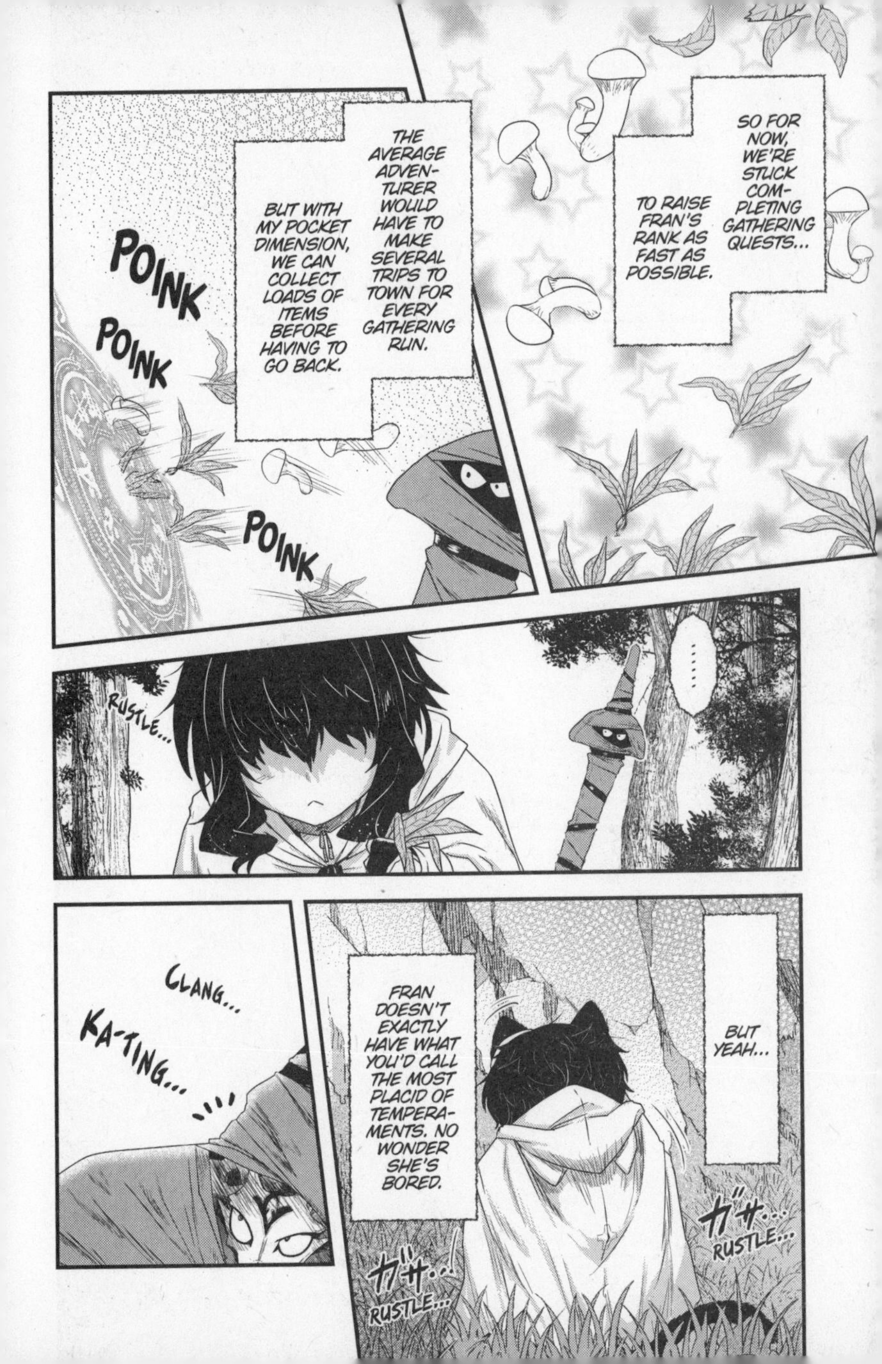
SO FOR NOW, WE'RE STUCK COMPLETING GATHERING QUESTS...
TO RAISE FRAN'S RANK AS FAST AS POSSIBLE.
THE AVERAGE ADVENTURER WOULD HAVE TO MAKE SEVERAL TRIPS TO TOWN FOR EVERY GATHERING RUN.
BUT WITH MY POCKET DIMENSION, WE CAN COLLECT LOADS OF ITEMS BEFORE HAVING TO GO BACK.
POINK
POINK
POINK
......
RUSTLE...
BUT YEAH...
FRAN DOESN'T EXACTLY HAVE WHAT YOU'D CALL THE MOST PLACID OF TEMPERAMENTS. NO WONDER SHE'S BORED.
ガサ... RUSTLE...
ガサ...! RUSTLE...
CLANG...
KA-TING...

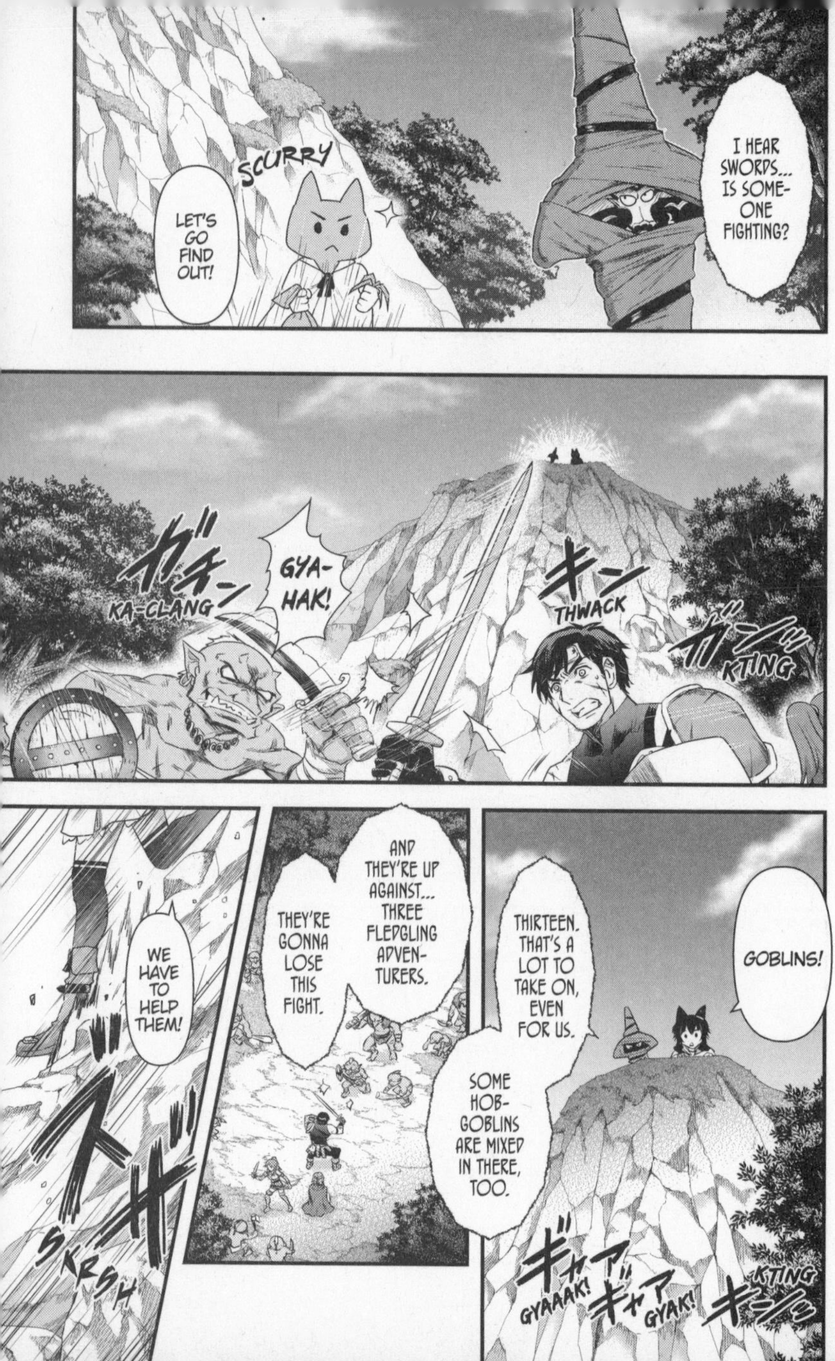
I HEAR SWORDS... IS SOME-ONE FIGHTING?
SCURRY
LET'S GO FIND OUT!
KTING
THWACK
GYA-HAK!
KA-CLANG
GOBLINS!
THIRTEEN. THAT'S A LOT TO TAKE ON, EVEN FOR US.
SOME HOB-GOBLINS ARE MIXED IN THERE, TOO.
KTING
GYAK!
GYAAAK!
AND THEY'RE UP AGAINST... THREE FLEDGLING ADVEN-TURERS.
THEY'RE GONNA LOSE THIS FIGHT.
WE HAVE TO HELP THEM!
SRSH

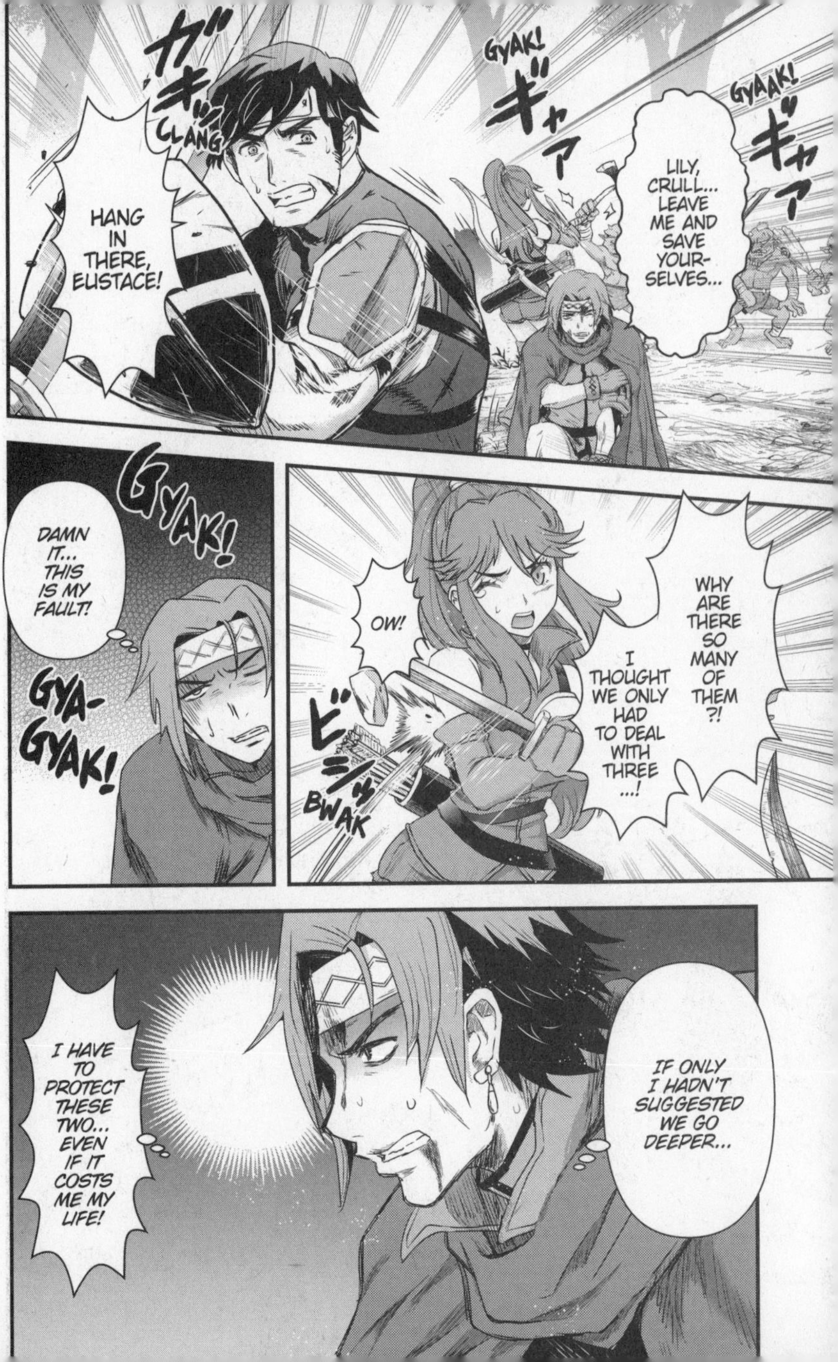
GYAAK!
ギャア
LILY, CRULL... LEAVE ME AND SAVE YOURSELVES...
GYAK!
ギャア
ガキッ
CLANG
HANG IN THERE, EUSTACE!
WHY ARE THERE SO MANY OF THEM?!
I THOUGHT WE ONLY HAD TO DEAL WITH THREE ...!
OW!
ビシッ
BWAK
GYAK!
DAMN IT... THIS IS MY FAULT!
GYA-GYAK!
IF ONLY I HADN'T SUGGESTED WE GO DEEPER...
I HAVE TO PROTECT THESE TWO... EVEN IF IT COSTS ME MY LIFE!

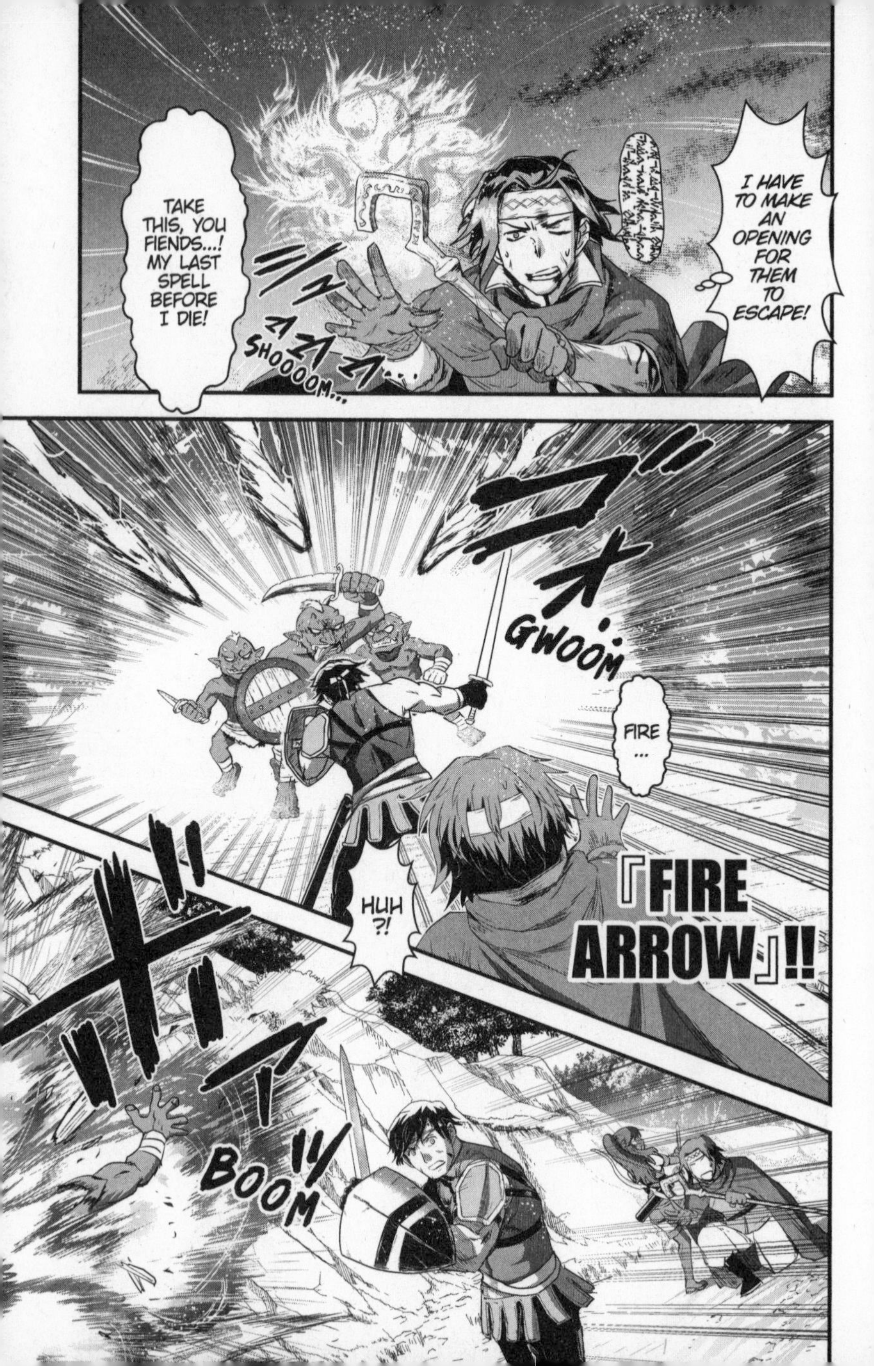
I HAVE TO MAKE AN OPENING FOR THEM TO ESCAPE!
TAKE THIS, YOU FIENDS...! MY LAST SPELL BEFORE I DIE!
SHOOOOM...
GWOOM
FIRE ...
『FIRE ARROW』!!
HUH ?!
BOOM

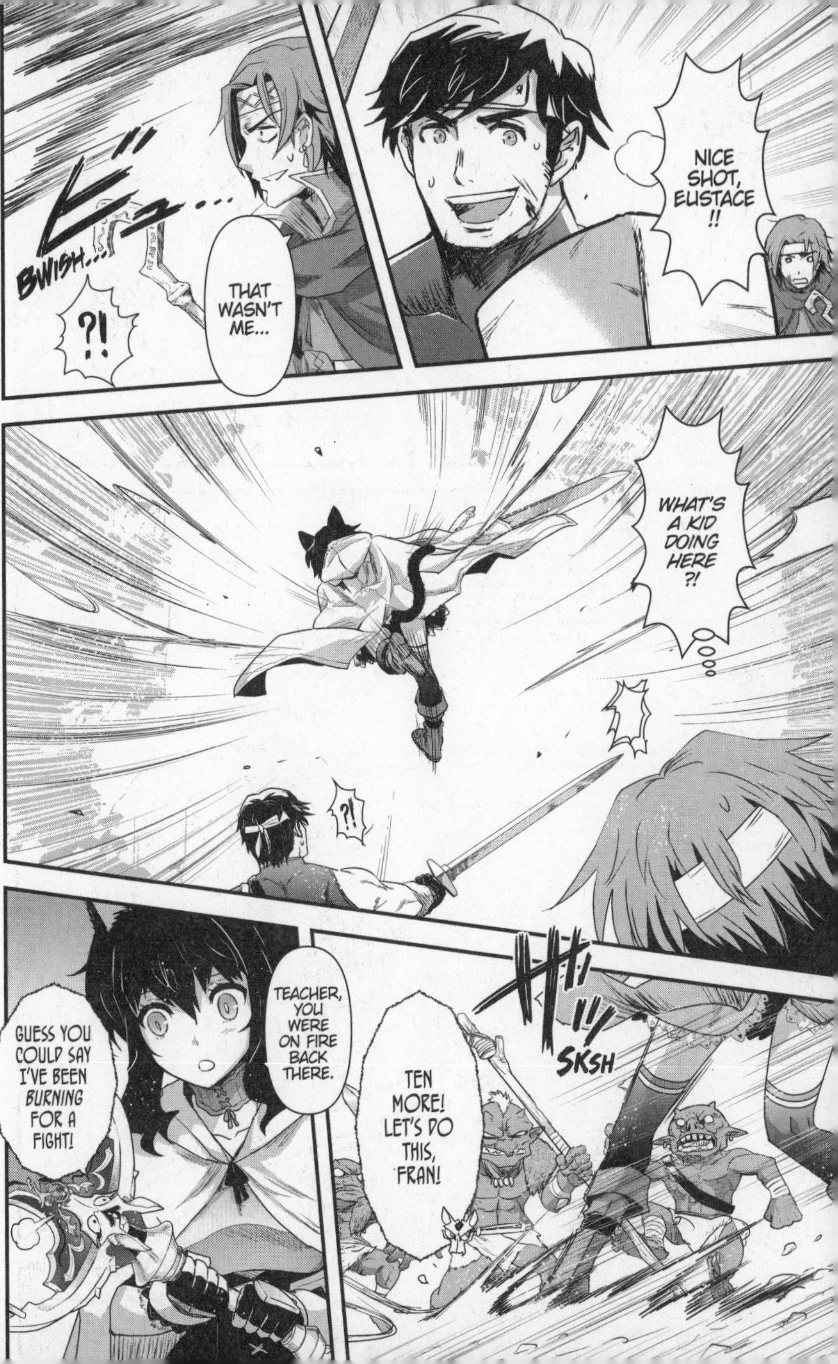

NICE SHOT, EUSTACE!!
THAT WASN'T ME...
BWISH...
?!
WHAT'S A KID DOING HERE?!
?!
SKSH
TEN MORE! LET'S DO THIS, FRAN!
TEACHER, YOU WERE ON FIRE BACK THERE.
GUESS YOU COULD SAY I'VE BEEN *BURNING* FOR A FIGHT!

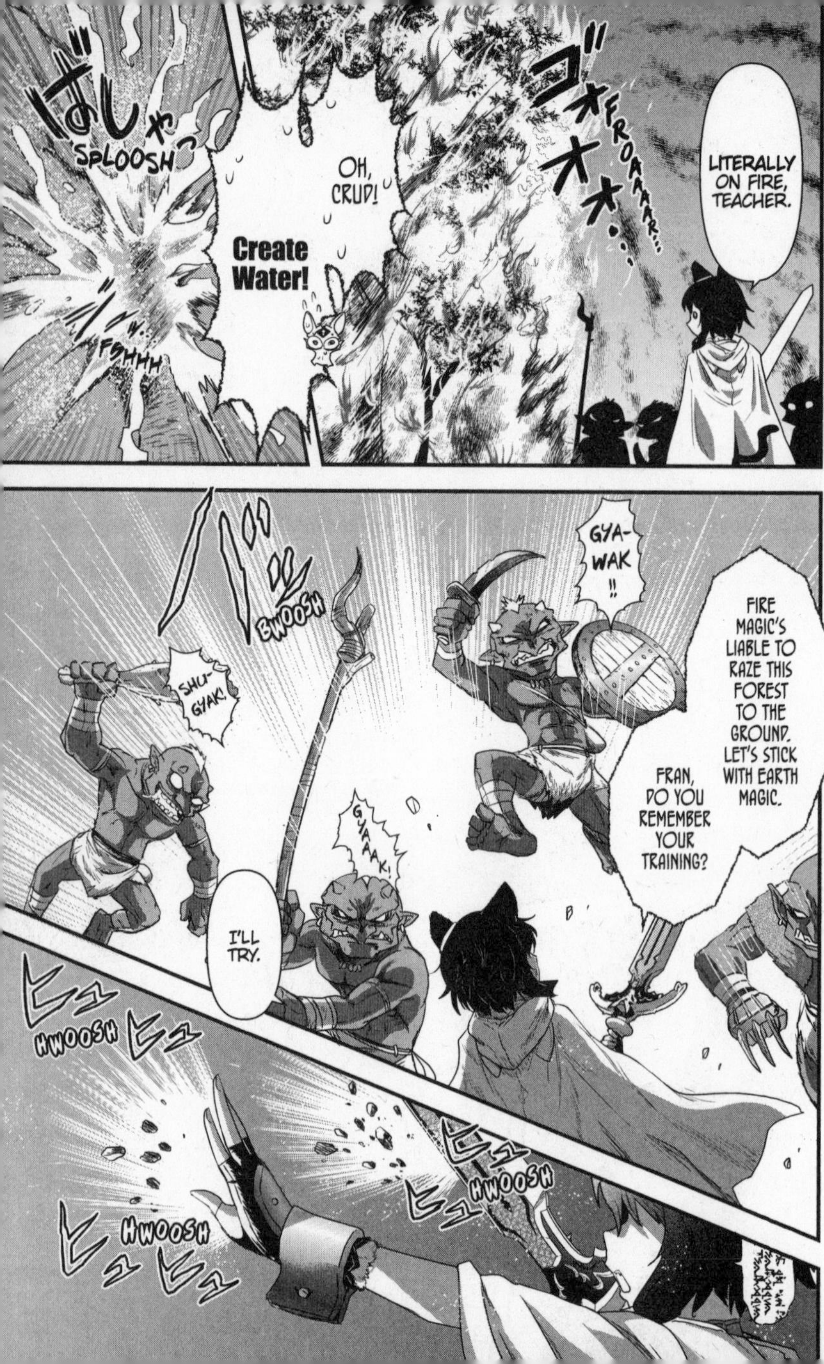
LITERALLY ON FIRE, TEACHER.
FROAAAAAR...
OH, CRUD!
Create Water!
SPLOOSH
FSHHH
FIRE MAGIC'S LIABLE TO RAZE THIS FOREST TO THE GROUND. LET'S STICK WITH EARTH MAGIC.
FRAN, DO YOU REMEMBER YOUR TRAINING?
GYA-WAK!!
BWOOSH
GYAAAAK!
SHU-GYAK!
I'LL TRY.
HWOOSH
HWOOSH
HWOOSH

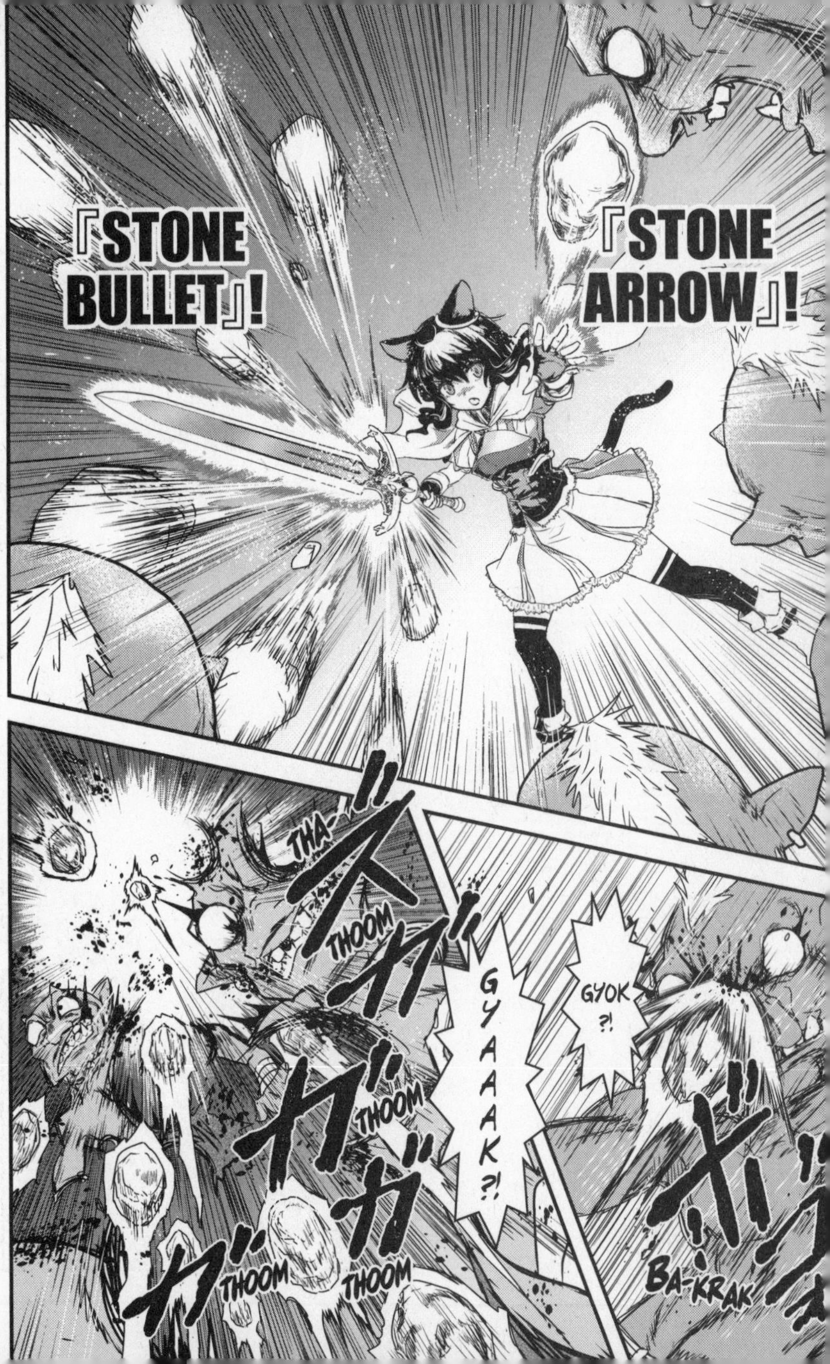
『STONE ARROW』!
『STONE BULLET』!
GYOK?!
BA-KRAK
THA-
THOOM
GYAAAK?!
THOOM
THOOM
THOOM

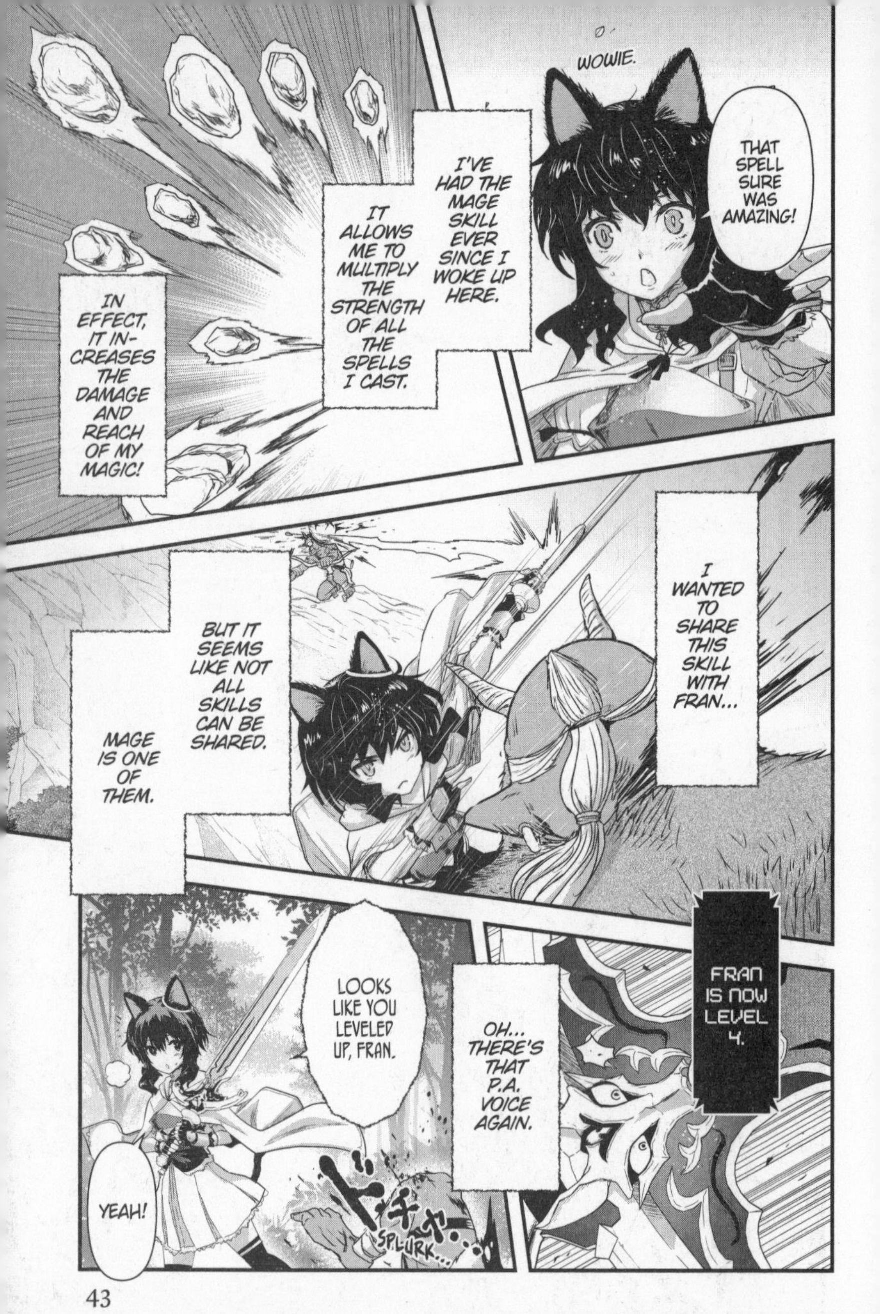
WOWIE.
THAT SPELL SURE WAS AMAZING!
I'VE HAD THE MAGE SKILL EVER SINCE I WOKE UP HERE.
IT ALLOWS ME TO MULTIPLY THE STRENGTH OF ALL THE SPELLS I CAST.
IN EFFECT, IT IN-CREASES THE DAMAGE AND REACH OF MY MAGIC!
I WANTED TO SHARE THIS SKILL WITH FRAN...
BUT IT SEEMS LIKE NOT ALL SKILLS CAN BE SHARED.
MAGE IS ONE OF THEM.
FRAN IS NOW LEVEL 4.
OH... THERE'S THAT P.A. VOICE AGAIN.
LOOKS LIKE YOU LEVELED UP, FRAN.
SPLURK...
YEAH!

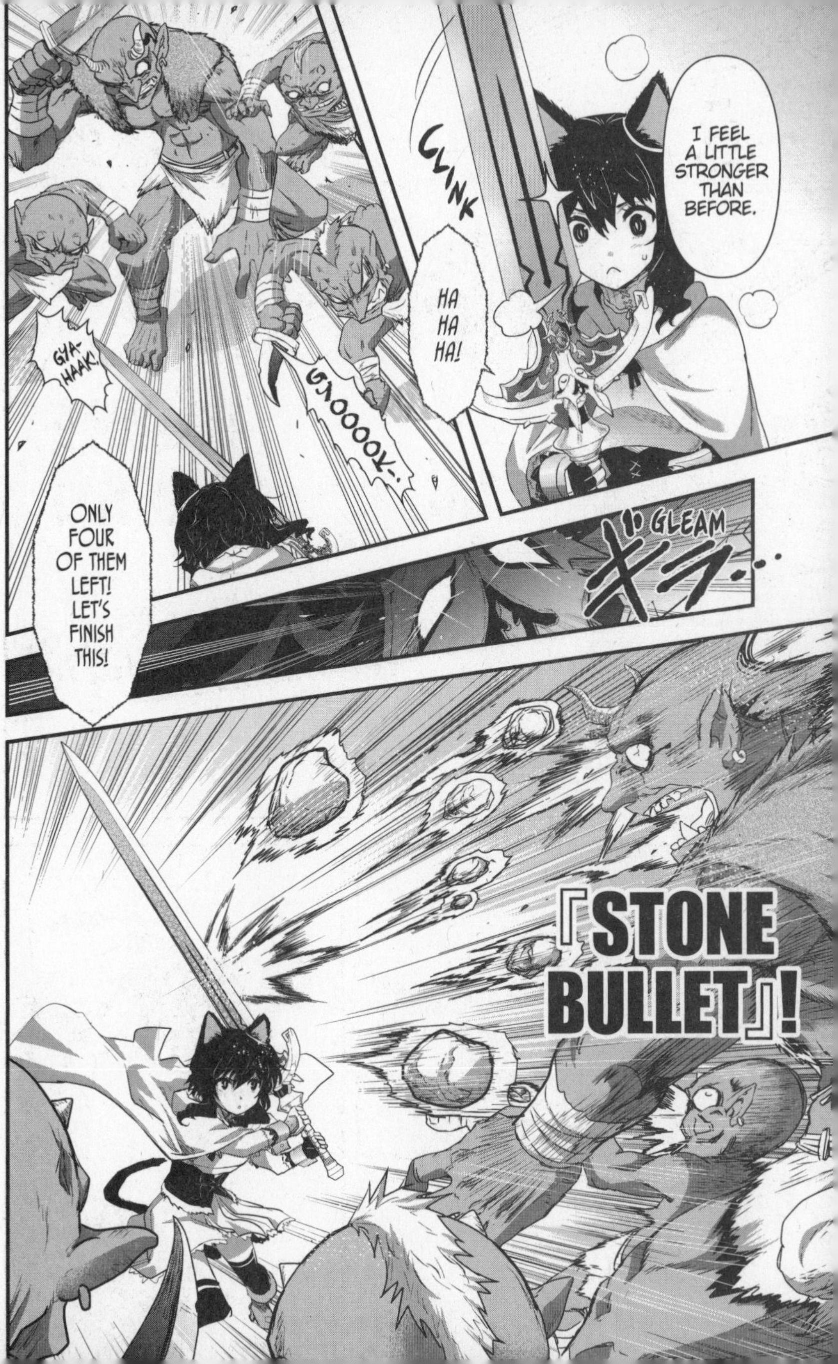
I FEEL A LITTLE STRONGER THAN BEFORE.
CLINK
HA HA HA!
GROOOOOK!
GYA-HAAK!
ONLY FOUR OF THEM LEFT! LET'S FINISH THIS!
GLEAM
『STONE BULLET』!

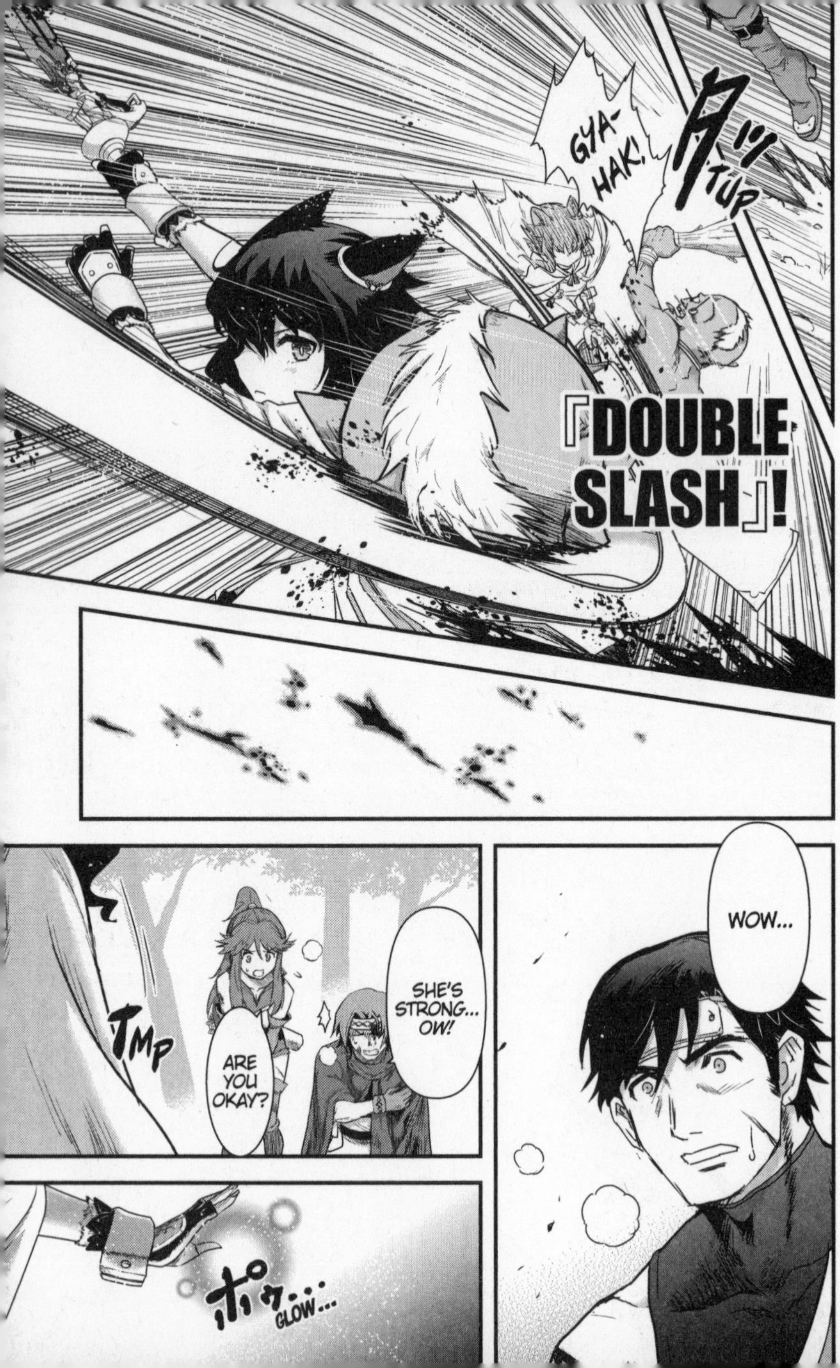
TUP
GYA-HAK!
『DOUBLE SLASH』!
WOW...
SHE'S STRONG... OW!
ARE YOU OKAY?
TMP
GLOW...

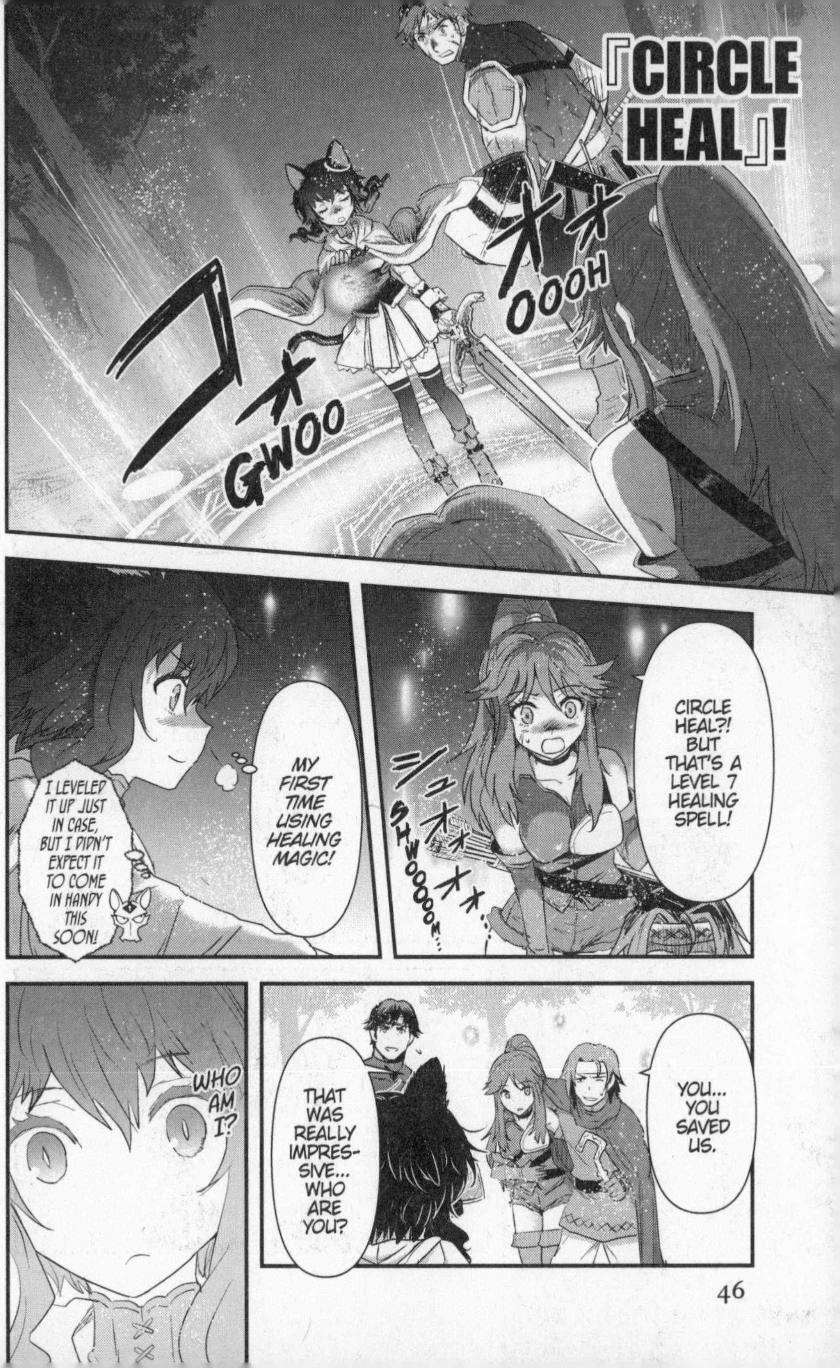
『CIRCLE HEAL』!
OOOH
GWOO
CIRCLE HEAL?! BUT THAT'S A LEVEL 7 HEALING SPELL!
SHWOOOOOM...
MY FIRST TIME USING HEALING MAGIC!
I LEVELED IT UP JUST IN CASE, BUT I DIDN'T EXPECT IT TO COME IN HANDY THIS SOON!
YOU... YOU SAVED US.
THAT WAS REALLY IMPRES-SIVE... WHO ARE YOU?
WHO AM I?

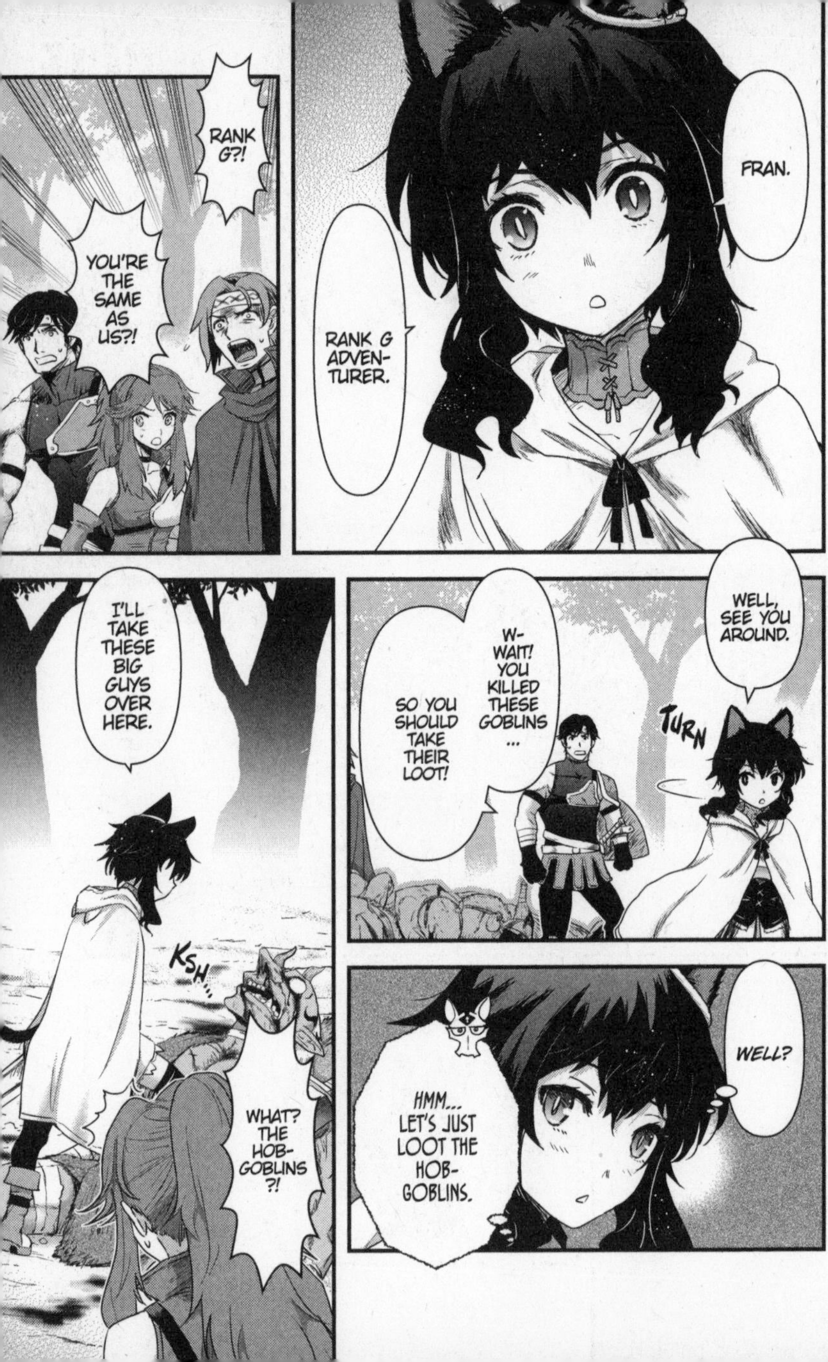
FRAN.
RANK G ADVENTURER.
RANK G?!
YOU'RE THE SAME AS US?!
WELL, SEE YOU AROUND.
TURN
W-WAIT! YOU KILLED THESE GOBLINS ...
SO YOU SHOULD TAKE THEIR LOOT!
WELL?
HMM... LET'S JUST LOOT THE HOB-GOBLINS.
I'LL TAKE THESE BIG GUYS OVER HERE.
KSH...
WHAT? THE HOB-GOBLINS ?!

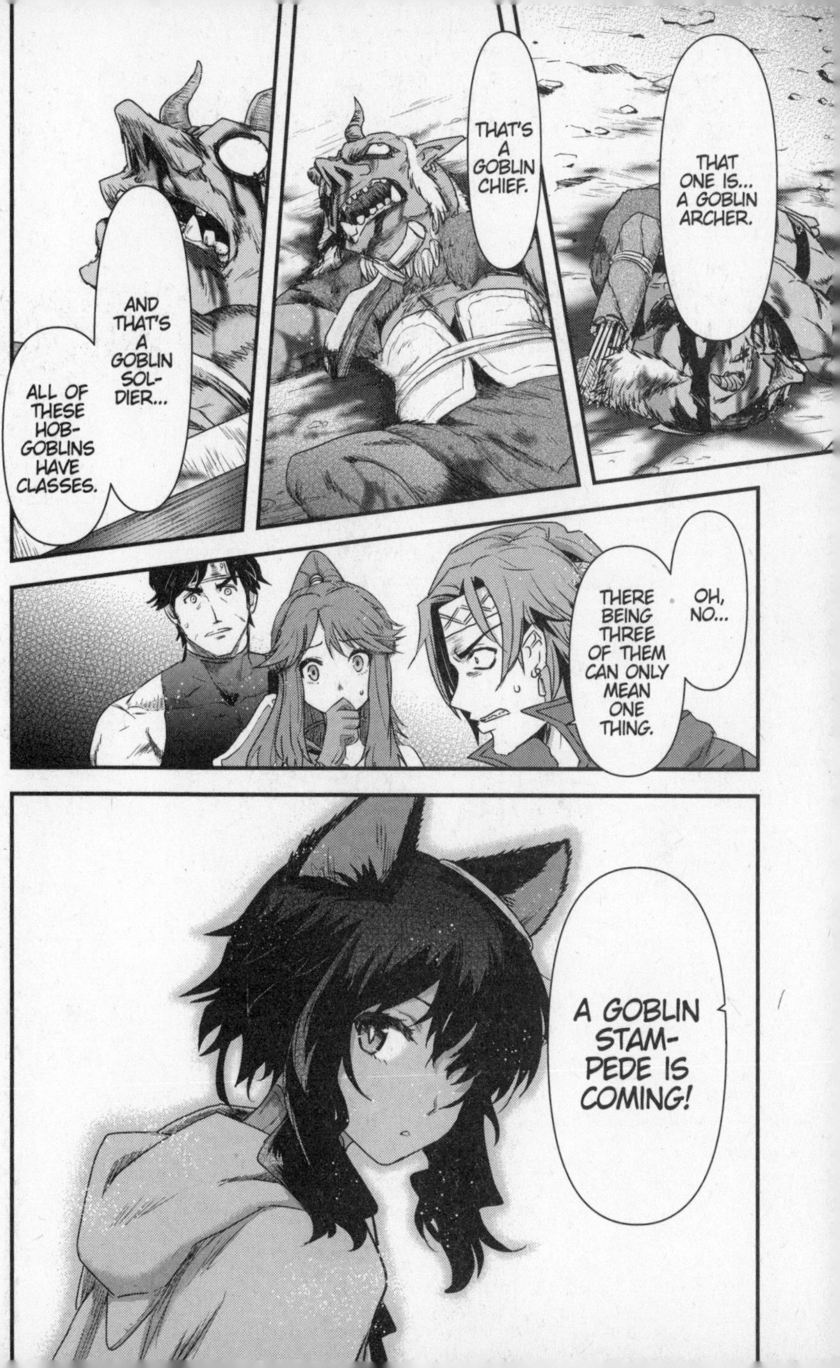
THAT ONE IS... A GOBLIN ARCHER.
THAT'S A GOBLIN CHIEF.
AND THAT'S A GOBLIN SOLDIER...
ALL OF THESE HOBGOBLINS HAVE CLASSES.
OH, NO...
THERE BEING THREE OF THEM CAN ONLY MEAN ONE THING.
A GOBLIN STAMPEDE IS COMING!

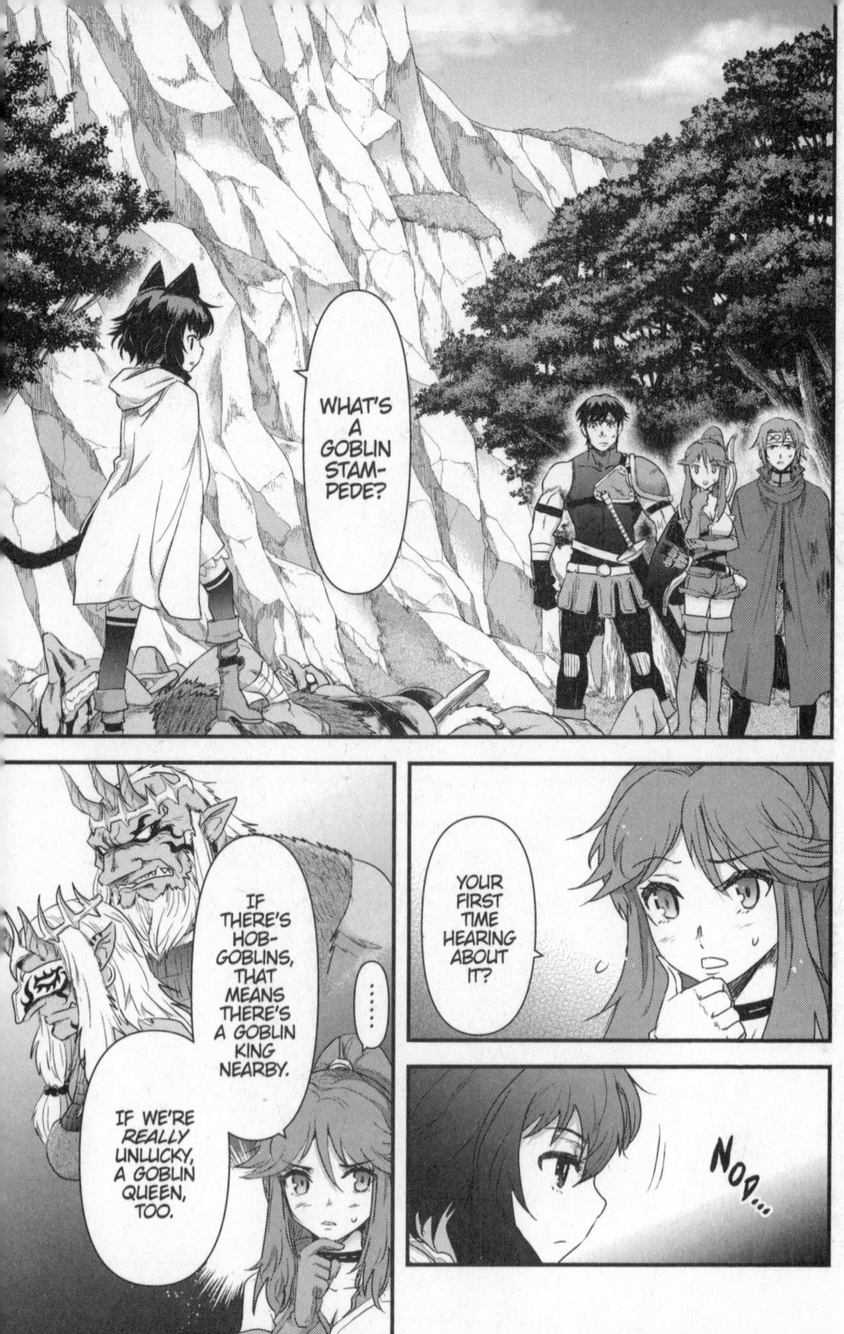
WHAT'S A GOBLIN STAMPEDE?
YOUR FIRST TIME HEARING ABOUT IT?
NOD...
IF THERE'S HOBGOBLINS, THAT MEANS THERE'S A GOBLIN KING NEARBY.
......
IF WE'RE *REALLY* UNLUCKY, A GOBLIN QUEEN, TOO.

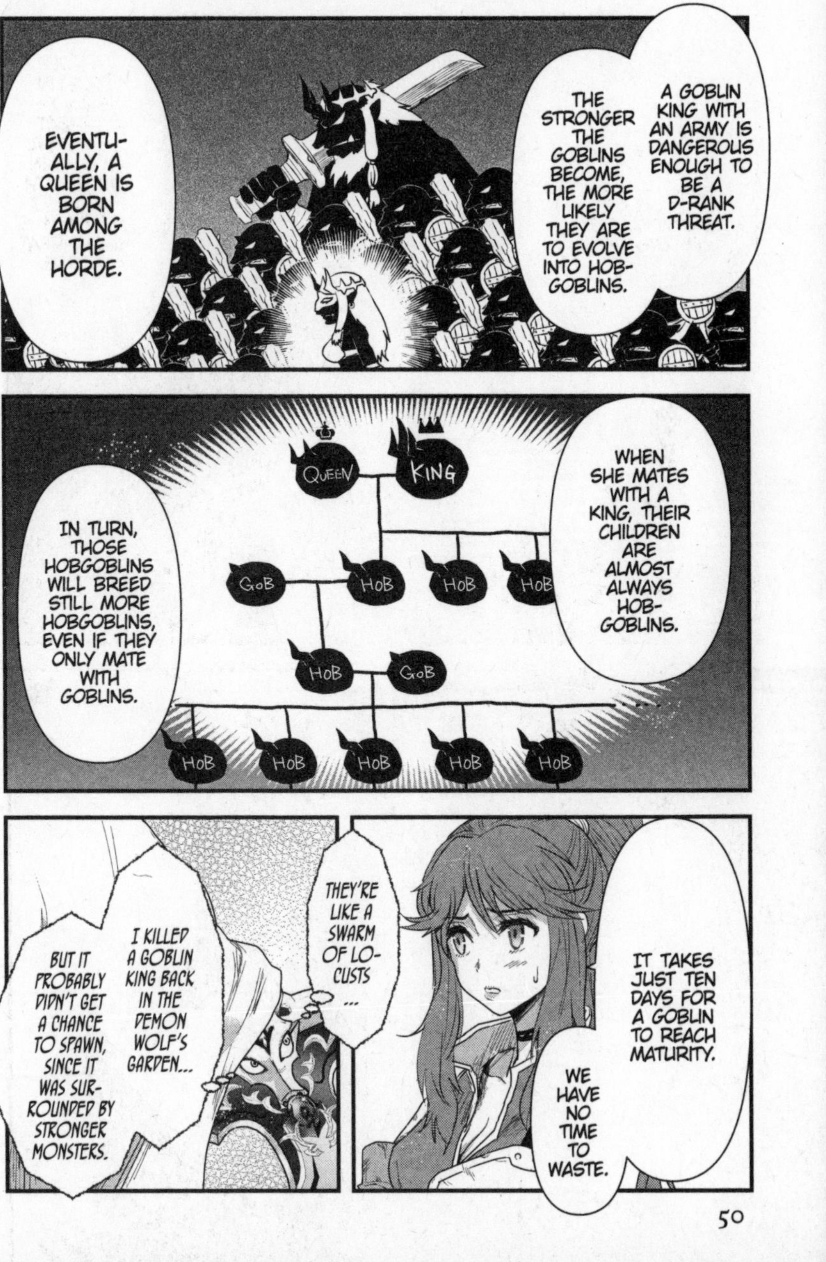
A GOBLIN KING WITH AN ARMY IS DANGEROUS ENOUGH TO BE A D-RANK THREAT.
THE STRONGER THE GOBLINS BECOME, THE MORE LIKELY THEY ARE TO EVOLVE INTO HOB-GOBLINS.
EVENTU-ALLY, A QUEEN IS BORN AMONG THE HORDE.
WHEN SHE MATES WITH A KING, THEIR CHILDREN ARE ALMOST ALWAYS HOB-GOBLINS.
QUEEN
KING
GOB
HOB
HOB
HOB
HOB
GOB
HOB
HOB
HOB
HOB
HOB
IN TURN, THOSE HOBGOBLINS WILL BREED STILL MORE HOBGOBLINS, EVEN IF THEY ONLY MATE WITH GOBLINS.
IT TAKES JUST TEN DAYS FOR A GOBLIN TO REACH MATURITY.
WE HAVE NO TIME TO WASTE.
THEY'RE LIKE A SWARM OF LO-CUSTS ...
I KILLED A GOBLIN KING BACK IN THE DEMON WOLF'S GARDEN...
BUT IT PROBABLY DIDN'T GET A CHANCE TO SPAWN, SINCE IT WAS SUR-ROUNDED BY STRONGER MONSTERS.

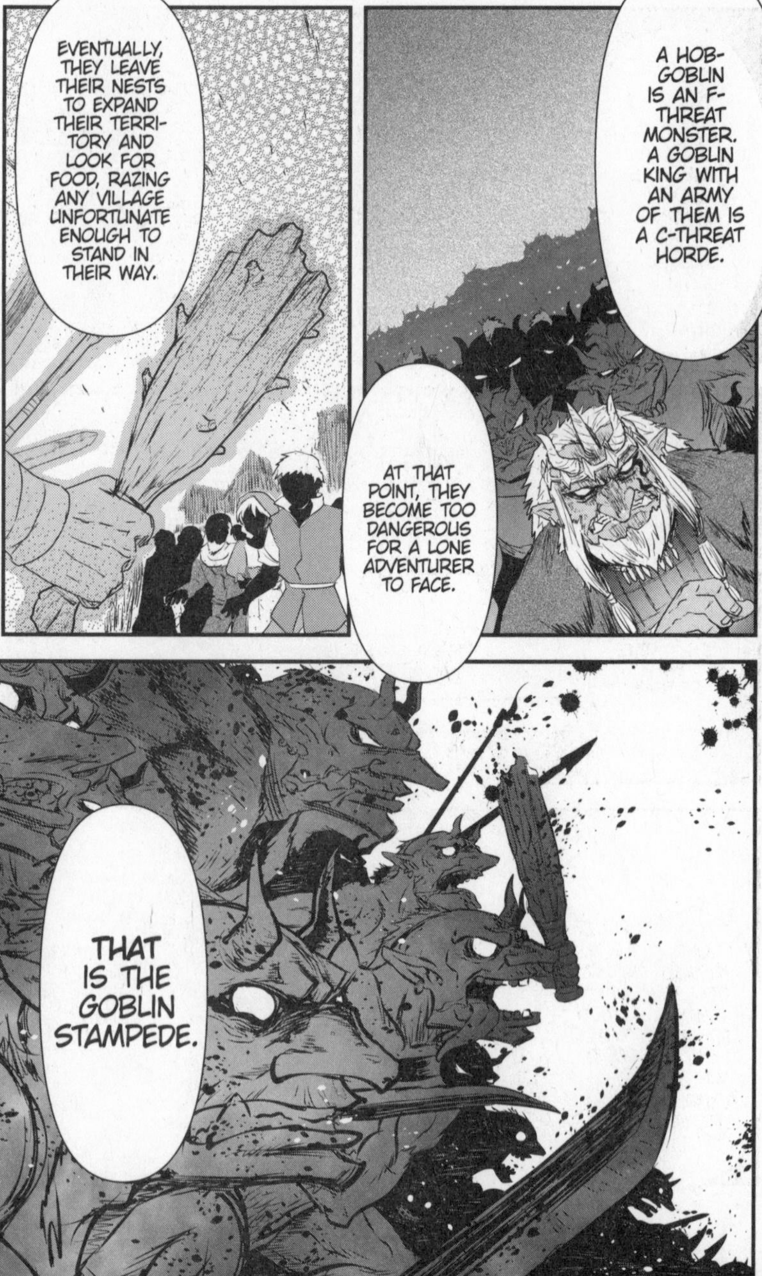
A HOB-GOBLIN IS AN F-THREAT MONSTER. A GOBLIN KING WITH AN ARMY OF THEM IS A C-THREAT HORDE.
EVENTUALLY, THEY LEAVE THEIR NESTS TO EXPAND THEIR TERRITORY AND LOOK FOR FOOD, RAZING ANY VILLAGE UNFORTUNATE ENOUGH TO STAND IN THEIR WAY.
AT THAT POINT, THEY BECOME TOO DANGEROUS FOR A LONE ADVENTURER TO FACE.
THAT IS THE GOBLIN STAMPEDE.

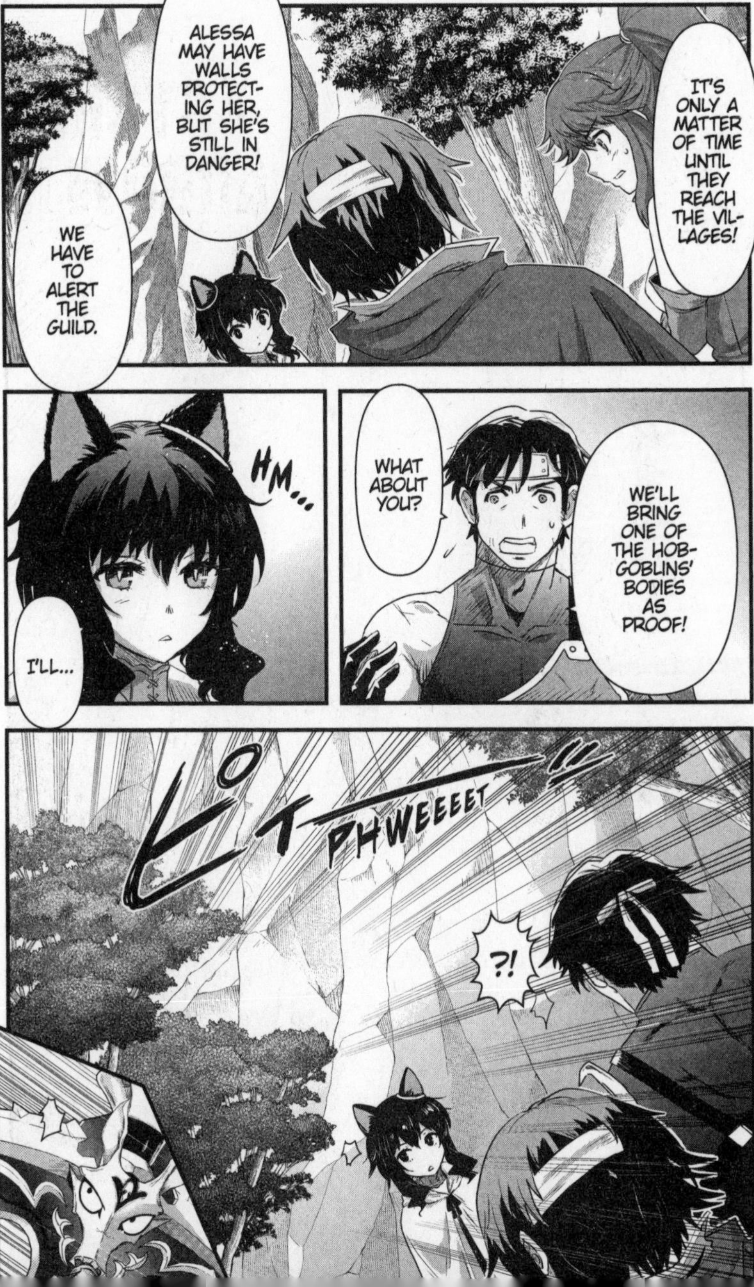
IT'S ONLY A MATTER OF TIME UNTIL THEY REACH THE VILLAGES!
ALESSA MAY HAVE WALLS PROTECTING HER, BUT SHE'S STILL IN DANGER!
WE HAVE TO ALERT THE GUILD.
WE'LL BRING ONE OF THE HOBGOBLINS' BODIES AS PROOF!
WHAT ABOUT YOU?
HM...
I'LL...
PHWEEEET
?!

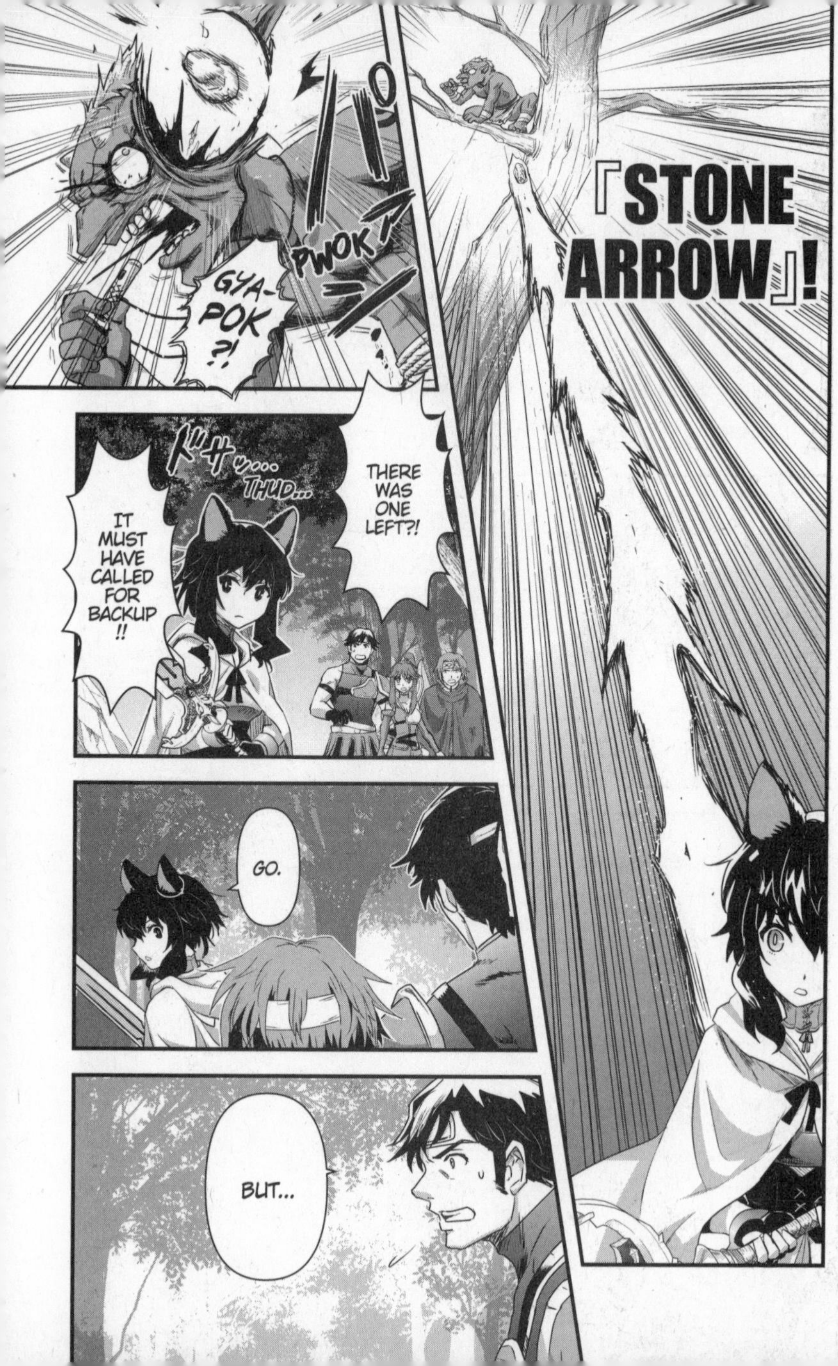
『STONE ARROW』!
PWOK
GYA-POK ?!
THERE WAS ONE LEFT?!
ドサッ... THUD...
IT MUST HAVE CALLED FOR BACKUP !!
GO.
BUT...

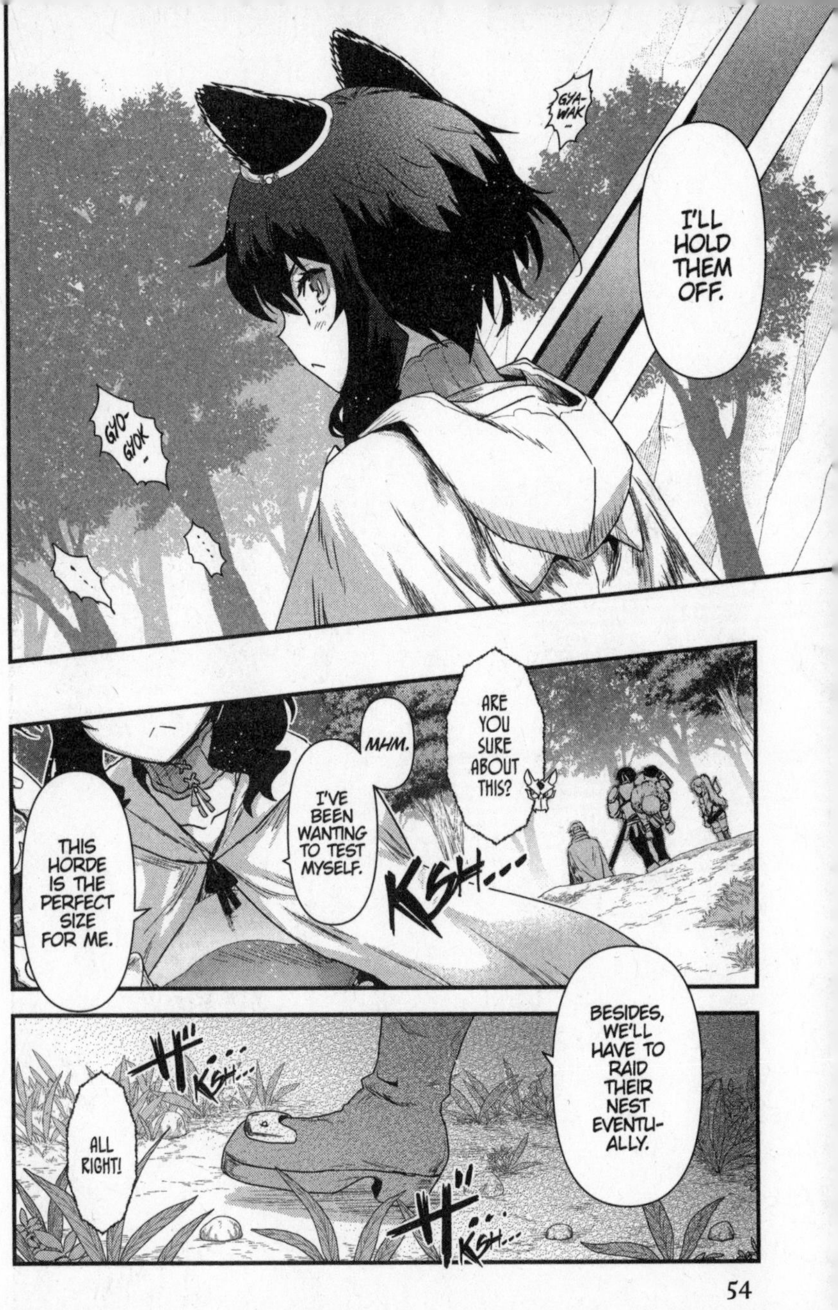
GYA-WAK...
I'LL HOLD THEM OFF.
GYO-GYOK...
...
...
ARE YOU SURE ABOUT THIS?
MHM.
I'VE BEEN WANTING TO TEST MYSELF.
KSH...
THIS HORDE IS THE PERFECT SIZE FOR ME.
BESIDES, WE'LL HAVE TO RAID THEIR NEST EVENTUALLY.
KSH...
ALL RIGHT!
KSH...

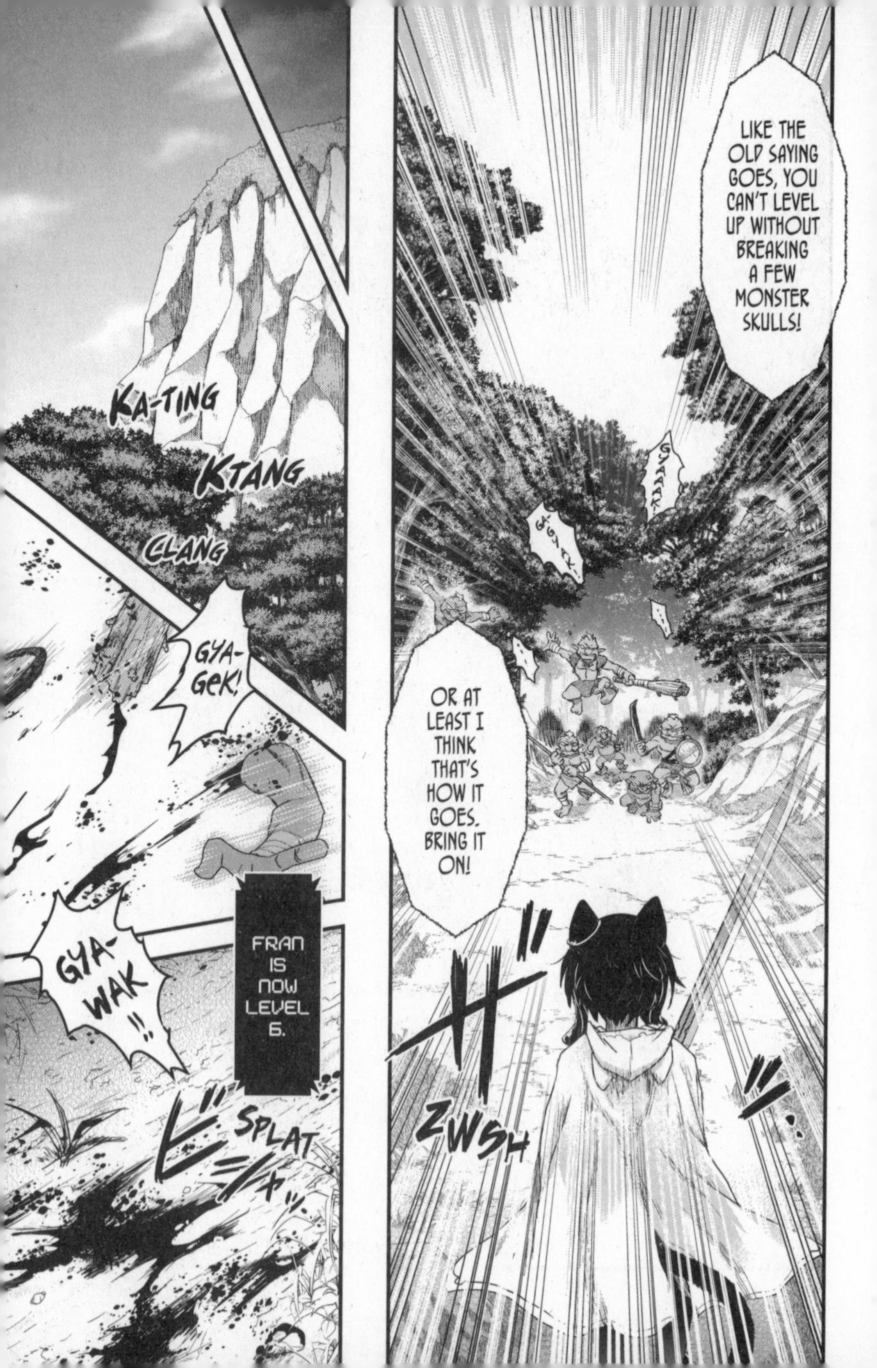
LIKE THE OLD SAYING GOES, YOU CAN'T LEVEL UP WITHOUT BREAKING A FEW MONSTER SKULLS!
OR AT LEAST I THINK THAT'S HOW IT GOES. BRING IT ON!
ZWSH
KA-TING
KTANG
CLANG
GYA-GEK!
FRAN IS NOW LEVEL 6.
GYA-WAK!!
SPLAT

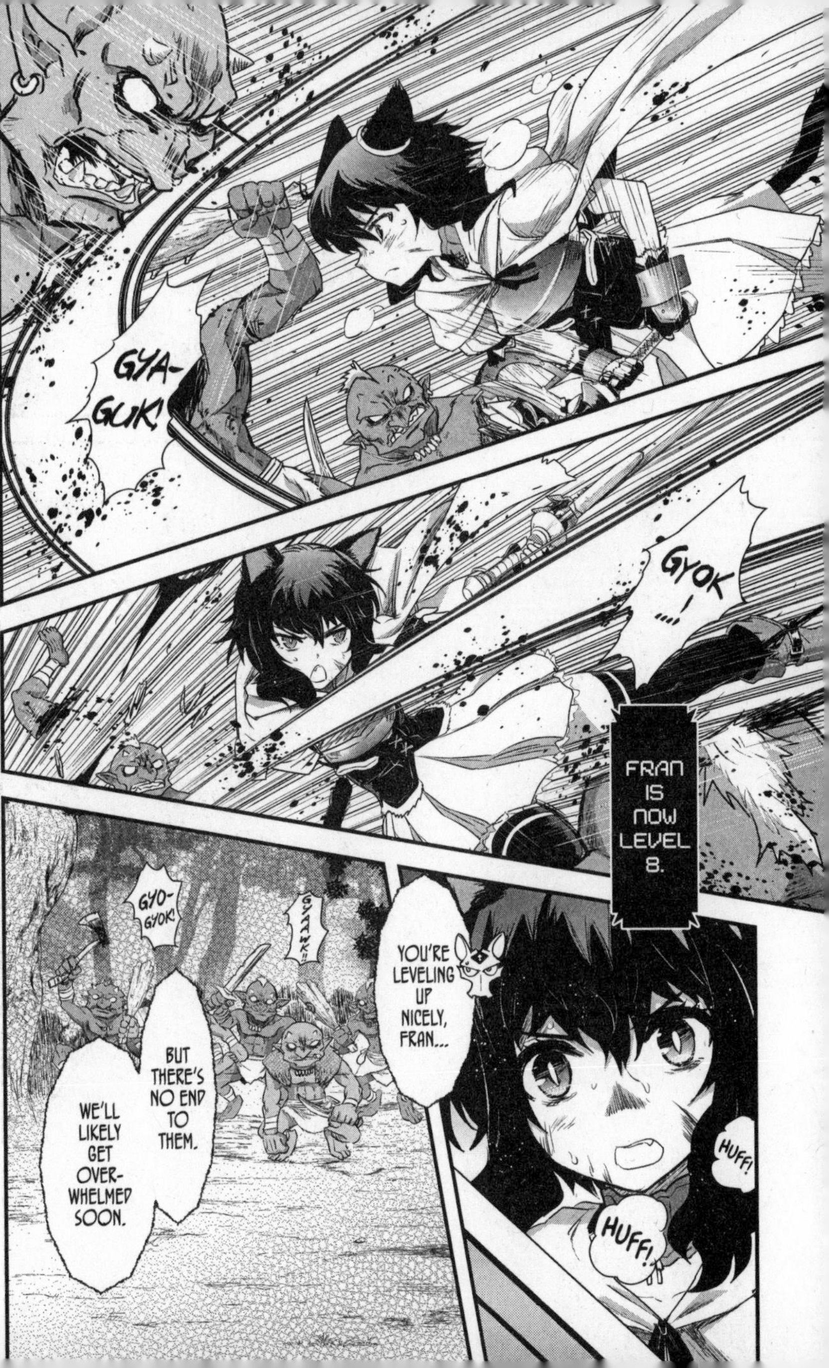
GYA-GUK!
GYOK...!
FRAN IS NOW LEVEL 8.
YOU'RE LEVELING UP NICELY, FRAN...
BUT THERE'S NO END TO THEM.
WE'LL LIKELY GET OVER-WHELMED SOON.
HUFF!
HUFF!
GYAAWK!!
GYO-GYOK!

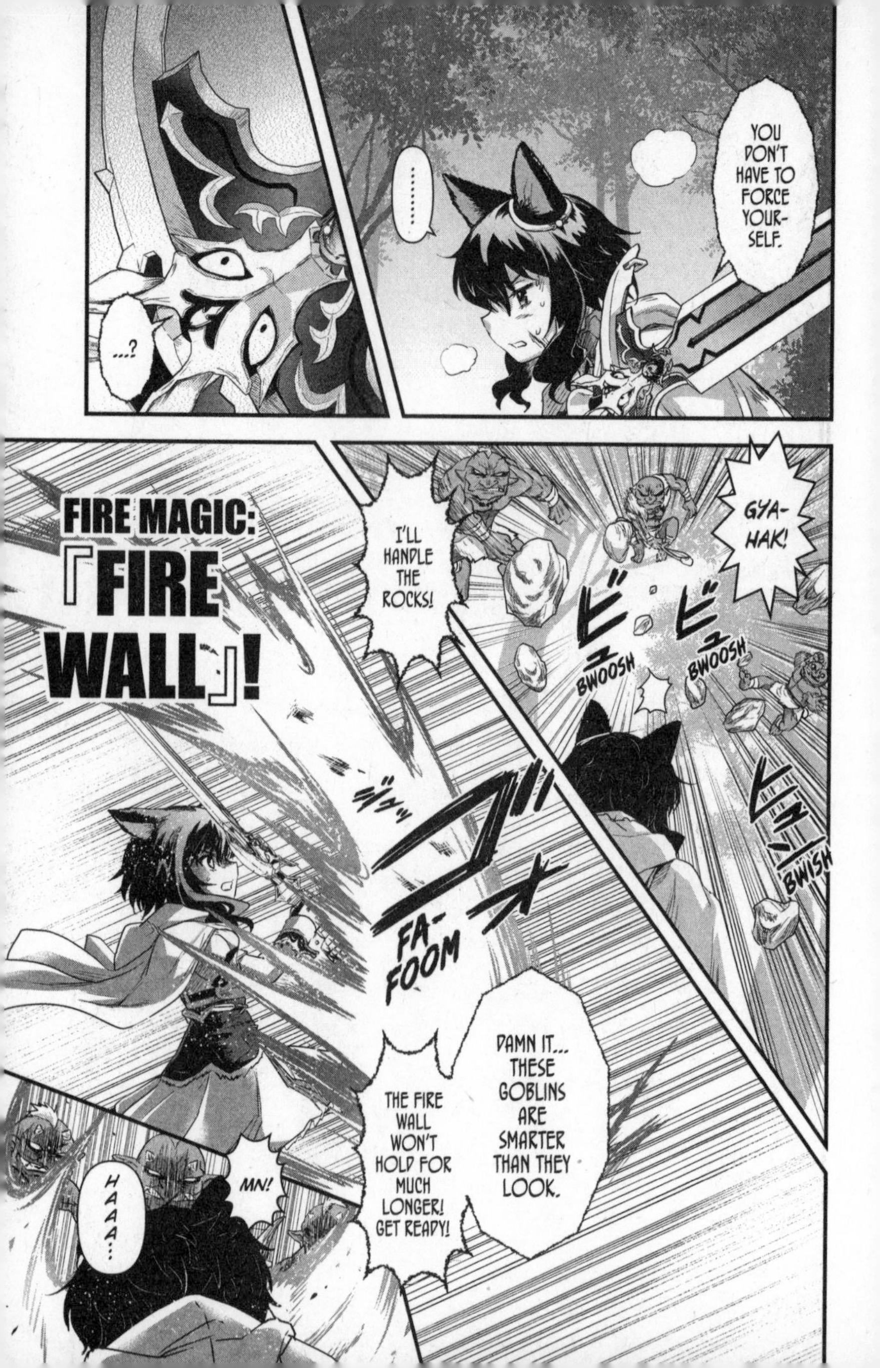
YOU DON'T HAVE TO FORCE YOURSELF.
......
...?
GYA-HAK!
BWOOSH
BWOOSH
BWISH
I'LL HANDLE THE ROCKS!
FIRE MAGIC: 『FIRE WALL』!
FA-FOOM
DAMN IT... THESE GOBLINS ARE SMARTER THAN THEY LOOK.
THE FIRE WALL WON'T HOLD FOR MUCH LONGER! GET READY!
MN!
HAAAA...

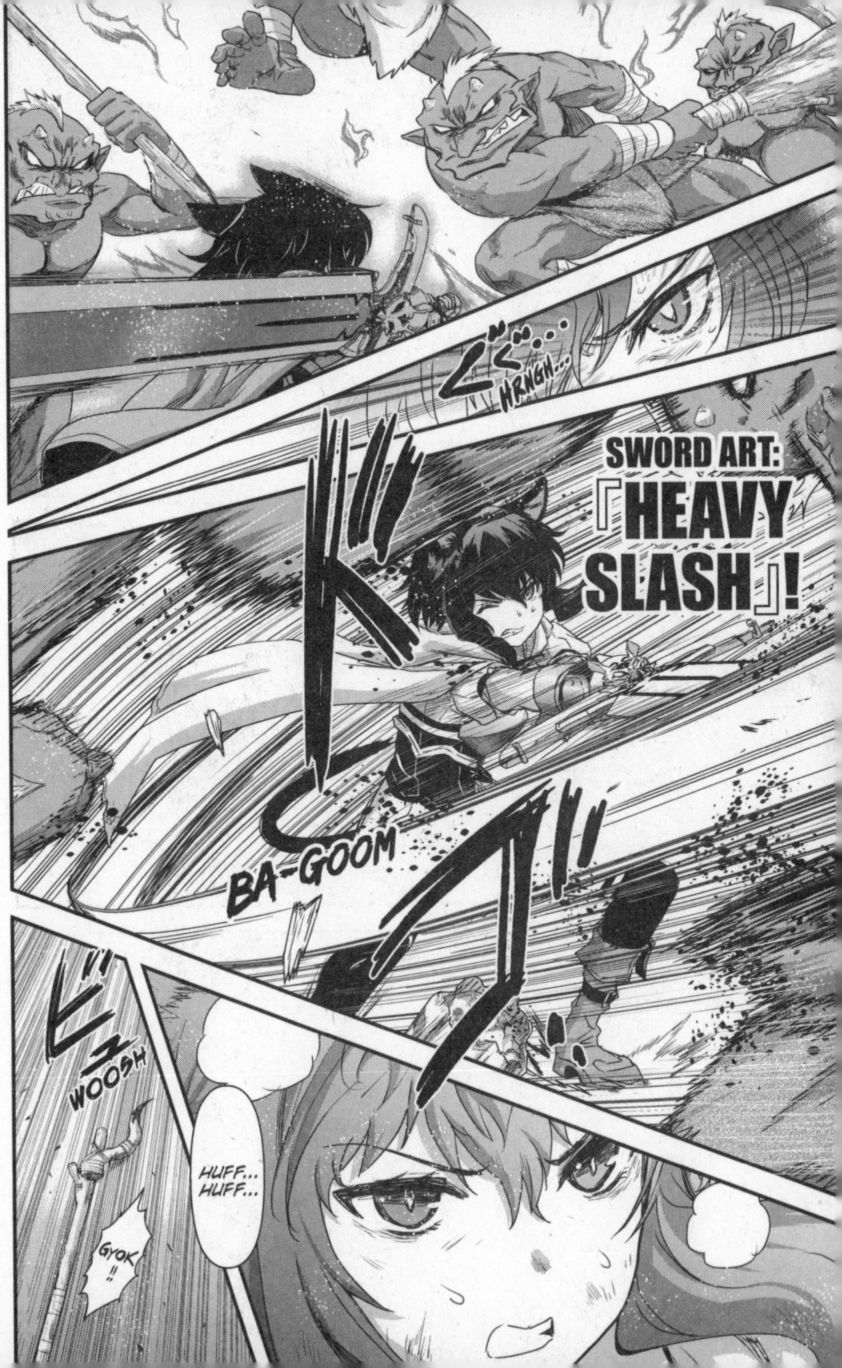
HRNGH...
SWORD ART:
『HEAVY SLASH』!
BA-GOOM
HUFF... HUFF...
WOOSH
GYOK!!

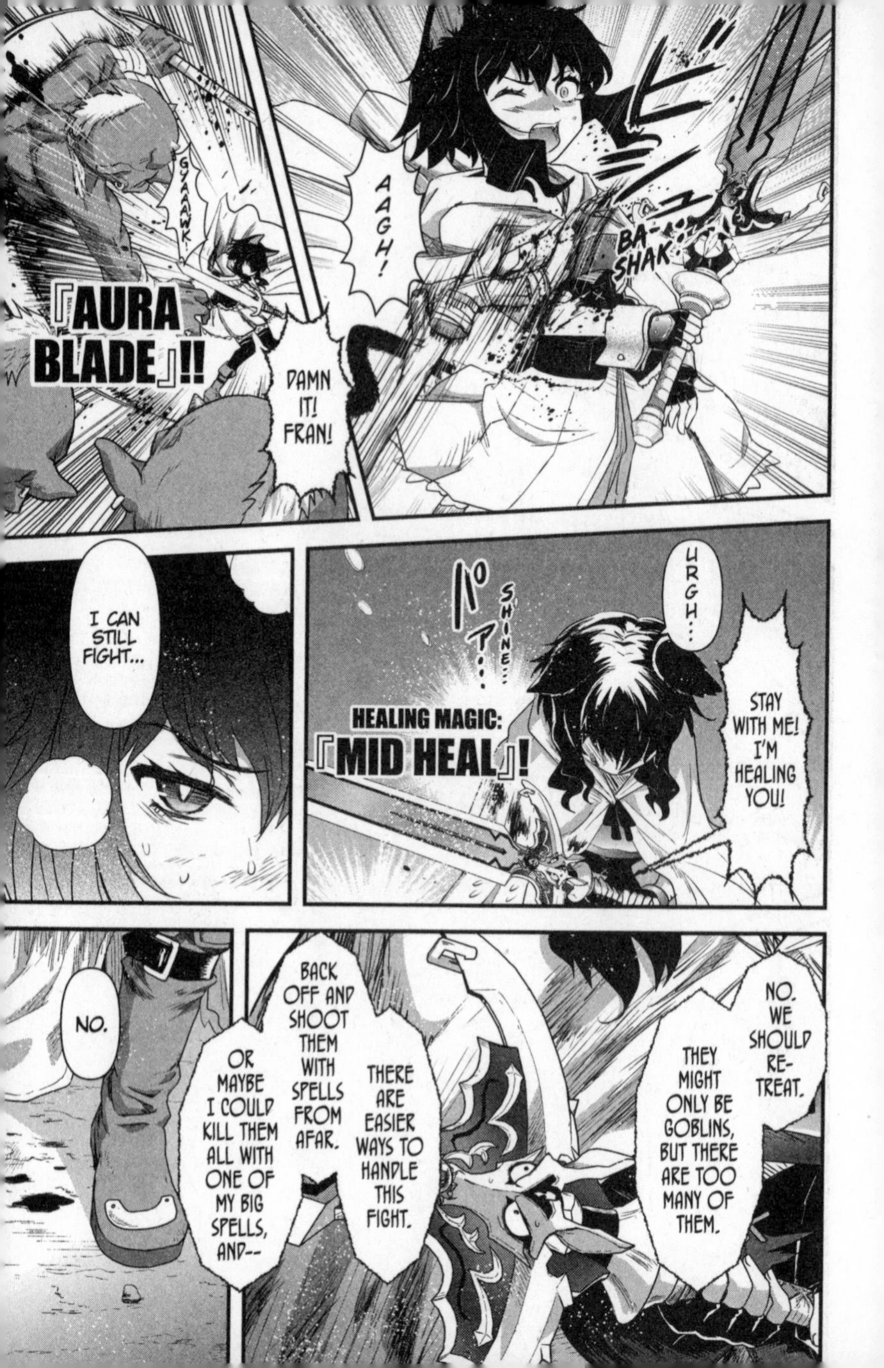
BA-SHAK
AAGH!
DAMN IT! FRAN!
GYAAAWK!
『AURA BLADE』!!
URGH...
SHINE...
STAY WITH ME! I'M HEALING YOU!
HEALING MAGIC: 『MID HEAL』!
I CAN STILL FIGHT...
NO. WE SHOULD RE-TREAT.
THEY MIGHT ONLY BE GOBLINS, BUT THERE ARE TOO MANY OF THEM.
THERE ARE EASIER WAYS TO HANDLE THIS FIGHT.
BACK OFF AND SHOOT THEM WITH SPELLS FROM AFAR.
OR MAYBE I COULD KILL THEM ALL WITH ONE OF MY BIG SPELLS, AND--
NO.

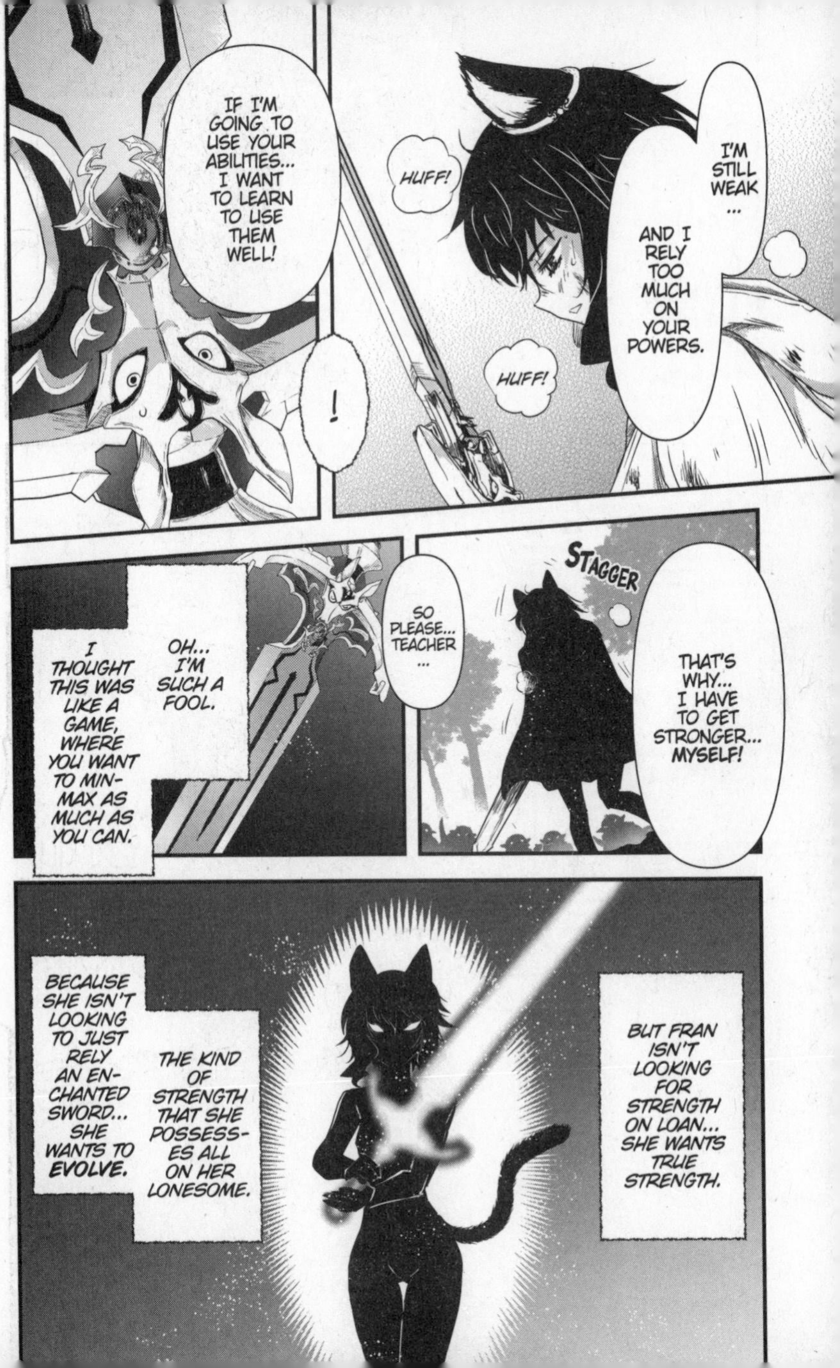
HUFF!
I'M STILL WEAK... AND I RELY TOO MUCH ON YOUR POWERS.
HUFF!
IF I'M GOING TO USE YOUR ABILITIES... I WANT TO LEARN TO USE THEM WELL!
!
STAGGER
THAT'S WHY... I HAVE TO GET STRONGER... MYSELF!
SO PLEASE... TEACHER...
OH... I'M SUCH A FOOL.
I THOUGHT THIS WAS LIKE A GAME, WHERE YOU WANT TO MIN-MAX AS MUCH AS YOU CAN.
BUT FRAN ISN'T LOOKING FOR STRENGTH ON LOAN... SHE WANTS TRUE STRENGTH.
THE KIND OF STRENGTH THAT SHE POSSESSES ALL ON HER LONESOME.
BECAUSE SHE ISN'T LOOKING TO JUST RELY AN ENCHANTED SWORD... SHE WANTS TO **EVOLVE.**

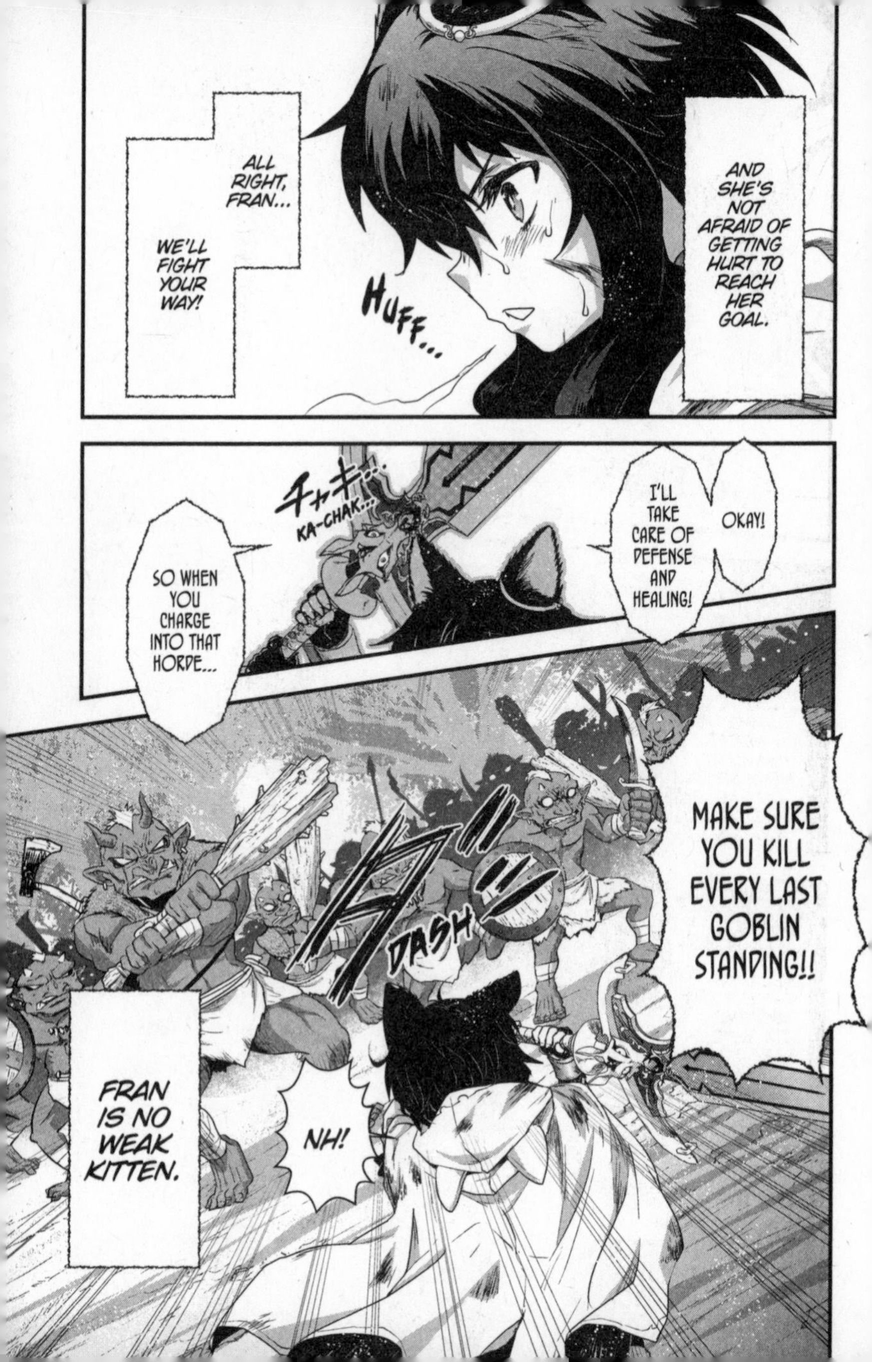
AND SHE'S NOT AFRAID OF GETTING HURT TO REACH HER GOAL.
HUFF...
ALL RIGHT, FRAN...
WE'LL FIGHT YOUR WAY!
OKAY!
I'LL TAKE CARE OF DEFENSE AND HEALING!
チャキ...
KA-CHAK...
SO WHEN YOU CHARGE INTO THAT HORDE...
MAKE SURE YOU KILL EVERY LAST GOBLIN STANDING!!
DASH
NH!
FRAN IS NO WEAK KITTEN.

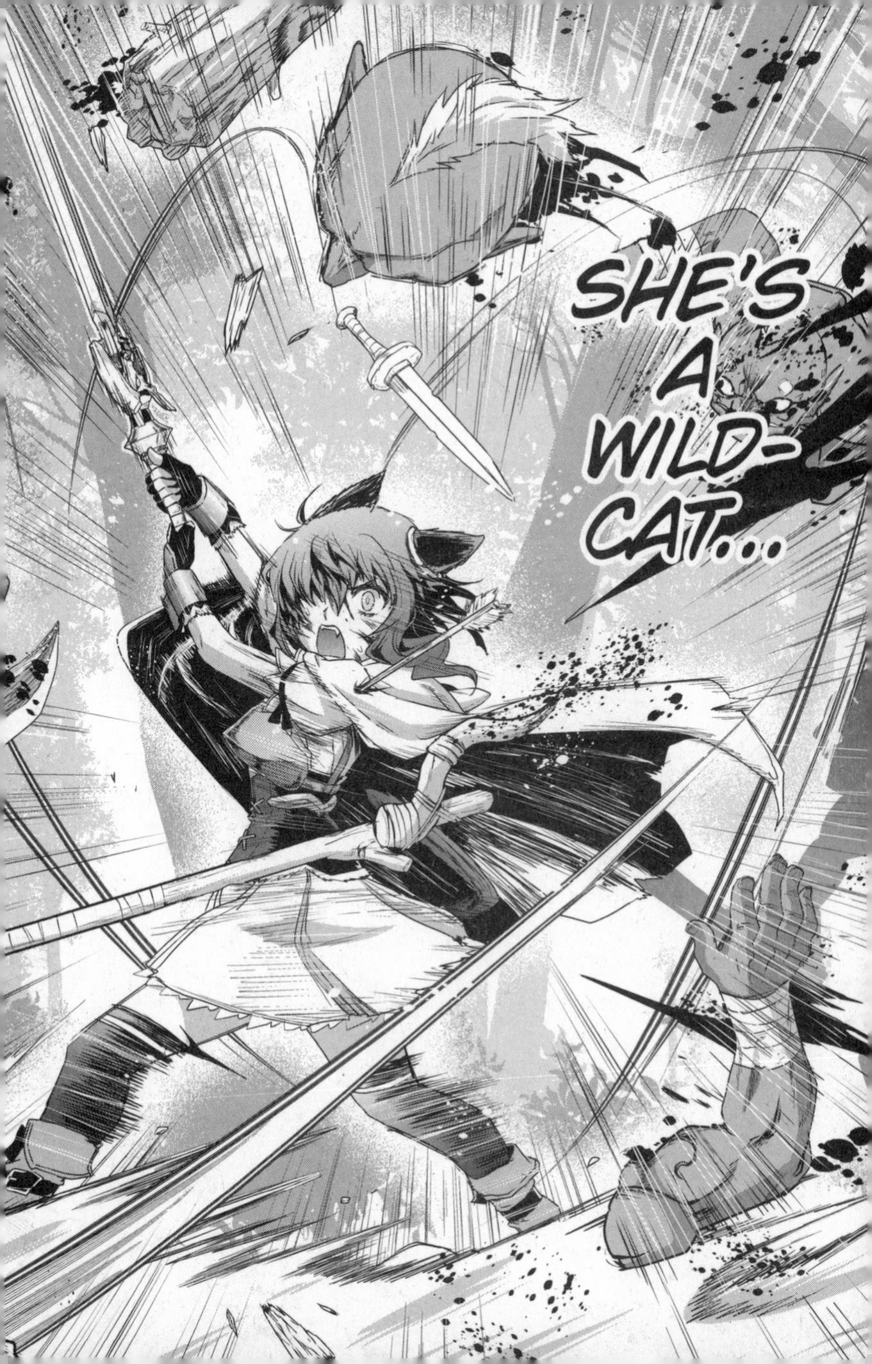
SHE'S A WILD-CAT...

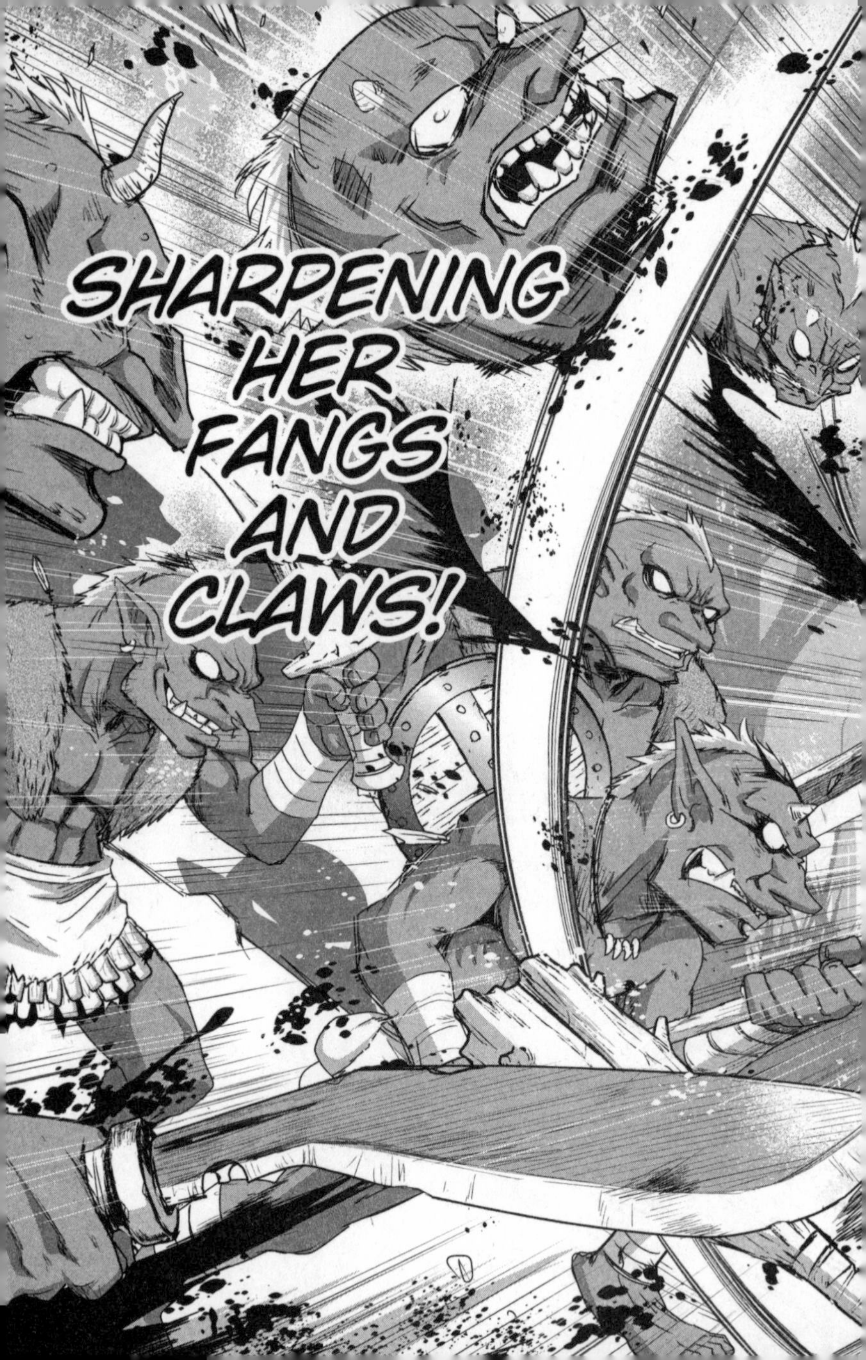
SHARPENING HER FANGS AND CLAWS!

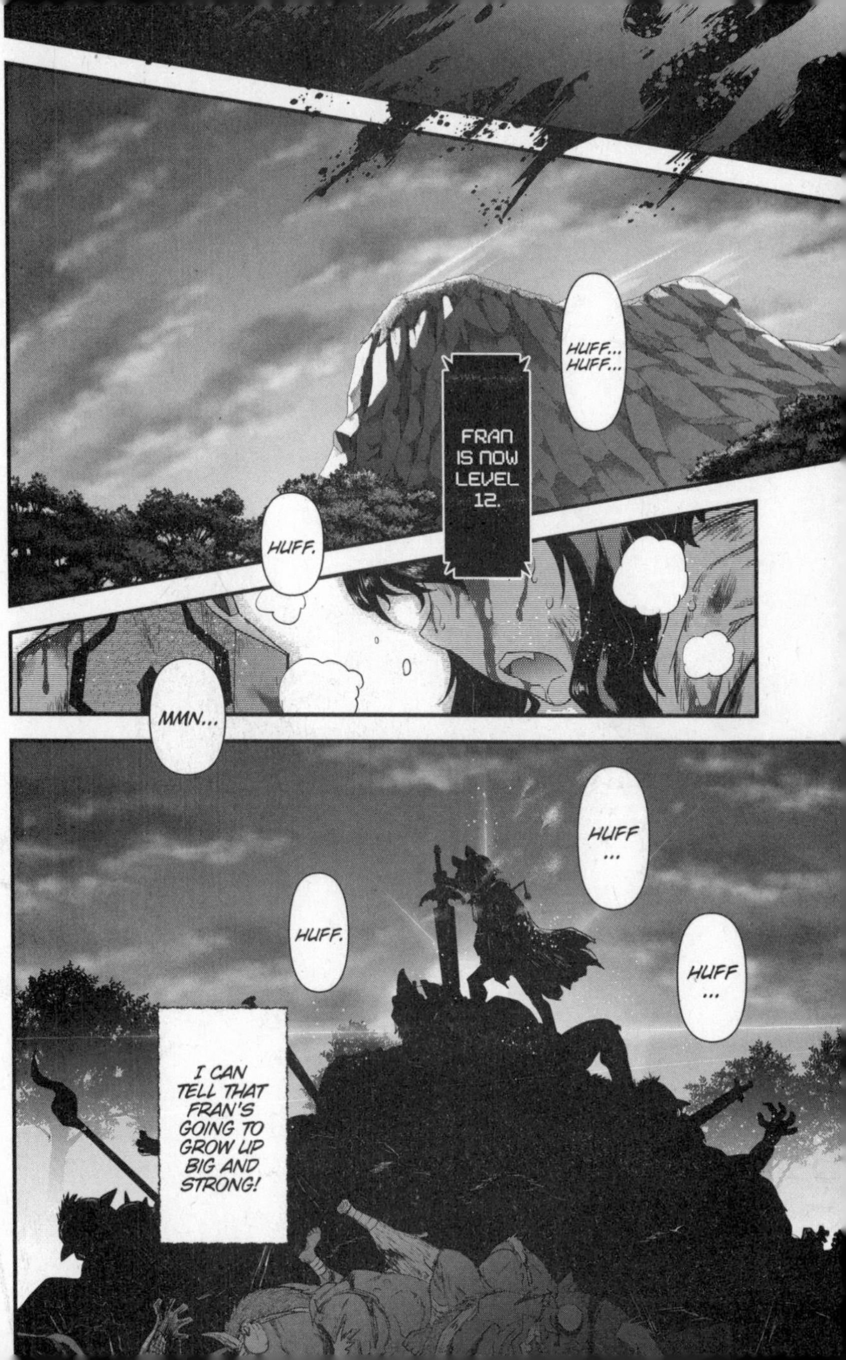
HUFF... HUFF...
FRAN IS NOW LEVEL 12.
HUFF.
MMN...
HUFF ...
HUFF ...
HUFF.
I CAN TELL THAT FRAN'S GOING TO GROW UP BIG AND STRONG!

Chapter 9: Gods and Dungeons

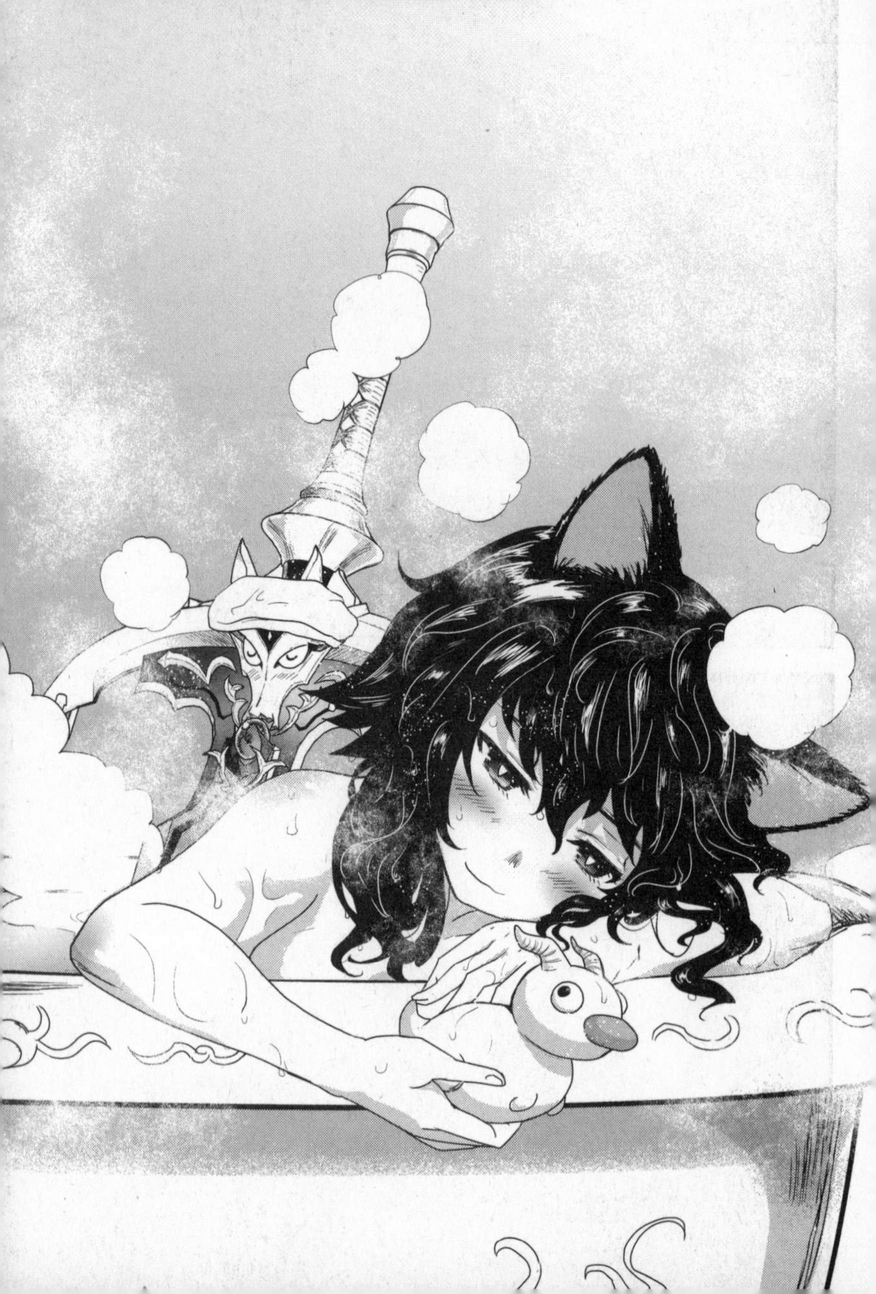

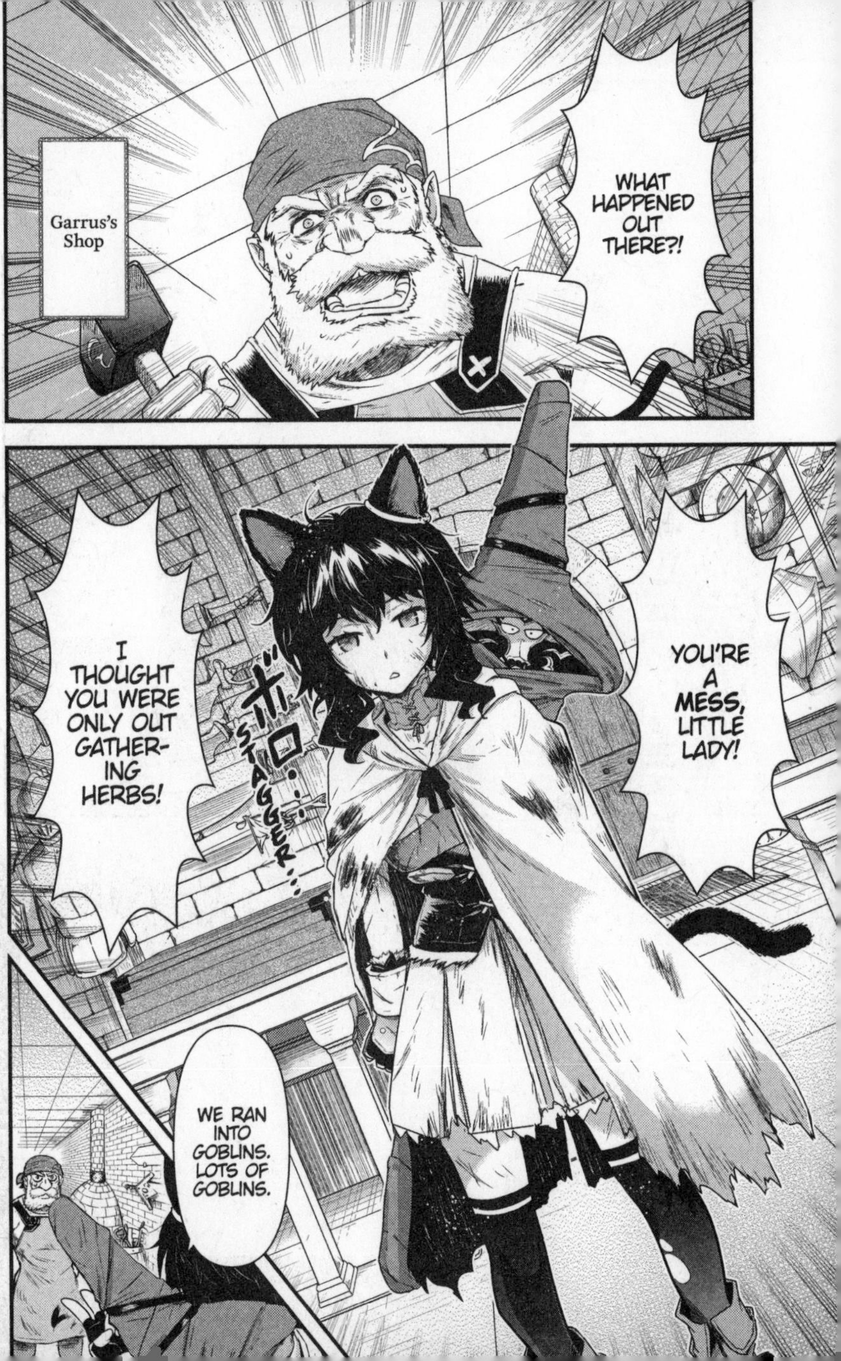
WHAT HAPPENED OUT THERE?!
Garrus's Shop
YOU'RE A MESS, LITTLE LADY!
I THOUGHT YOU WERE ONLY OUT GATHERING HERBS!
STAGGER...
WE RAN INTO GOBLINS. LOTS OF GOBLINS.

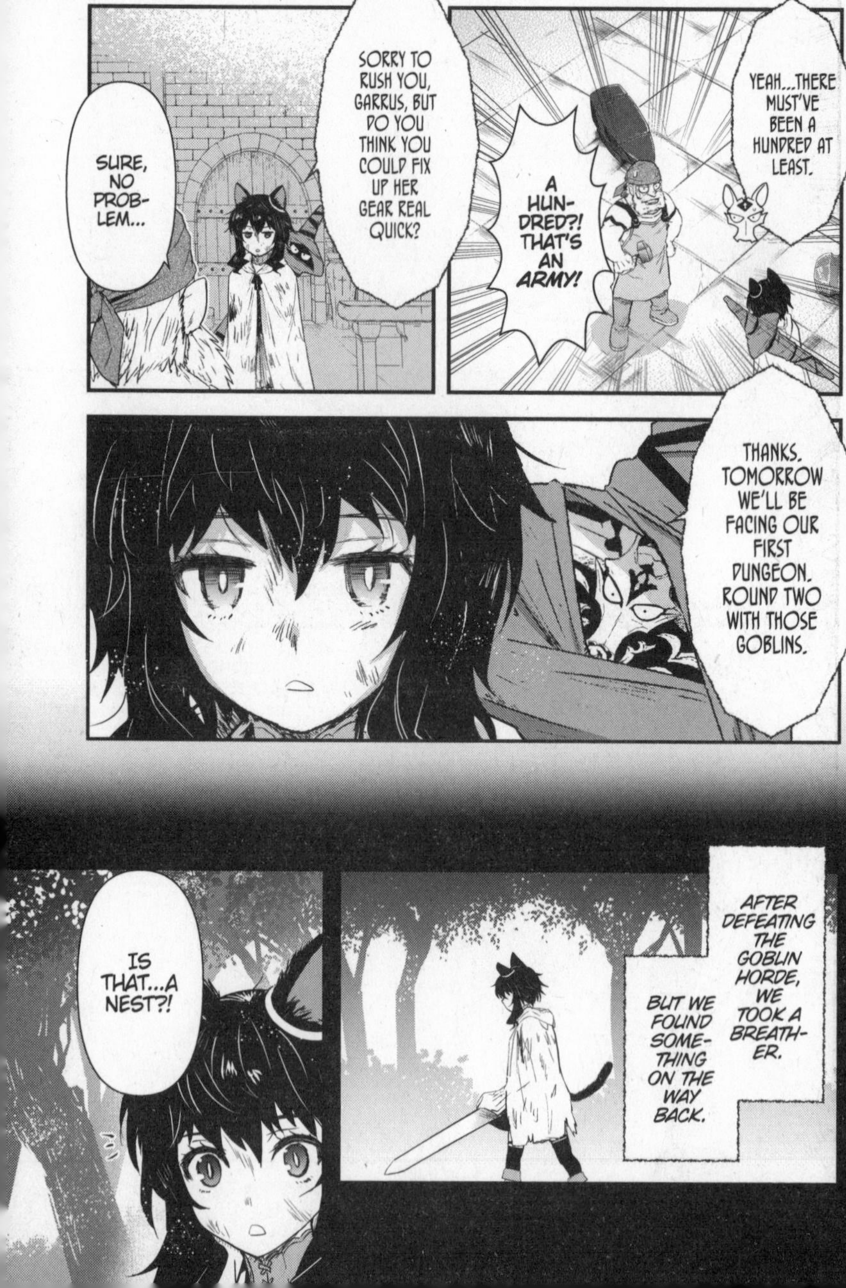
YEAH...THERE MUST'VE BEEN A HUNDRED AT LEAST.
A HUN-DRED?! THAT'S AN *ARMY!*
SORRY TO RUSH YOU, GARRUS, BUT DO YOU THINK YOU COULD FIX UP HER GEAR REAL QUICK?
SURE, NO PROB-LEM...
THANKS. TOMORROW WE'LL BE FACING OUR FIRST DUNGEON. ROUND TWO WITH THOSE GOBLINS.
AFTER DEFEATING THE GOBLIN HORDE, WE TOOK A BREATH-ER.
BUT WE FOUND SOME-THING ON THE WAY BACK.
IS THAT...A NEST?!

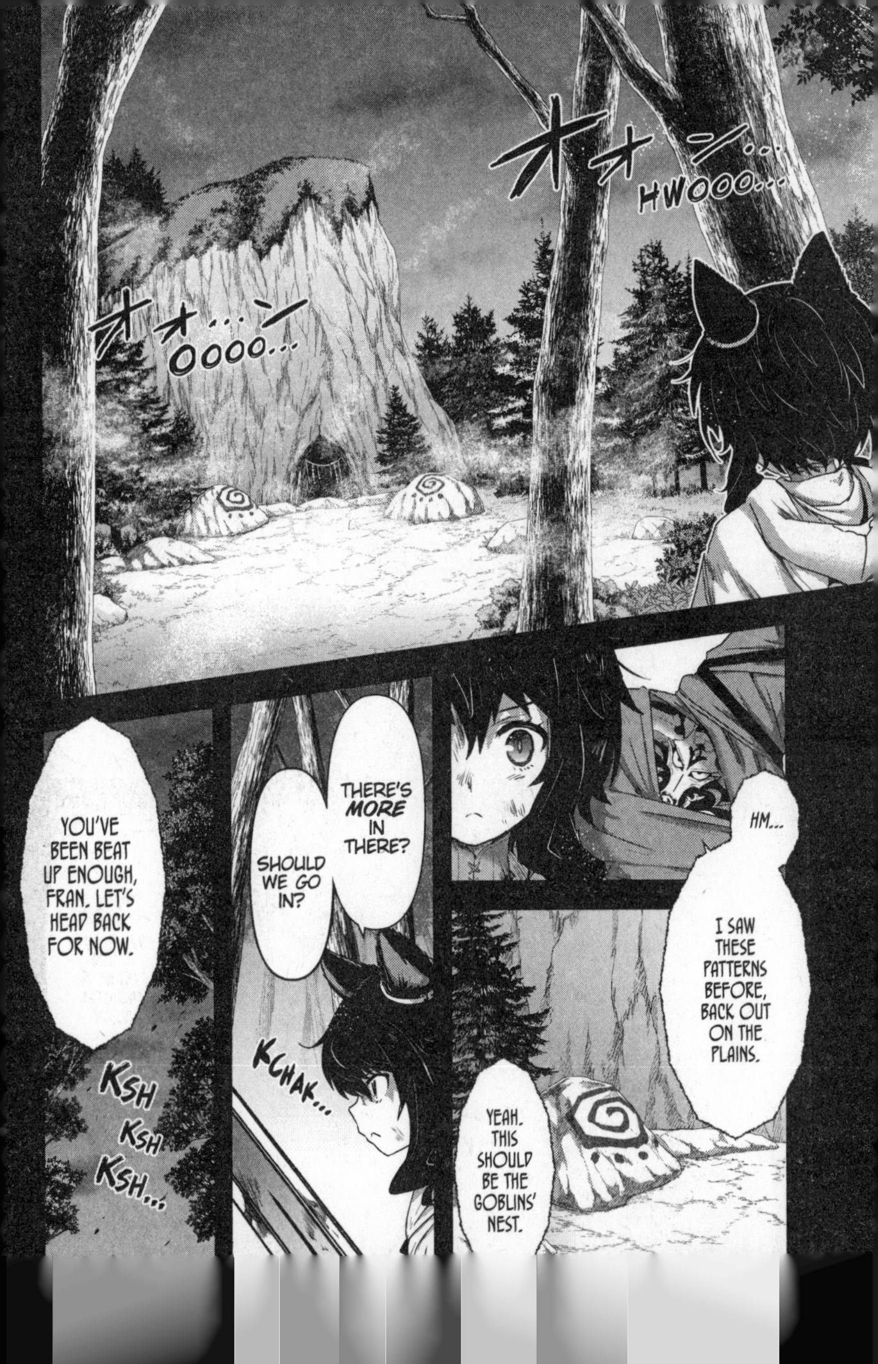
オオン...
HWOOO...
オオ...ン
OOOO...
HM...
I SAW THESE PATTERNS BEFORE, BACK OUT ON THE PLAINS.
YEAH. THIS SHOULD BE THE GOBLINS' NEST.
THERE'S **MORE** IN THERE?
SHOULD WE GO IN?
KCHAK...
YOU'VE BEEN BEAT UP ENOUGH, FRAN. LET'S HEAD BACK FOR NOW.
KSH KSH KSH...

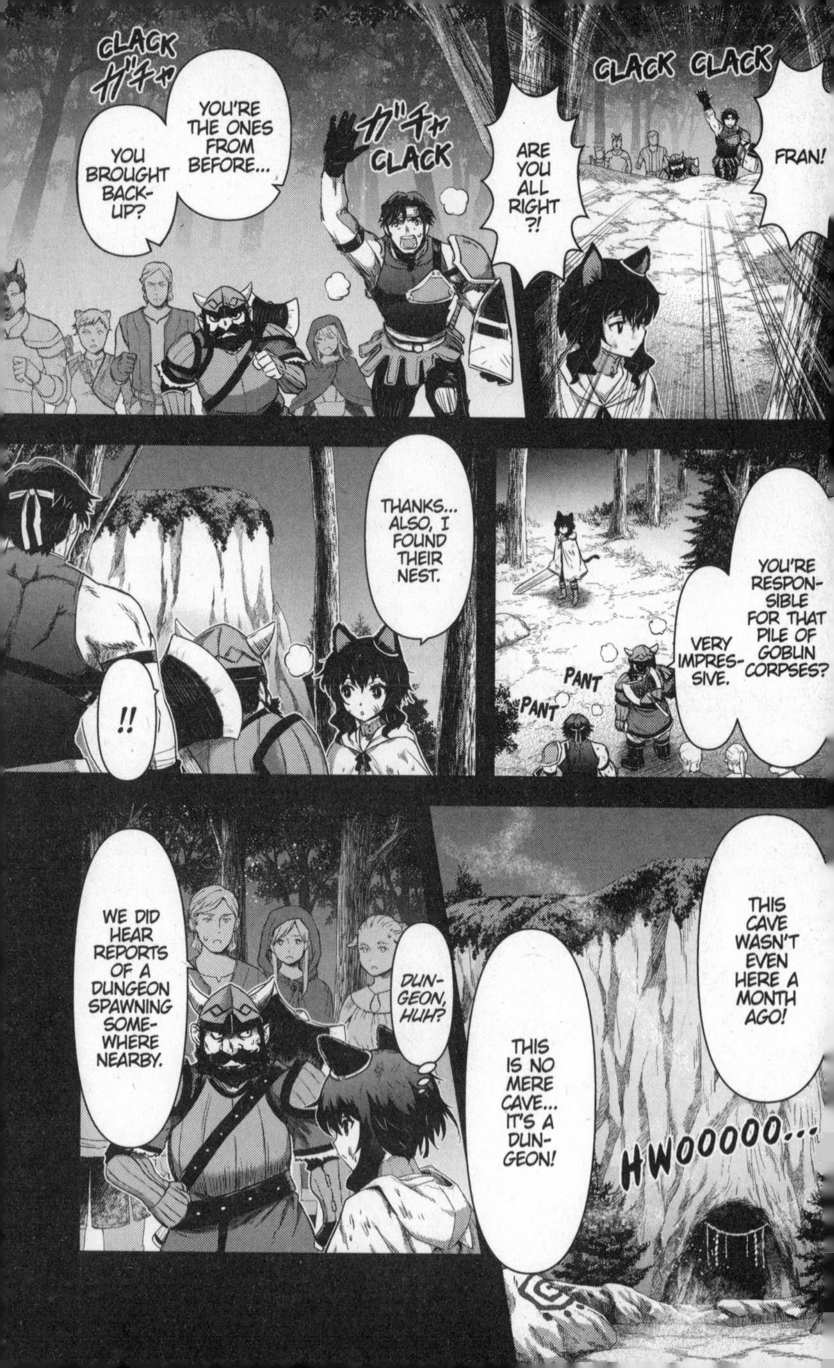
CLACK CLACK
FRAN!
ARE YOU ALL RIGHT?!
ガチャ CLACK
YOU'RE THE ONES FROM BEFORE...
YOU BROUGHT BACK-UP?
CLACK ガチャ
YOU'RE RESPONSIBLE FOR THAT PILE OF GOBLIN CORPSES?
VERY IMPRESSIVE.
PANT PANT
THANKS... ALSO, I FOUND THEIR NEST.
!!
THIS CAVE WASN'T EVEN HERE A MONTH AGO!
THIS IS NO MERE CAVE... IT'S A DUNGEON!
HWOOOOO...
DUNGEON, HUH?
WE DID HEAR REPORTS OF A DUNGEON SPAWNING SOMEWHERE NEARBY.

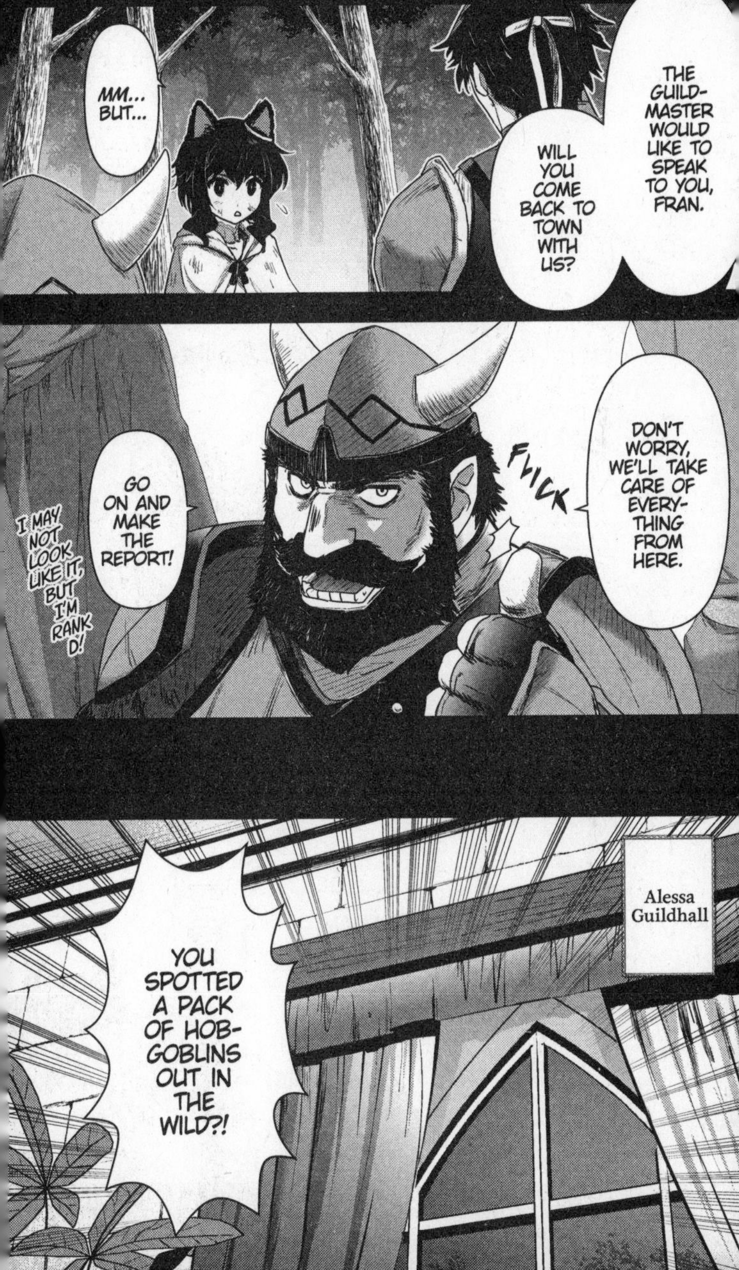
THE GUILD-MASTER WOULD LIKE TO SPEAK TO YOU, FRAN.
WILL YOU COME BACK TO TOWN WITH US?
MM... BUT...
DON'T WORRY, WE'LL TAKE CARE OF EVERY-THING FROM HERE.
FLICK
GO ON AND MAKE THE REPORT!
I MAY NOT LOOK LIKE IT, BUT I'M RANK D!
Alessa Guildhall
YOU SPOTTED A PACK OF HOB-GOBLINS OUT IN THE WILD?!

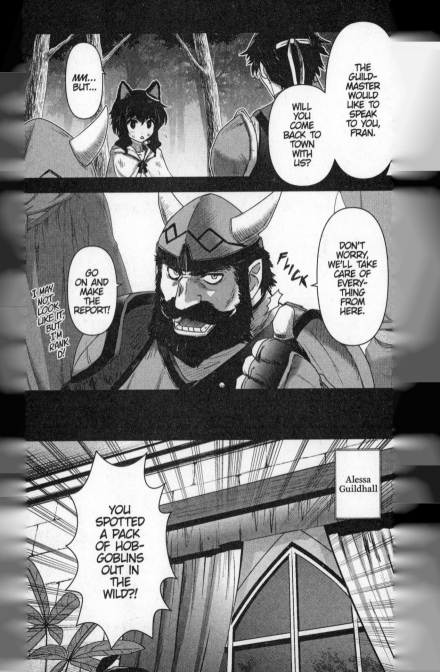

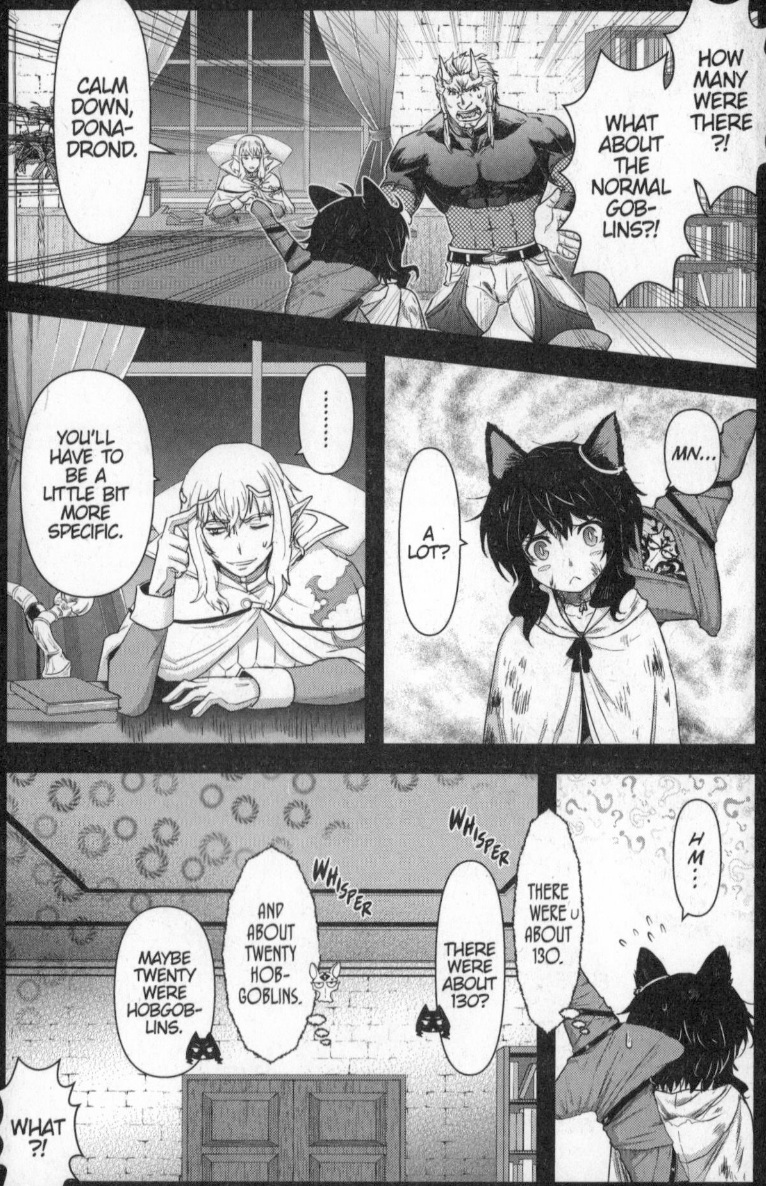
HOW MANY WERE THERE?!
WHAT ABOUT THE NORMAL GOB-LINS?!
CALM DOWN, DONA-DROND.
MN...
A LOT?
......
YOU'LL HAVE TO BE A LITTLE BIT MORE SPECIFIC.
HM...
THERE WERE ABOUT 130.
WHISPER
THERE WERE ABOUT 130?
WHISPER
AND ABOUT TWENTY HOB-GOBLINS.
MAYBE TWENTY WERE HOBGOB-LINS.
WHAT?!

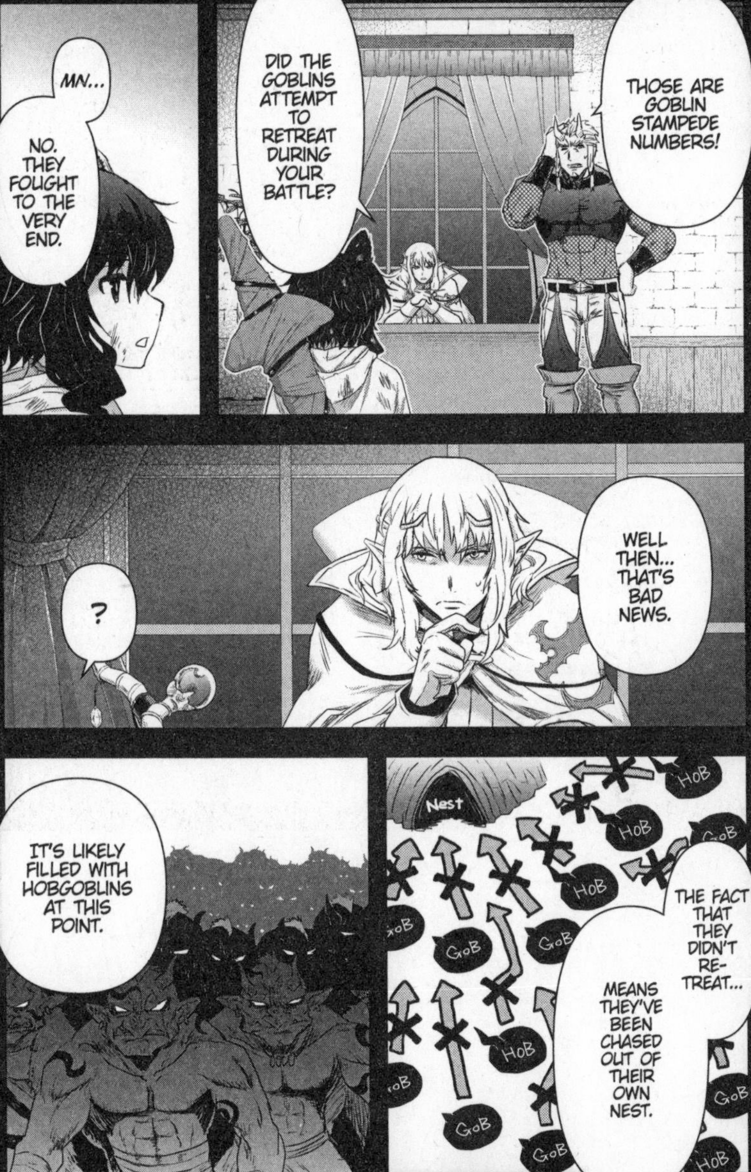
THOSE ARE GOBLIN STAMPEDE NUMBERS!
DID THE GOBLINS ATTEMPT TO RETREAT DURING YOUR BATTLE?
MN...
NO. THEY FOUGHT TO THE VERY END.
WELL THEN... THAT'S BAD NEWS.
?
Nest
HoB
GoB
THE FACT THAT THEY DIDN'T RE-TREAT...
MEANS THEY'VE BEEN CHASED OUT OF THEIR OWN NEST.
IT'S LIKELY FILLED WITH HOBGOBLINS AT THIS POINT.

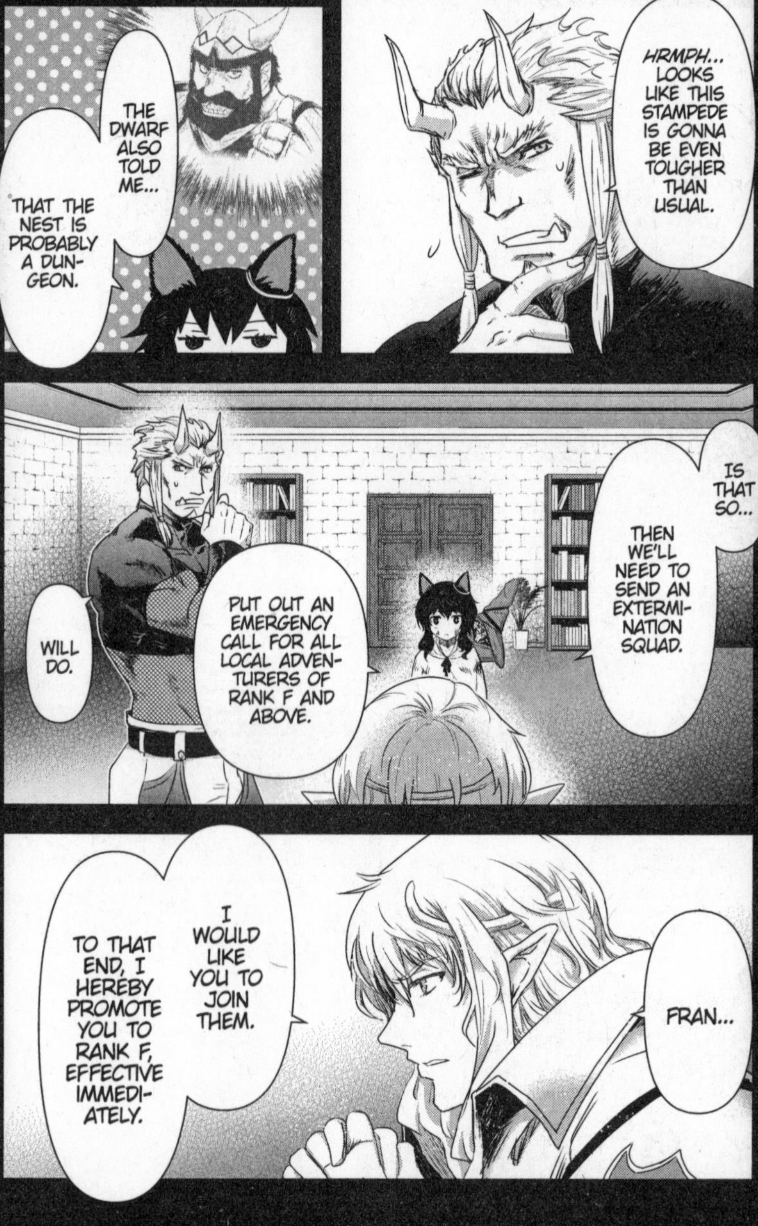
HRMPH... LOOKS LIKE THIS STAMPEDE IS GONNA BE EVEN TOUGHER THAN USUAL.
THE DWARF ALSO TOLD ME...
THAT THE NEST IS PROBABLY A DUNGEON.
IS THAT SO...
THEN WE'LL NEED TO SEND AN EXTERMINATION SQUAD.
PUT OUT AN EMERGENCY CALL FOR ALL LOCAL ADVENTURERS OF RANK F AND ABOVE.
WILL DO.
FRAN...
I WOULD LIKE YOU TO JOIN THEM.
TO THAT END, I HEREBY PROMOTE YOU TO RANK F, EFFECTIVE IMMEDIATELY.

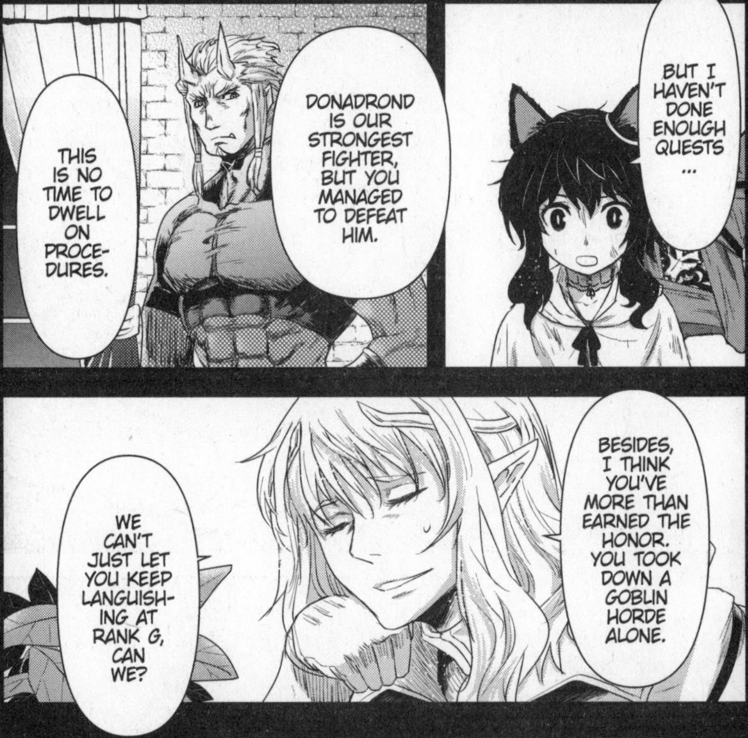
BUT I HAVEN'T DONE ENOUGH QUESTS ...
DONADROND IS OUR STRONGEST FIGHTER, BUT YOU MANAGED TO DEFEAT HIM.
THIS IS NO TIME TO DWELL ON PROCE-DURES.
BESIDES, I THINK YOU'VE MORE THAN EARNED THE HONOR. YOU TOOK DOWN A GOBLIN HORDE ALONE.
WE CAN'T JUST LET YOU KEEP LANGUISH-ING AT RANK G, CAN WE?
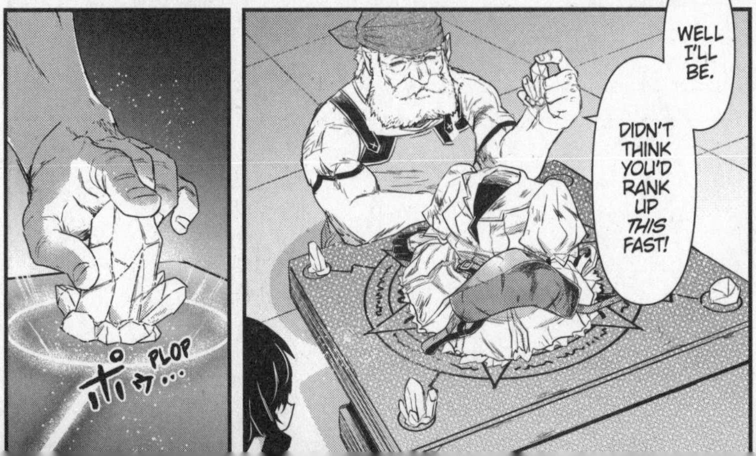
WELL I'LL BE.
DIDN'T THINK YOU'D RANK UP *THIS* FAST!
PLOP...

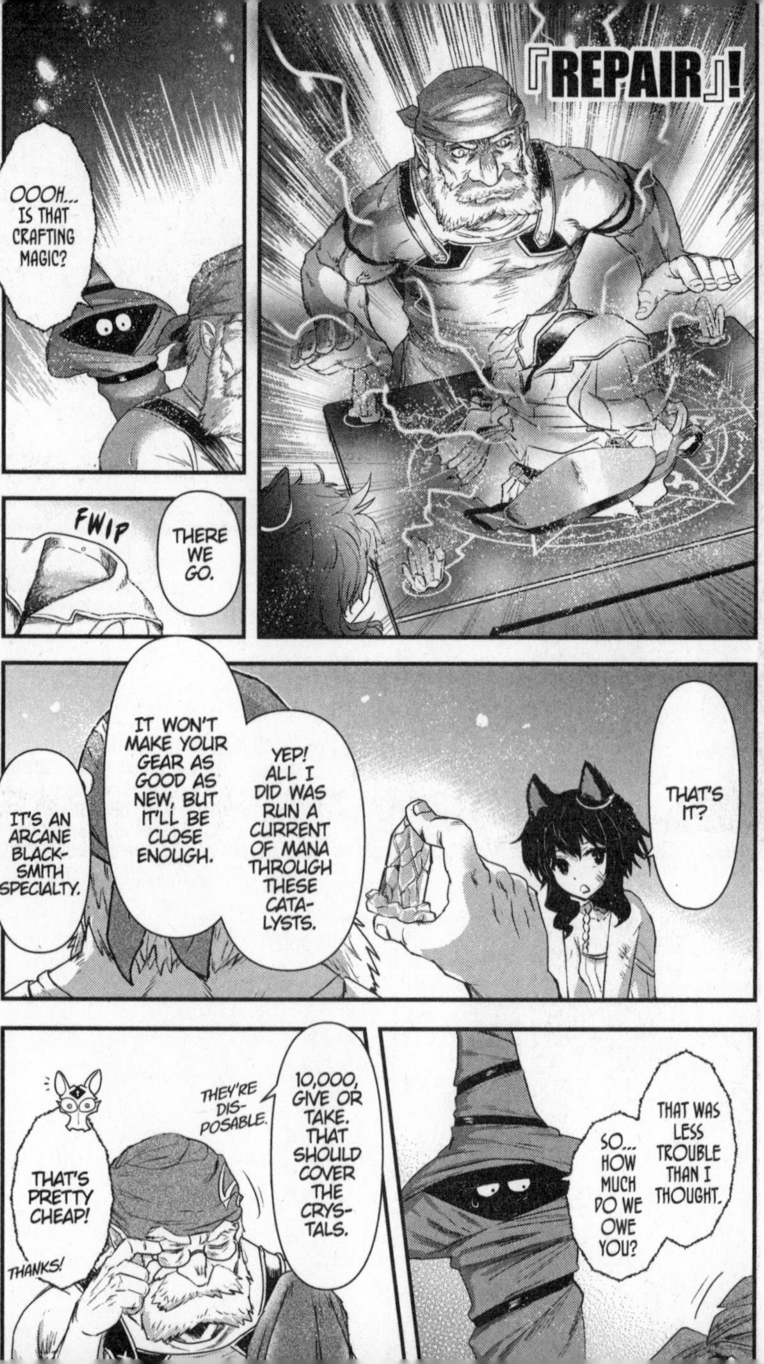
『REPAIR』!
OOOH... IS THAT CRAFTING MAGIC?
FWIP
THERE WE GO.
THAT'S IT?
YEP! ALL I DID WAS RUN A CURRENT OF MANA THROUGH THESE CATA-LYSTS.
IT WON'T MAKE YOUR GEAR AS GOOD AS NEW, BUT IT'LL BE CLOSE ENOUGH.
IT'S AN ARCANE BLACK-SMITH SPECIALTY.
THAT WAS LESS TROUBLE THAN I THOUGHT.
SO... HOW MUCH DO WE OWE YOU?
10,000, GIVE OR TAKE. THAT SHOULD COVER THE CRYS-TALS.
THEY'RE DIS-POSABLE.
THAT'S PRETTY CHEAP!
THANKS!

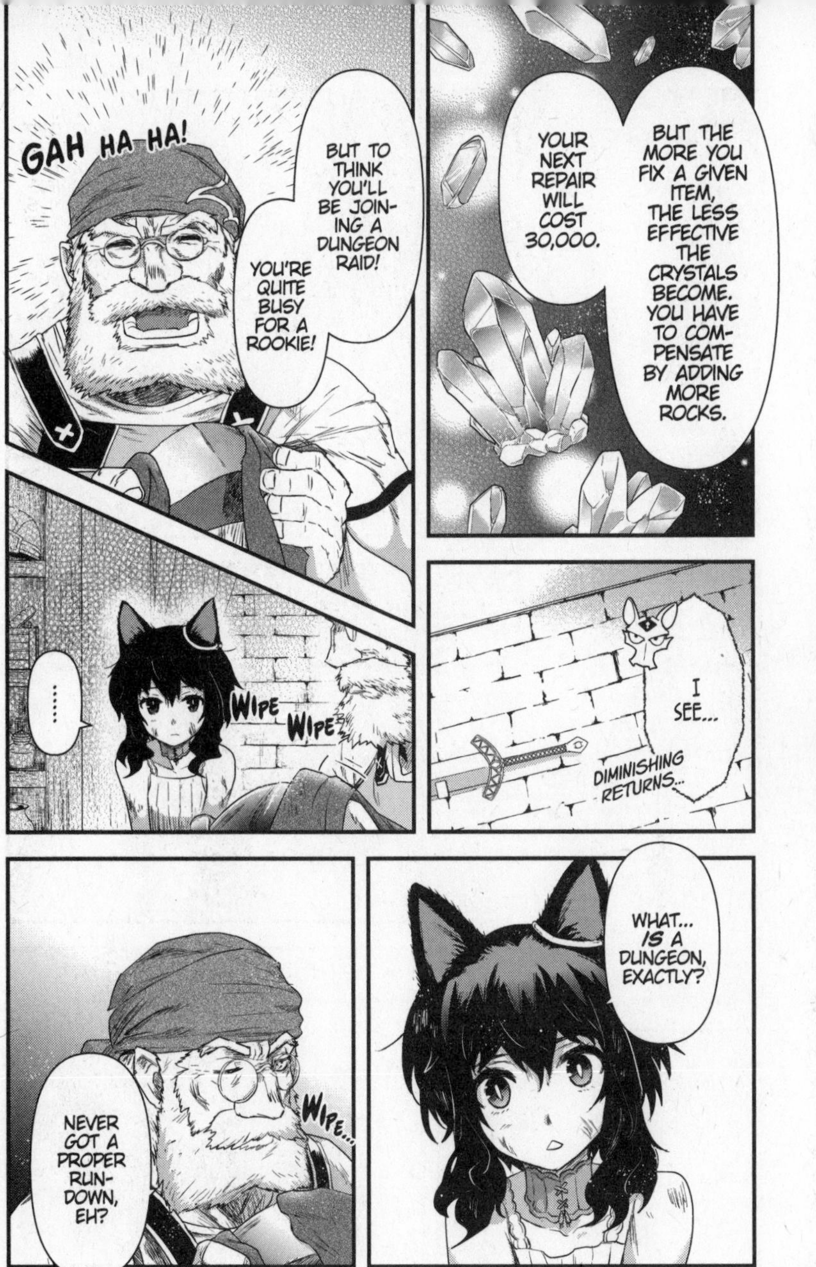
BUT THE MORE YOU FIX A GIVEN ITEM, THE LESS EFFECTIVE THE CRYSTALS BECOME. YOU HAVE TO COMPENSATE BY ADDING MORE ROCKS.
YOUR NEXT REPAIR WILL COST 30,000.
BUT TO THINK YOU'LL BE JOINING A DUNGEON RAID!
YOU'RE QUITE BUSY FOR A ROOKIE!
GAH HA HA!
I SEE...
DIMINISHING RETURNS...
WIPE
WIPE
......
WHAT... *IS* A DUNGEON, EXACTLY?
WIPE...
NEVER GOT A PROPER RUNDOWN, EH?

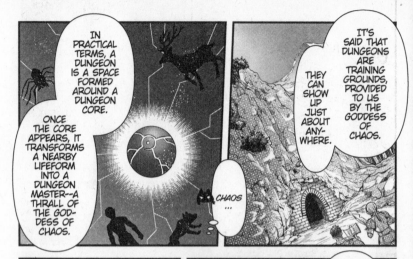

IT'S SAID THAT DUNGEONS ARE TRAINING GROUNDS, PROVIDED TO US BY THE GODDESS OF CHAOS.
THEY CAN SHOW UP JUST ABOUT ANY-WHERE.
IN PRACTICAL TERMS, A DUNGEON IS A SPACE FORMED AROUND A DUNGEON CORE.
ONCE THE CORE APPEARS, IT TRANSFORMS A NEARBY LIFEFORM INTO A DUNGEON MASTER--A THRALL OF THE GOD-DESS OF CHAOS.
CHAOS ...
DUNGEON MASTERS USE THE CORE TO MANIPULATE AND MANAGE THE DUNGEON.
THERE ARE REPORTS OF TRULY RARE MONSTERS INHABITING SOME OF THE OLDER DUNGEONS, TOO.
BUT YOU CAN COUNT ON EACH DUNGEON CONTAINING A HOARD OF TREASURE: MAGICAL ITEMS AND WEAPONS AND THE LIKE.
PEOPLE SAY THE GODDESS OF CHAOS PROVIDES THIS AS A REWARD FOR ANYONE BOLD ENOUGH TO CONQUER A DUNGEON.

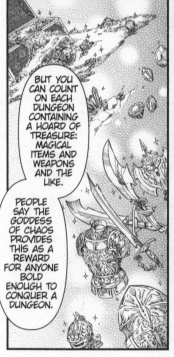

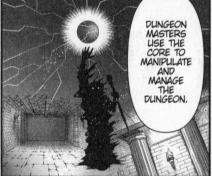

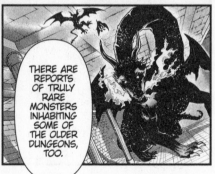

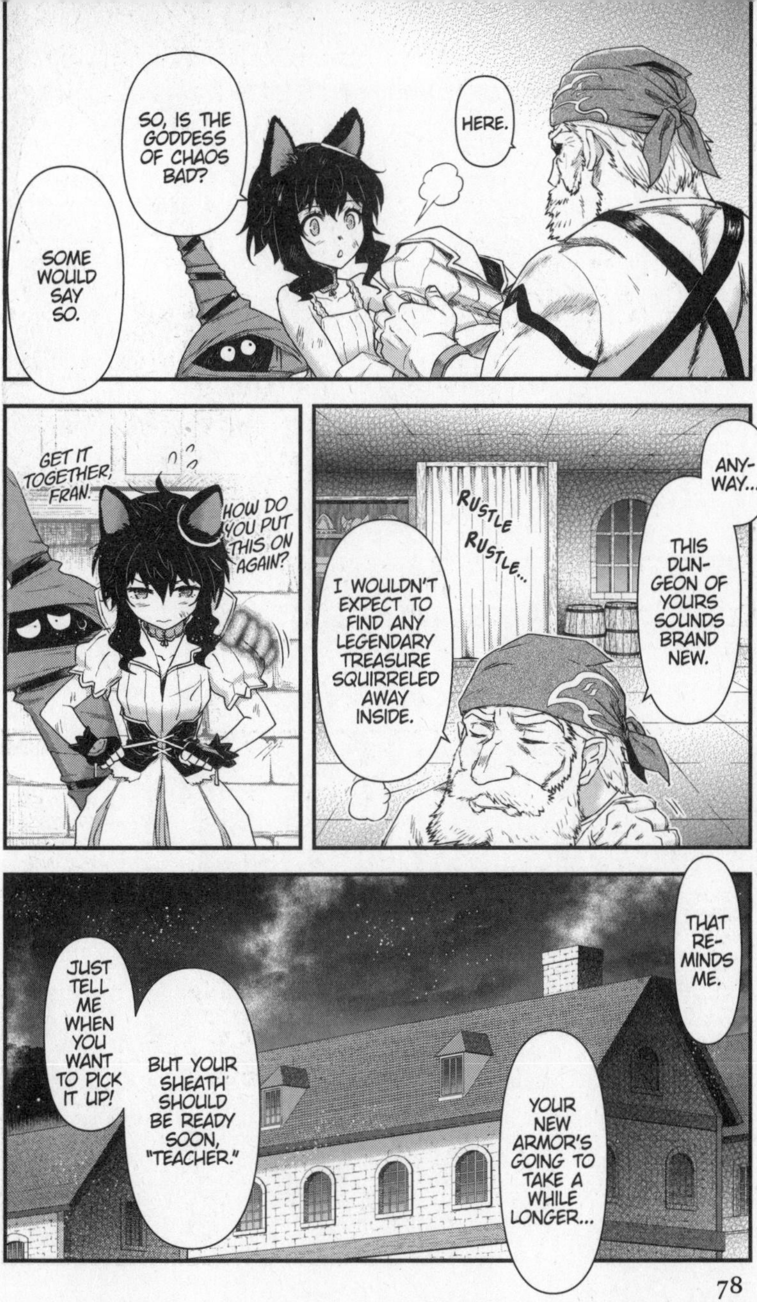

HERE.
SO, IS THE GODDESS OF CHAOS BAD?
SOME WOULD SAY SO.
ANY-WAY...
THIS DUN-GEON OF YOURS SOUNDS BRAND NEW.
RUSTLE RUSTLE...
I WOULDN'T EXPECT TO FIND ANY LEGENDARY TREASURE SQUIRRELED AWAY INSIDE.
HOW DO YOU PUT THIS ON AGAIN?
GET IT TOGETHER, FRAN.
THAT RE-MINDS ME.
YOUR NEW ARMOR'S GOING TO TAKE A WHILE LONGER...
BUT YOUR SHEATH SHOULD BE READY SOON, "TEACHER."
JUST TELL ME WHEN YOU WANT TO PICK IT UP!

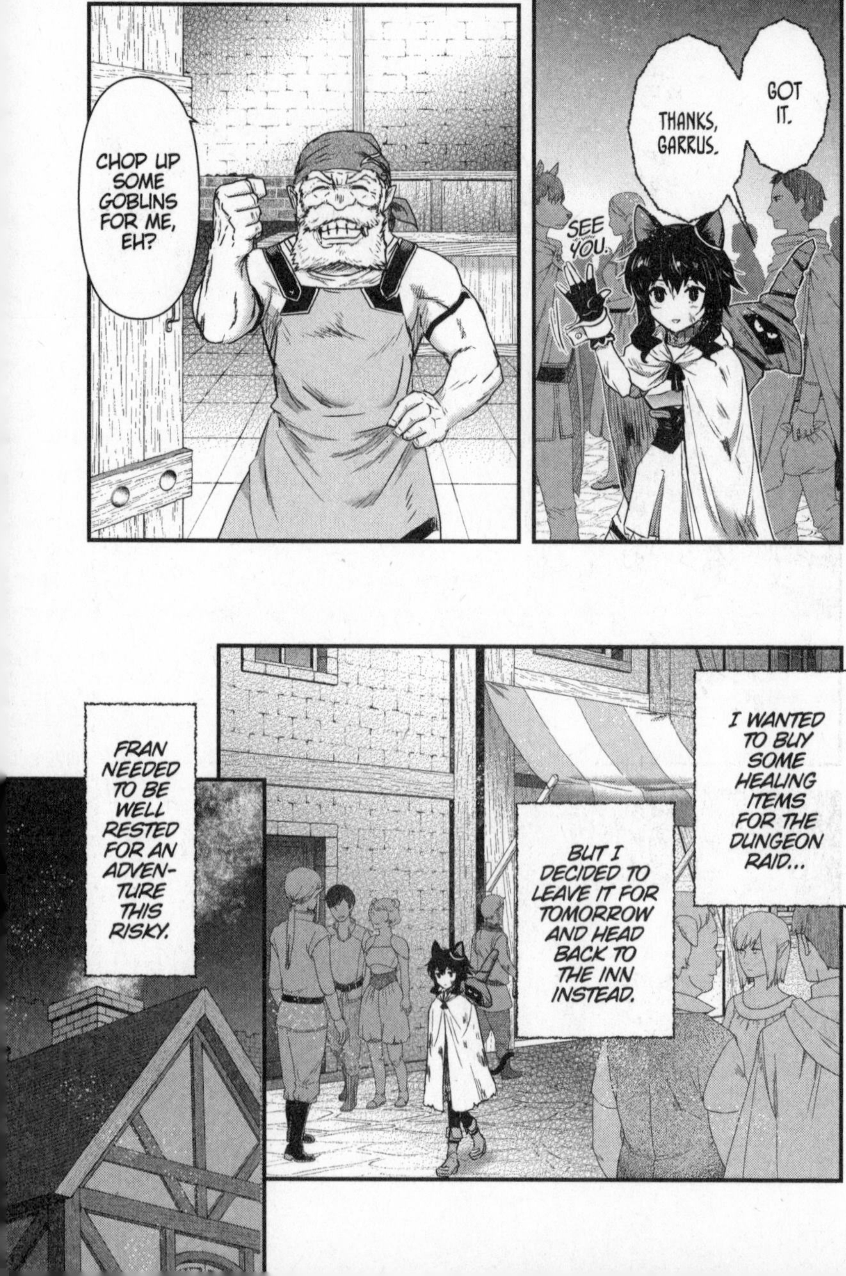
GOT IT.
THANKS, GARRUS.
SEE YOU.
CHOP UP SOME GOBLINS FOR ME, EH?
I WANTED TO BUY SOME HEALING ITEMS FOR THE DUNGEON RAID...
BUT I DECIDED TO LEAVE IT FOR TOMORROW AND HEAD BACK TO THE INN INSTEAD.
FRAN NEEDED TO BE WELL RESTED FOR AN ADVEN-TURE THIS RISKY.

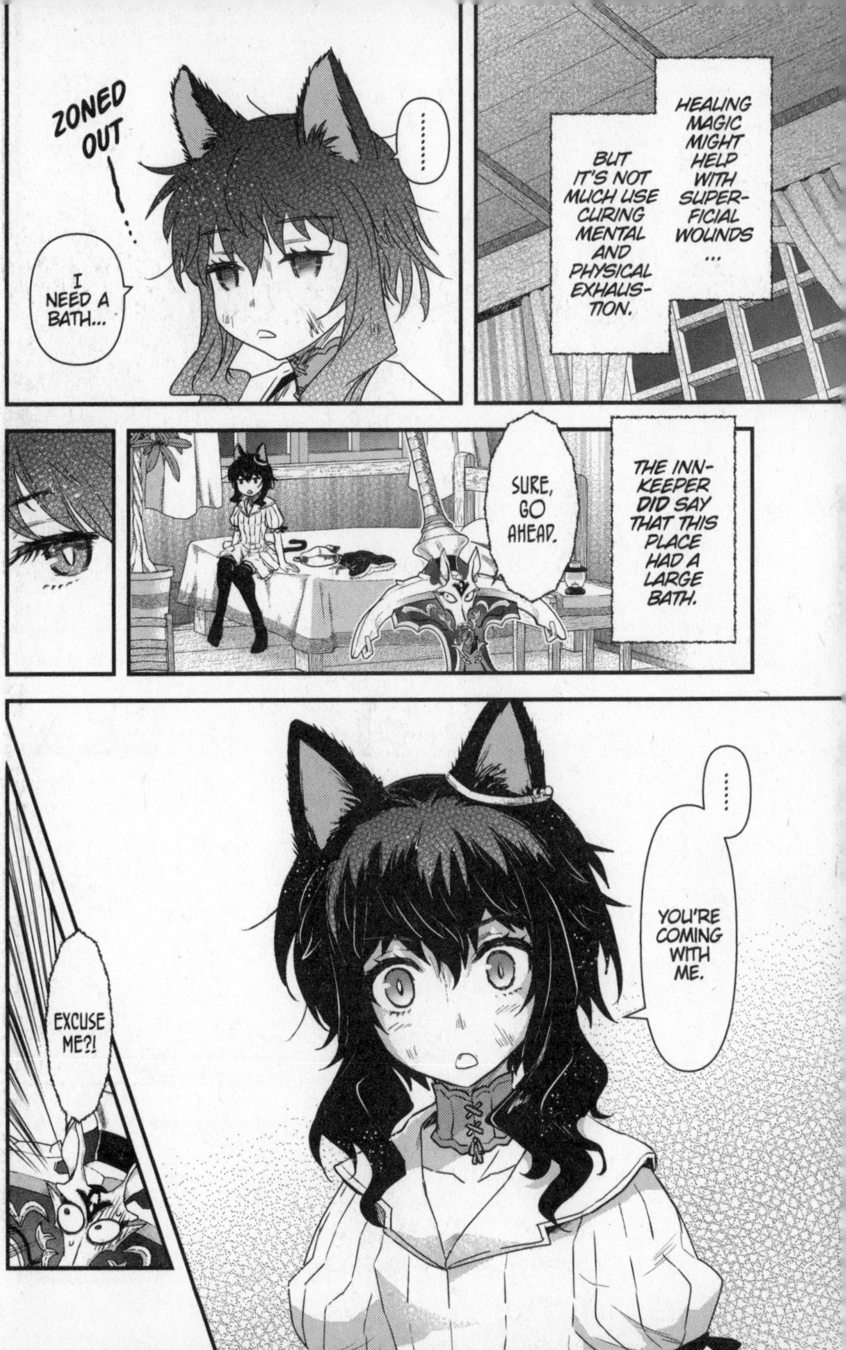
HEALING MAGIC MIGHT HELP WITH SUPERFICIAL WOUNDS...
BUT IT'S NOT MUCH USE CURING MENTAL AND PHYSICAL EXHAUSTION.
......
ZONED OUT
I NEED A BATH...
THE INNKEEPER DID SAY THAT THIS PLACE HAD A LARGE BATH.
SURE, GO AHEAD.
......
YOU'RE COMING WITH ME.
EXCUSE ME?!

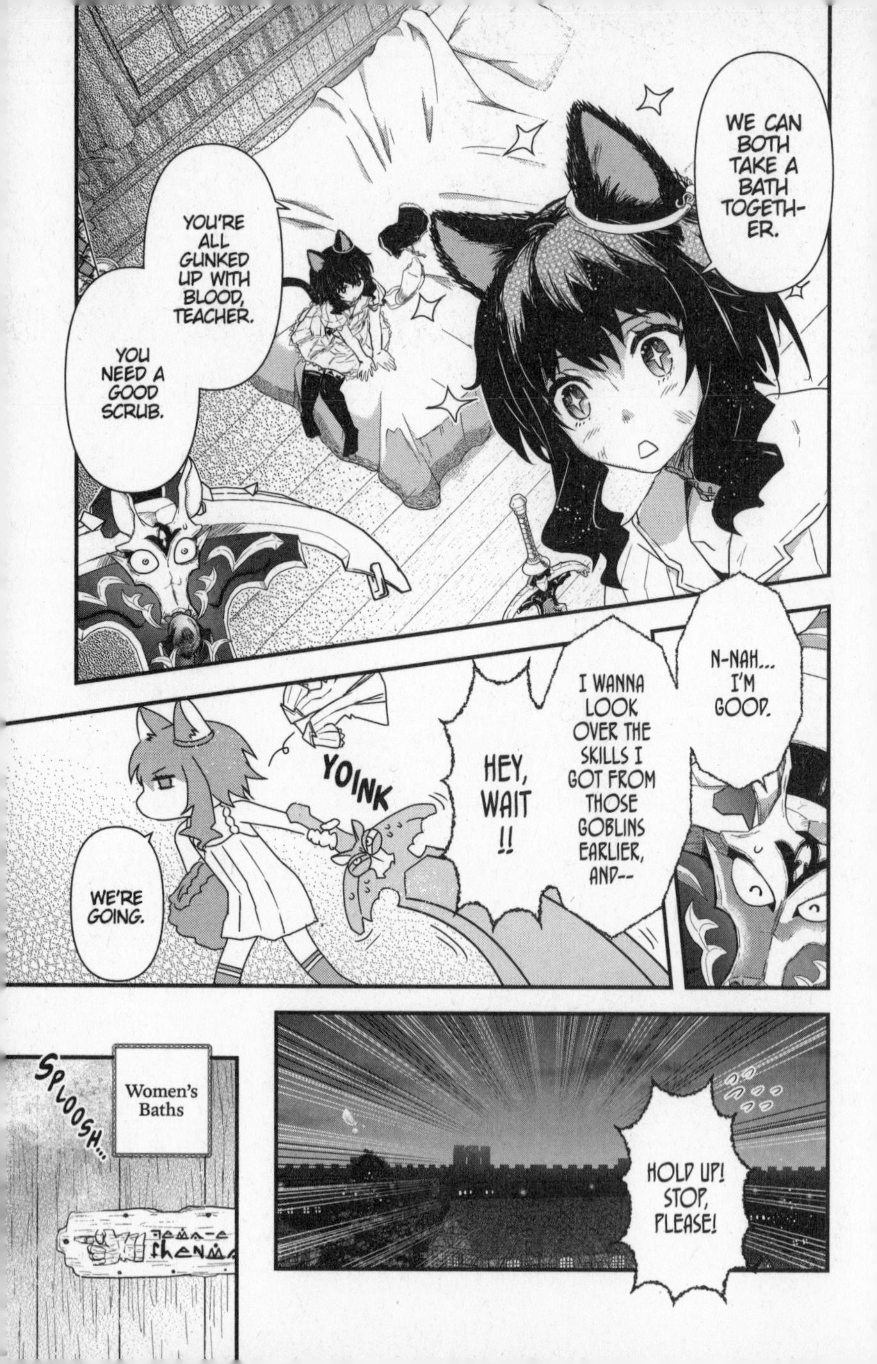
WE CAN BOTH TAKE A BATH TOGETHER.
YOU'RE ALL GUNKED UP WITH BLOOD, TEACHER.
YOU NEED A GOOD SCRUB.
N-NAH... I'M GOOD.
I WANNA LOOK OVER THE SKILLS I GOT FROM THOSE GOBLINS EARLIER, AND--
HEY, WAIT!!
YOINK
WE'RE GOING.
HOLD UP! STOP, PLEASE!
Women's Baths
SPLOOSH...

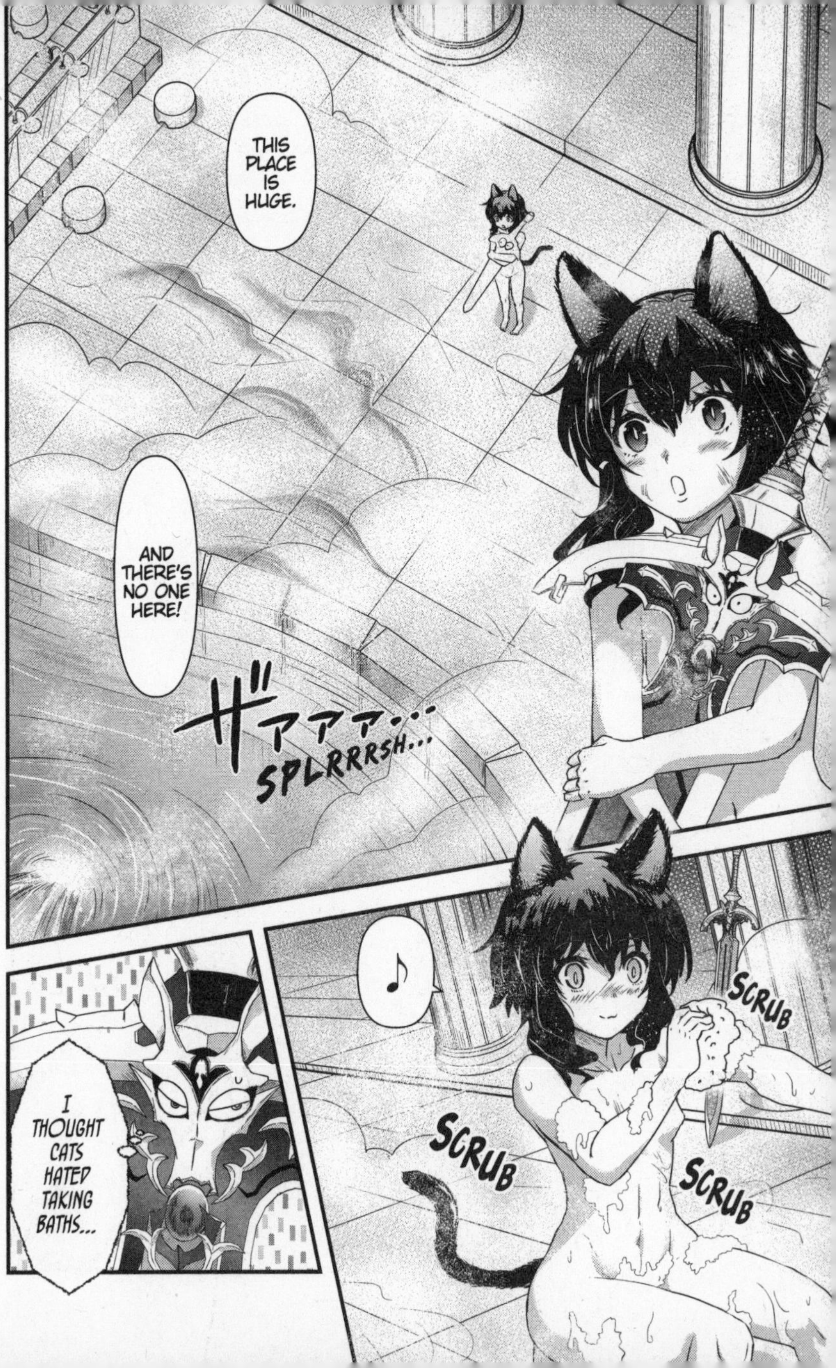
THIS PLACE IS HUGE.
AND THERE'S NO ONE HERE!
ザァァァ…
SPLRRRSH...
♪
SCRUB
SCRUB
SCRUB
I THOUGHT CATS HATED TAKING BATHS...

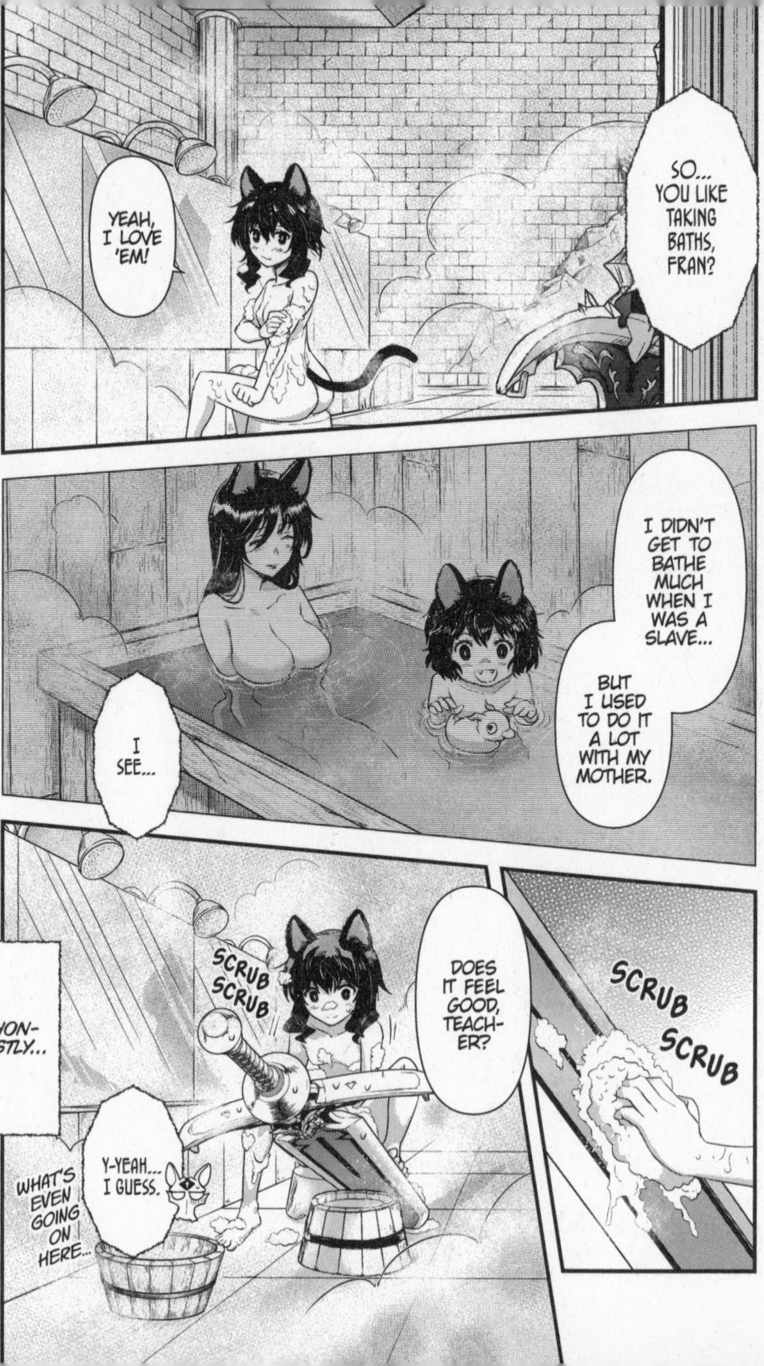
SO... YOU LIKE TAKING BATHS, FRAN?
YEAH, I LOVE 'EM!
I DIDN'T GET TO BATHE MUCH WHEN I WAS A SLAVE...
BUT I USED TO DO IT A LOT WITH MY MOTHER.
I SEE...
SCRUB SCRUB
DOES IT FEEL GOOD, TEACHER?
SCRUB SCRUB
HONESTLY...
Y-YEAH... I GUESS.
WHAT'S EVEN GOING ON HERE...

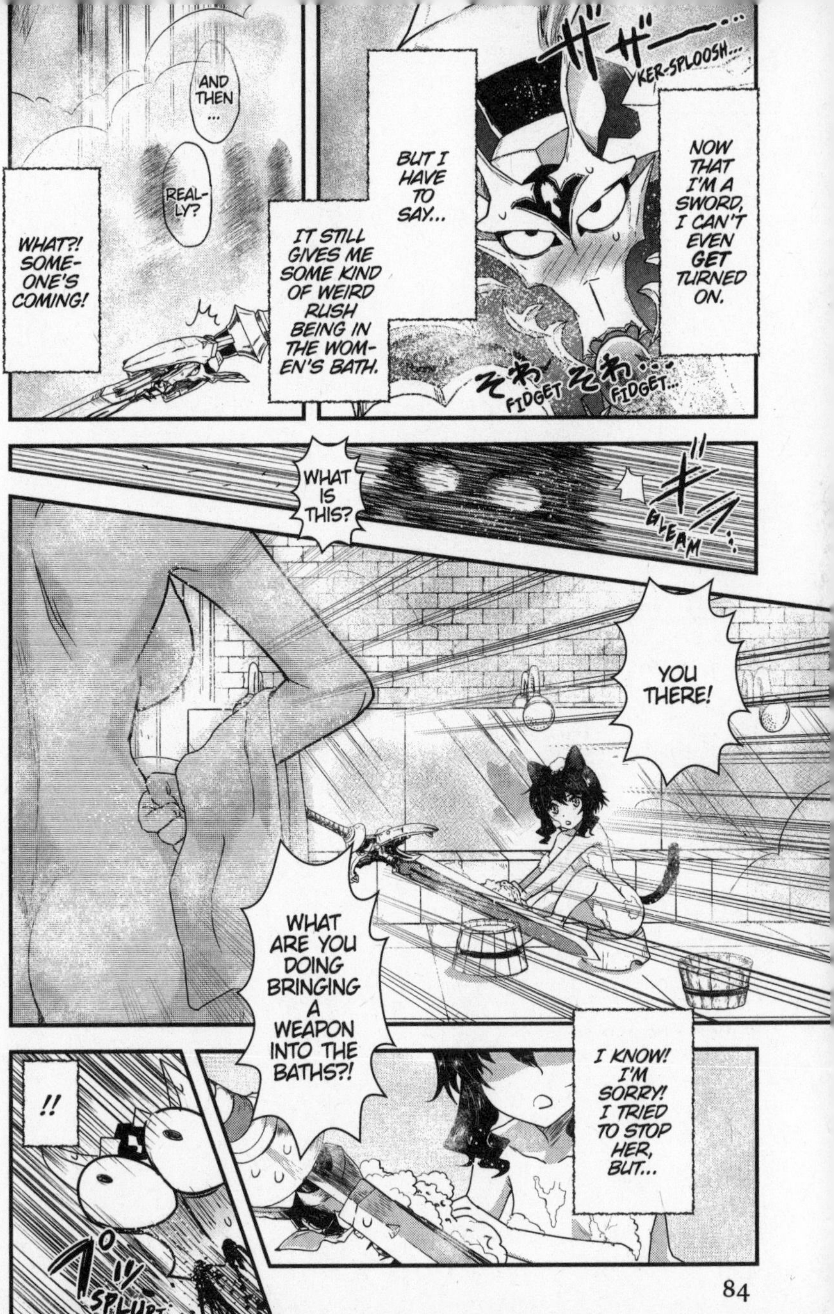
KER-SPLOOSH...
NOW THAT I'M A SWORD, I CAN'T EVEN GET TURNED ON.
BUT I HAVE TO SAY...
IT STILL GIVES ME SOME KIND OF WEIRD RUSH BEING IN THE WOMEN'S BATH.
FIDGET FIDGET...
AND THEN...
REAL-LY?
WHAT?! SOME-ONE'S COMING!
WHAT IS THIS?
GLEAM
YOU THERE!
WHAT ARE YOU DOING BRINGING A WEAPON INTO THE BATHS?!
I KNOW! I'M SORRY! I TRIED TO STOP HER, BUT...
!!
SPLURT

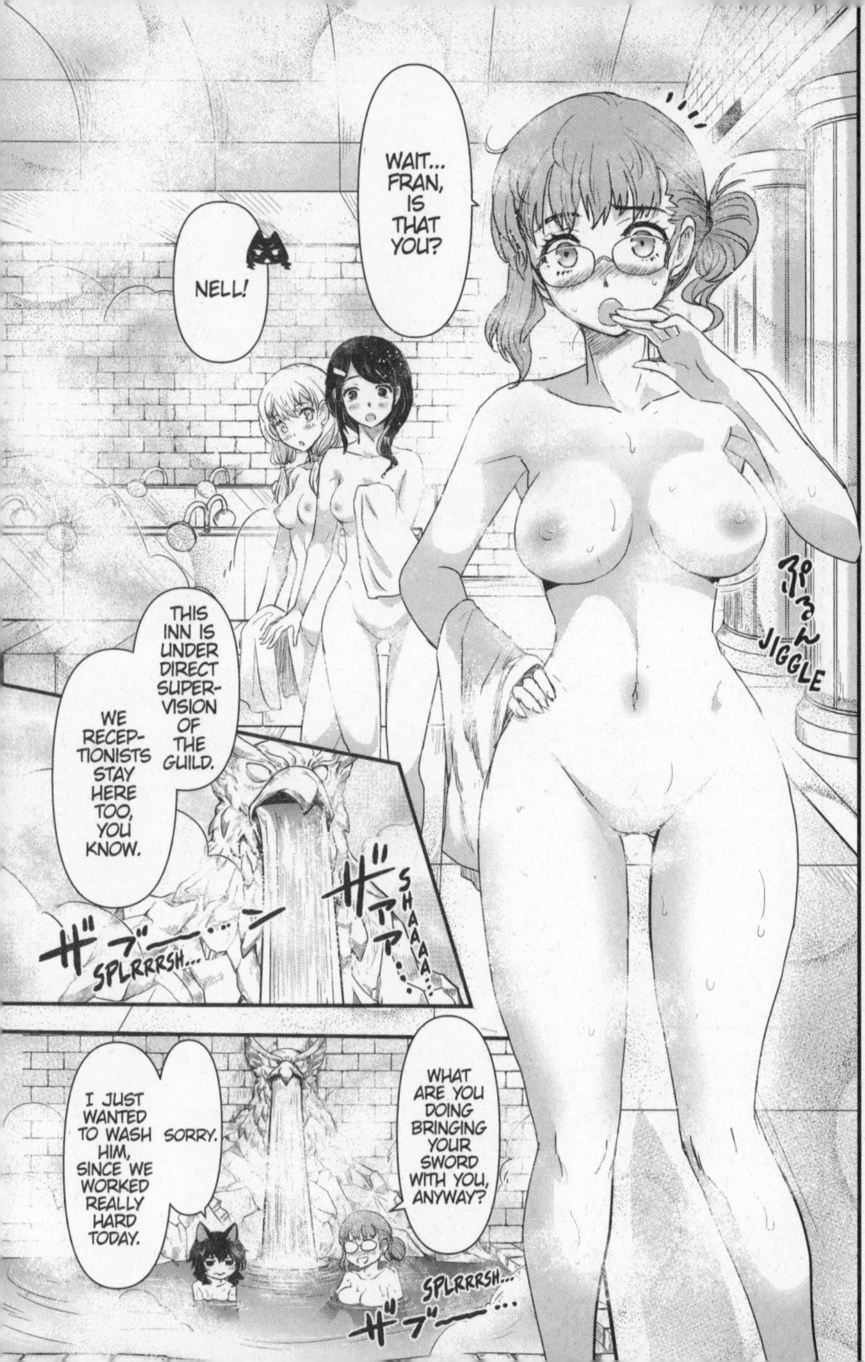
WAIT... FRAN, IS THAT YOU?
NELL!
ぷるん
JIGGLE
THIS INN IS UNDER DIRECT SUPER-VISION OF THE GUILD.
WE RECEP-TIONISTS STAY HERE TOO, YOU KNOW.
ザァァ
SHAAAA...
ザブーーン
SPLRRRSH...
WHAT ARE YOU DOING BRINGING YOUR SWORD WITH YOU, ANYWAY?
SORRY.
I JUST WANTED TO WASH HIM, SINCE WE WORKED REALLY HARD TODAY.
SPLRRRSH...
ザブーー...

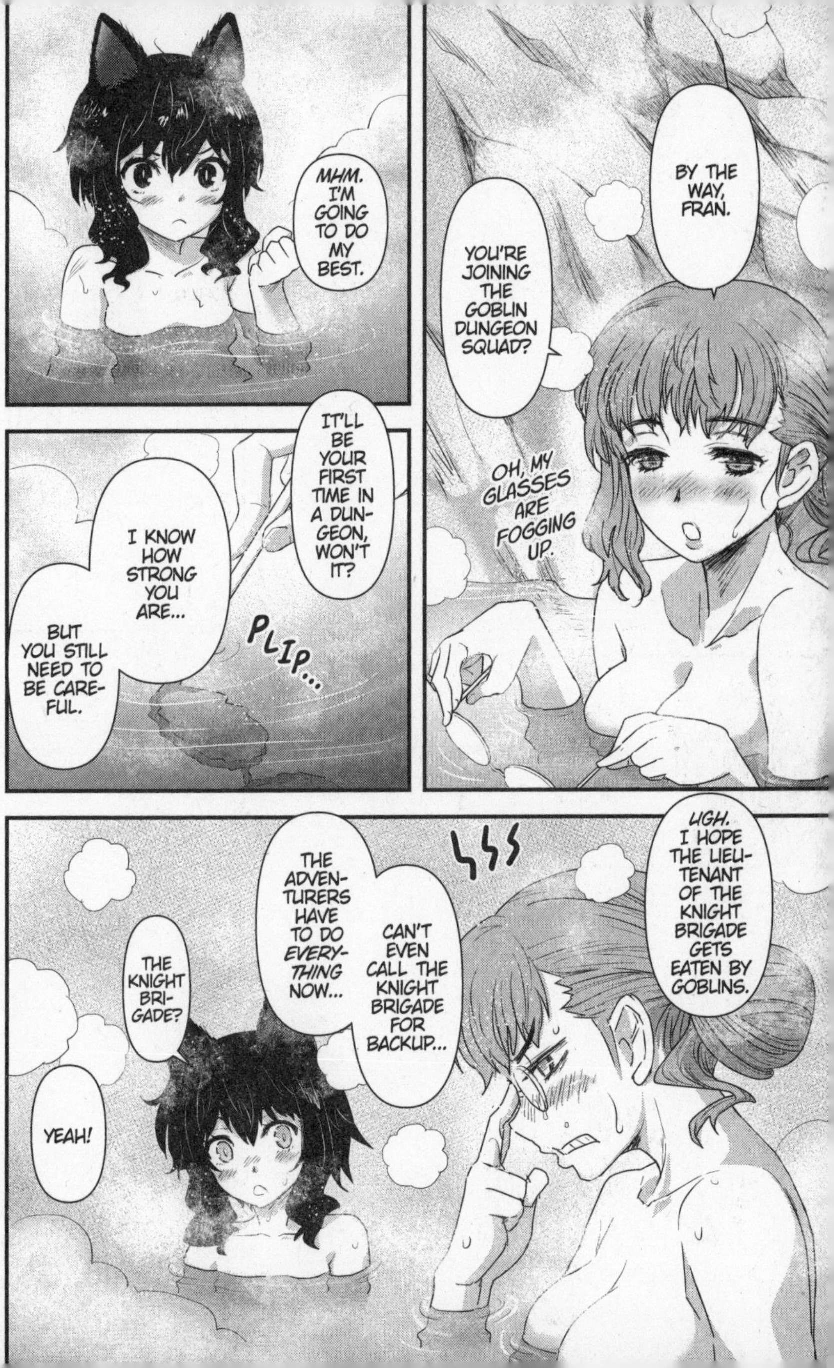
BY THE WAY, FRAN.
YOU'RE JOINING THE GOBLIN DUNGEON SQUAD?
OH, MY GLASSES ARE FOGGING UP.
MHM. I'M GOING TO DO MY BEST.
IT'LL BE YOUR FIRST TIME IN A DUN-GEON, WON'T IT?
I KNOW HOW STRONG YOU ARE...
BUT YOU STILL NEED TO BE CARE-FUL.
PLIP...
UGH. I HOPE THE LIEU-TENANT OF THE KNIGHT BRIGADE GETS EATEN BY GOBLINS.
CAN'T EVEN CALL THE KNIGHT BRIGADE FOR BACKUP...
THE ADVEN-TURERS HAVE TO DO *EVERY-THING* NOW...
THE KNIGHT BRI-GADE?
YEAH!

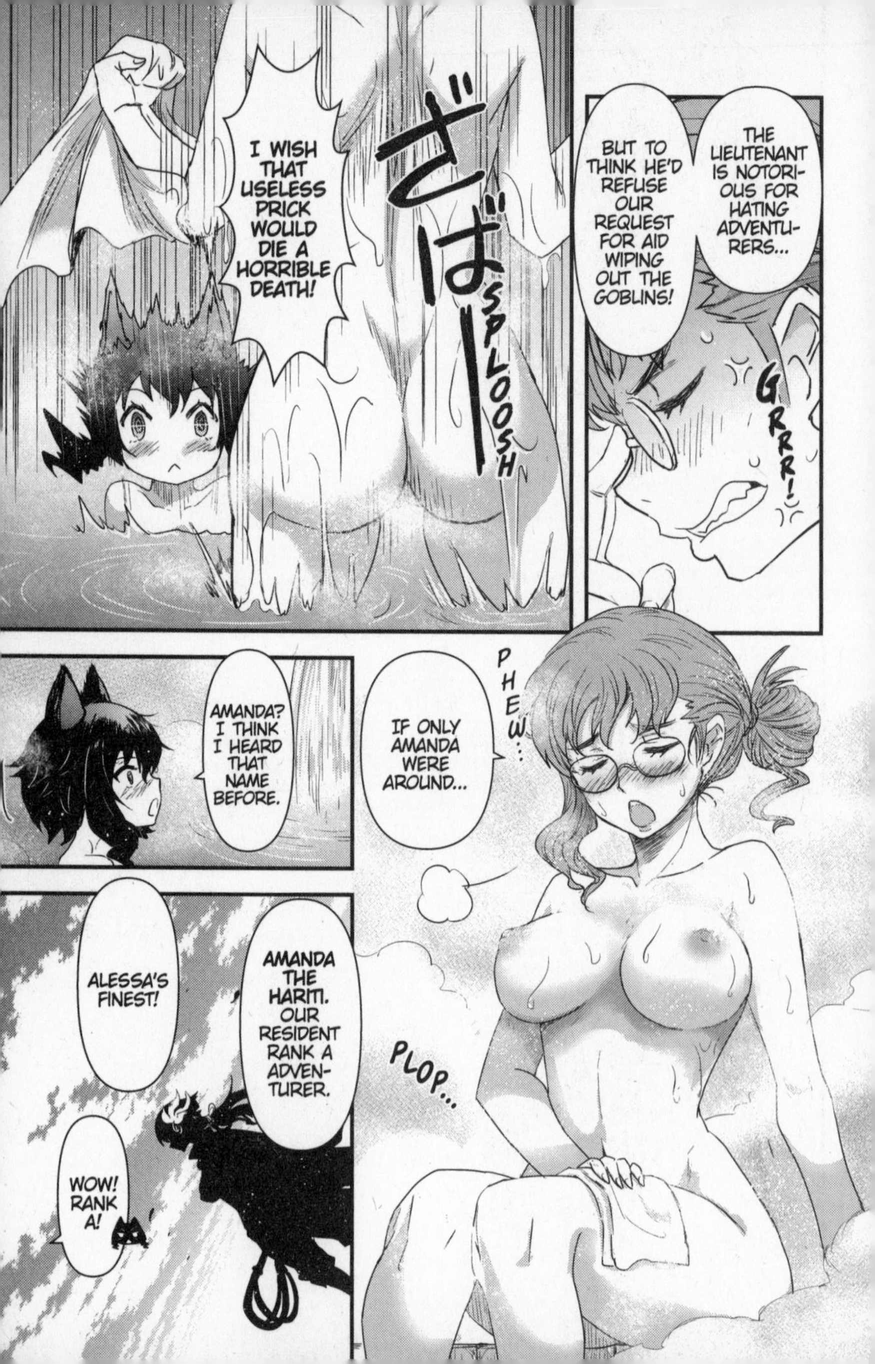
THE LIEUTENANT IS NOTORIOUS FOR HATING ADVENTURERS...
BUT TO THINK HE'D REFUSE OUR REQUEST FOR AID WIPING OUT THE GOBLINS!
GRRR!
I WISH THAT USELESS PRICK WOULD DIE A HORRIBLE DEATH!
ざばー
SPLOOSH
PHEW...
IF ONLY AMANDA WERE AROUND...
PLOP...
AMANDA? I THINK I HEARD THAT NAME BEFORE.
AMANDA THE HARITI. OUR RESIDENT RANK A ADVENTURER.
ALESSA'S FINEST!
WOW! RANK A!

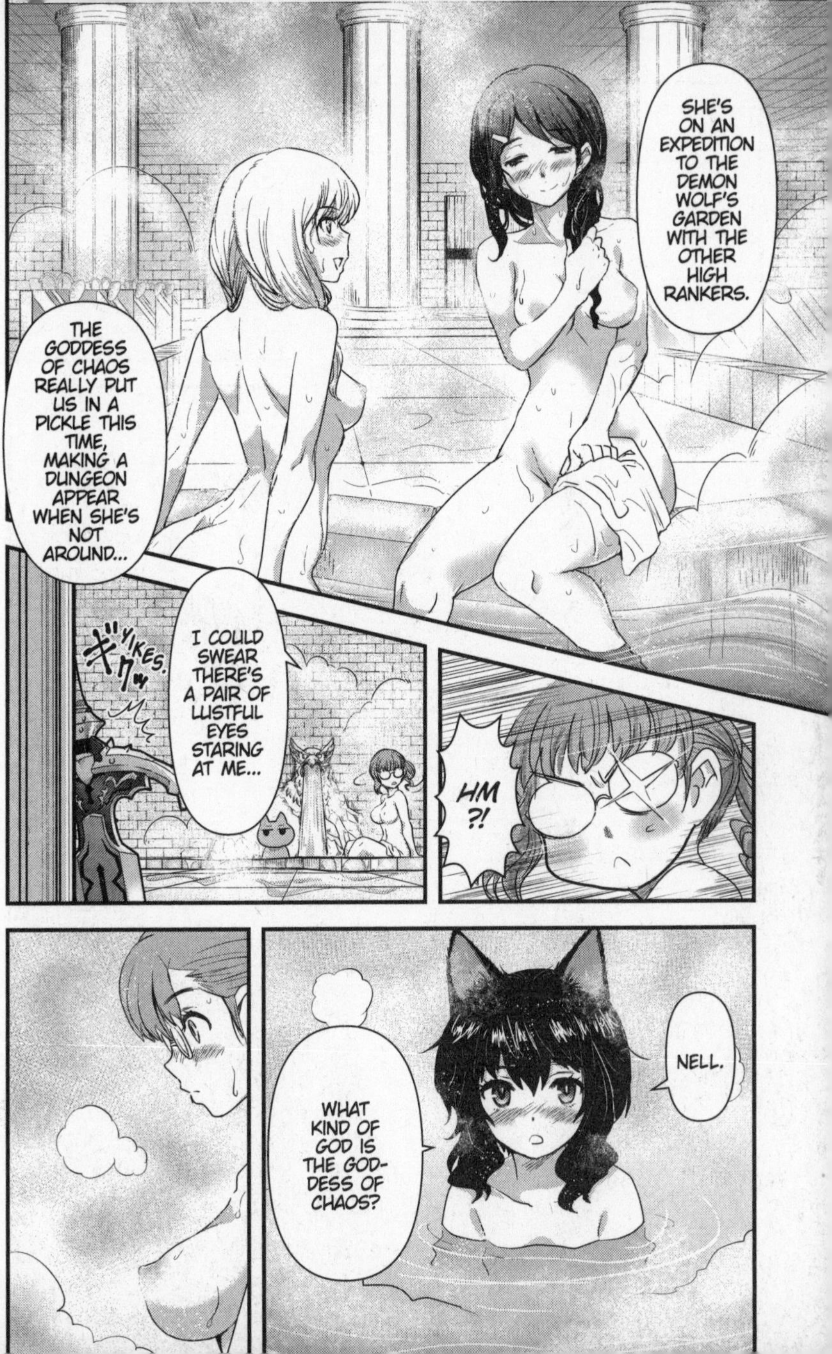
SHE'S ON AN EXPEDITION TO THE DEMON WOLF'S GARDEN WITH THE OTHER HIGH RANKERS.
THE GODDESS OF CHAOS REALLY PUT US IN A PICKLE THIS TIME, MAKING A DUNGEON APPEAR WHEN SHE'S NOT AROUND...
HM ?!
I COULD SWEAR THERE'S A PAIR OF LUSTFUL EYES STARING AT ME...
YIKES.
NELL.
WHAT KIND OF GOD IS THE GOD-DESS OF CHAOS?

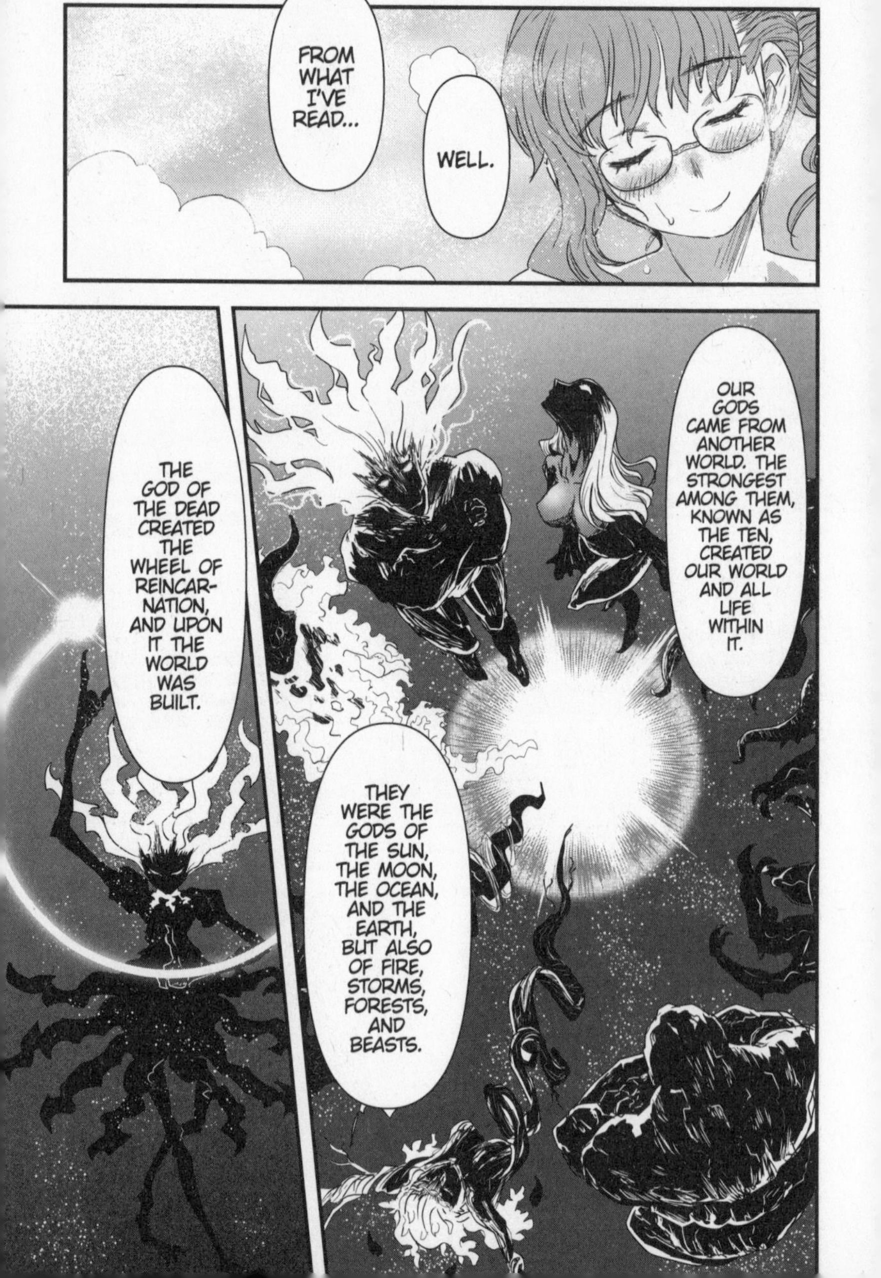
WELL.
FROM WHAT I'VE READ...
OUR GODS CAME FROM ANOTHER WORLD. THE STRONGEST AMONG THEM, KNOWN AS THE TEN, CREATED OUR WORLD AND ALL LIFE WITHIN IT.
THEY WERE THE GODS OF THE SUN, THE MOON, THE OCEAN, AND THE EARTH, BUT ALSO OF FIRE, STORMS, FORESTS, AND BEASTS.
THE GOD OF THE DEAD CREATED THE WHEEL OF REINCAR-NATION, AND UPON IT THE WORLD WAS BUILT.

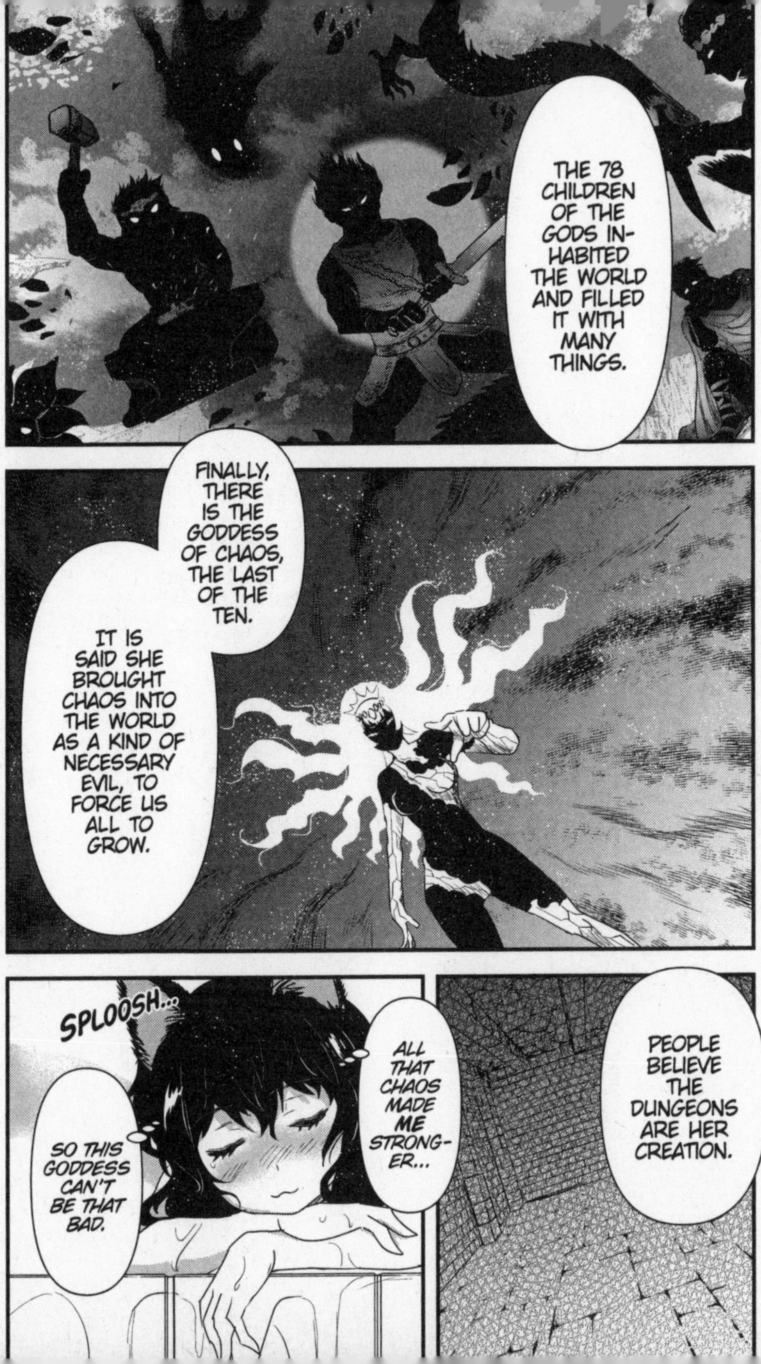
THE 78 CHILDREN OF THE GODS IN-HABITED THE WORLD AND FILLED IT WITH MANY THINGS.
FINALLY, THERE IS THE GODDESS OF CHAOS, THE LAST OF THE TEN.
IT IS SAID SHE BROUGHT CHAOS INTO THE WORLD AS A KIND OF NECESSARY EVIL, TO FORCE US ALL TO GROW.
PEOPLE BELIEVE THE DUNGEONS ARE HER CREATION.
SPLOOSH...
ALL THAT CHAOS MADE ME STRONG-ER...
SO THIS GODDESS CAN'T BE THAT BAD.

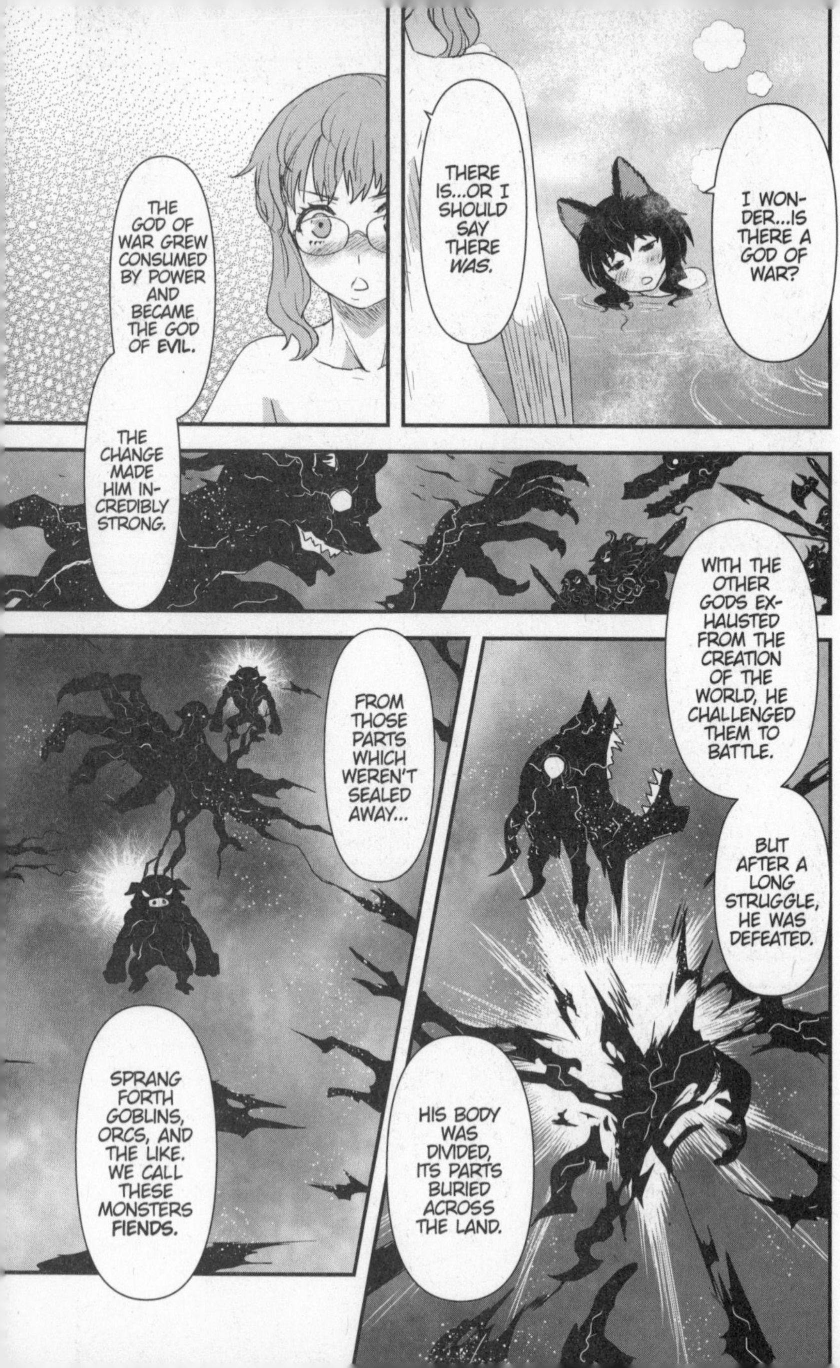
I WONDER...IS THERE A GOD OF WAR?
THERE IS...OR I SHOULD SAY THERE *WAS*.
THE GOD OF WAR GREW CONSUMED BY POWER AND BECAME THE GOD OF **EVIL**.
THE CHANGE MADE HIM INCREDIBLY STRONG.
WITH THE OTHER GODS EXHAUSTED FROM THE CREATION OF THE WORLD, HE CHALLENGED THEM TO BATTLE.
BUT AFTER A LONG STRUGGLE, HE WAS DEFEATED.
HIS BODY WAS DIVIDED, ITS PARTS BURIED ACROSS THE LAND.
FROM THOSE PARTS WHICH WEREN'T SEALED AWAY...
SPRANG FORTH GOBLINS, ORCS, AND THE LIKE. WE CALL THESE MONSTERS FIENDS.

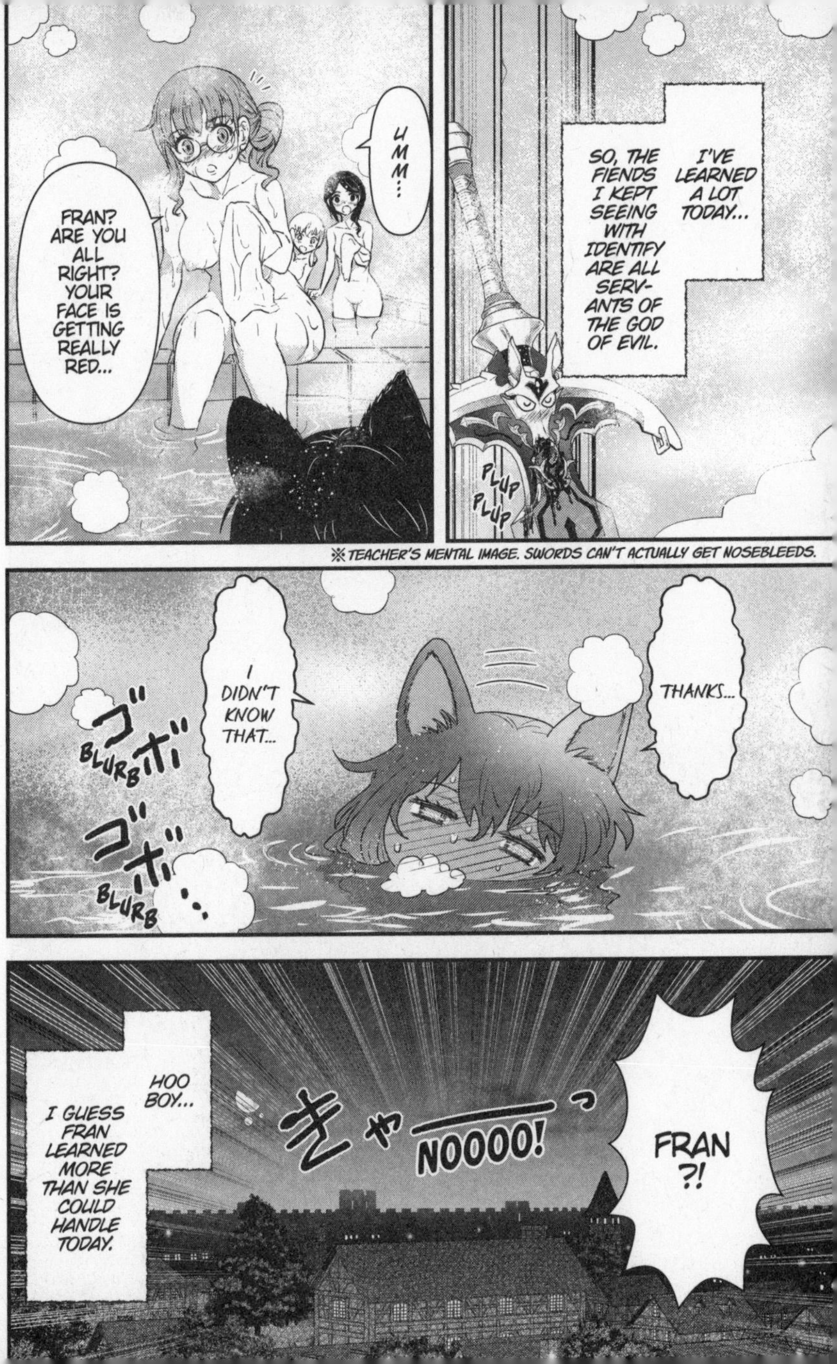
I'VE LEARNED A LOT TODAY...
SO, THE FIENDS I KEPT SEEING WITH IDENTIFY ARE ALL SERV-ANTS OF THE GOD OF EVIL.
PLUP PLUP
UMM...
FRAN? ARE YOU ALL RIGHT? YOUR FACE IS GETTING REALLY RED...
※TEACHER'S MENTAL IMAGE. SWORDS CAN'T ACTUALLY GET NOSEBLEEDS.
THANKS...
I DIDN'T KNOW THAT...
ゴボ BLURB
ゴボ BLURB
...
FRAN?!
きゃ――っ NOOOO!
HOO BOY...
I GUESS FRAN LEARNED MORE THAN SHE COULD HANDLE TODAY.

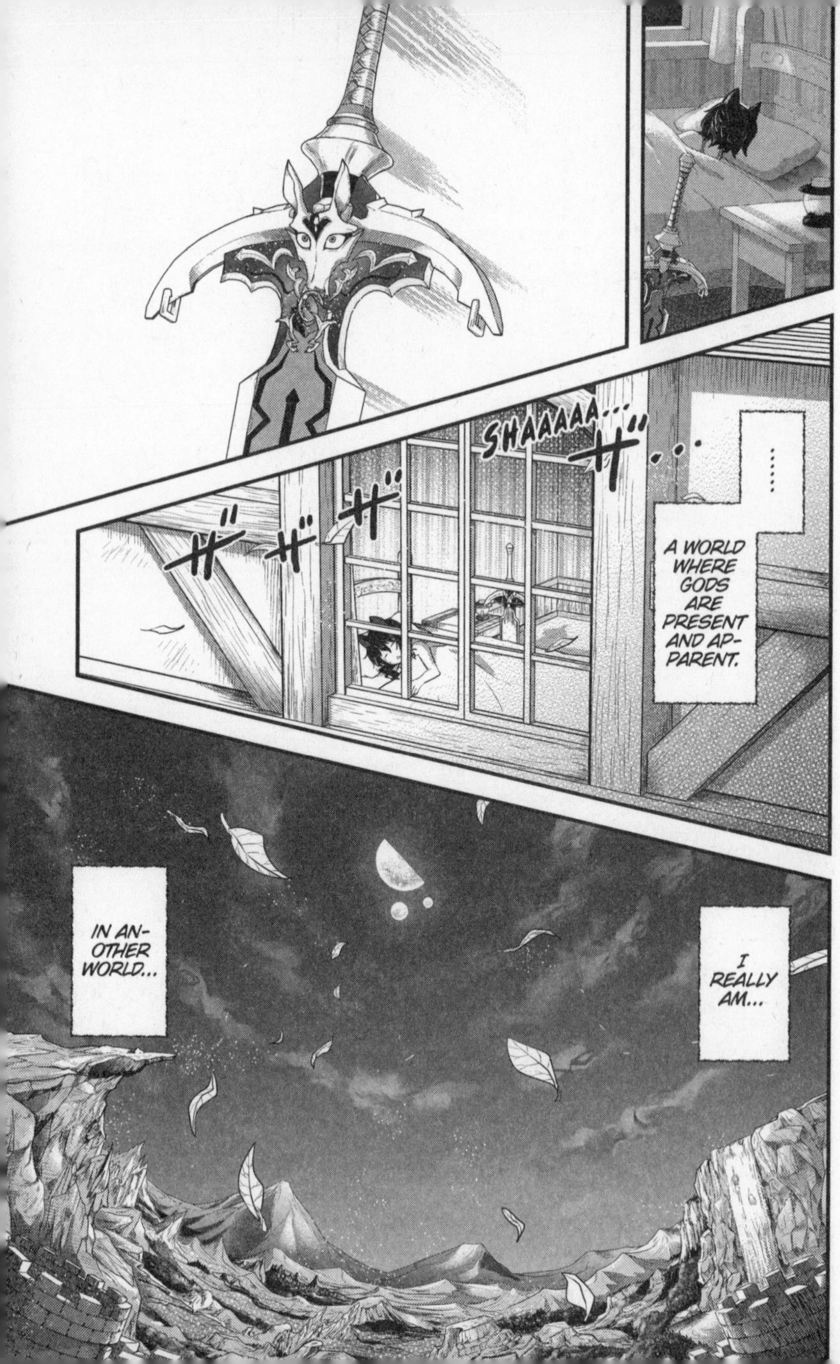
......
SHAAAAA...
ザ
ザ ザ ザ
A WORLD WHERE GODS ARE PRESENT AND APPARENT.
I REALLY AM...
IN ANOTHER WORLD...

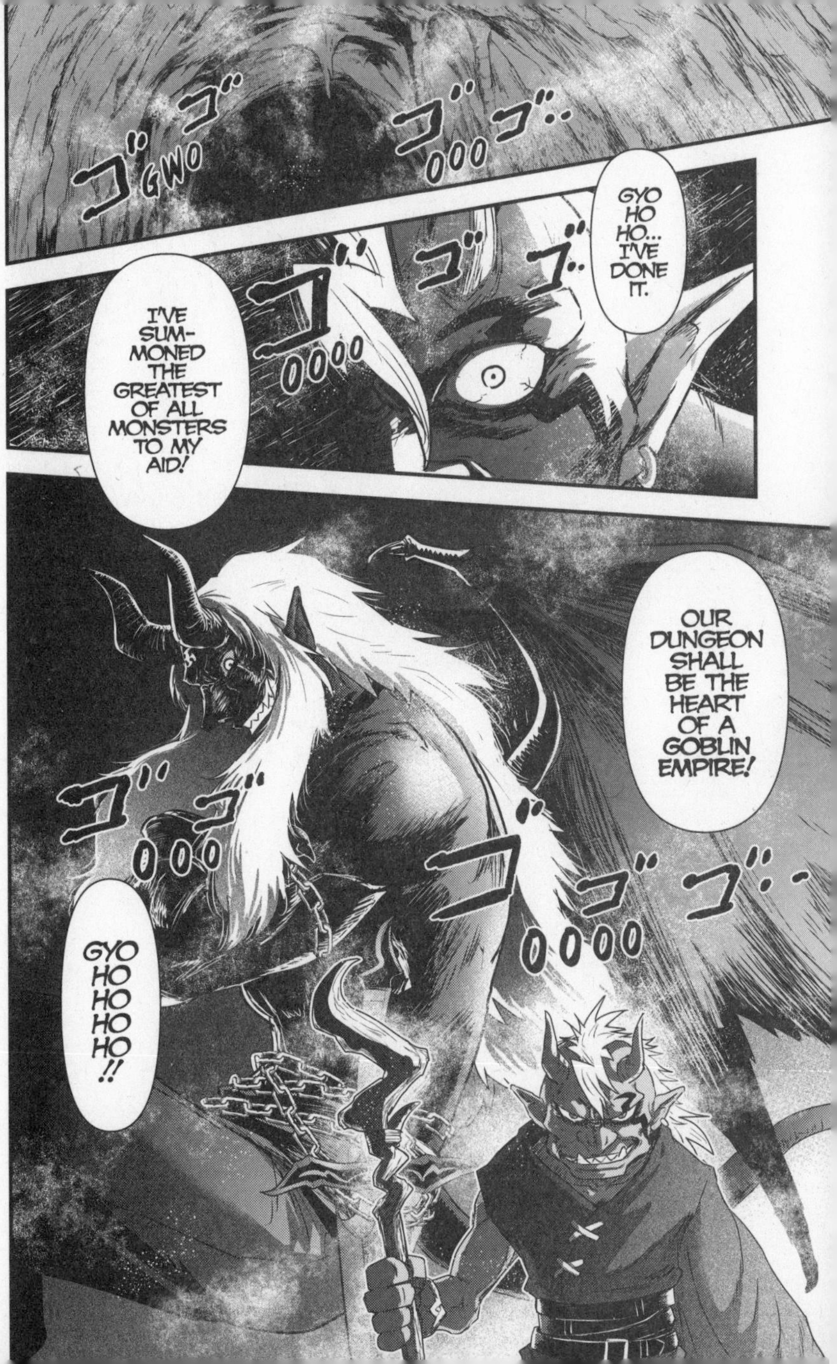
GWO
OOO
GYO HO HO... I'VE DONE IT.
OOOO
I'VE SUMMONED THE GREATEST OF ALL MONSTERS TO MY AID!
OUR DUNGEON SHALL BE THE HEART OF A GOBLIN EMPIRE!
OOOO
OOO
GYO HO HO HO HO!!

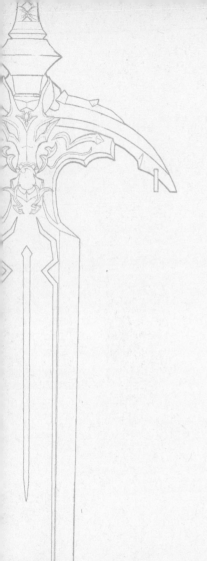

Reincarnated
as a sword

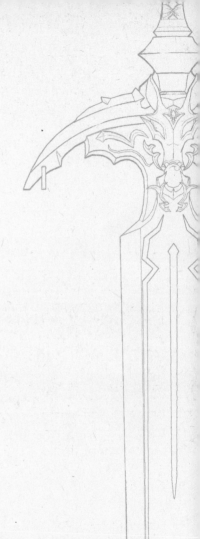

Reincarnated
as a sword

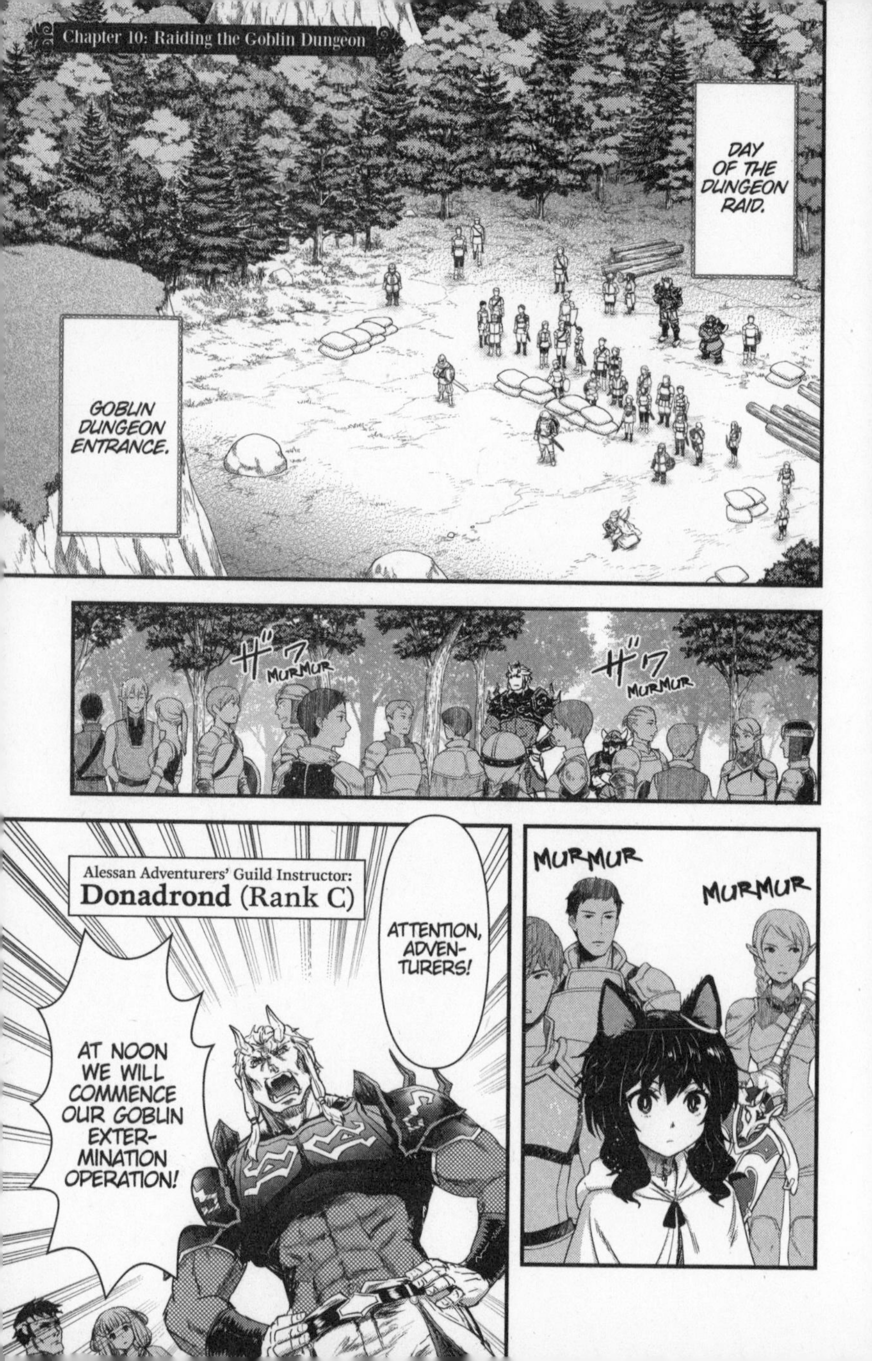
Chapter 10: Raiding the Goblin Dungeon
DAY OF THE DUNGEON RAID.
GOBLIN DUNGEON ENTRANCE.
ザワ
MURMUR
ザワ
MURMUR
MURMUR
MURMUR
ATTENTION, ADVEN-TURERS!
Alessan Adventurers' Guild Instructor: Donadrond (Rank C)
AT NOON WE WILL COMMENCE OUR GOBLIN EXTER-MINATION OPERATION!

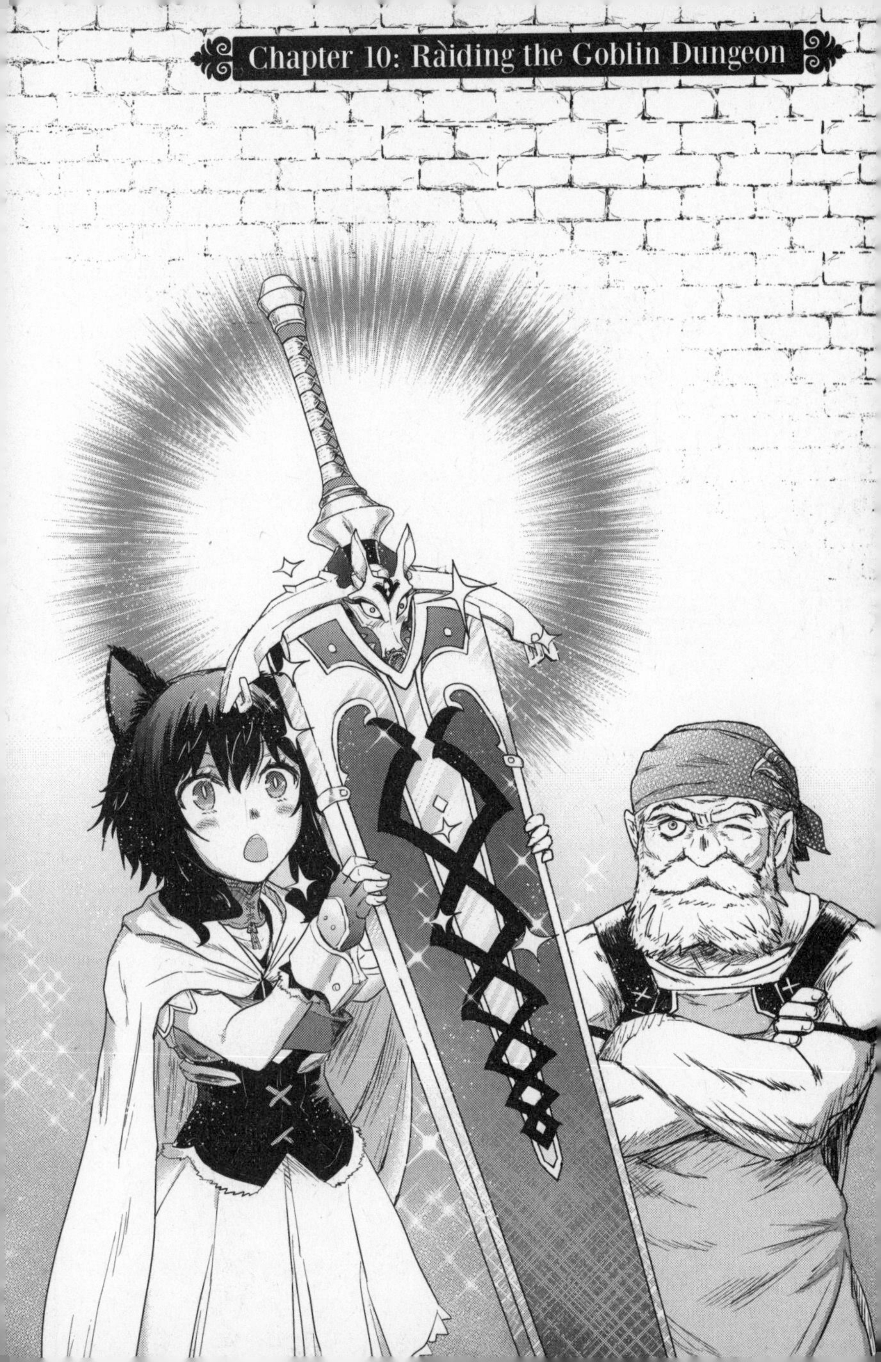
Chapter 10: Raiding the Goblin Dungeon

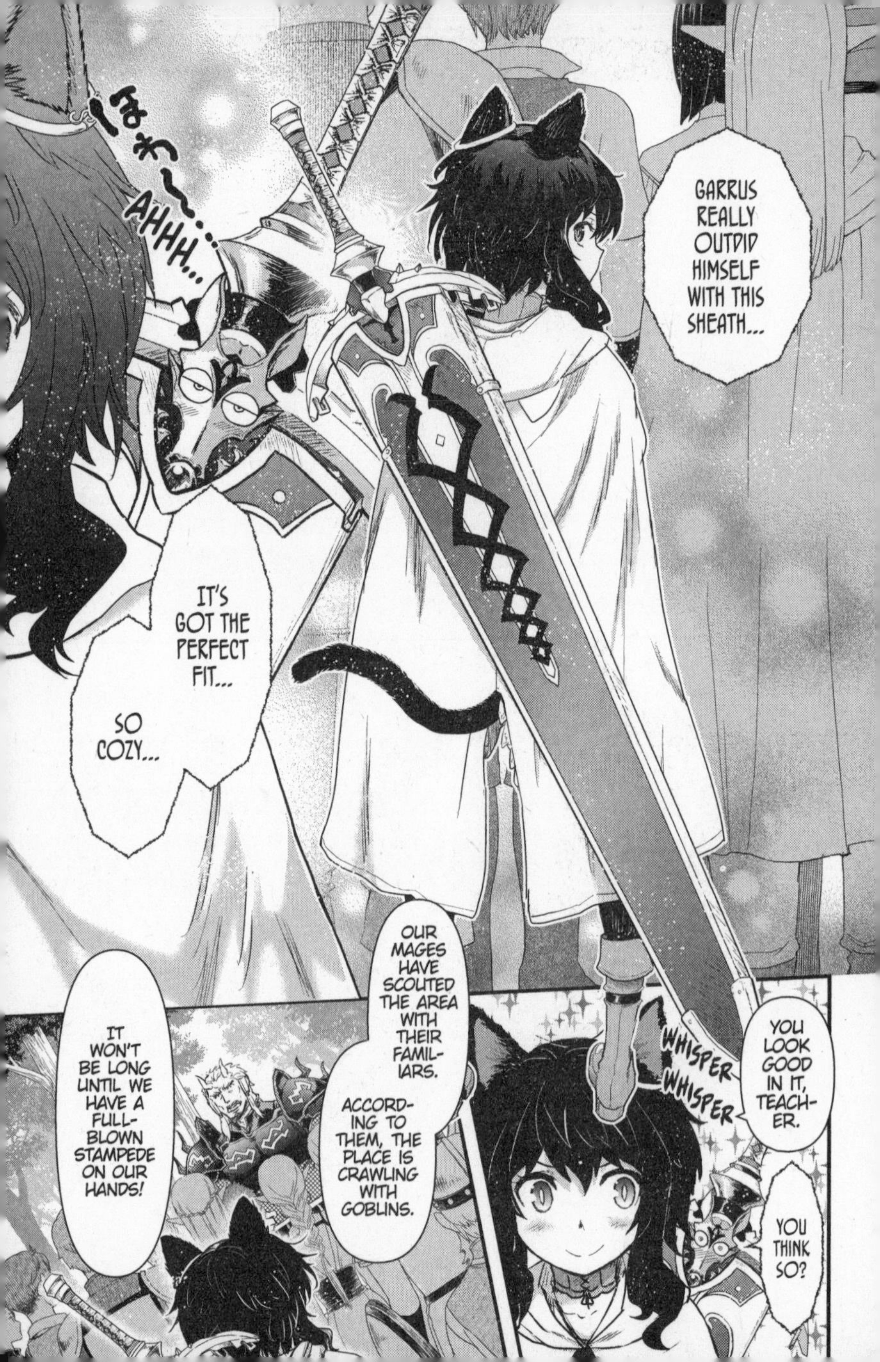
GARRUS REALLY OUTDID HIMSELF WITH THIS SHEATH...
ほわ~~ AHHH...
IT'S GOT THE PERFECT FIT...
SO COZY...
YOU LOOK GOOD IN IT, TEACHER.
WHISPER WHISPER
YOU THINK SO?
OUR MAGES HAVE SCOUTED THE AREA WITH THEIR FAMILIARS.
ACCORDING TO THEM, THE PLACE IS CRAWLING WITH GOBLINS.
IT WON'T BE LONG UNTIL WE HAVE A FULL-BLOWN STAMPEDE ON OUR HANDS!

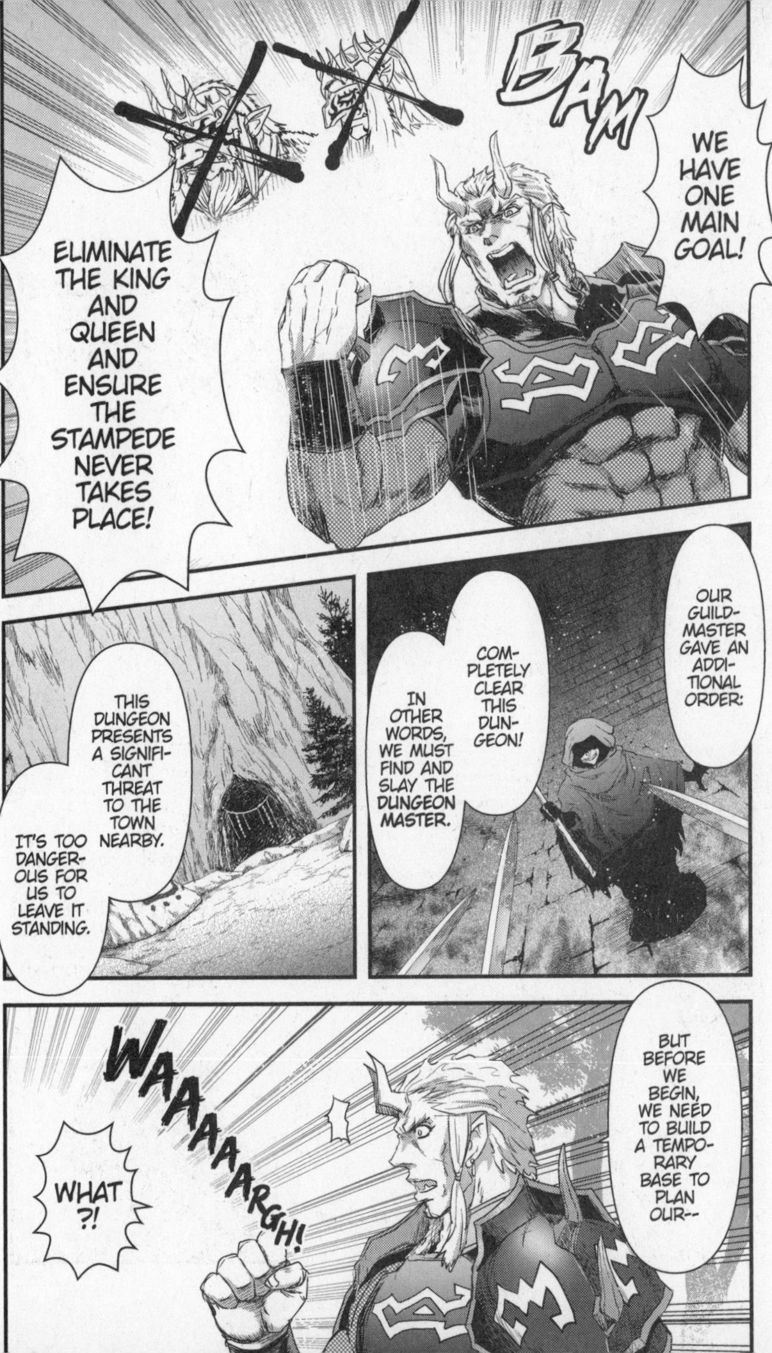
BAM
WE HAVE ONE MAIN GOAL!
ELIMINATE THE KING AND QUEEN AND ENSURE THE STAMPEDE NEVER TAKES PLACE!
OUR GUILD-MASTER GAVE AN ADDITIONAL ORDER:
COMPLETELY CLEAR THIS DUNGEON!
IN OTHER WORDS, WE MUST FIND AND SLAY THE DUNGEON MASTER.
THIS DUNGEON PRESENTS A SIGNIFICANT THREAT TO THE TOWN NEARBY.
IT'S TOO DANGEROUS FOR US TO LEAVE IT STANDING.
BUT BEFORE WE BEGIN, WE NEED TO BUILD A TEMPORARY BASE TO PLAN OUR--
!
WAAAAAARGH!
WHAT?!

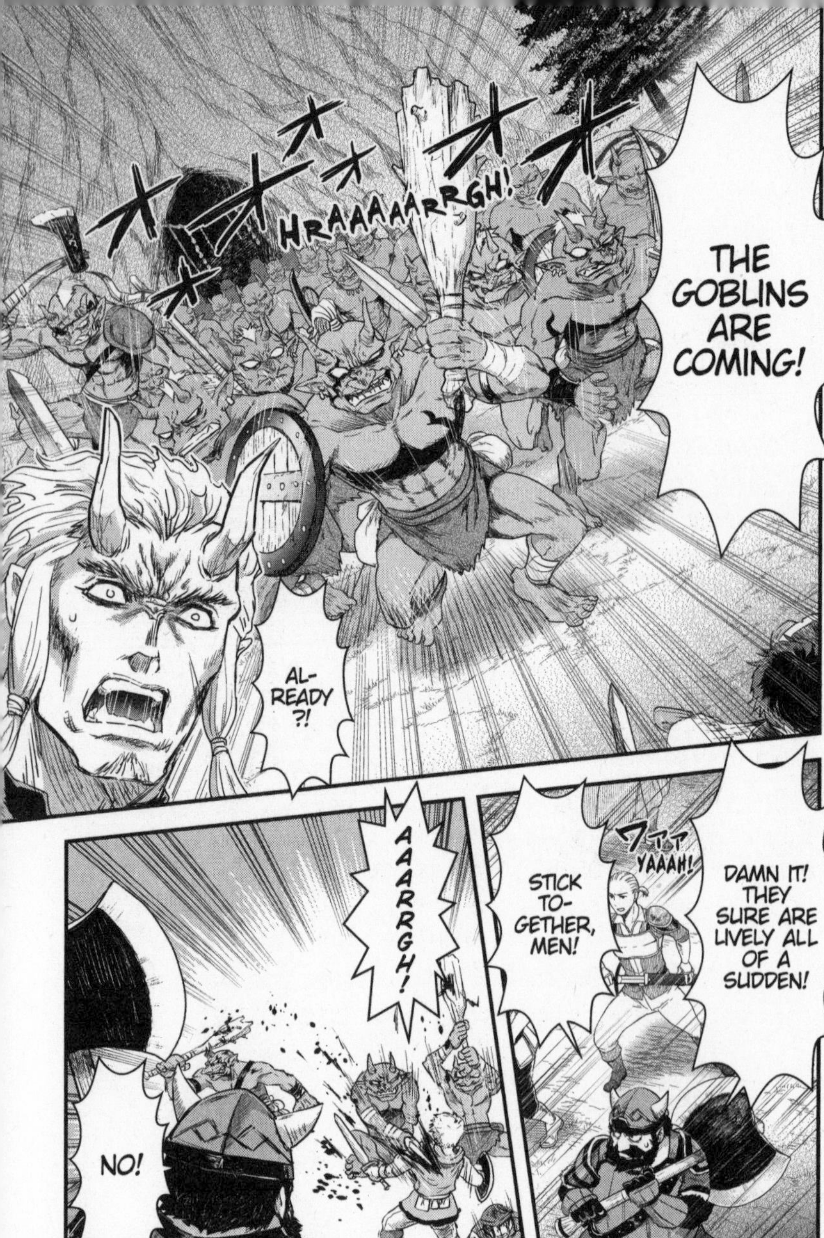
THE GOBLINS ARE COMING!
HRAAAAARRGH!
AL-READY?!
DAMN IT! THEY SURE ARE LIVELY ALL OF A SUDDEN!
YAAAH!
STICK TO-GETHER, MEN!
AAAARRGH!
NO!

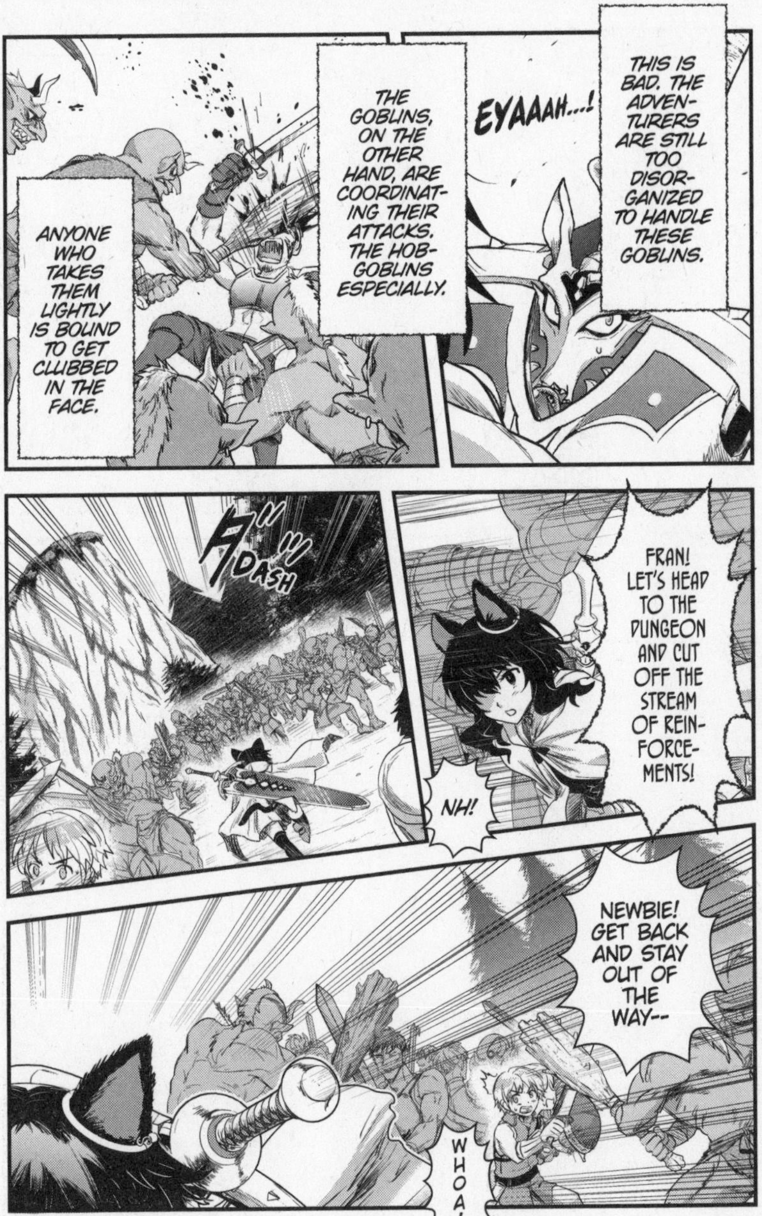
THIS IS BAD. THE ADVENTURERS ARE STILL TOO DISORGANIZED TO HANDLE THESE GOBLINS.
EYAAAH...!
THE GOBLINS, ON THE OTHER HAND, ARE COORDINATING THEIR ATTACKS. THE HOBGOBLINS ESPECIALLY.
ANYONE WHO TAKES THEM LIGHTLY IS BOUND TO GET CLUBBED IN THE FACE.
FRAN! LET'S HEAD TO THE DUNGEON AND CUT OFF THE STREAM OF REINFORCEMENTS!
NH!
DASH
NEWBIE! GET BACK AND STAY OUT OF THE WAY--
WHOA!

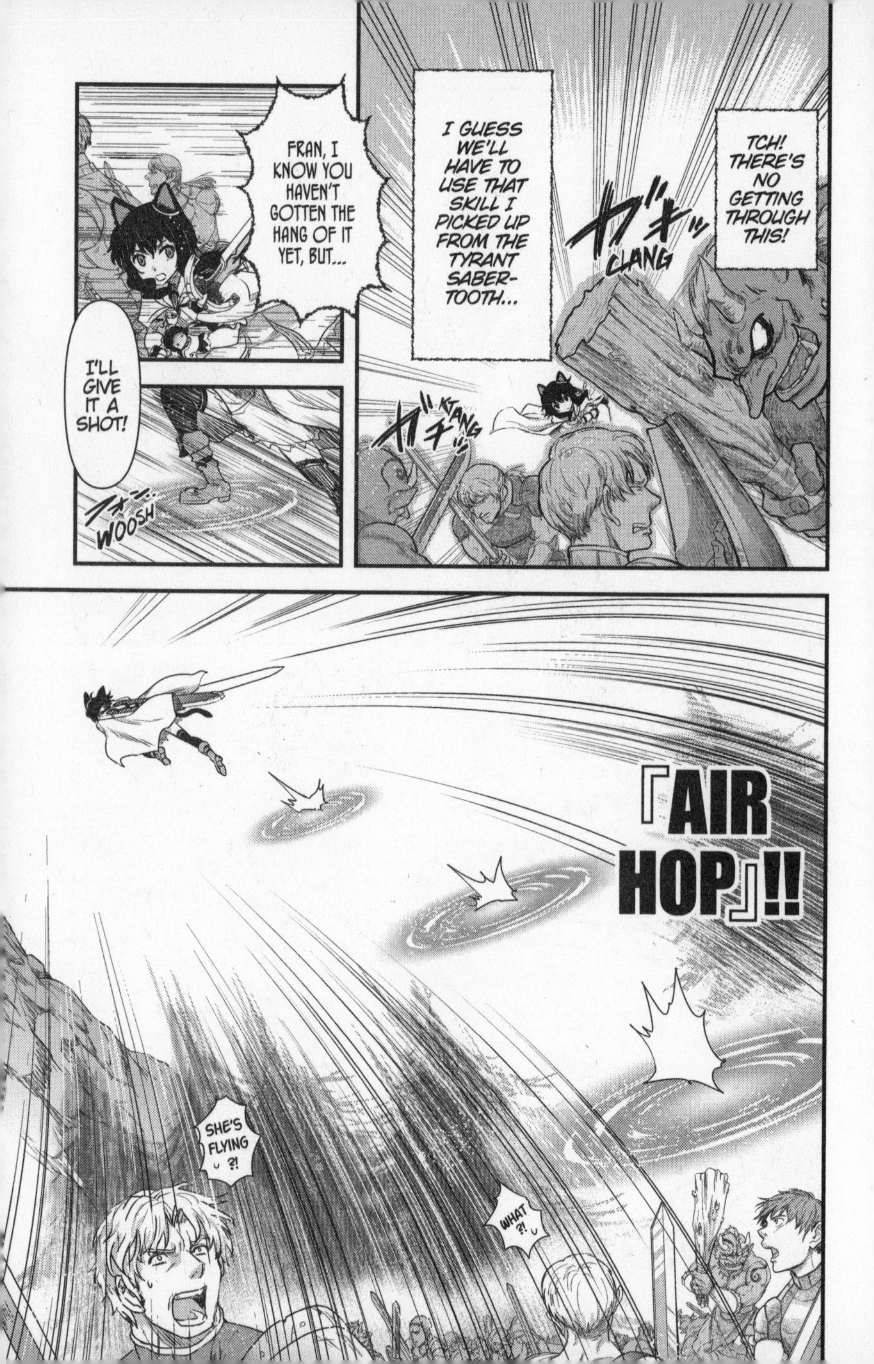
TCH! THERE'S NO GETTING THROUGH THIS!
I GUESS WE'LL HAVE TO USE THAT SKILL I PICKED UP FROM THE TYRANT SABER-TOOTH...
CLANG
KTANG
FRAN, I KNOW YOU HAVEN'T GOTTEN THE HANG OF IT YET, BUT...
I'LL GIVE IT A SHOT!
WOOSH
「AIR HOP」!!
WHAT?!
SHE'S FLYING?!

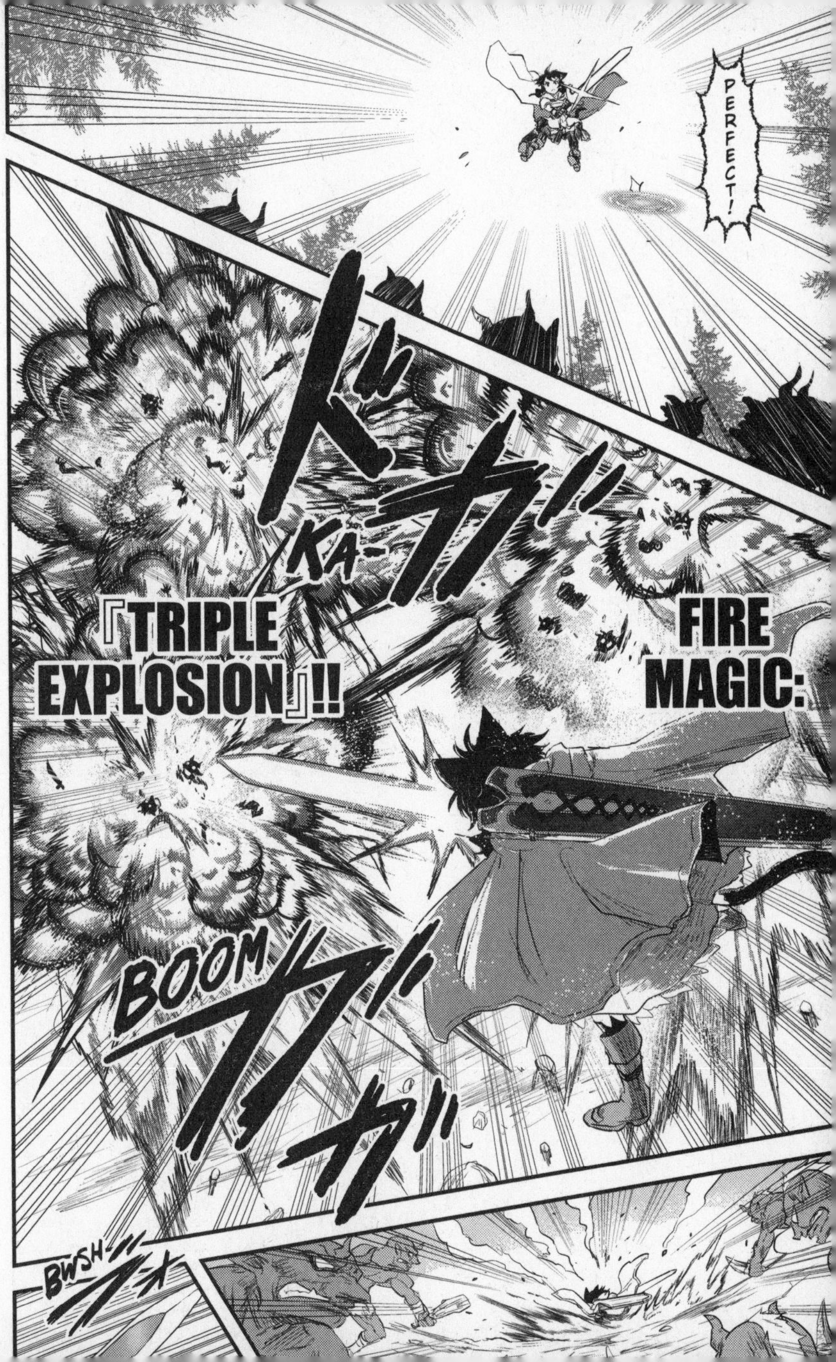
PERFECT!
KA-
FIRE MAGIC:
『TRIPLE EXPLOSION』!!
BOOM
BWSH-

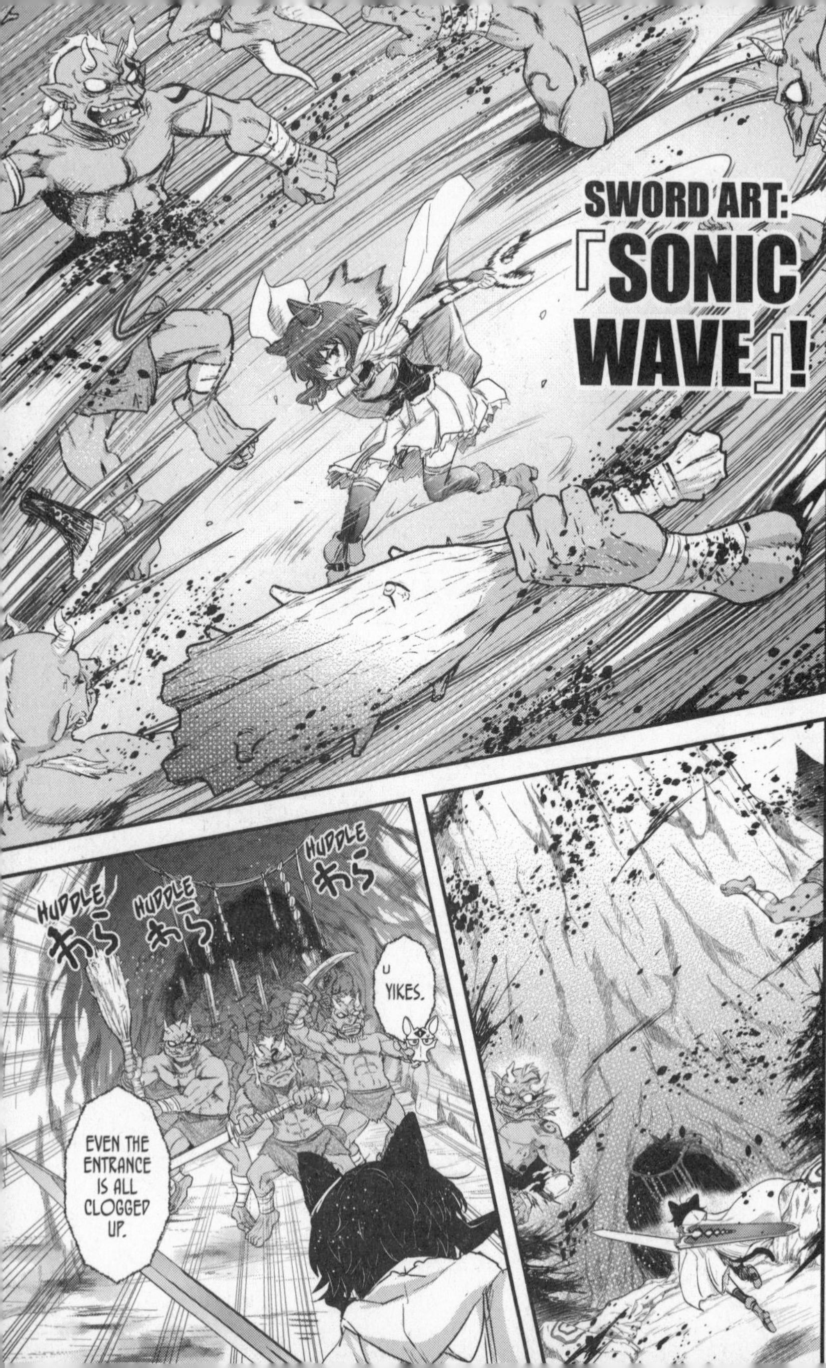
SWORD ART: 『SONIC WAVE』!
HUDDLE わら
YIKES.
HUDDLE わら
HUDDLE わら
EVEN THE ENTRANCE IS ALL CLOGGED UP.

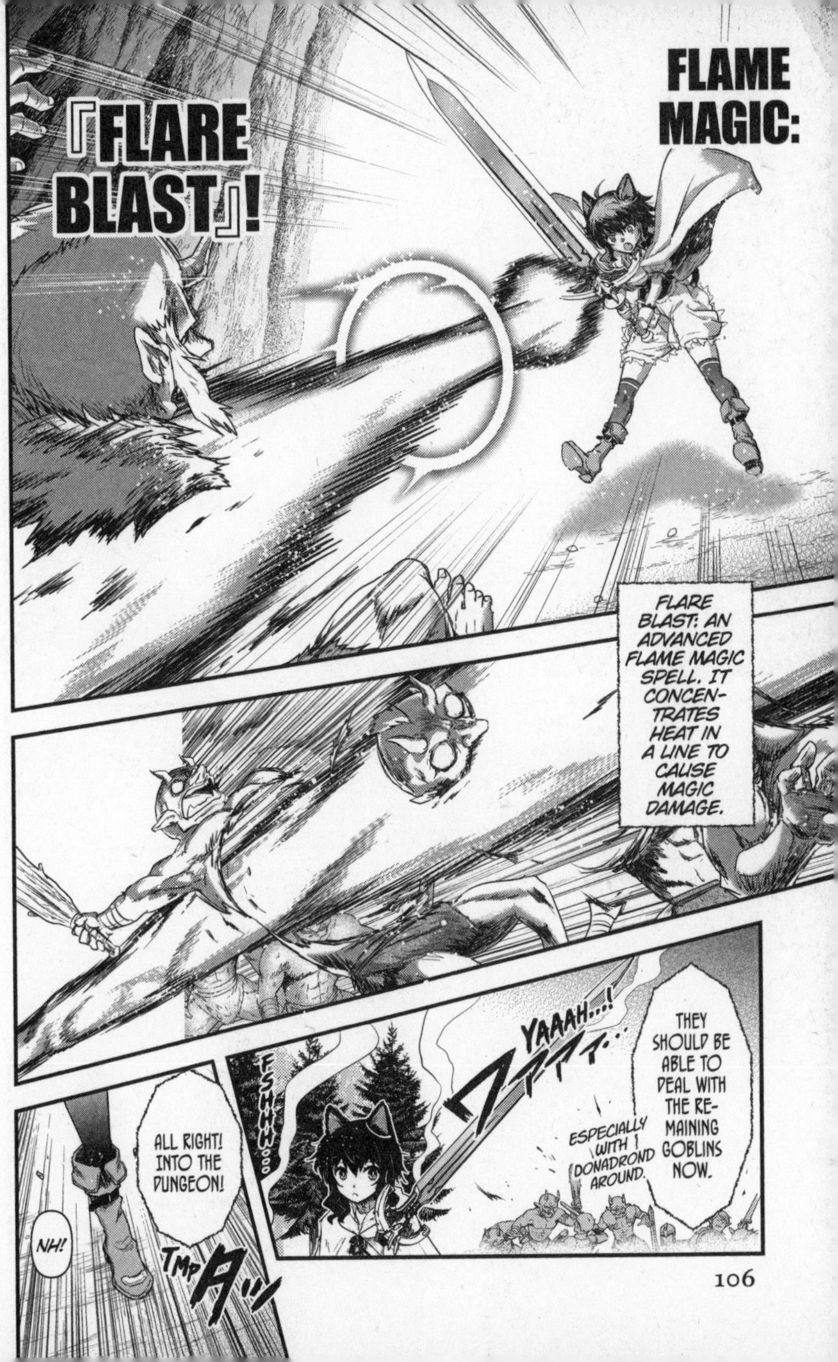
FLAME MAGIC:
『FLARE BLAST』!
FLARE BLAST: AN ADVANCED FLAME MAGIC SPELL. IT CONCEN-TRATES HEAT IN A LINE TO CAUSE MAGIC DAMAGE.
THEY SHOULD BE ABLE TO DEAL WITH THE RE-MAINING GOBLINS NOW.
ESPECIALLY WITH DONADROND AROUND.
YAAAH...!
FSHHHH...
ALL RIGHT! INTO THE DUNGEON!
NH!
TMP

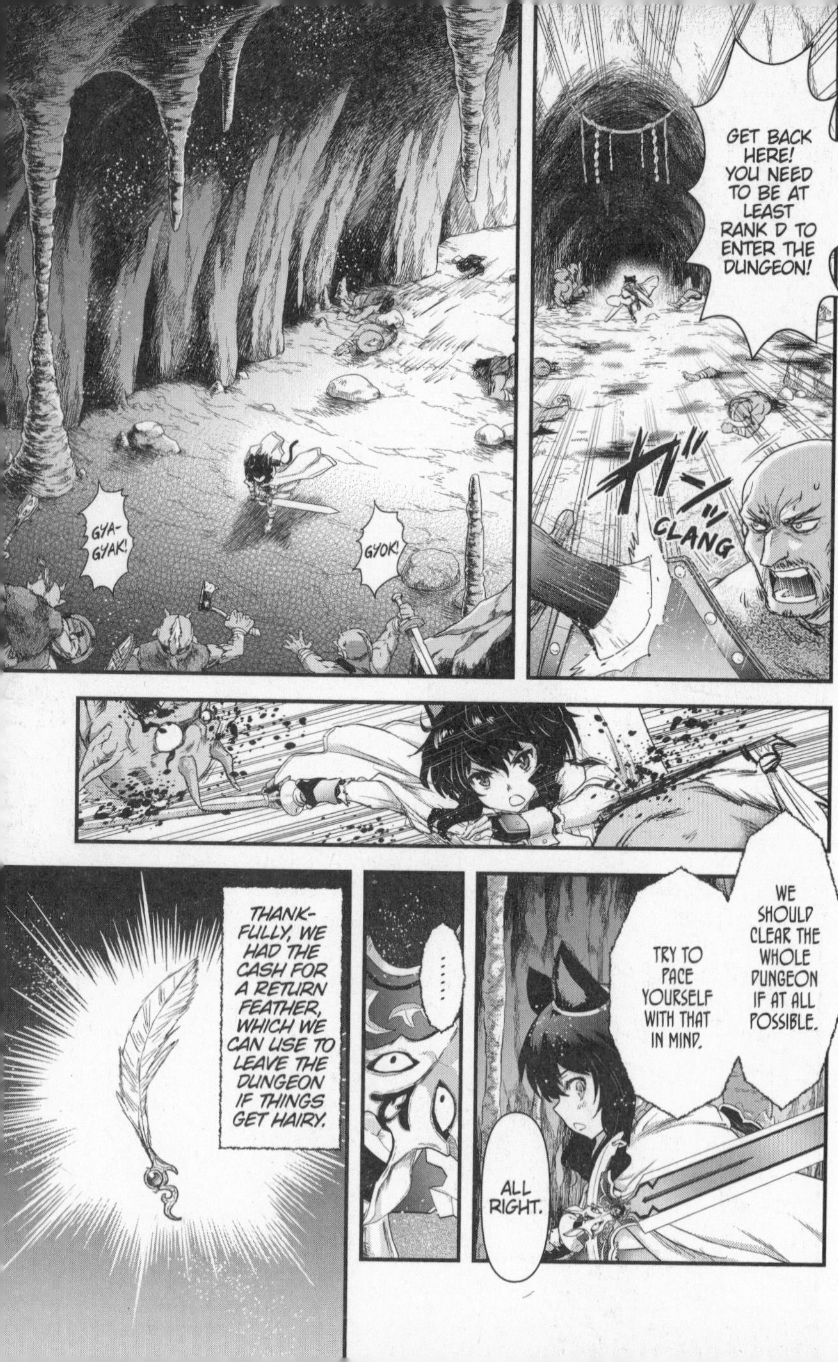
GET BACK HERE! YOU NEED TO BE AT LEAST RANK D TO ENTER THE DUNGEON!
CLANG
GYOK!
GYA-GYAK!
WE SHOULD CLEAR THE WHOLE DUNGEON IF AT ALL POSSIBLE.
TRY TO PACE YOURSELF WITH THAT IN MIND.
ALL RIGHT.
......
THANK-FULLY, WE HAD THE CASH FOR A RETURN FEATHER, WHICH WE CAN USE TO LEAVE THE DUNGEON IF THINGS GET HAIRY.

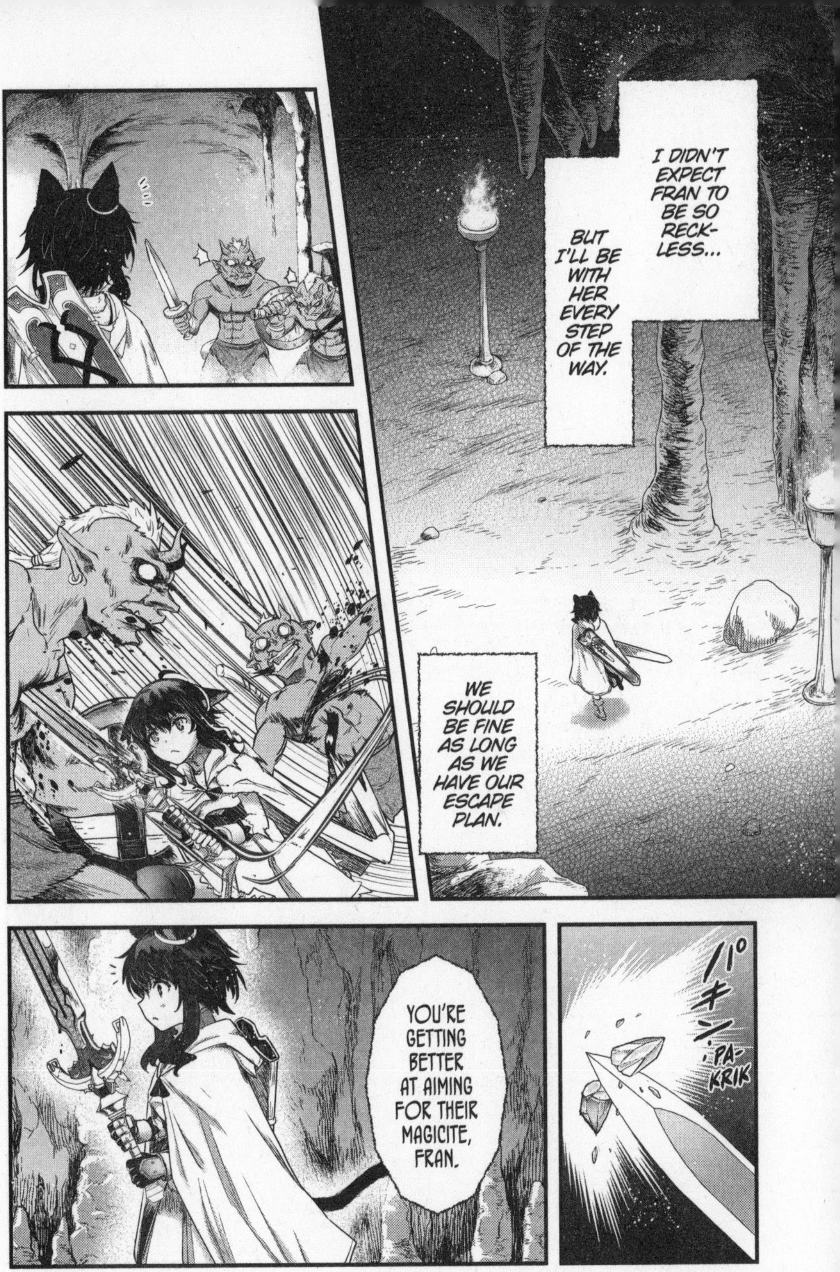
I DIDN'T EXPECT FRAN TO BE SO RECK-LESS...
BUT I'LL BE WITH HER EVERY STEP OF THE WAY.
WE SHOULD BE FINE AS LONG AS WE HAVE OUR ESCAPE PLAN.
パキン
PA-KRIK
YOU'RE GETTING BETTER AT AIMING FOR THEIR MAGICITE, FRAN.

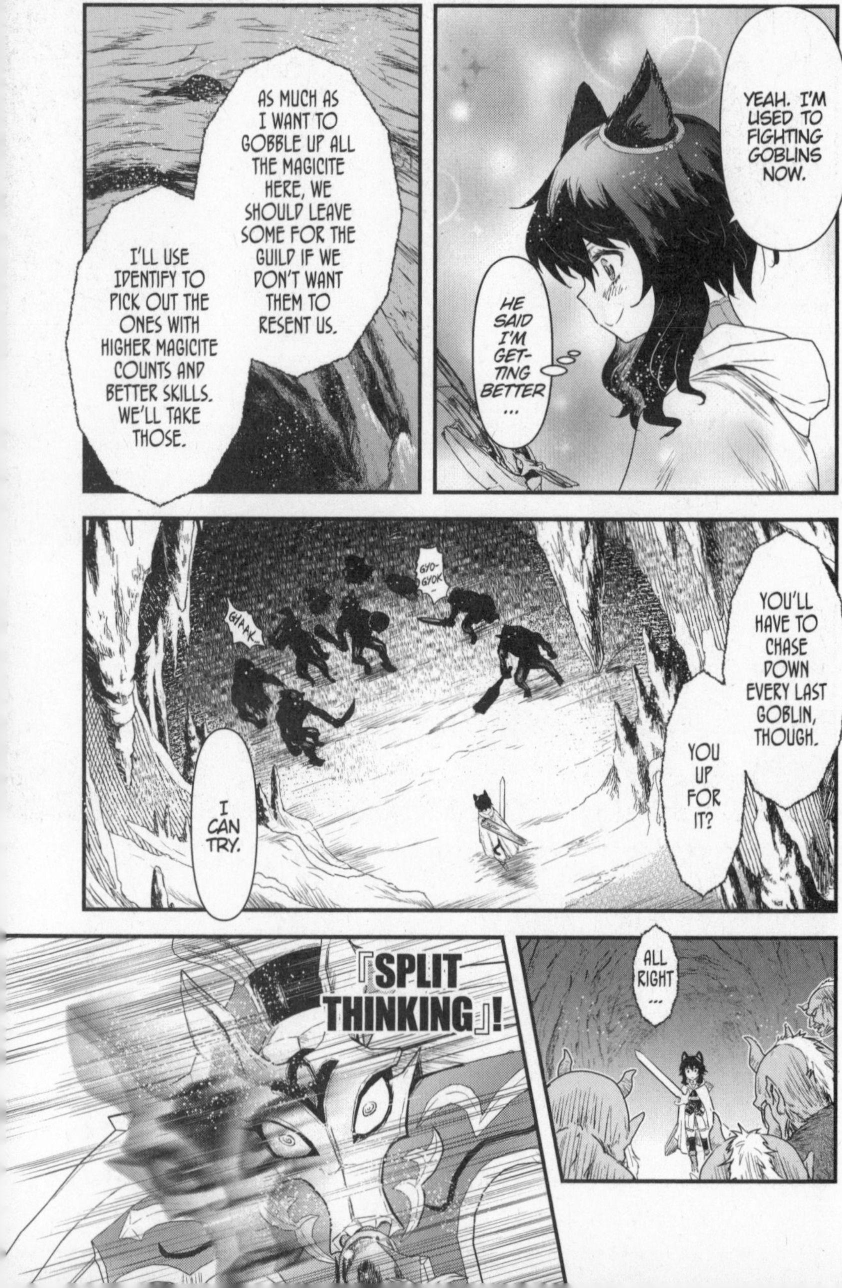
YEAH. I'M USED TO FIGHTING GOBLINS NOW.
HE SAID I'M GET-TING BETTER...
AS MUCH AS I WANT TO GOBBLE UP ALL THE MAGICITE HERE, WE SHOULD LEAVE SOME FOR THE GUILD IF WE DON'T WANT THEM TO RESENT US.
I'LL USE IDENTIFY TO PICK OUT THE ONES WITH HIGHER MAGICITE COUNTS AND BETTER SKILLS. WE'LL TAKE THOSE.
YOU'LL HAVE TO CHASE DOWN EVERY LAST GOBLIN, THOUGH.
YOU UP FOR IT?
GYO-GYOK...
GYAAK...
I CAN TRY.
ALL RIGHT...
『SPLIT THINKING』!

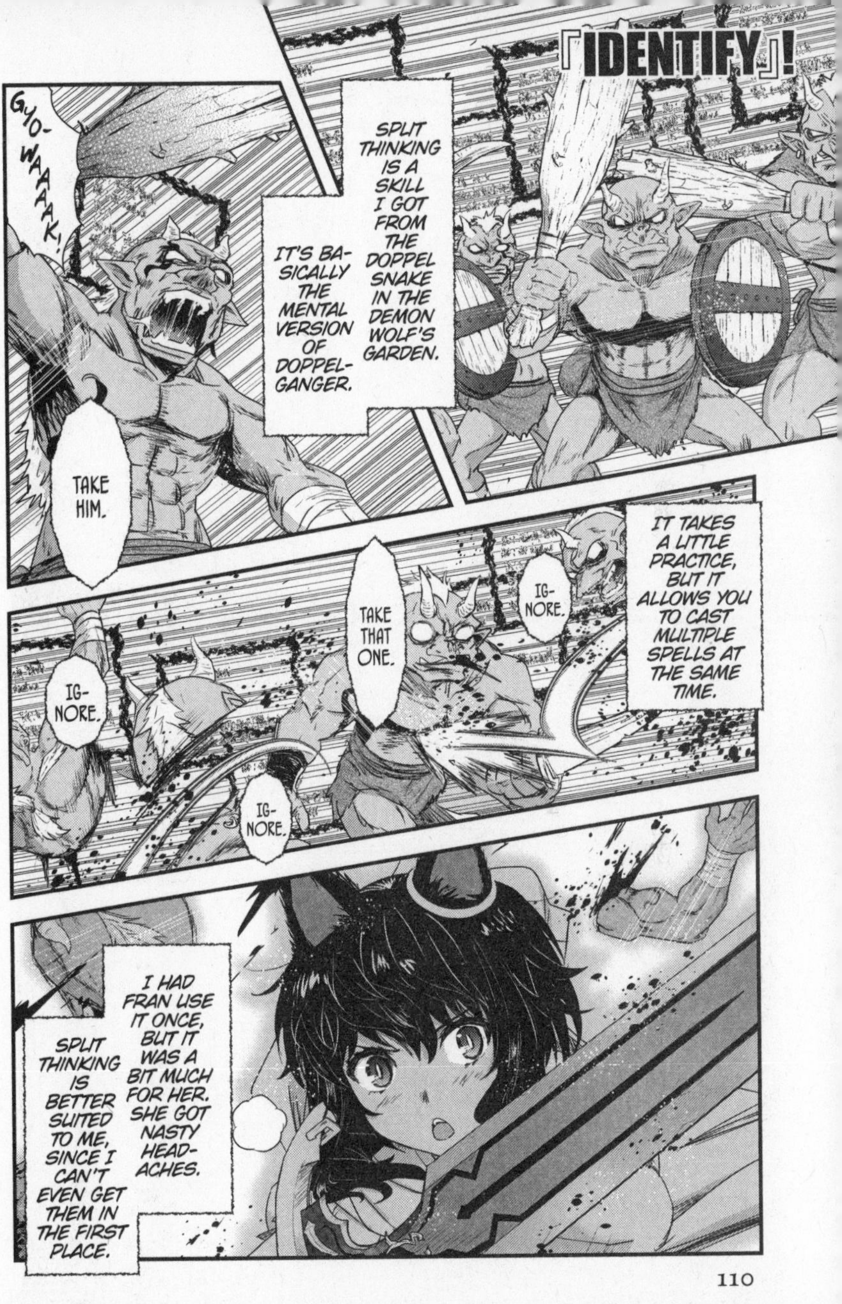

「IDENTIFY」!
SPLIT THINKING IS A SKILL I GOT FROM THE DOPPEL SNAKE IN THE DEMON WOLF'S GARDEN.
IT'S BASICALLY THE MENTAL VERSION OF DOPPEL-GANGER.
GYO-WAAAAAK!
TAKE HIM.
IT TAKES A LITTLE PRACTICE, BUT IT ALLOWS YOU TO CAST MULTIPLE SPELLS AT THE SAME TIME.
IG-NORE.
TAKE THAT ONE.
IG-NORE.
IG-NORE.
I HAD FRAN USE IT ONCE, BUT IT WAS A BIT MUCH FOR HER. SHE GOT NASTY HEAD-ACHES.
SPLIT THINKING IS BETTER SUITED TO ME, SINCE I CAN'T EVEN GET THEM IN THE FIRST PLACE.

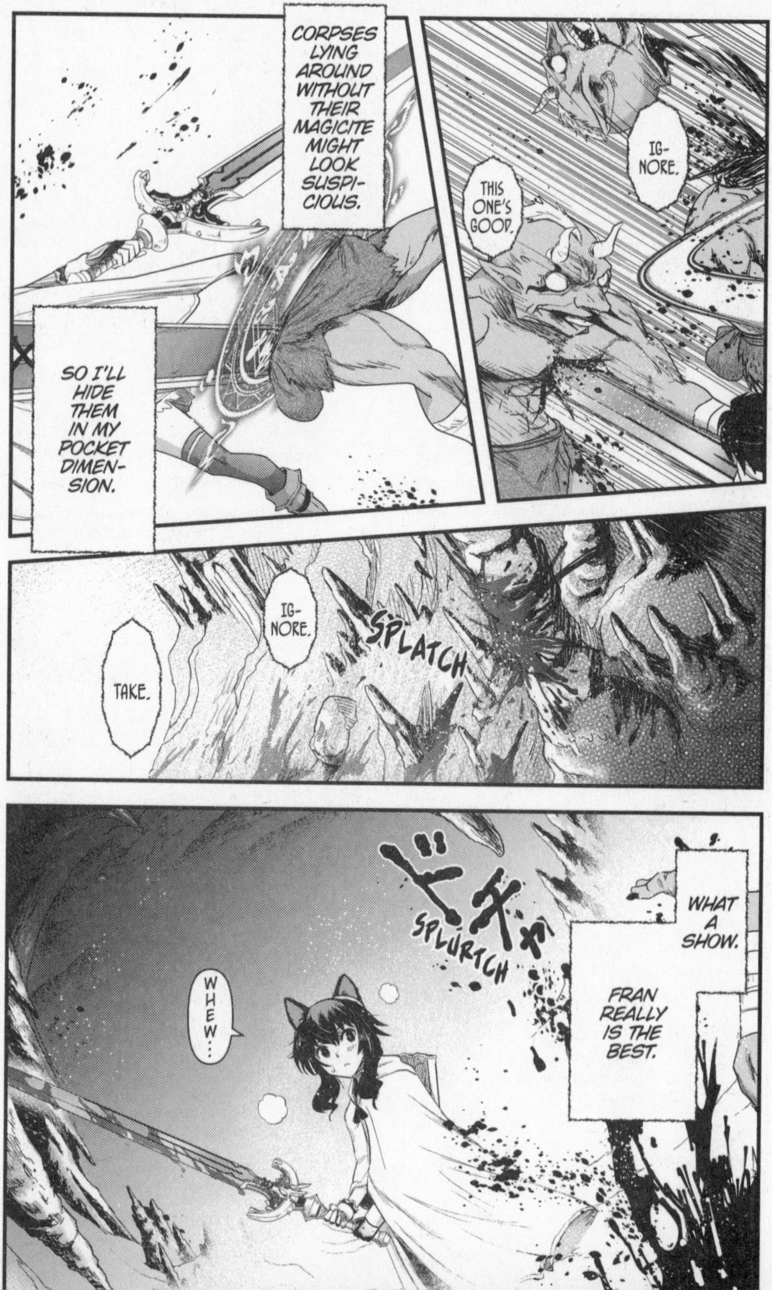
IG-NORE.
THIS ONE'S GOOD.
CORPSES LYING AROUND WITHOUT THEIR MAGICITE MIGHT LOOK SUSPICIOUS.
SO I'LL HIDE THEM IN MY POCKET DIMENSION.
SPLATCH
IG-NORE.
TAKE.
WHAT A SHOW.
FRAN REALLY IS THE BEST.
SPLURTCH
WHEW...

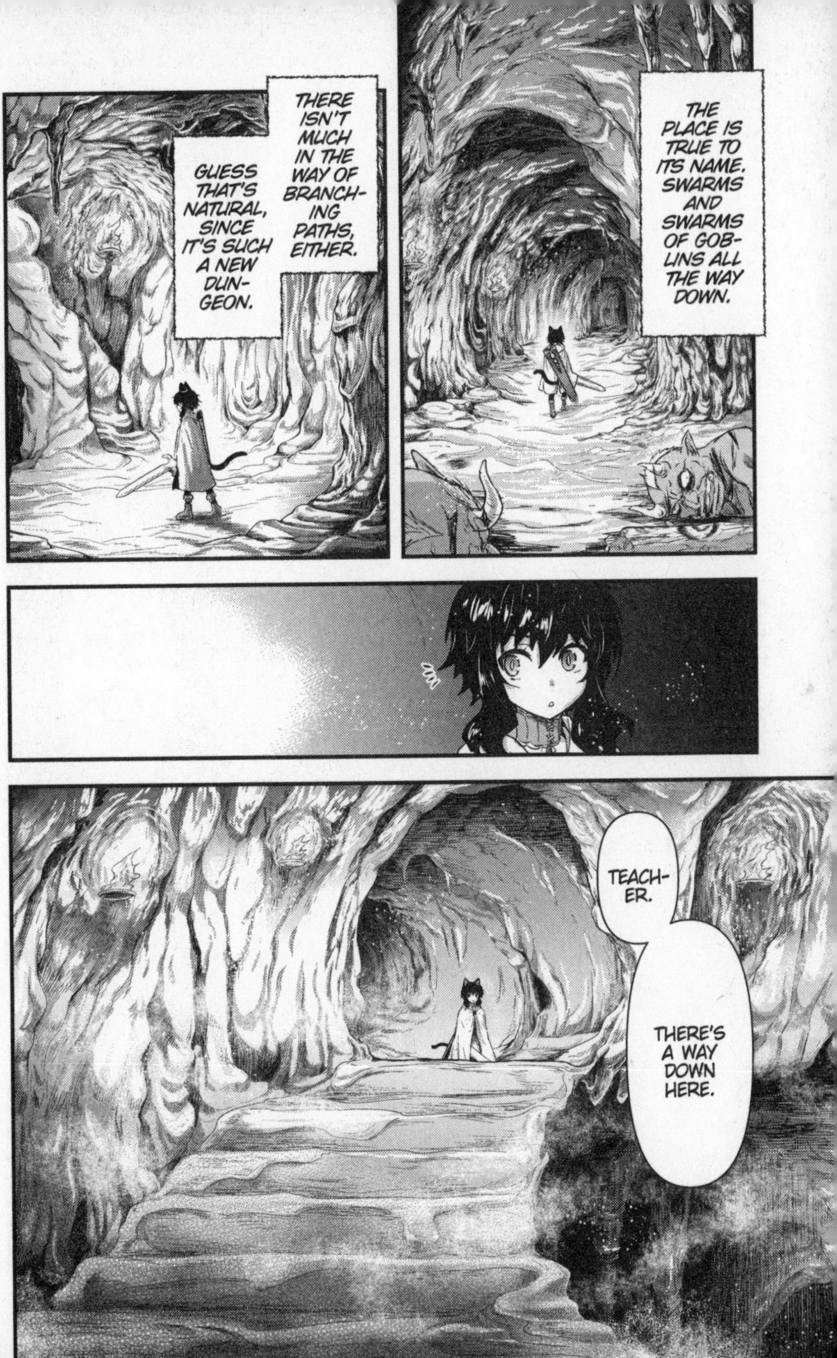
THE PLACE IS TRUE TO ITS NAME. SWARMS AND SWARMS OF GOB-LINS ALL THE WAY DOWN.
THERE ISN'T MUCH IN THE WAY OF BRANCH-ING PATHS, EITHER.
GUESS THAT'S NATURAL, SINCE IT'S SUCH A NEW DUN-GEON.
TEACH-ER.
THERE'S A WAY DOWN HERE.

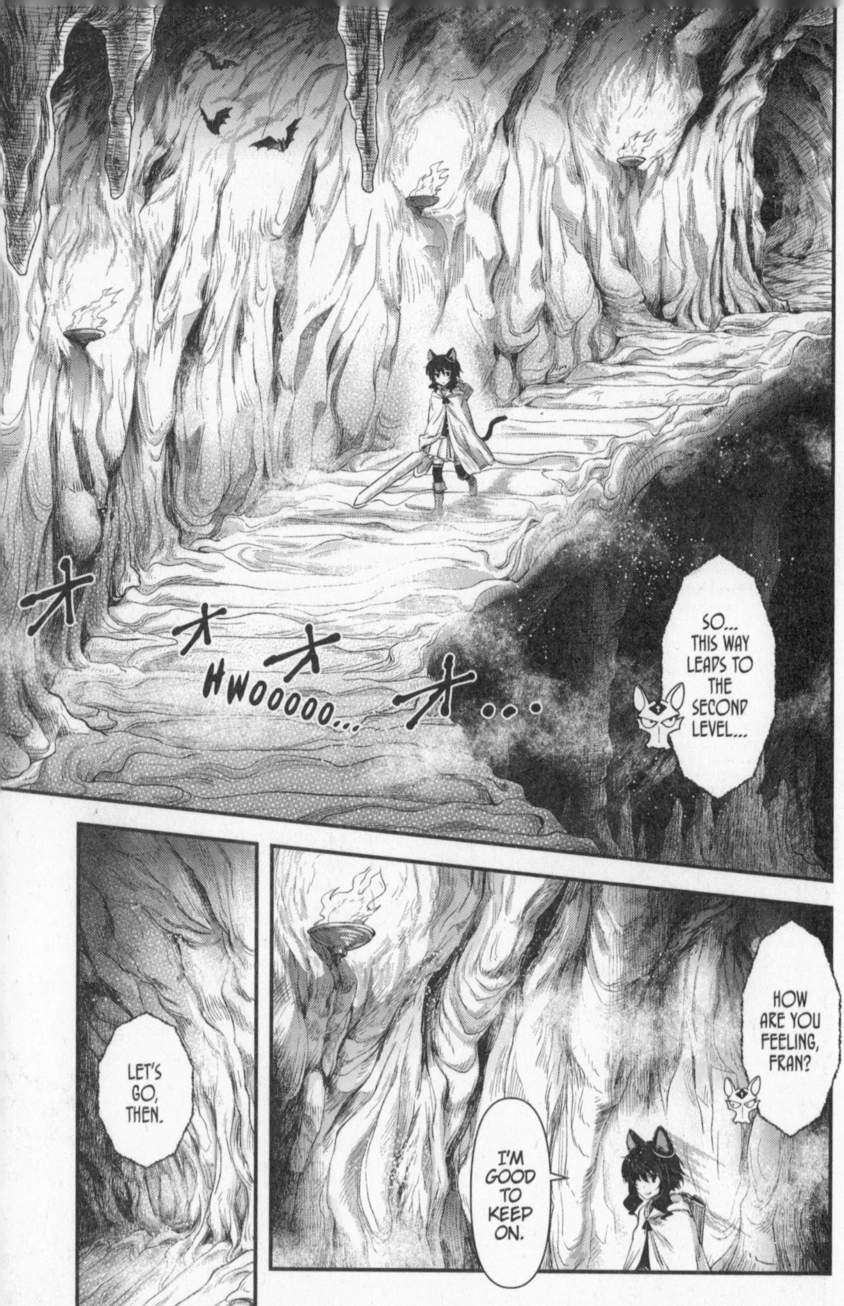
SO... THIS WAY LEADS TO THE SECOND LEVEL...
HWOOOOO...
HOW ARE YOU FEELING, FRAN?
I'M GOOD TO KEEP ON.
LET'S GO, THEN.

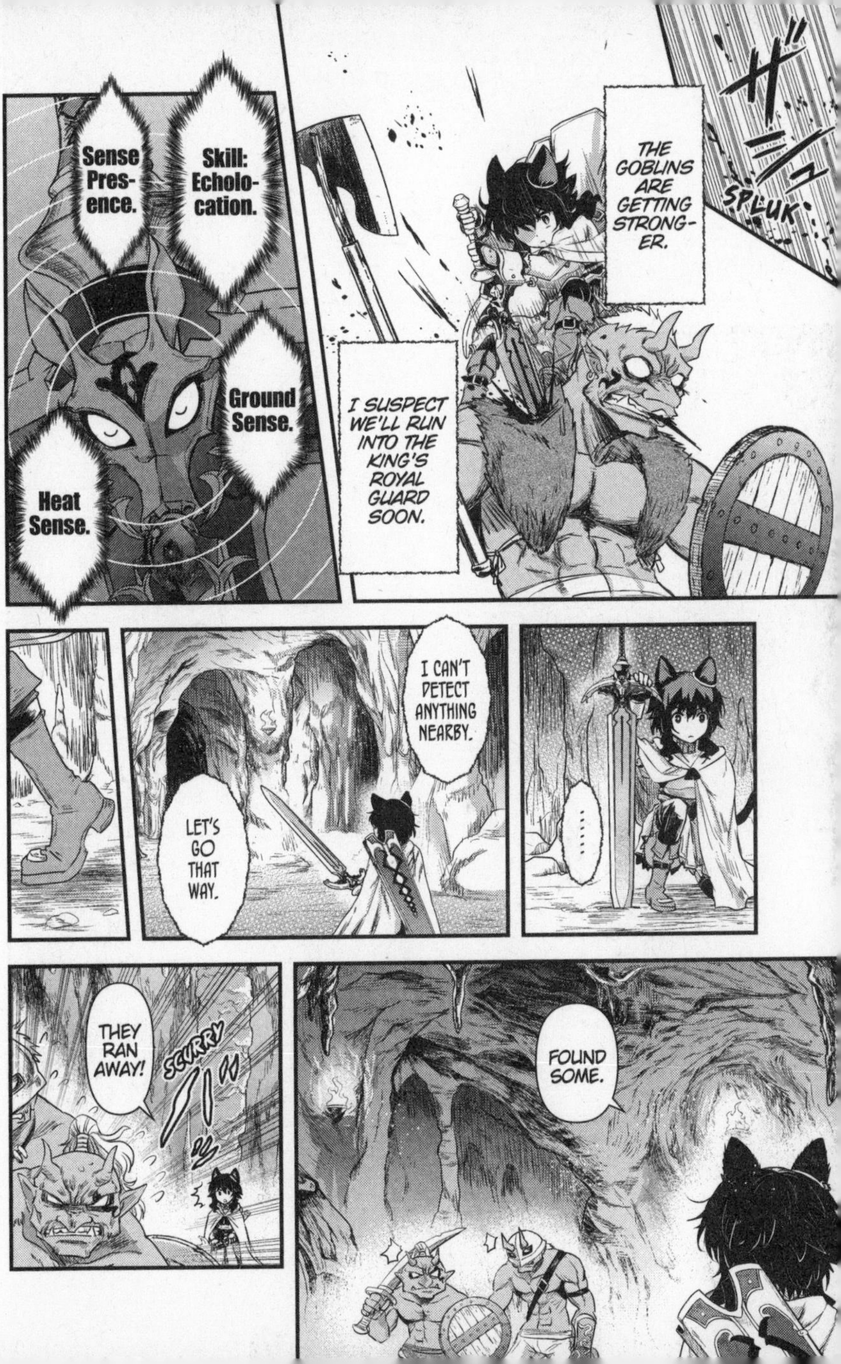
SPLUK
THE GOBLINS ARE GETTING STRONGER.
I SUSPECT WE'LL RUN INTO THE KING'S ROYAL GUARD SOON.
Skill: Echolocation.
Sense Presence.
Ground Sense.
Heat Sense.
......
I CAN'T DETECT ANYTHING NEARBY.
LET'S GO THAT WAY.
FOUND SOME.
THEY RAN AWAY!
SCURRY

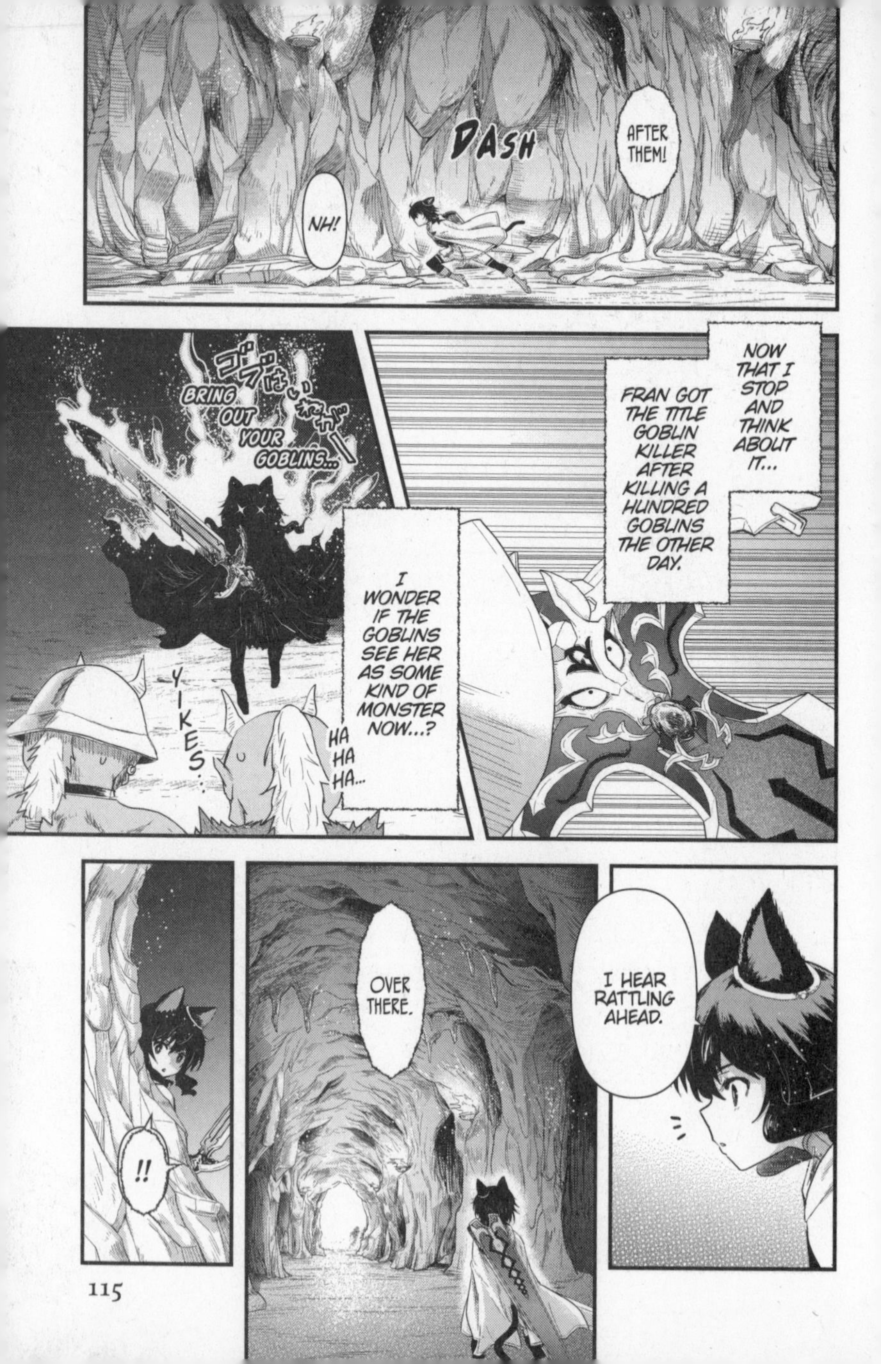
AFTER THEM!
DASH
NH!
NOW THAT I STOP AND THINK ABOUT IT...
FRAN GOT THE TITLE GOBLIN KILLER AFTER KILLING A HUNDRED GOBLINS THE OTHER DAY.
I WONDER IF THE GOBLINS SEE HER AS SOME KIND OF MONSTER NOW...?
ゴブはいねがー
BRING OUT YOUR GOBLINS...
HA HA HA...
YIKES...
I HEAR RATTLING AHEAD.
OVER THERE.
!!

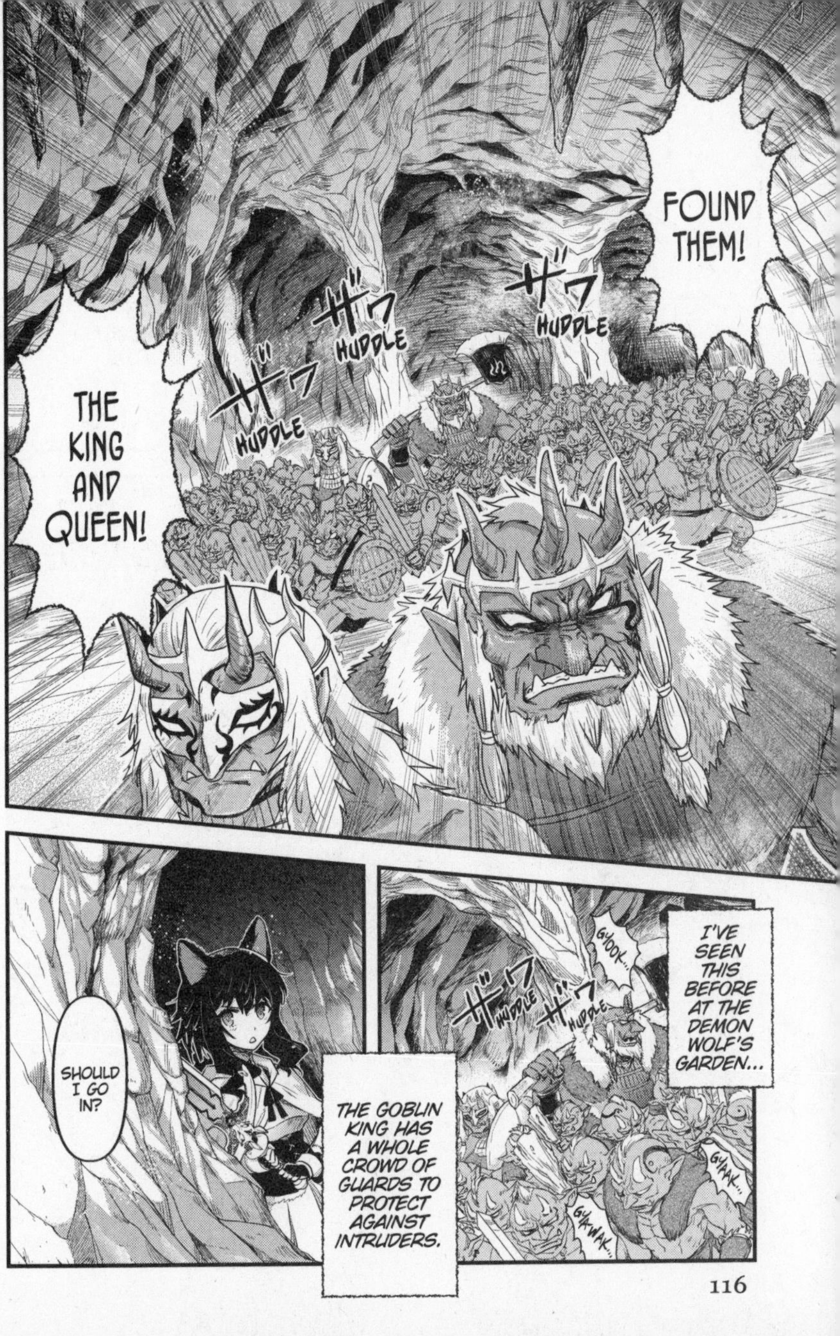
FOUND THEM!
ザワ HUDDLE
ザワ HUDDLE
ザワ HUDDLE
THE KING AND QUEEN!
I'VE SEEN THIS BEFORE AT THE DEMON WOLF'S GARDEN...
GYOOK...
ザワ HUDDLE
ザワ HUDDLE
GYAAK...
GYAWAK...
THE GOBLIN KING HAS A WHOLE CROWD OF GUARDS TO PROTECT AGAINST INTRUDERS.
SHOULD I GO IN?

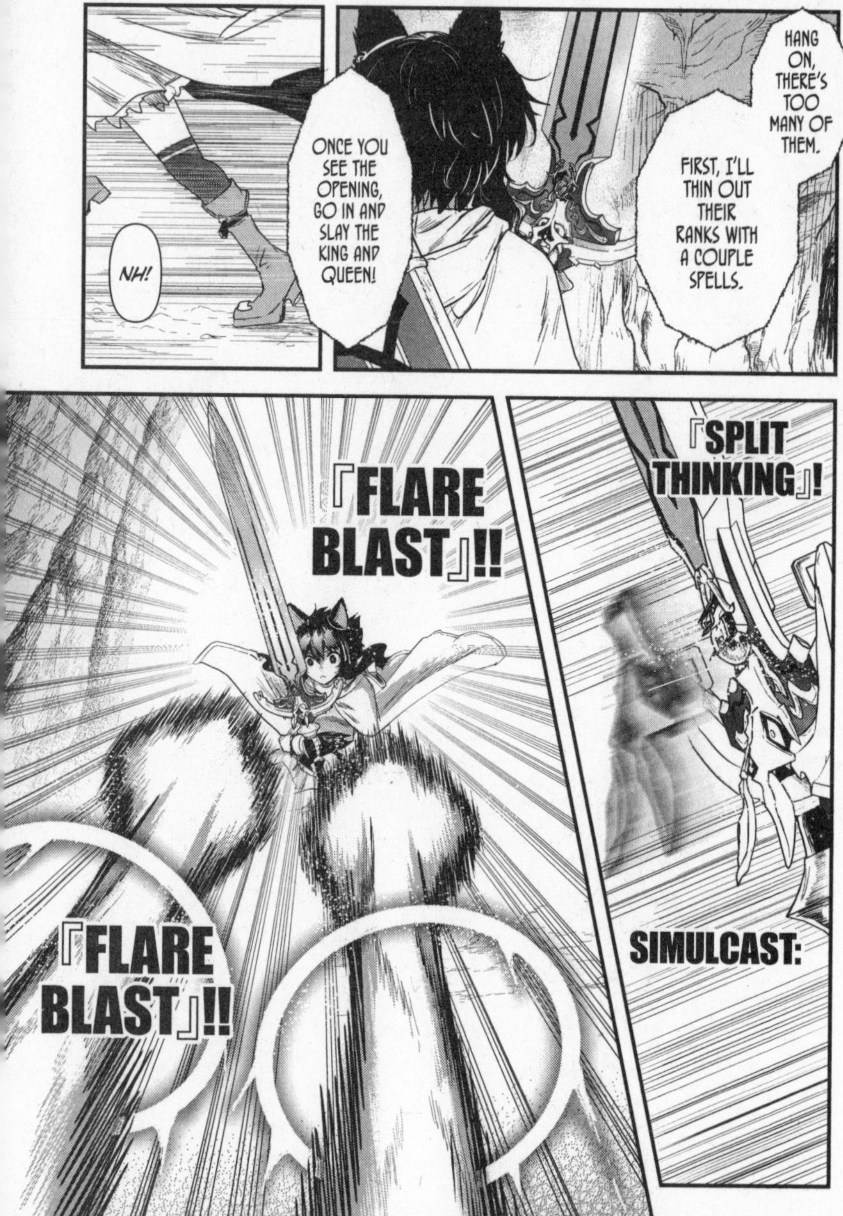

HANG ON, THERE'S TOO MANY OF THEM.
FIRST, I'LL THIN OUT THEIR RANKS WITH A COUPLE SPELLS.
ONCE YOU SEE THE OPENING, GO IN AND SLAY THE KING AND QUEEN!
NH!
『SPLIT THINKING』!
SIMULCAST:
『FLARE BLAST』!!
『FLARE BLAST』!!

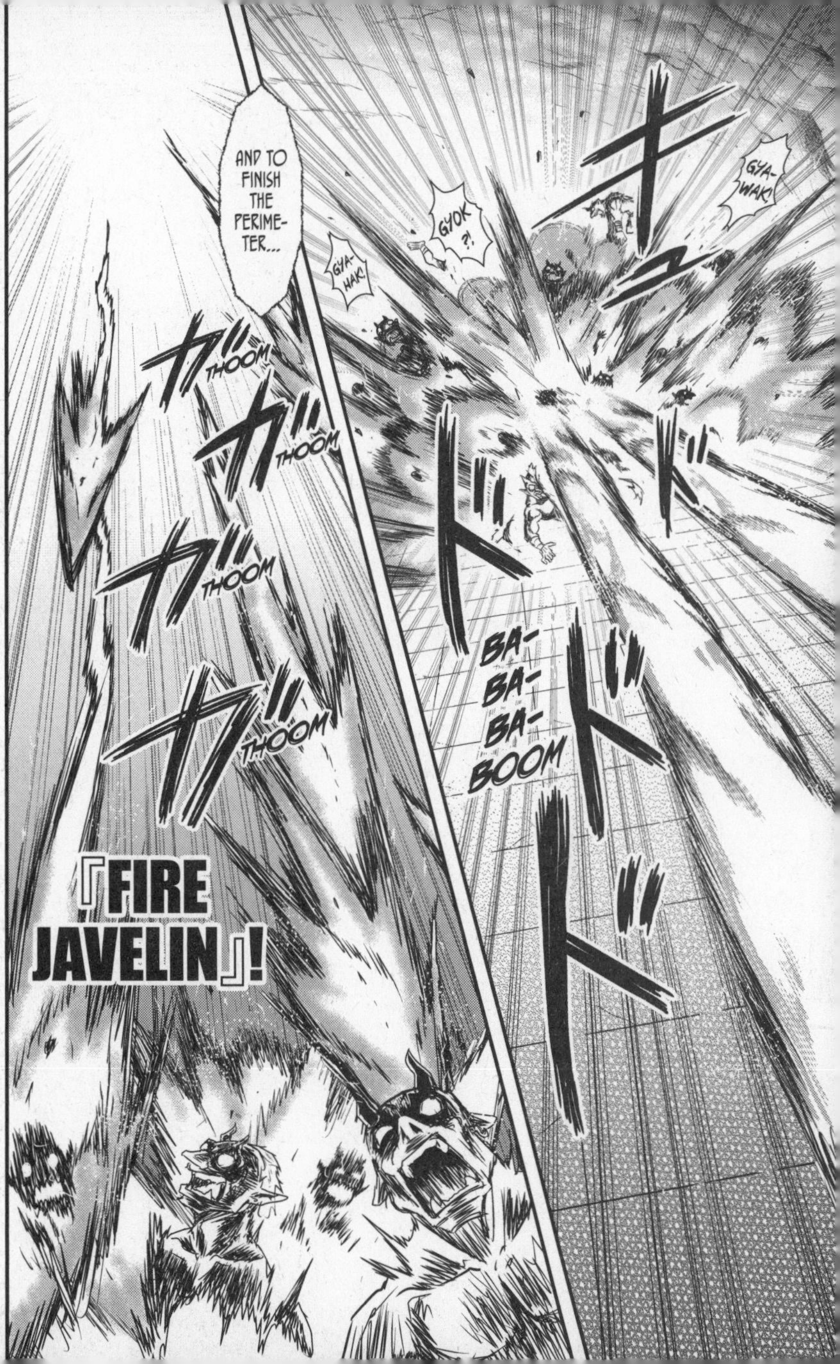
GYA-WAK!
GYOK?!
GYA-HAK!
BA-BA-BA-BOOM
AND TO FINISH THE PERIMETER...
THOOM
THOOM
THOOM
THOOM
『FIRE JAVELIN』!

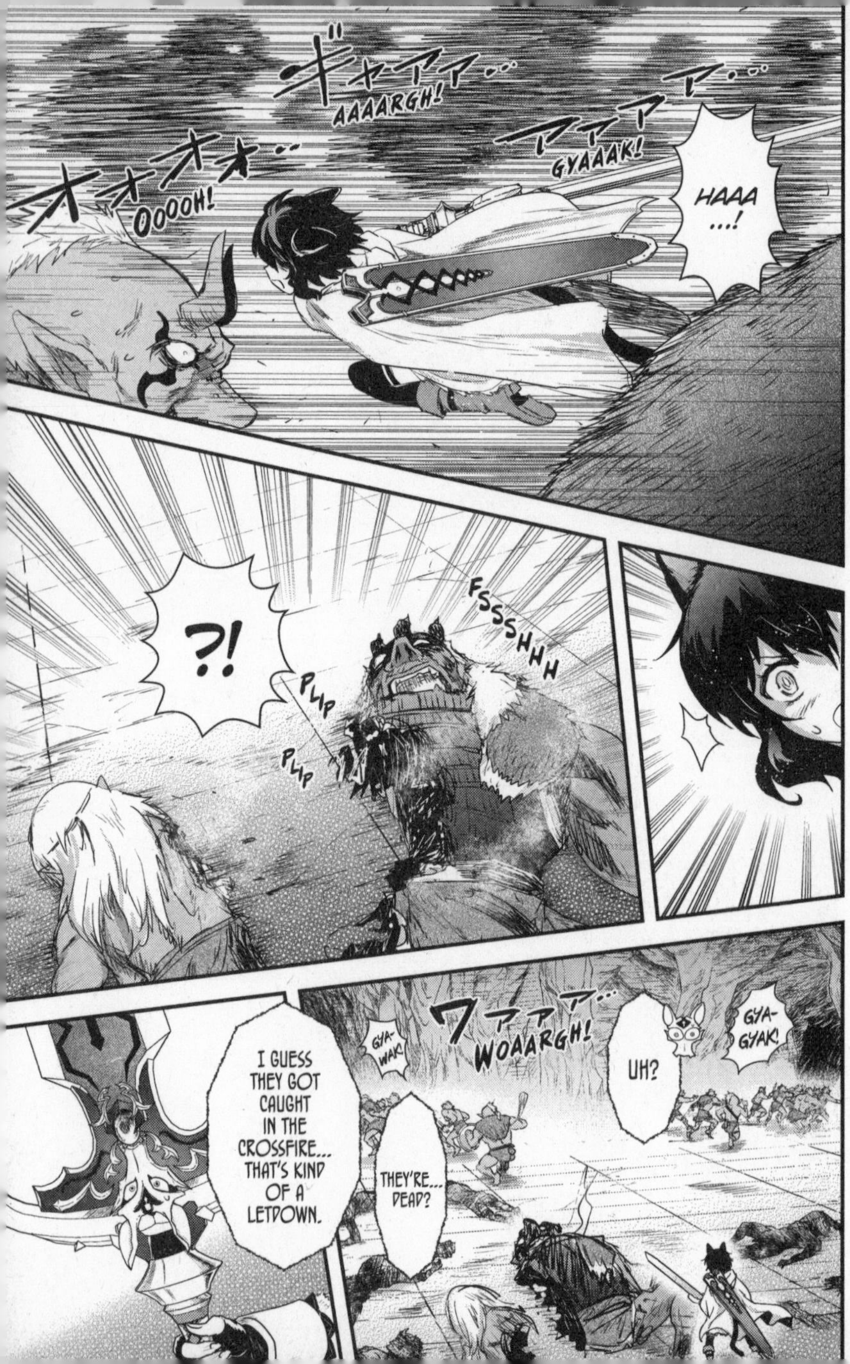
HAAA...!
アアアァ…
GYAAAK!
ギャアア…
AAAARGH!
オオオオ…
OOOOH!
?!
FSSSHHH
PLIP
PLIP
GYA-GYAK!
UH?
ワァァァ…
WOARGH!
GYA-WAK!
THEY'RE... DEAD?
I GUESS THEY GOT CAUGHT IN THE CROSSFIRE... THAT'S KIND OF A LETDOWN.

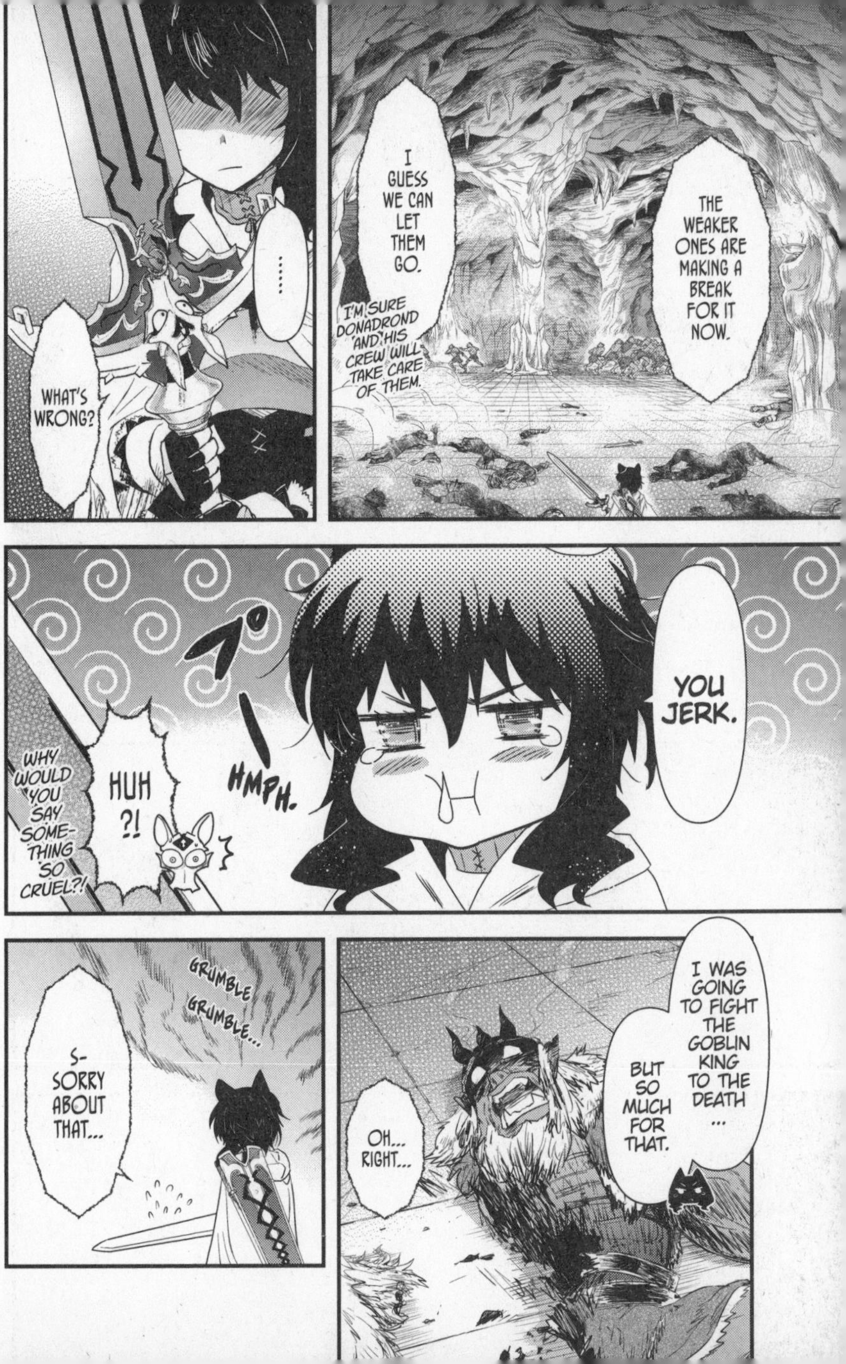
THE WEAKER ONES ARE MAKING A BREAK FOR IT NOW.
I GUESS WE CAN LET THEM GO.
I'M SURE DONADROND AND HIS CREW WILL TAKE CARE OF THEM.
......
WHAT'S WRONG?
YOU JERK.
HMPH.
HUH ?!
WHY WOULD YOU SAY SOME-THING SO CRUEL?!
I WAS GOING TO FIGHT THE GOBLIN KING TO THE DEATH ...
BUT SO MUCH FOR THAT.
OH... RIGHT...
GRUMBLE GRUMBLE...
S-SORRY ABOUT THAT...

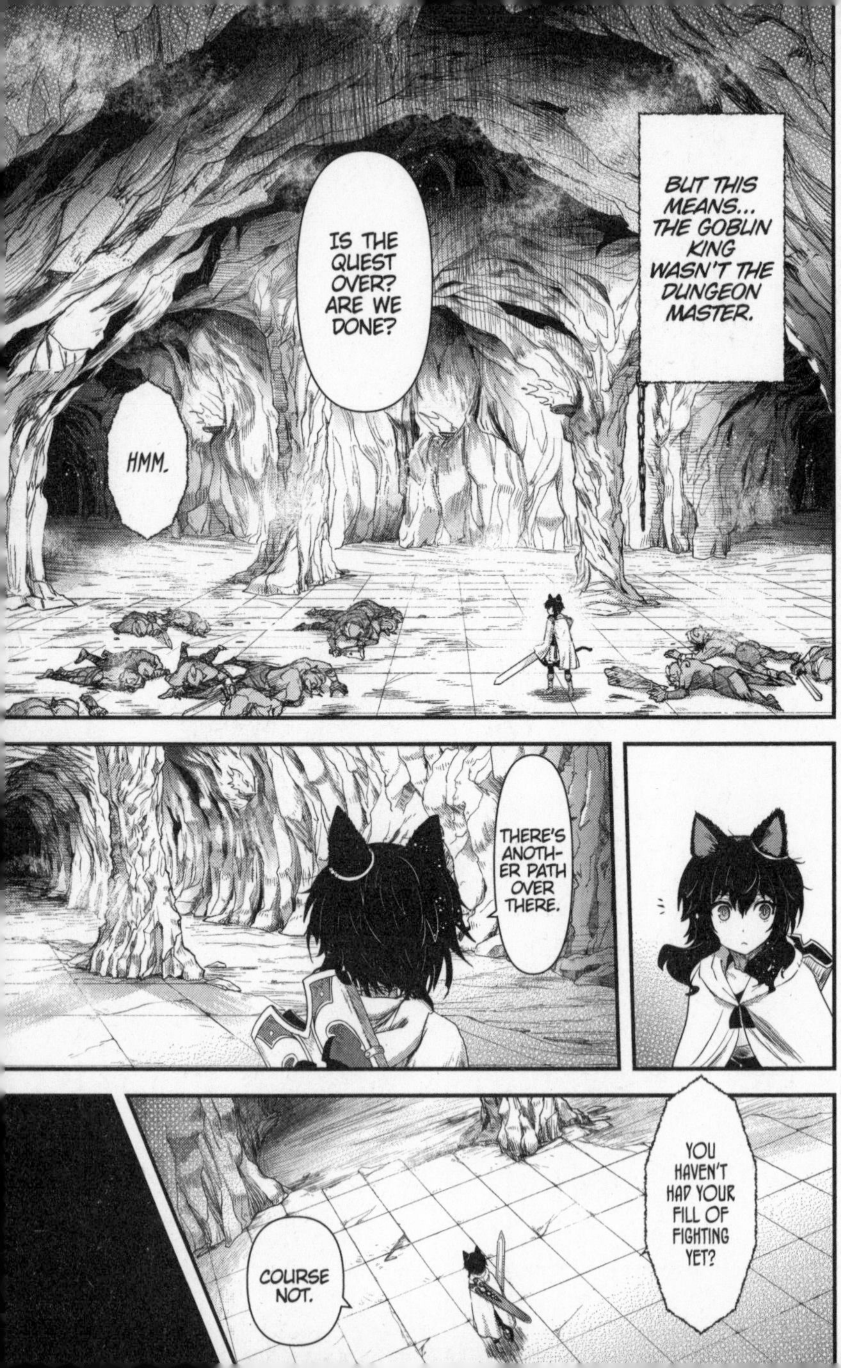
BUT THIS MEANS... THE GOBLIN KING WASN'T THE DUNGEON MASTER.
IS THE QUEST OVER? ARE WE DONE?
HMM.
THERE'S ANOTHER PATH OVER THERE.
YOU HAVEN'T HAD YOUR FILL OF FIGHTING YET?
COURSE NOT.

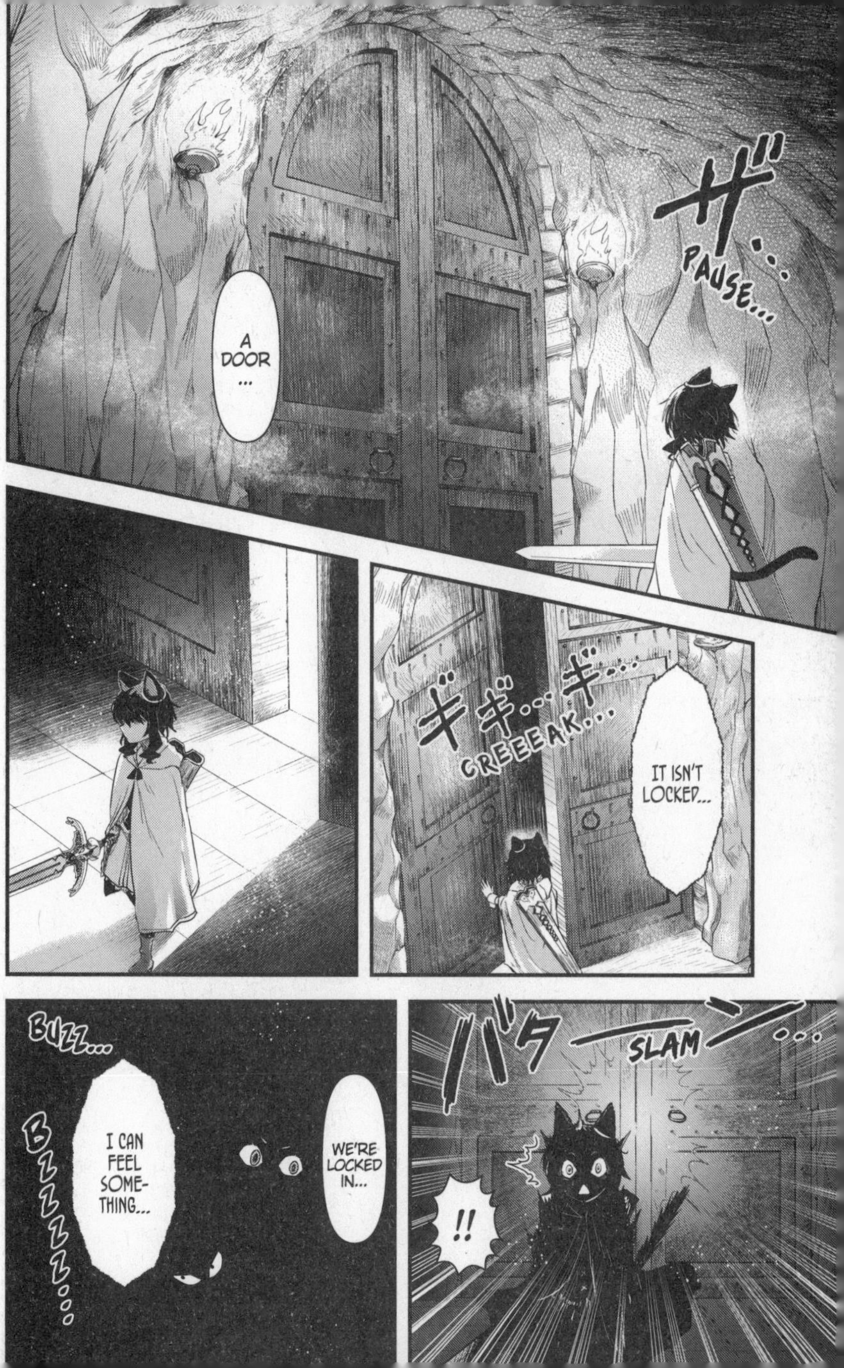
ザ…
PAUSE...
A DOOR ...
ギギ…ギ…
CREEEAK...
IT ISN'T LOCKED...
バタ―ン…
SLAM
!!
BUZZ...
WE'RE LOCKED IN...
I CAN FEEL SOME-THING...
BZZZZZ...

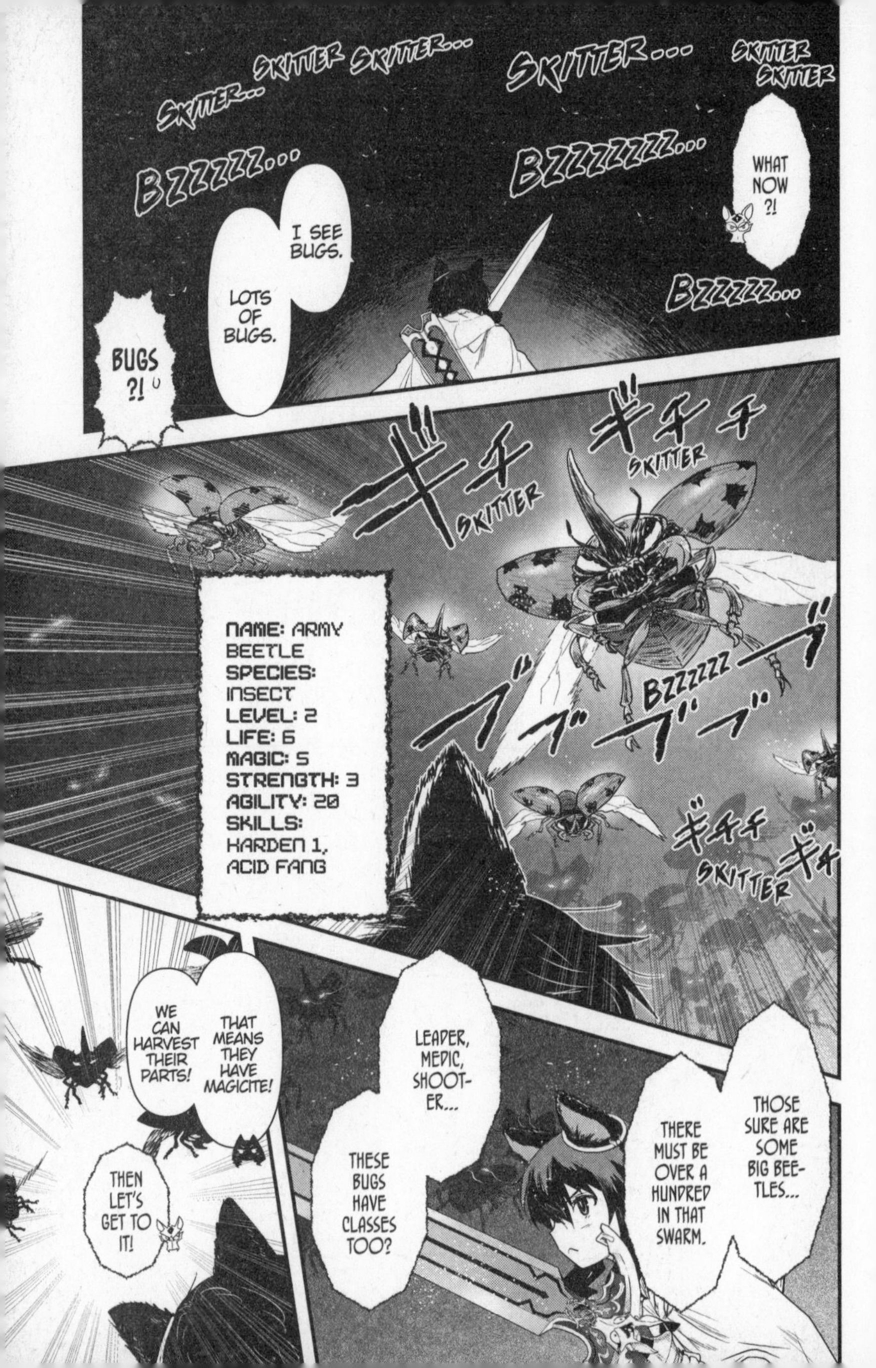
SKITTER SKITTER
WHAT NOW ?!
SKITTER...
BZZZZZZZ...
BZZZZZ...
SKITTER... SKITTER SKITTER...
BZZZZZ...
I SEE BUGS.
LOTS OF BUGS.
BUGS ?!
SKITTER
SKITTER
BZZZZZZ
SKITTER
NAME: ARMY BEETLE
SPECIES: INSECT
LEVEL: 2
LIFE: 6
MAGIC: 5
STRENGTH: 3
ABILITY: 20
SKILLS: HARDEN 1, ACID FANG
THOSE SURE ARE SOME BIG BEE-TLES...
THERE MUST BE OVER A HUNDRED IN THAT SWARM.
LEADER, MEDIC, SHOOT-ER...
THESE BUGS HAVE CLASSES TOO?
THAT MEANS THEY HAVE MAGICITE!
WE CAN HARVEST THEIR PARTS!
THEN LET'S GET TO IT!

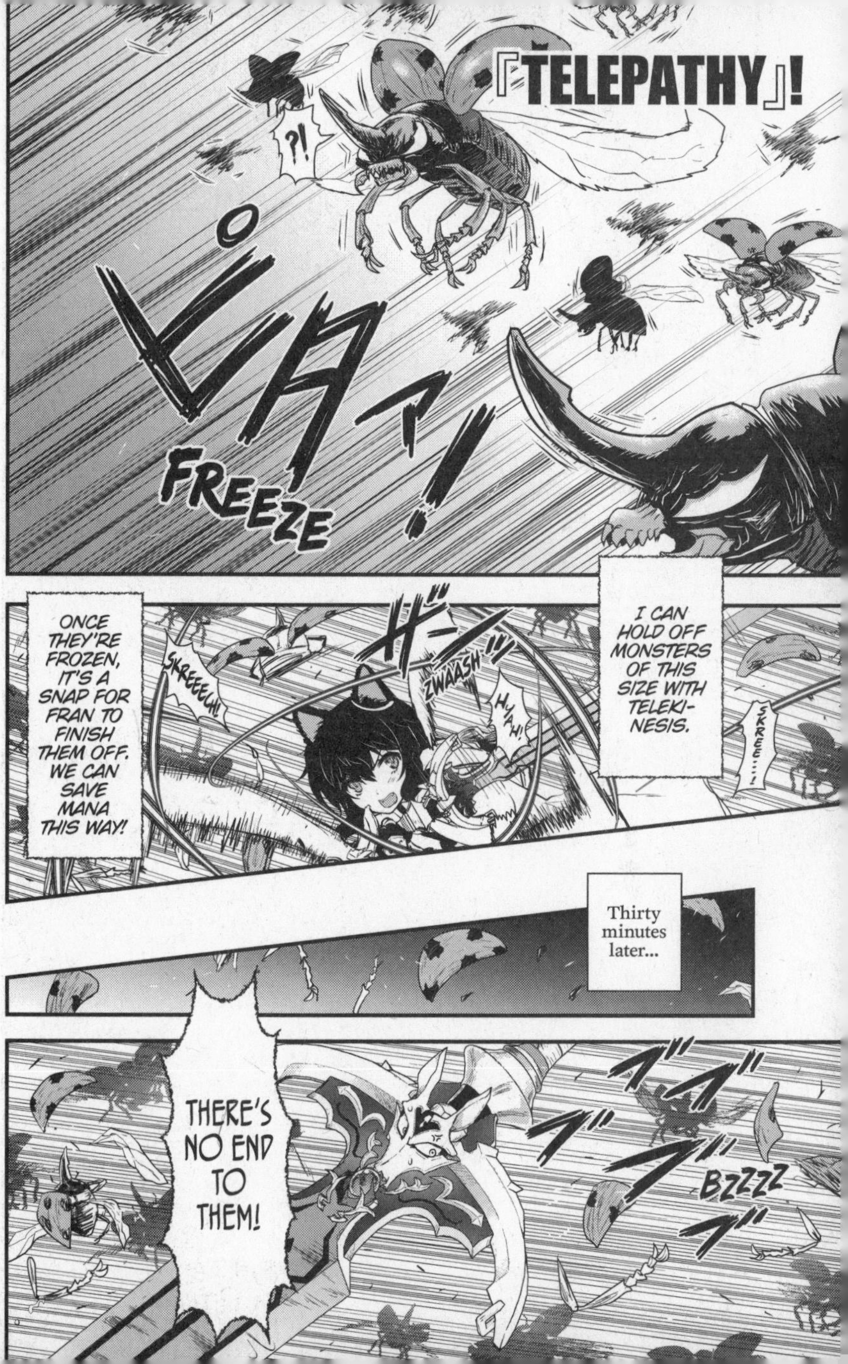
『TELEPATHY』!
?!
FREEZE
I CAN HOLD OFF MONSTERS OF THIS SIZE WITH TELEKI-NESIS.
SKREE...!
HYAH!
ZWAASH
SKREEECH!
ONCE THEY'RE FROZEN, IT'S A SNAP FOR FRAN TO FINISH THEM OFF. WE CAN SAVE MANA THIS WAY!
Thirty minutes later...
BZZZZ
THERE'S NO END TO THEM!

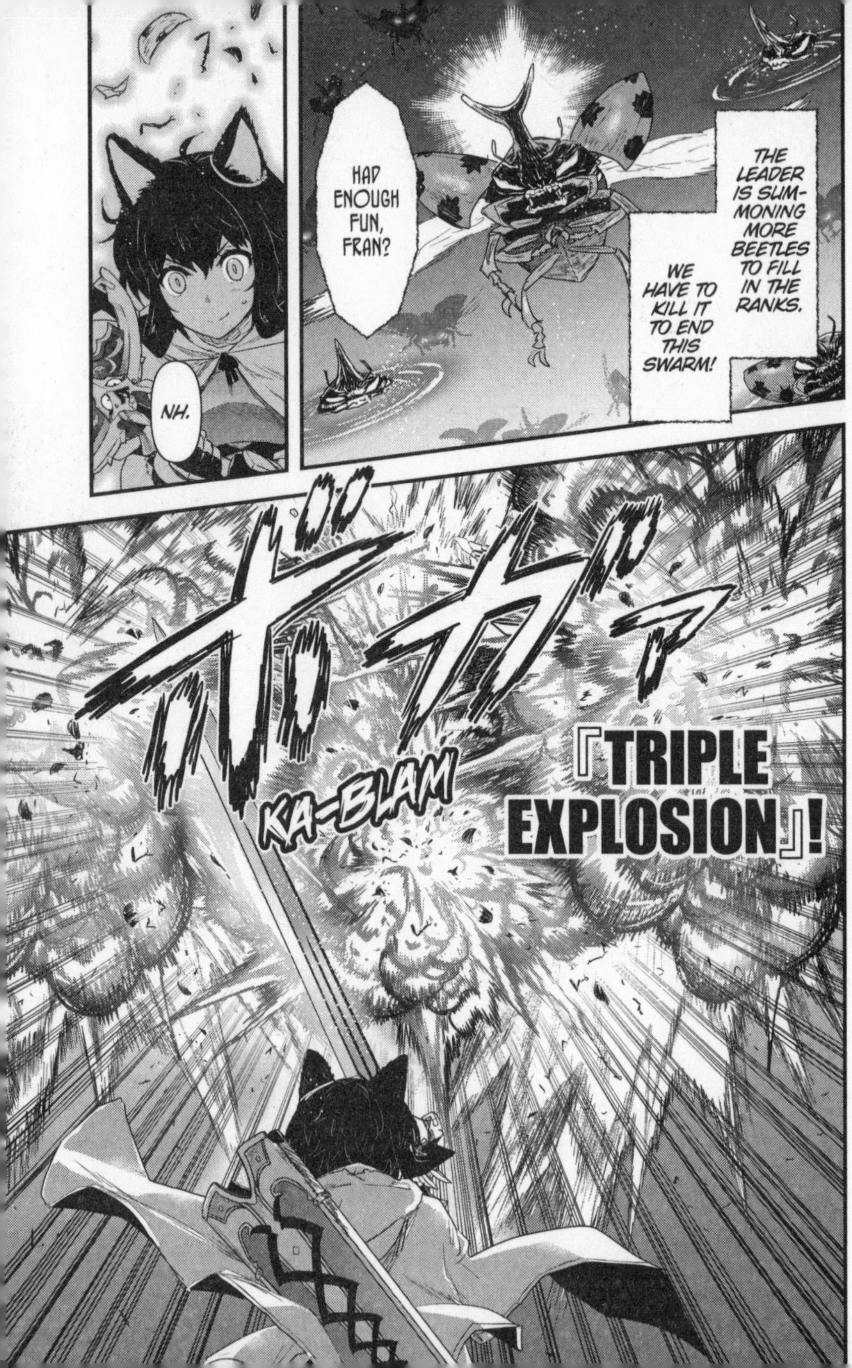
THE LEADER IS SUMMONING MORE BEETLES TO FILL IN THE RANKS.
WE HAVE TO KILL IT TO END THIS SWARM!
HAD ENOUGH FUN, FRAN?
NH.
『TRIPLE EXPLOSION』!
KA-BLAM

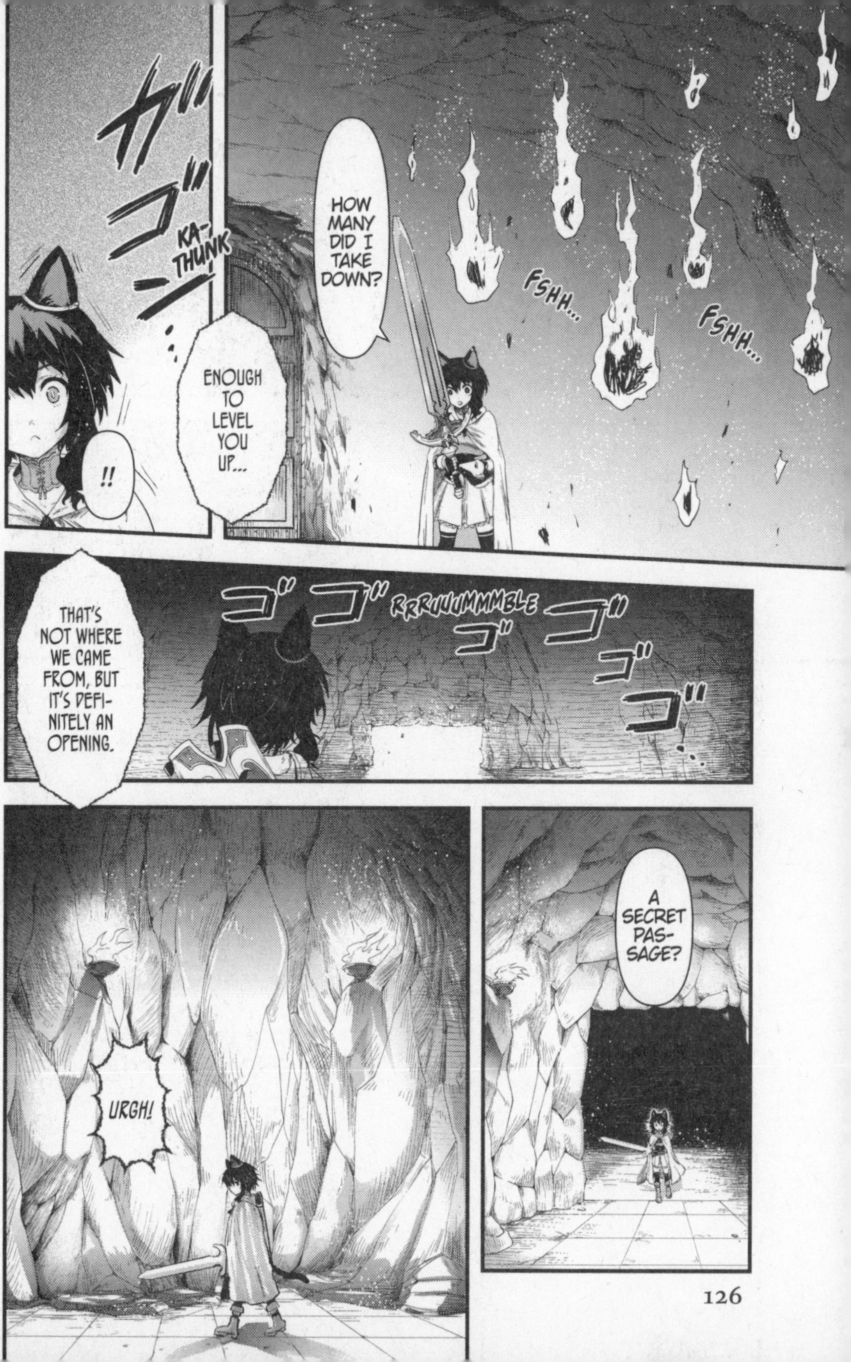
HOW MANY DID I TAKE DOWN?
FSHH...
FSHH...
ENOUGH TO LEVEL YOU UP...
KA-THUNK
!!
RRRUUUMMMBLE
THAT'S NOT WHERE WE CAME FROM, BUT IT'S DEFINITELY AN OPENING.
A SECRET PASSAGE?
URGH!

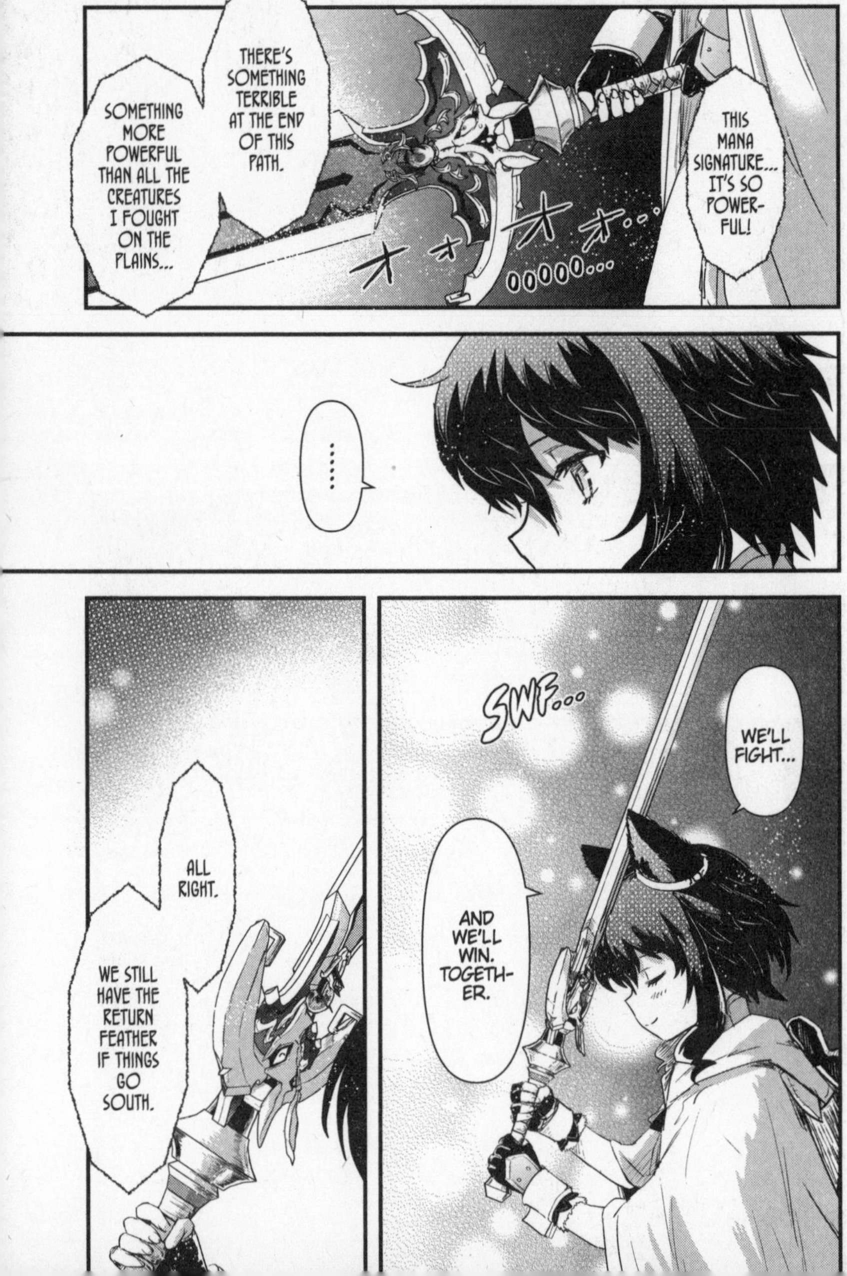
THIS MANA SIGNATURE... IT'S SO POWER-FUL!
OOOOO...
THERE'S SOMETHING TERRIBLE AT THE END OF THIS PATH.
SOMETHING MORE POWERFUL THAN ALL THE CREATURES I FOUGHT ON THE PLAINS...
......
SWF...
WE'LL FIGHT...
AND WE'LL WIN. TOGETH-ER.
ALL RIGHT.
WE STILL HAVE THE RETURN FEATHER IF THINGS GO SOUTH.

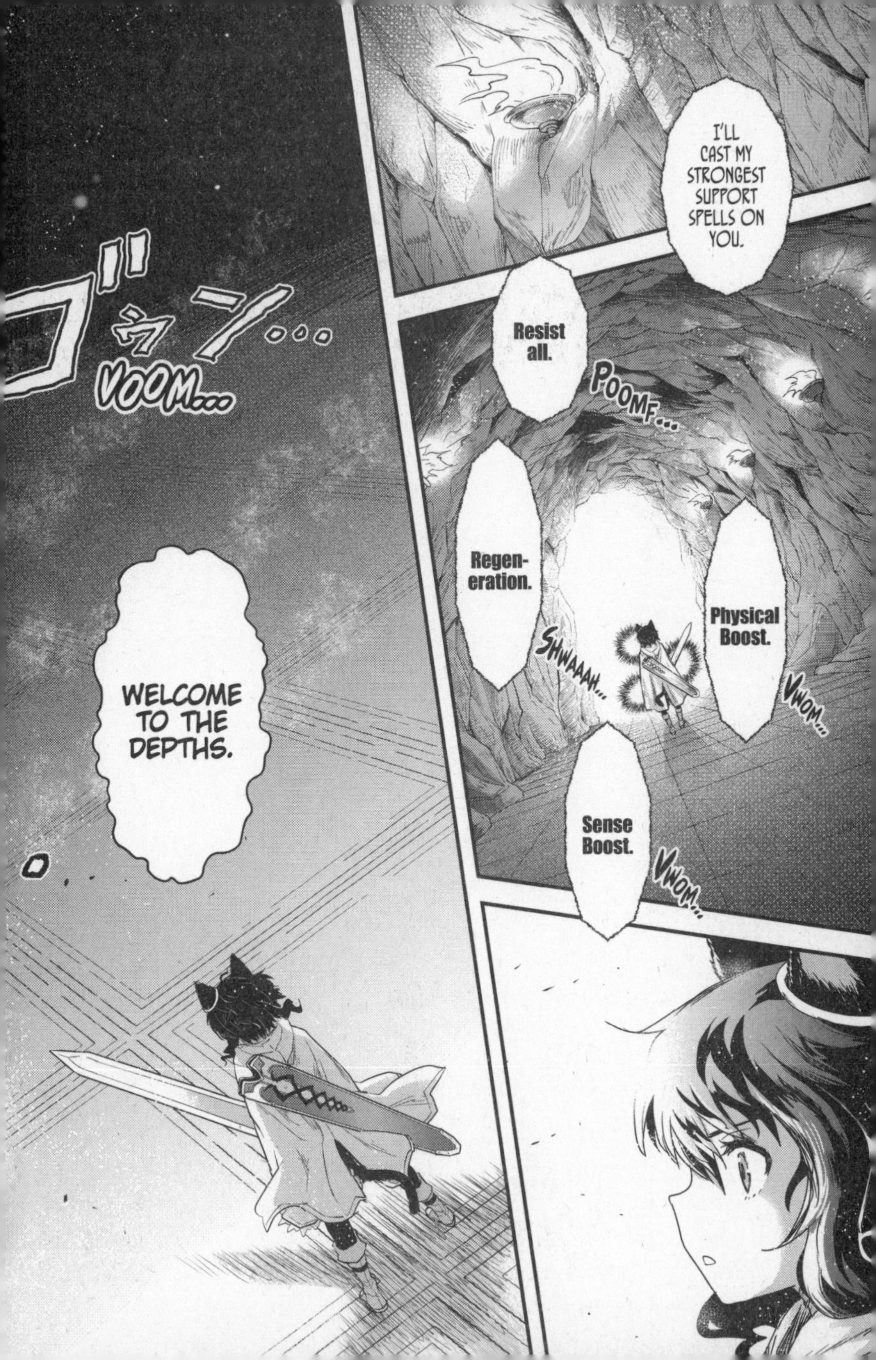
I'LL CAST MY STRONGEST SUPPORT SPELLS ON YOU.
Resist all.
POOMF...
Physical Boost.
Regen-eration.
VWOM...
SHWAAAH...
Sense Boost.
VWOM...
ゴゥン...
VOOM...
WELCOME TO THE DEPTHS.

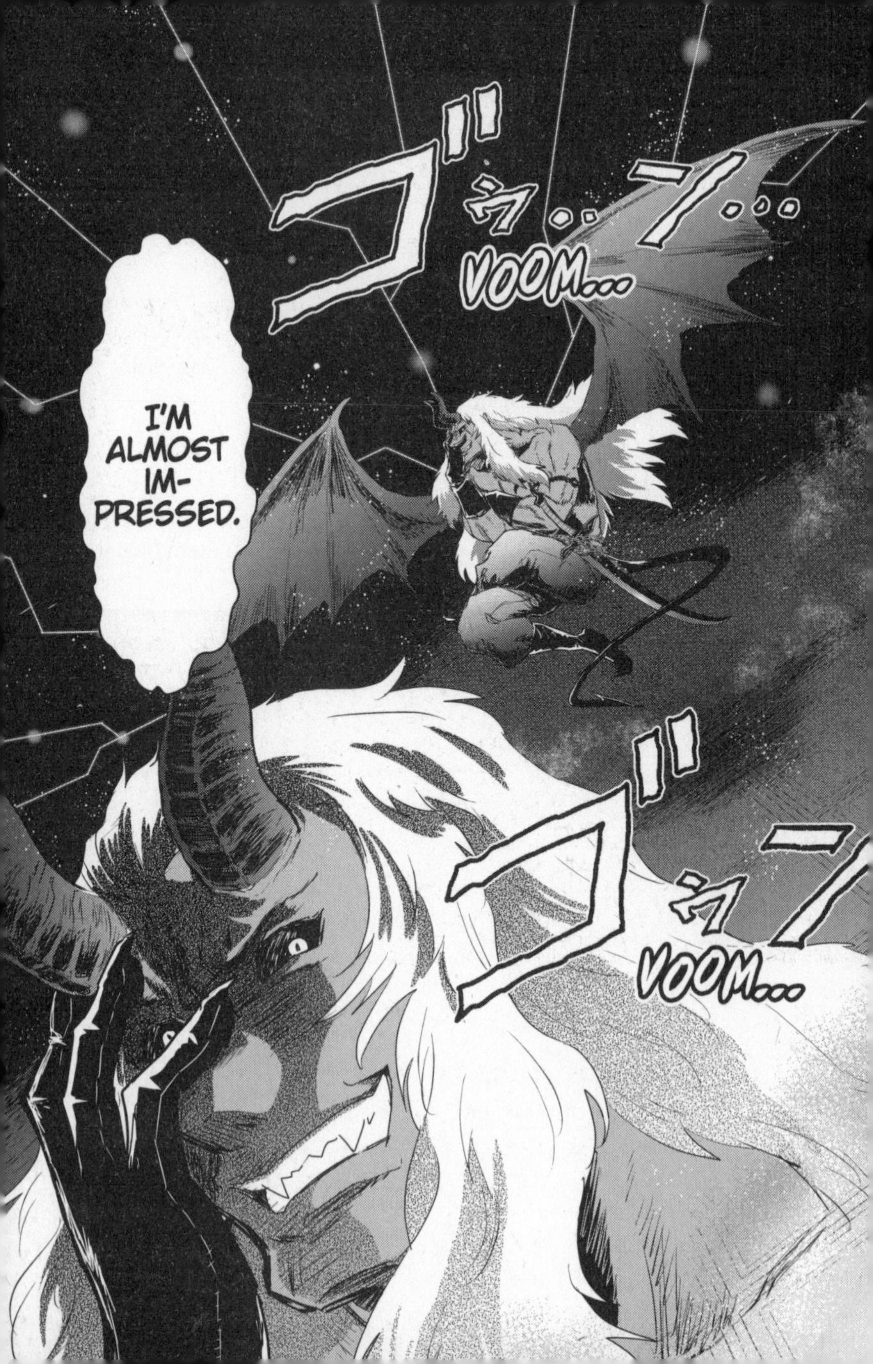
ゴォーン…
VOOM…
I'M ALMOST IM-PRESSED.
ゴォーン
VOOM…

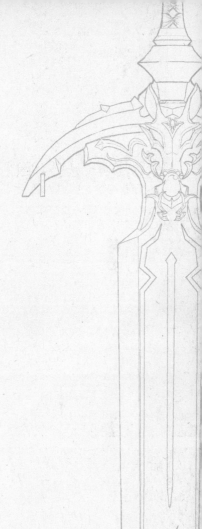

Reincarnated
as a sword

Chapter 11: Greater Demon

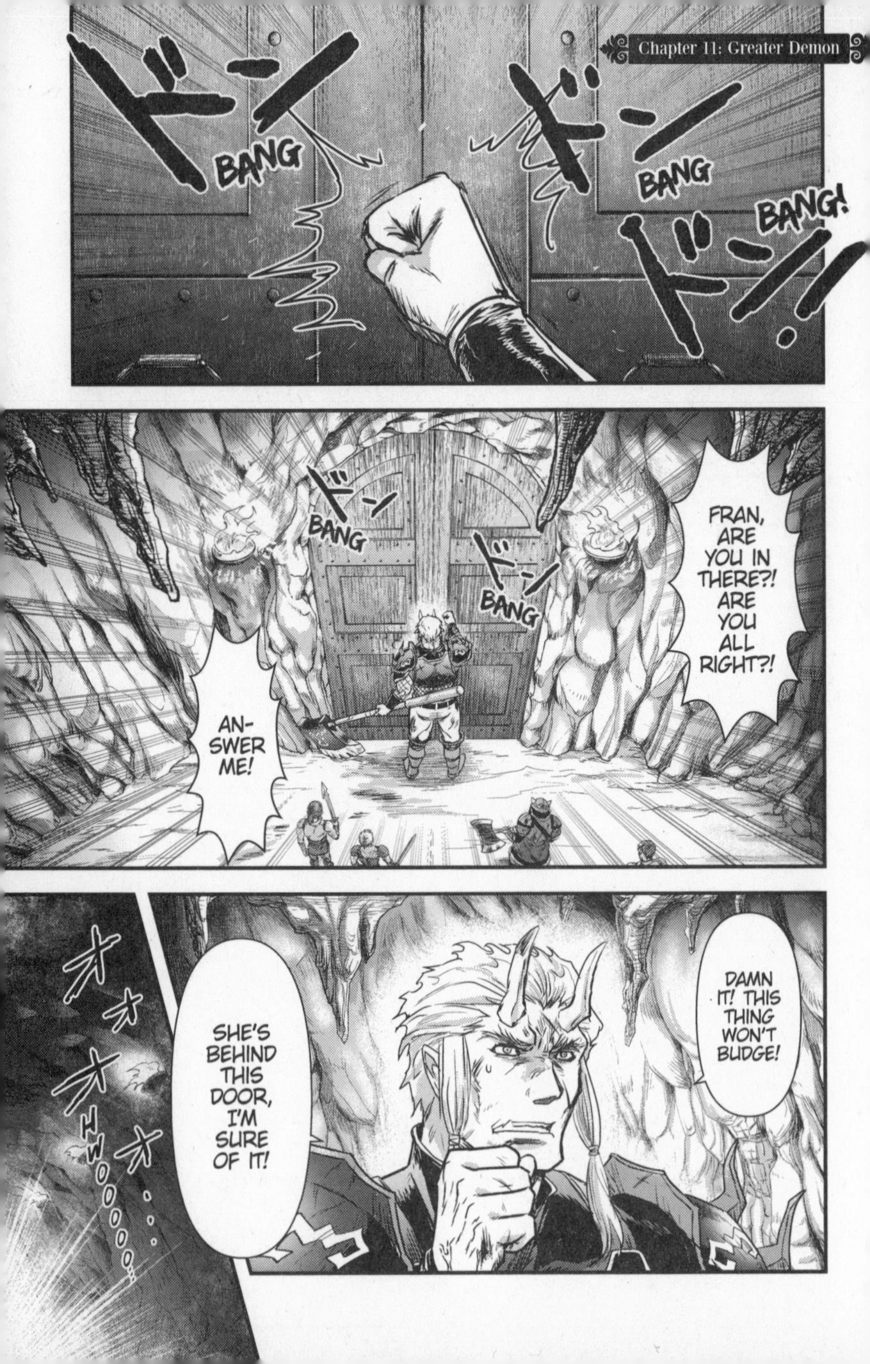
BANG!
BANG
BANG
BANG
BANG
FRAN, ARE YOU IN THERE?! ARE YOU ALL RIGHT?!
AN-SWER ME!
DAMN IT! THIS THING WON'T BUDGE!
SHE'S BEHIND THIS DOOR, I'M SURE OF IT!
HWOOOOOO...

Chapter 11: Greater Demon

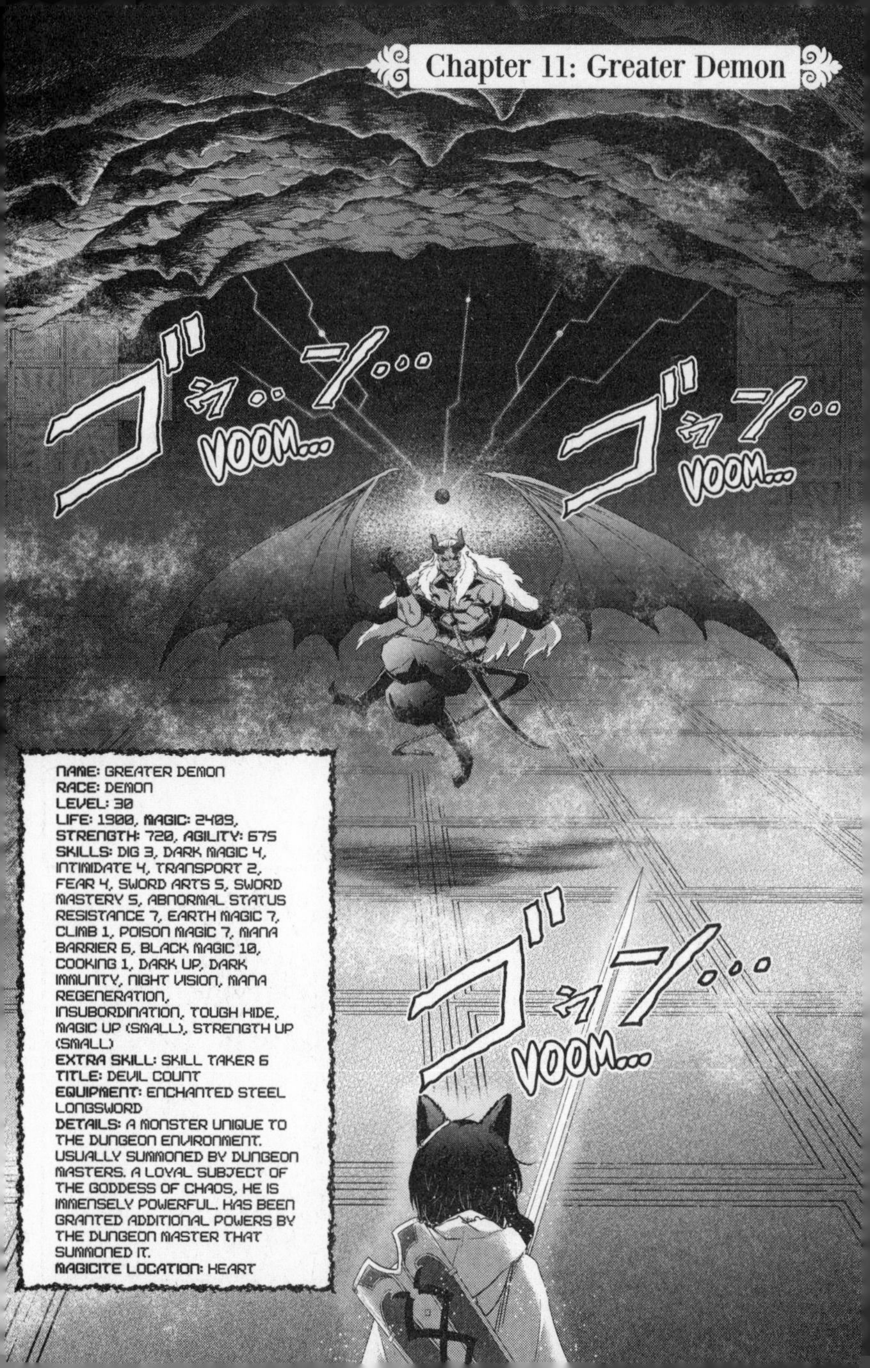
ゴォーン…
VOOM...
ゴォ‥ーン…
VOOM...
NAME: GREATER DEMON
RACE: DEMON
LEVEL: 30
LIFE: 1900, MAGIC: 2409,
STRENGTH: 720, AGILITY: 675
SKILLS: DIG 3, DARK MAGIC 4, INTIMIDATE 4, TRANSPORT 2, FEAR 4, SWORD ARTS 5, SWORD MASTERY 5, ABNORMAL STATUS RESISTANCE 7, EARTH MAGIC 7, CLIMB 1, POISON MAGIC 7, MANA BARRIER 6, BLACK MAGIC 10, COOKING 1, DARK UP, DARK IMMUNITY, NIGHT VISION, MANA REGENERATION, INSUBORDINATION, TOUGH HIDE, MAGIC UP (SMALL), STRENGTH UP (SMALL)
EXTRA SKILL: SKILL TAKER 6
TITLE: DEVIL COUNT
EQUIPMENT: ENCHANTED STEEL LONGSWORD
DETAILS: A MONSTER UNIQUE TO THE DUNGEON ENVIRONMENT. USUALLY SUMMONED BY DUNGEON MASTERS. A LOYAL SUBJECT OF THE GODDESS OF CHAOS, HE IS IMMENSELY POWERFUL. HAS BEEN GRANTED ADDITIONAL POWERS BY THE DUNGEON MASTER THAT SUMMONED IT.
MAGICITE LOCATION: HEART
ゴォーン…
VOOM...

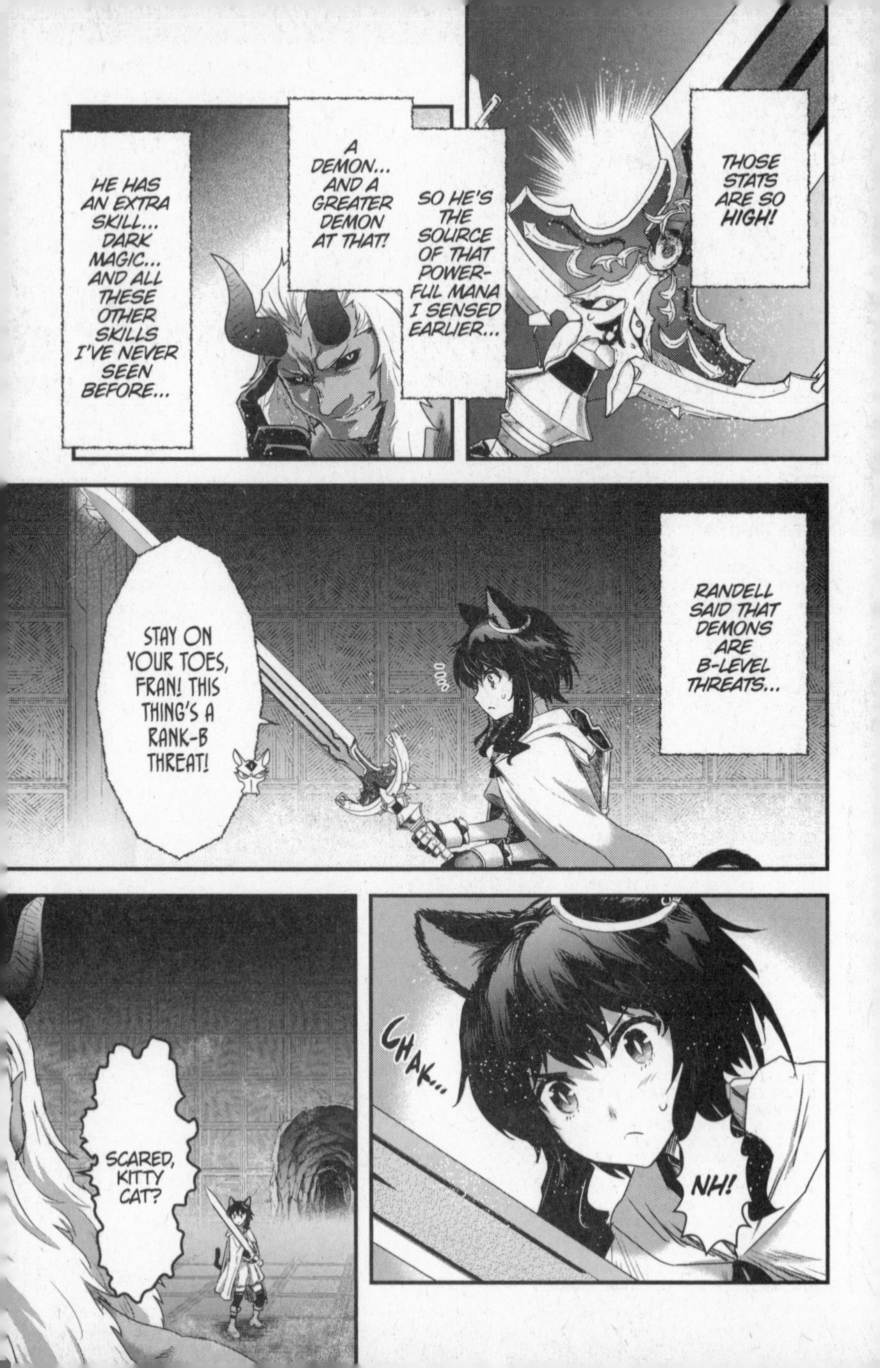
THOSE STATS ARE SO HIGH!
A DEMON... AND A GREATER DEMON AT THAT!
SO HE'S THE SOURCE OF THAT POWERFUL MANA I SENSED EARLIER...
HE HAS AN EXTRA SKILL... DARK MAGIC... AND ALL THESE OTHER SKILLS I'VE NEVER SEEN BEFORE...
RANDELL SAID THAT DEMONS ARE B-LEVEL THREATS...
STAY ON YOUR TOES, FRAN! THIS THING'S A RANK-B THREAT!
CHAK...
NH!
SCARED, KITTY CAT?

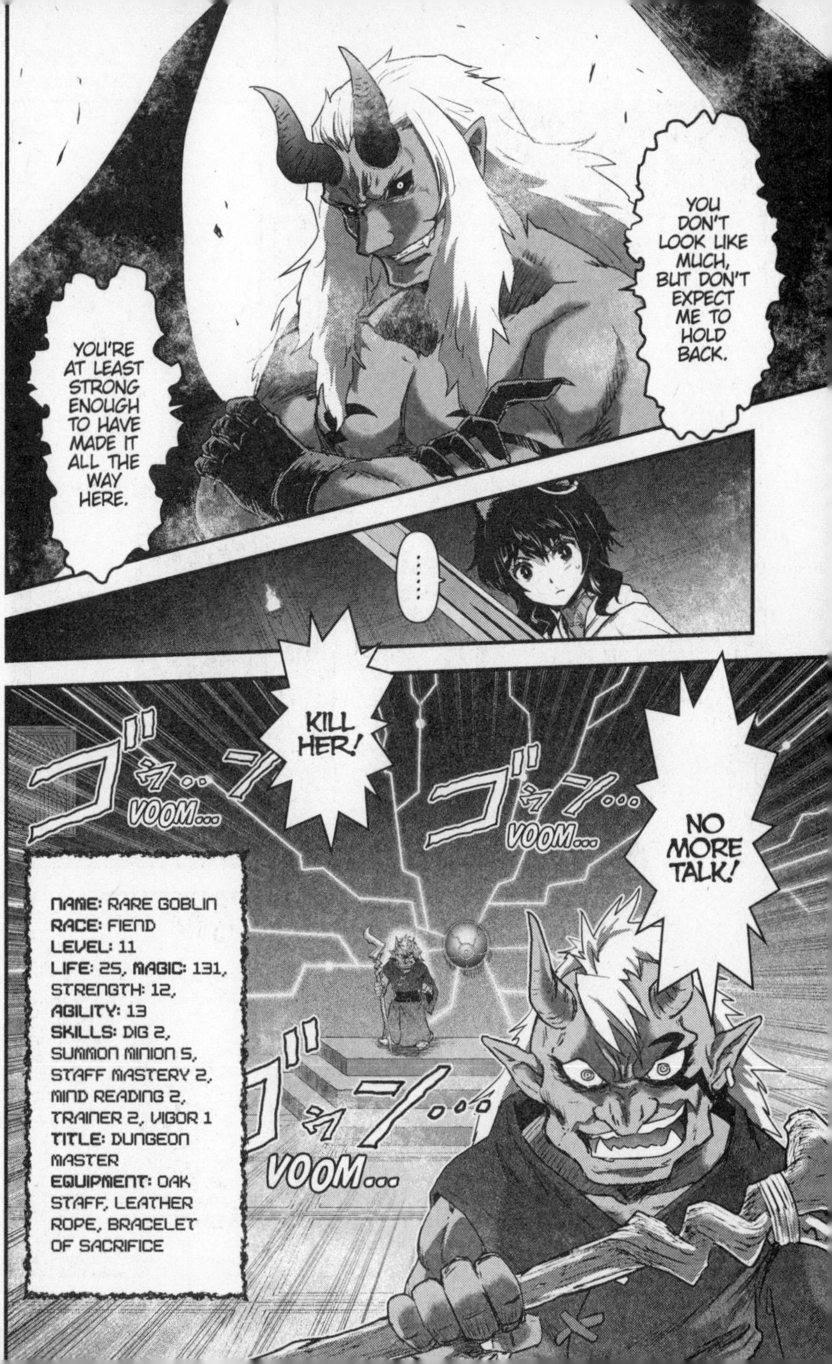
YOU DON'T LOOK LIKE MUCH, BUT DON'T EXPECT ME TO HOLD BACK.
YOU'RE AT LEAST STRONG ENOUGH TO HAVE MADE IT ALL THE WAY HERE.
......
KILL HER!
NO MORE TALK!
VOOM...
VOOM...
VOOM...
NAME: RARE GOBLIN
RACE: FIEND
LEVEL: 11
LIFE: 25, MAGIC: 131, STRENGTH: 12, ABILITY: 13
SKILLS: DIG 2, SUMMON MINION 5, STAFF MASTERY 2, MIND READING 2, TRAINER 2, VIGOR 1
TITLE: DUNGEON MASTER
EQUIPMENT: OAK STAFF, LEATHER ROPE, BRACELET OF SACRIFICE

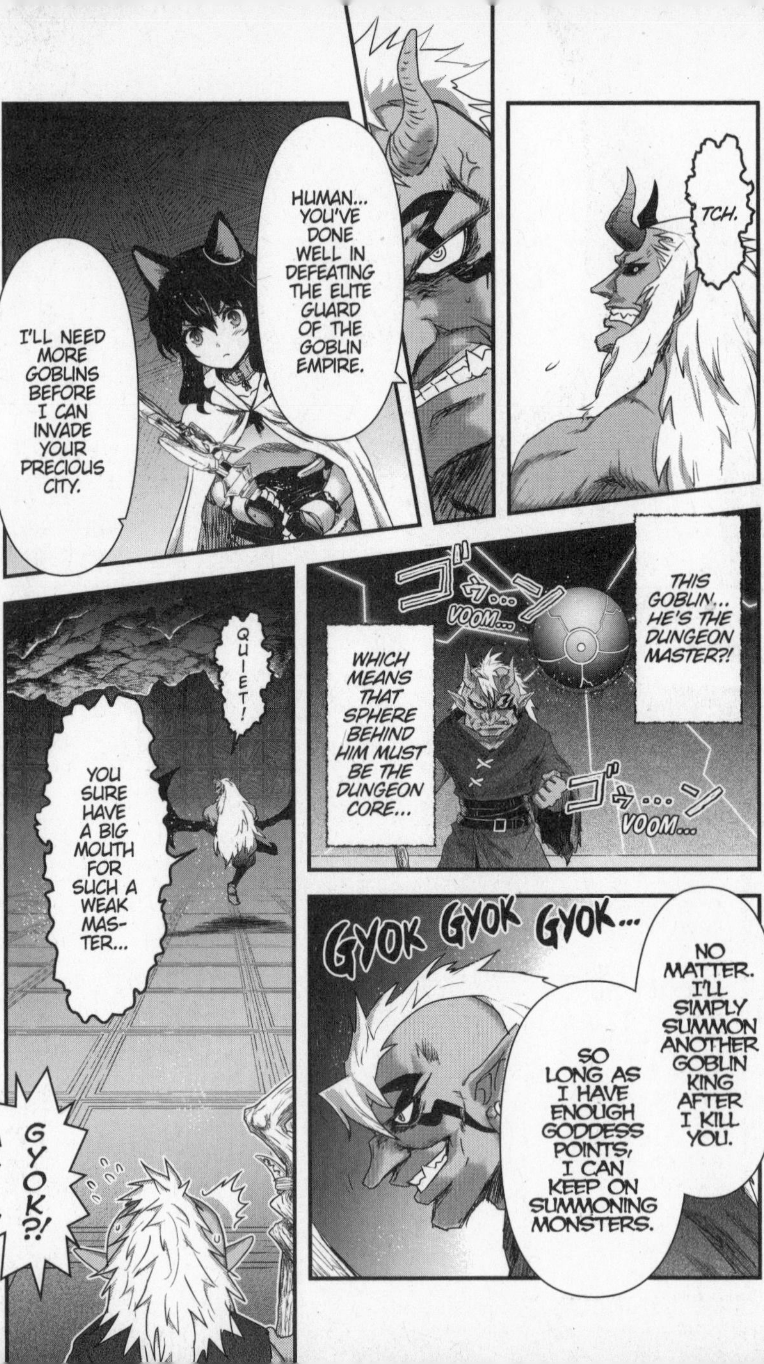
TCH.
HUMAN... YOU'VE DONE WELL IN DEFEATING THE ELITE GUARD OF THE GOBLIN EMPIRE.
I'LL NEED MORE GOBLINS BEFORE I CAN INVADE YOUR PRECIOUS CITY.
THIS GOBLIN... HE'S THE DUNGEON MASTER?!
ゴゥ...ン
VOOM...
WHICH MEANS THAT SPHERE BEHIND HIM MUST BE THE DUNGEON CORE...
ゴゥ...ン
VOOM...
NO MATTER. I'LL SIMPLY SUMMON ANOTHER GOBLIN KING AFTER I KILL YOU.
SO LONG AS I HAVE ENOUGH GODDESS POINTS, I CAN KEEP ON SUMMONING MONSTERS.
GYOK GYOK GYOK...
QUIET!
YOU SURE HAVE A BIG MOUTH FOR SUCH A WEAK MASTER...
GYOK?!

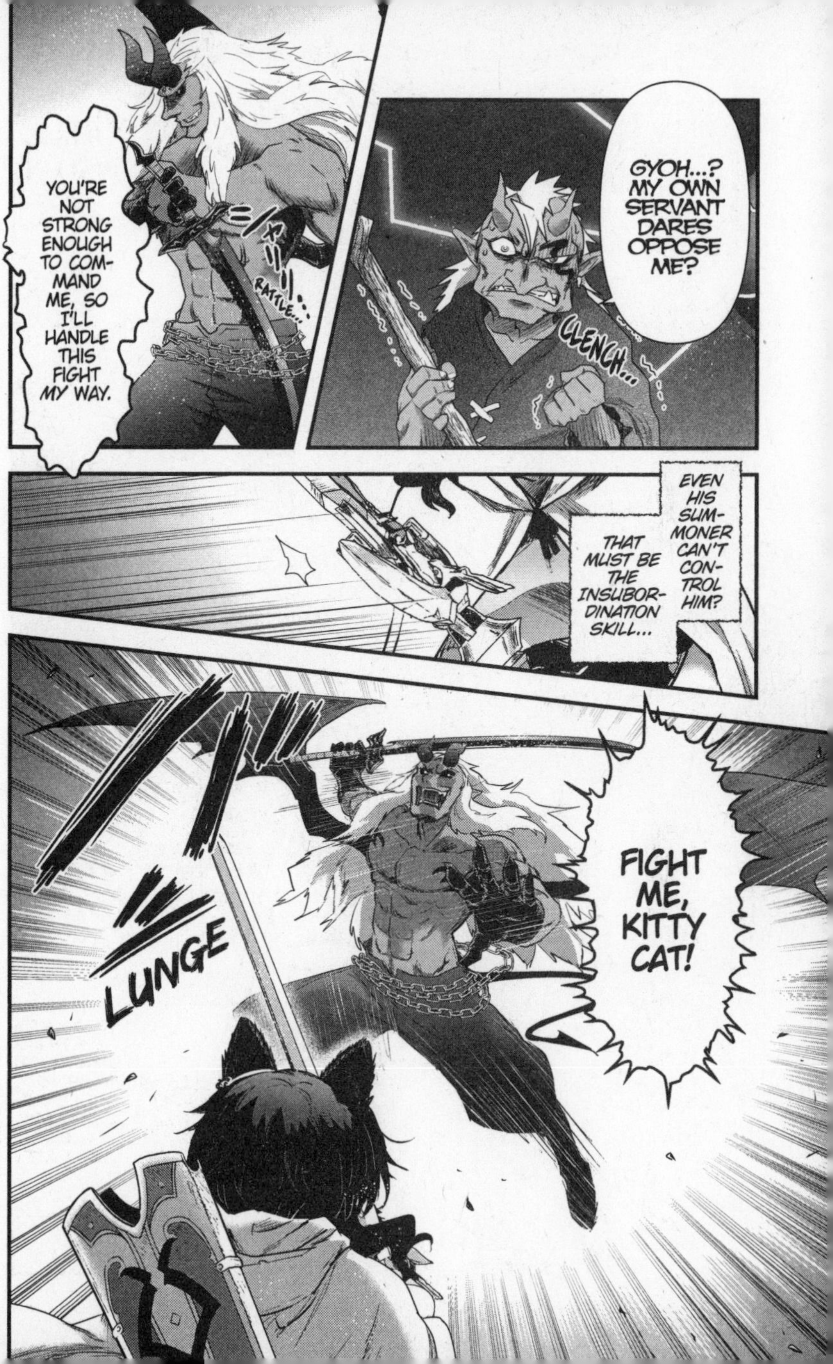
GYOH...? MY OWN SERVANT DARES OPPOSE ME?
CLENCH...
YOU'RE NOT STRONG ENOUGH TO COM-MAND ME, SO I'LL HANDLE THIS FIGHT MY WAY.
RATTLE...
EVEN HIS SUM-MONER CAN'T CON-TROL HIM?
THAT MUST BE THE INSUBOR-DINATION SKILL...
FIGHT ME, KITTY CAT!
LUNGE

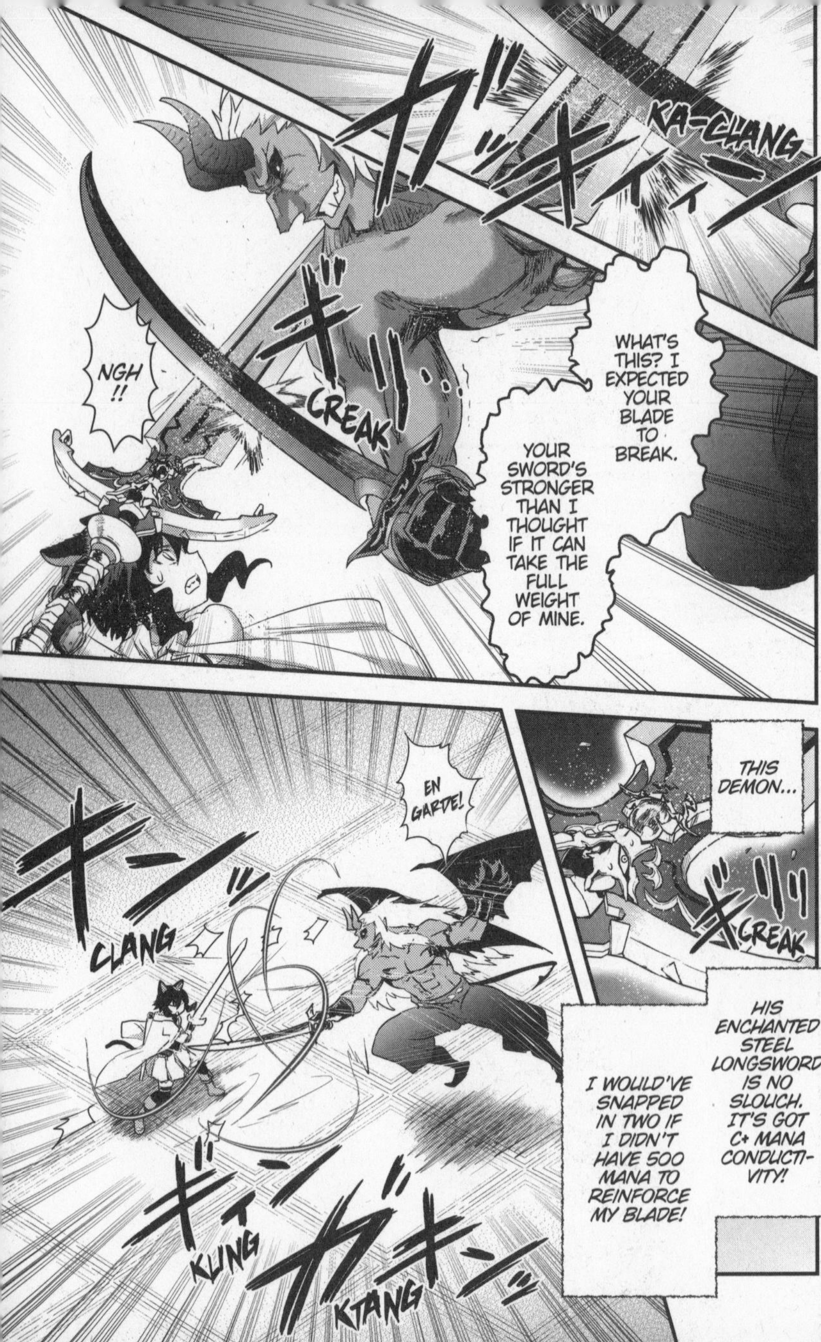

KA-CLANG
WHAT'S THIS? I EXPECTED YOUR BLADE TO BREAK.
YOUR SWORD'S STRONGER THAN I THOUGHT IF IT CAN TAKE THE FULL WEIGHT OF MINE.
CREAK
NGH !!
THIS DEMON...
CREAK
HIS ENCHANTED STEEL LONGSWORD IS NO SLOUCH. IT'S GOT C+ MANA CONDUCTI-VITY!
I WOULD'VE SNAPPED IN TWO IF I DIDN'T HAVE 500 MANA TO REINFORCE MY BLADE!
EN GARDE!
CLANG
KLING
KTANG

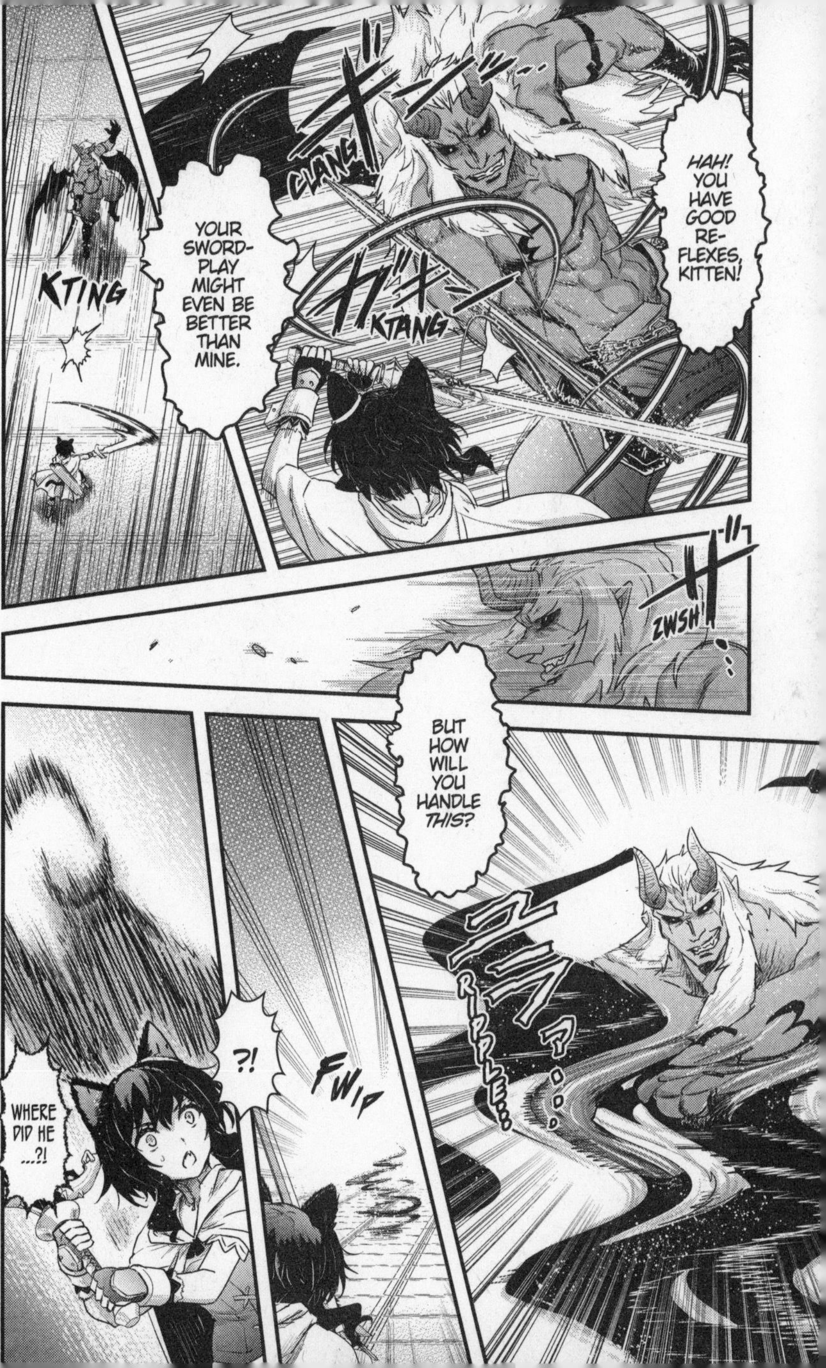
HAH! YOU HAVE GOOD RE-FLEXES, KITTEN!
CLANG
KTANG
YOUR SWORD-PLAY MIGHT EVEN BE BETTER THAN MINE.
KTING
ZWSH
BUT HOW WILL YOU HANDLE *THIS?*
RIPPLE...
?!
FWIP
WHERE DID HE ...?!

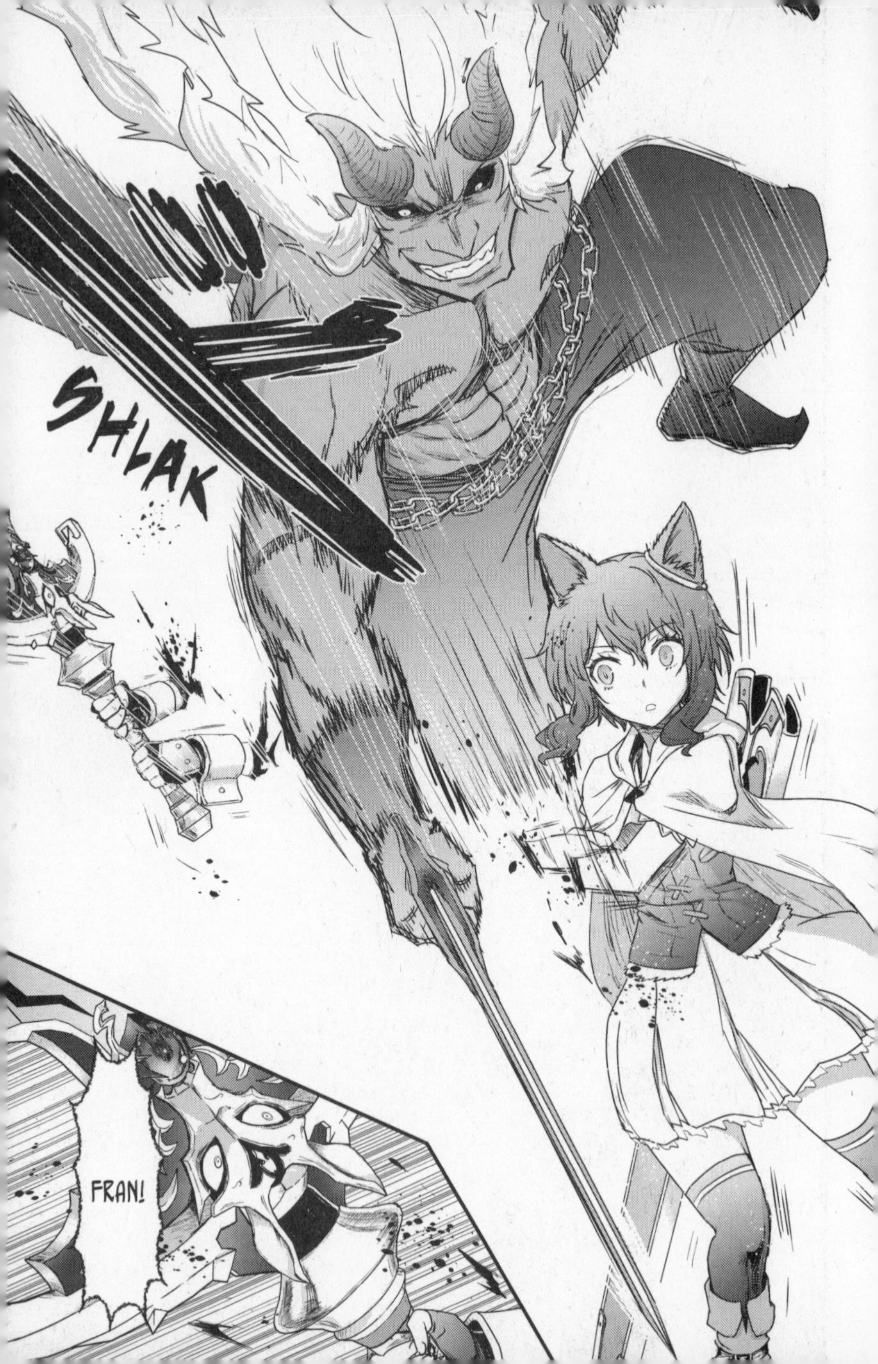
SHLAK
FRAN!

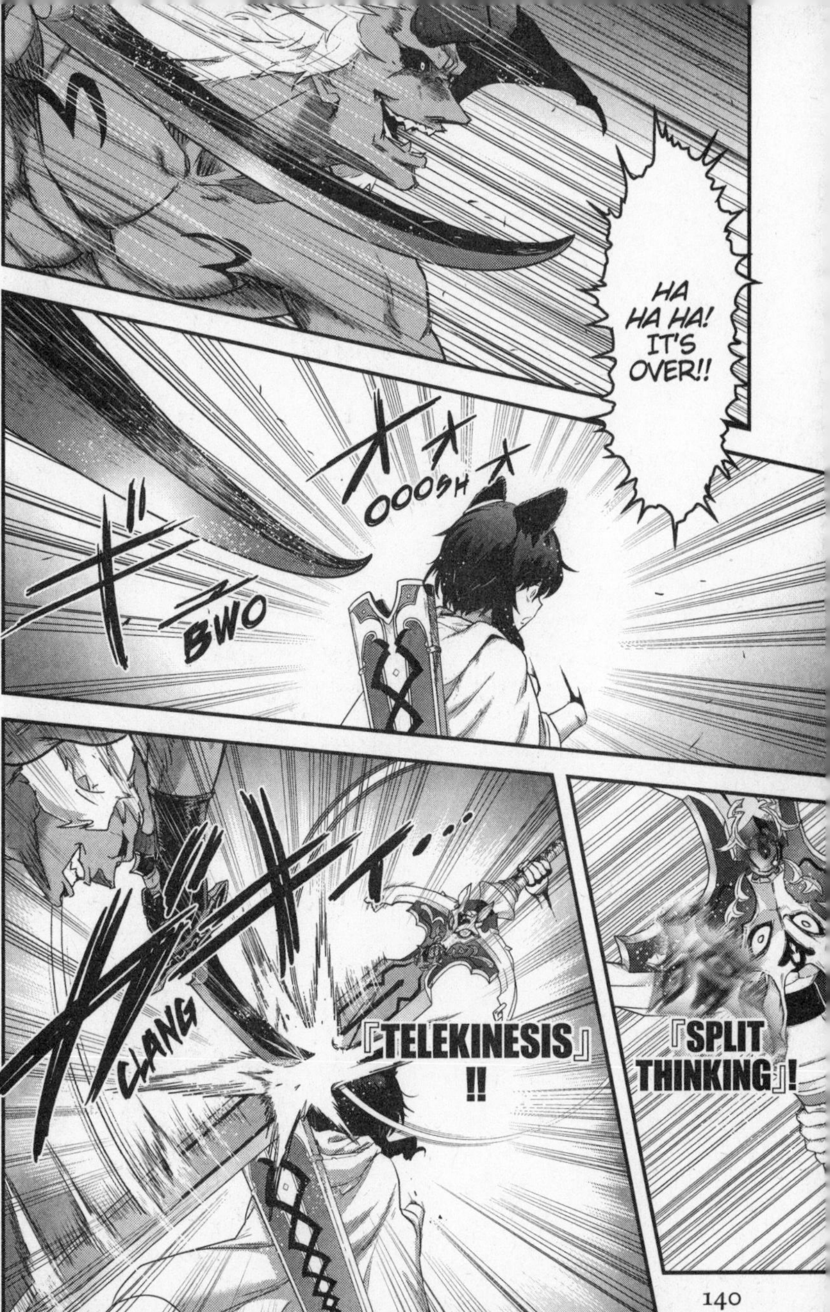
HA HA HA! IT'S OVER!!
OOOSH
BWO
『SPLIT THINKING』!
CLANG
『TELEKINESIS』!!

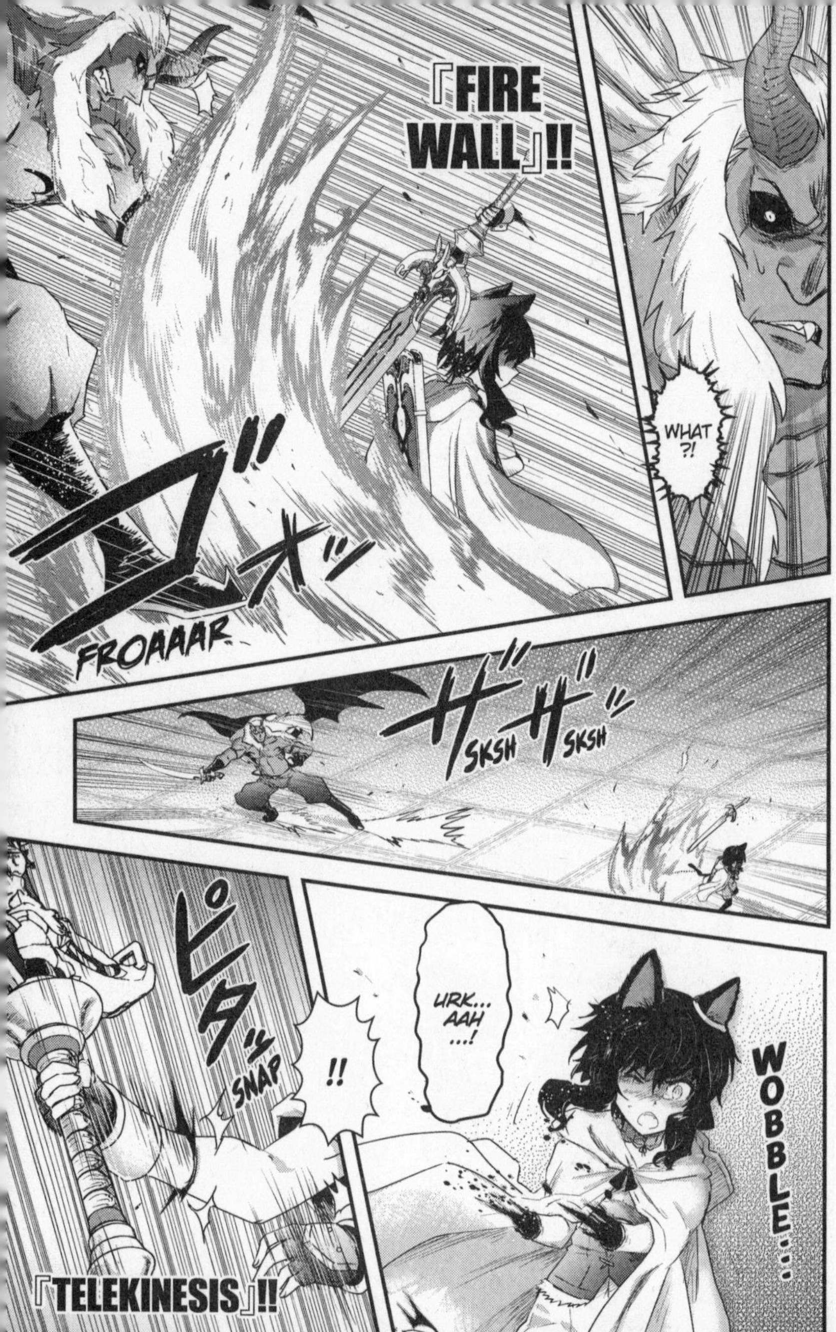
WHAT ?!
『FIRE WALL』!!
FROAAAR
SKSH
SKSH
WOBBLE....
URK... AAH ...!
!!
SNAP
『TELEKINESIS』!!

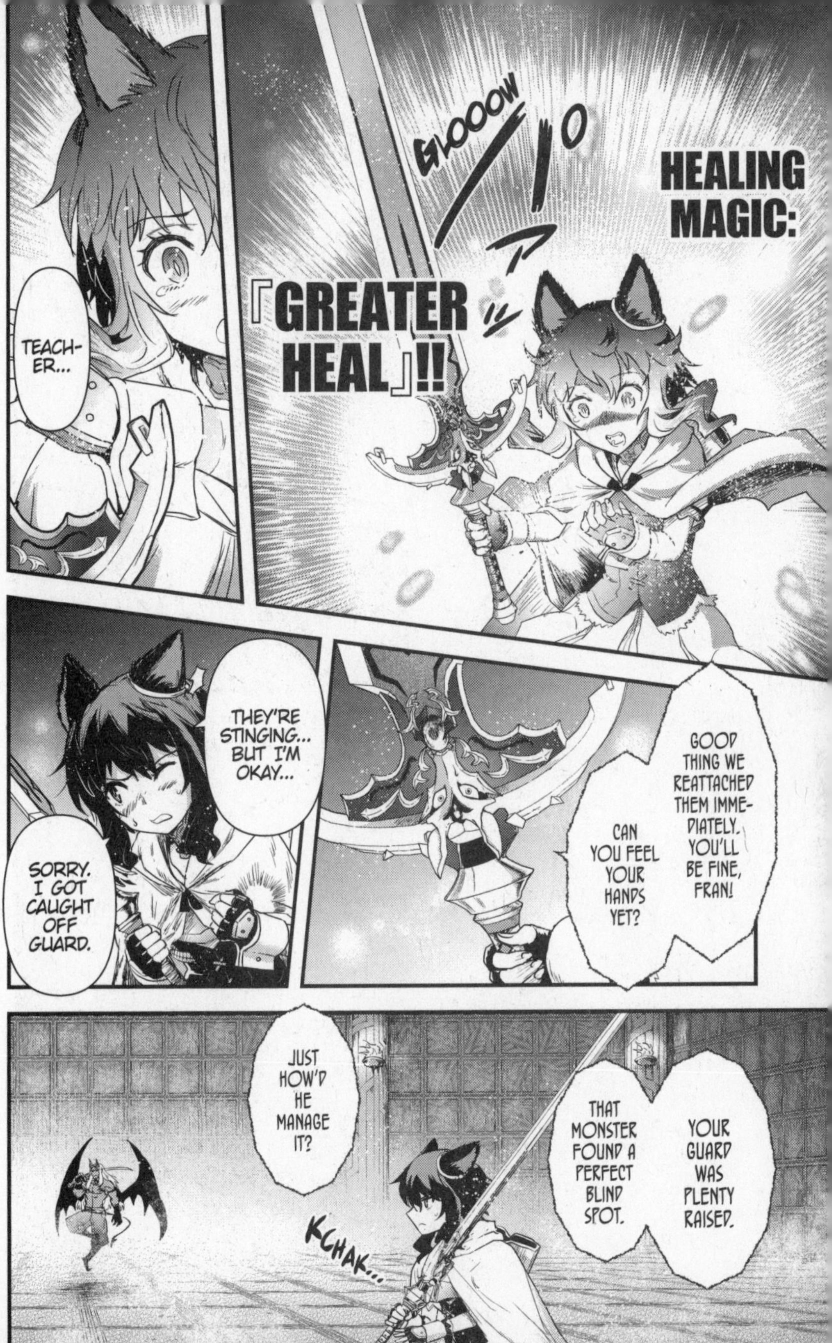
GLOOOW
HEALING MAGIC:
『GREATER HEAL』!!
TEACHER...
GOOD THING WE REATTACHED THEM IMMEDIATELY. YOU'LL BE FINE, FRAN!
CAN YOU FEEL YOUR HANDS YET?
THEY'RE STINGING... BUT I'M OKAY...
SORRY. I GOT CAUGHT OFF GUARD.
YOUR GUARD WAS PLENTY RAISED.
THAT MONSTER FOUND A PERFECT BLIND SPOT.
JUST HOW'D HE MANAGE IT?
KCHAK...

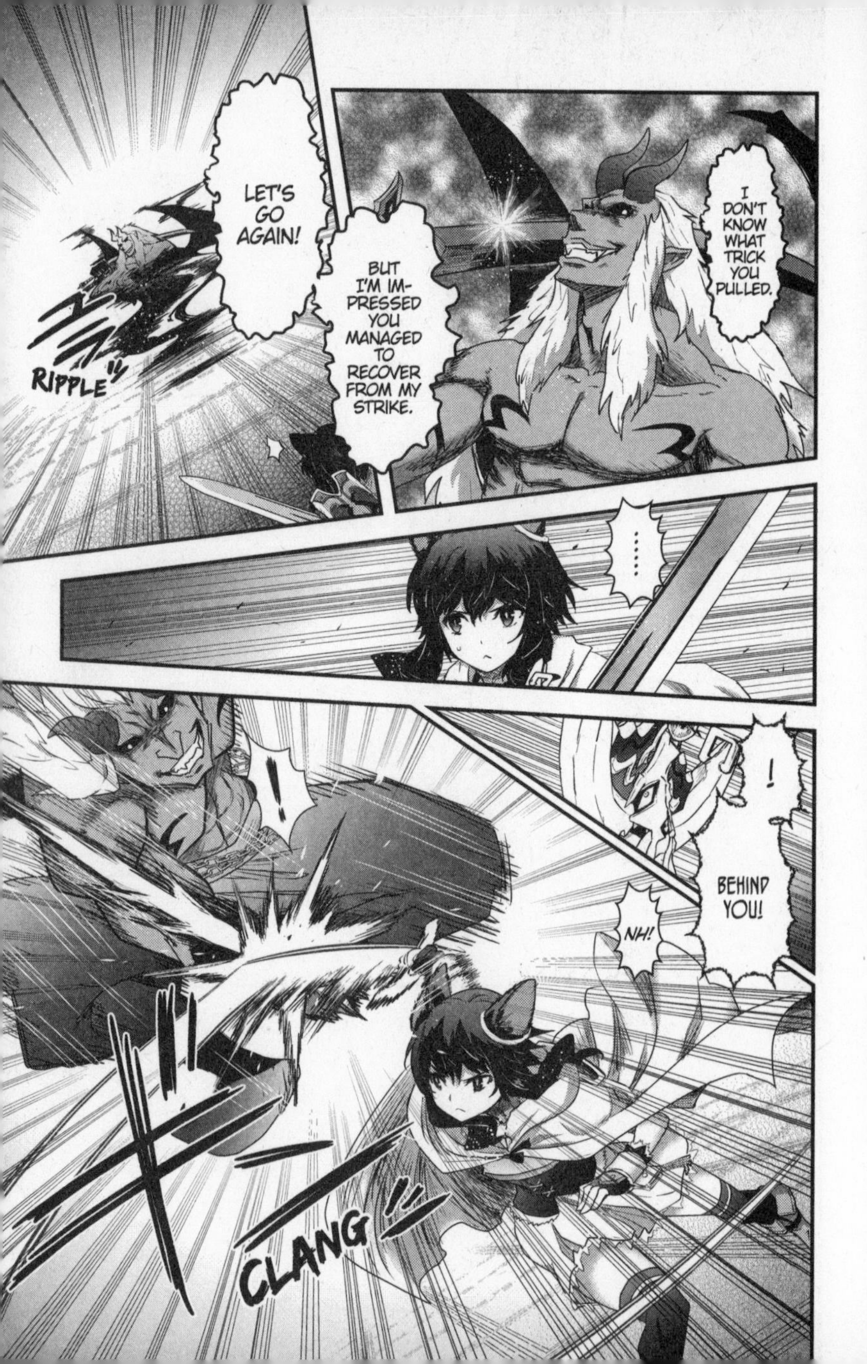
I DON'T KNOW WHAT TRICK YOU PULLED.
BUT I'M IM-PRESSED YOU MANAGED TO RECOVER FROM MY STRIKE.
LET'S GO AGAIN!
RIPPLE
......
!
BEHIND YOU!
!
NH!
CLANG

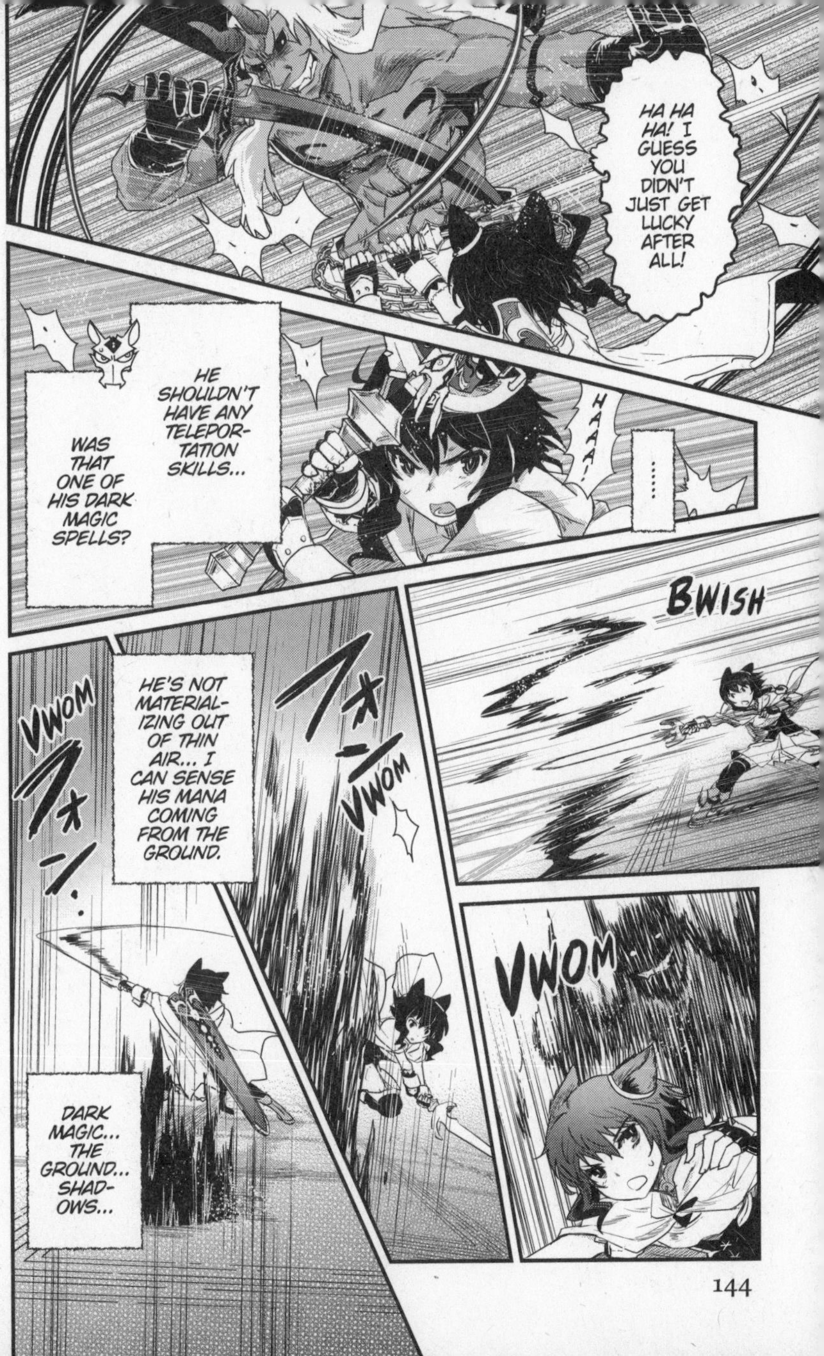
HA HA HA! I GUESS YOU DIDN'T JUST GET LUCKY AFTER ALL!
HAAA!
.....
HE SHOULDN'T HAVE ANY TELEPORTATION SKILLS...
WAS THAT ONE OF HIS DARK MAGIC SPELLS?
BWISH
VWOM
VWOM
HE'S NOT MATERIALIZING OUT OF THIN AIR... I CAN SENSE HIS MANA COMING FROM THE GROUND.
VWOM
DARK MAGIC... THE GROUND... SHADOWS...

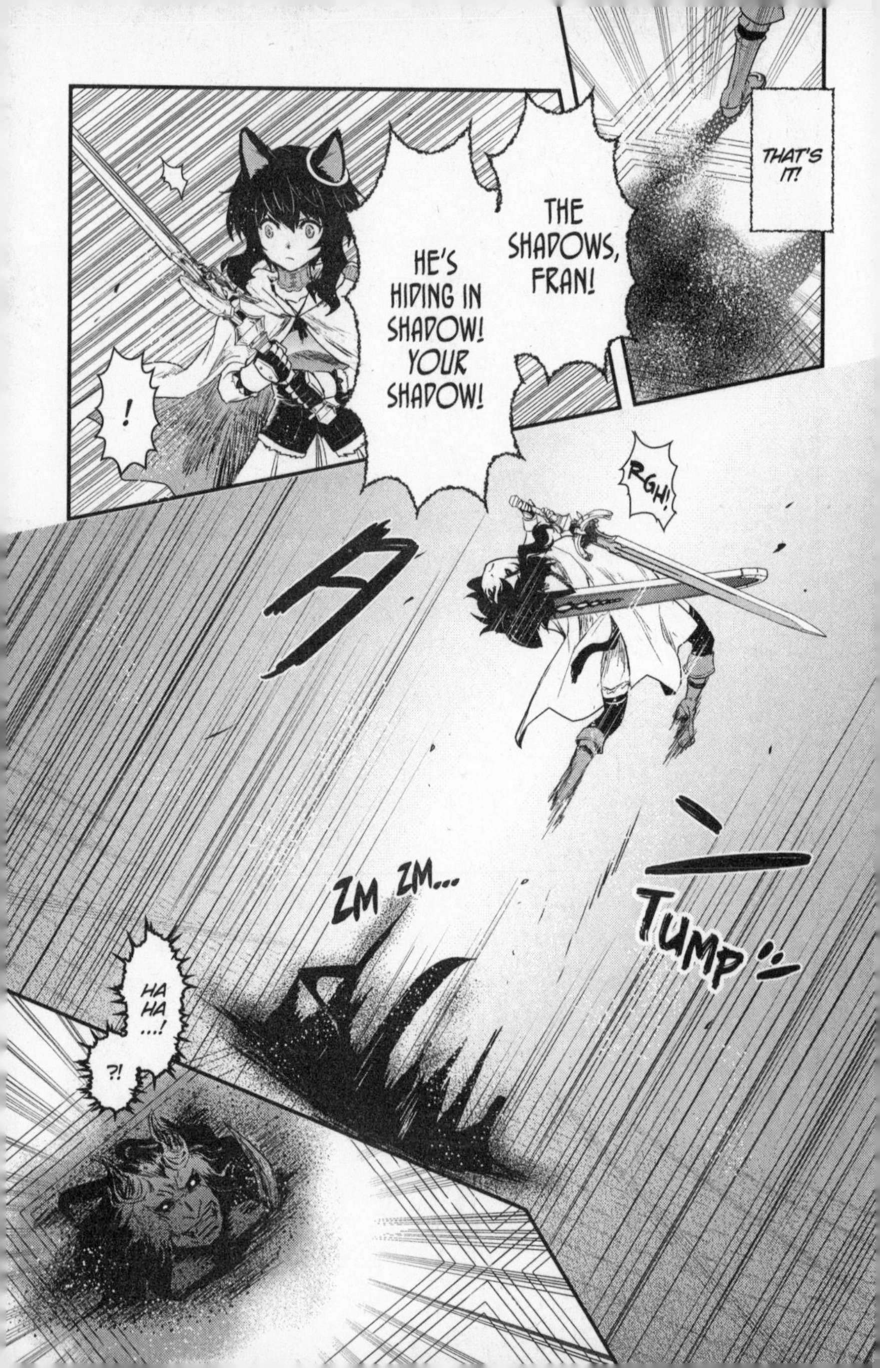

THAT'S IT!
THE SHADOWS, FRAN!
HE'S HIDING IN SHADOW! YOUR SHADOW!
!
RGH!
TUMP
ZM ZM...
HA HA ...!
?!

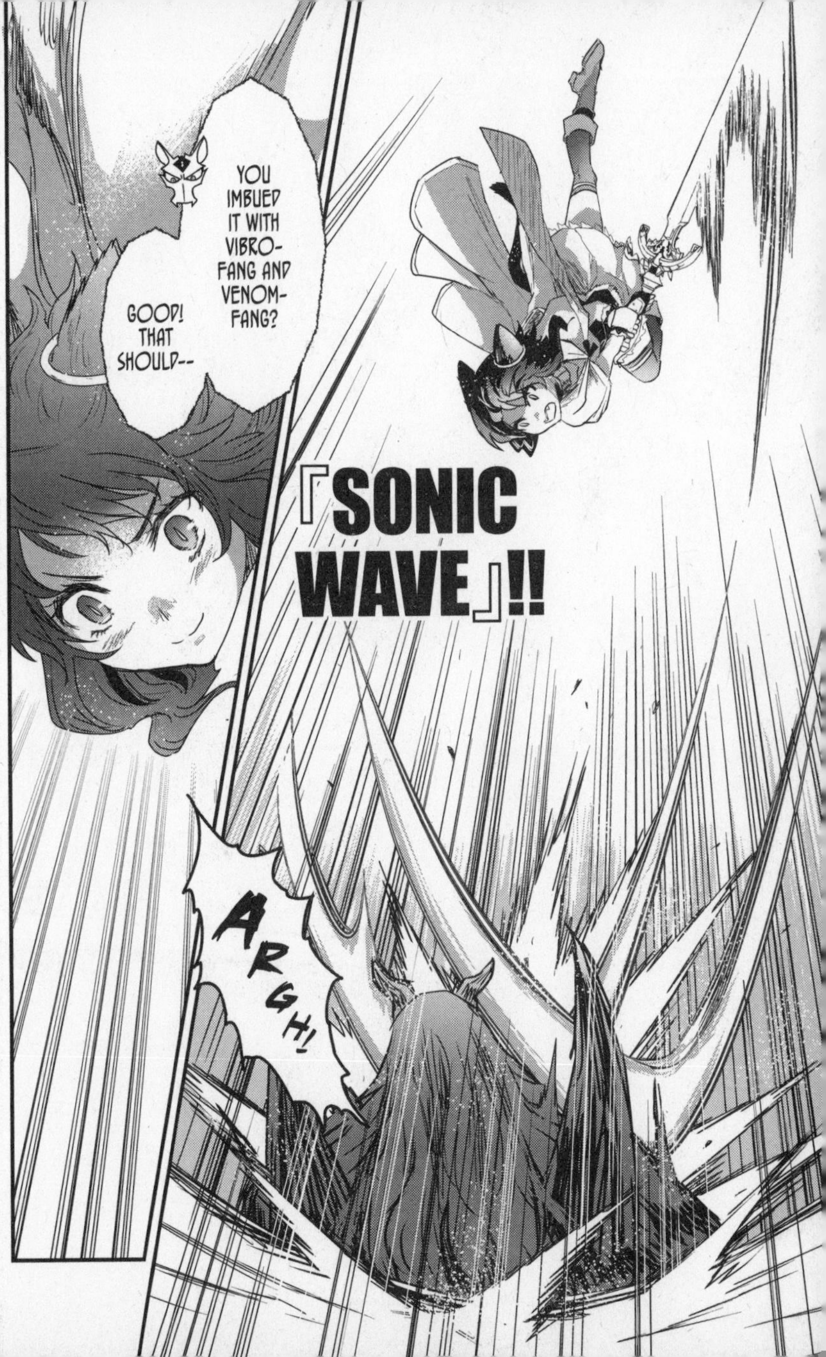
『SONIC WAVE』!!
ARGH!
YOU IMBUED IT WITH VIBRO-FANG AND VENOM-FANG?
GOOD! THAT SHOULD--

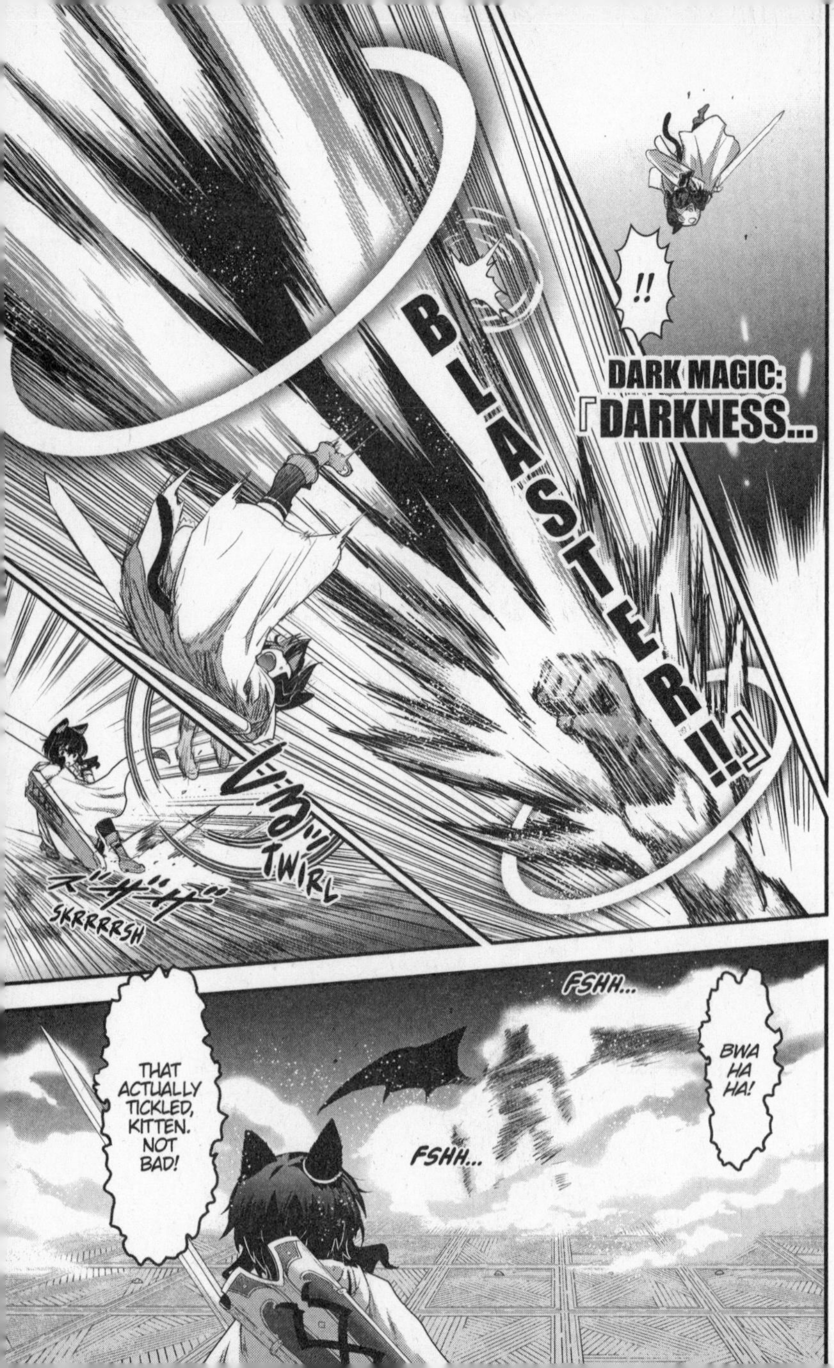
!!
DARK MAGIC:
『DARKNESS...
BLASTER!!』
TWIRL
SKRRRRSH
FSHH...
BWA HA HA!
FSHH...
THAT ACTUALLY TICKLED, KITTEN. NOT BAD!

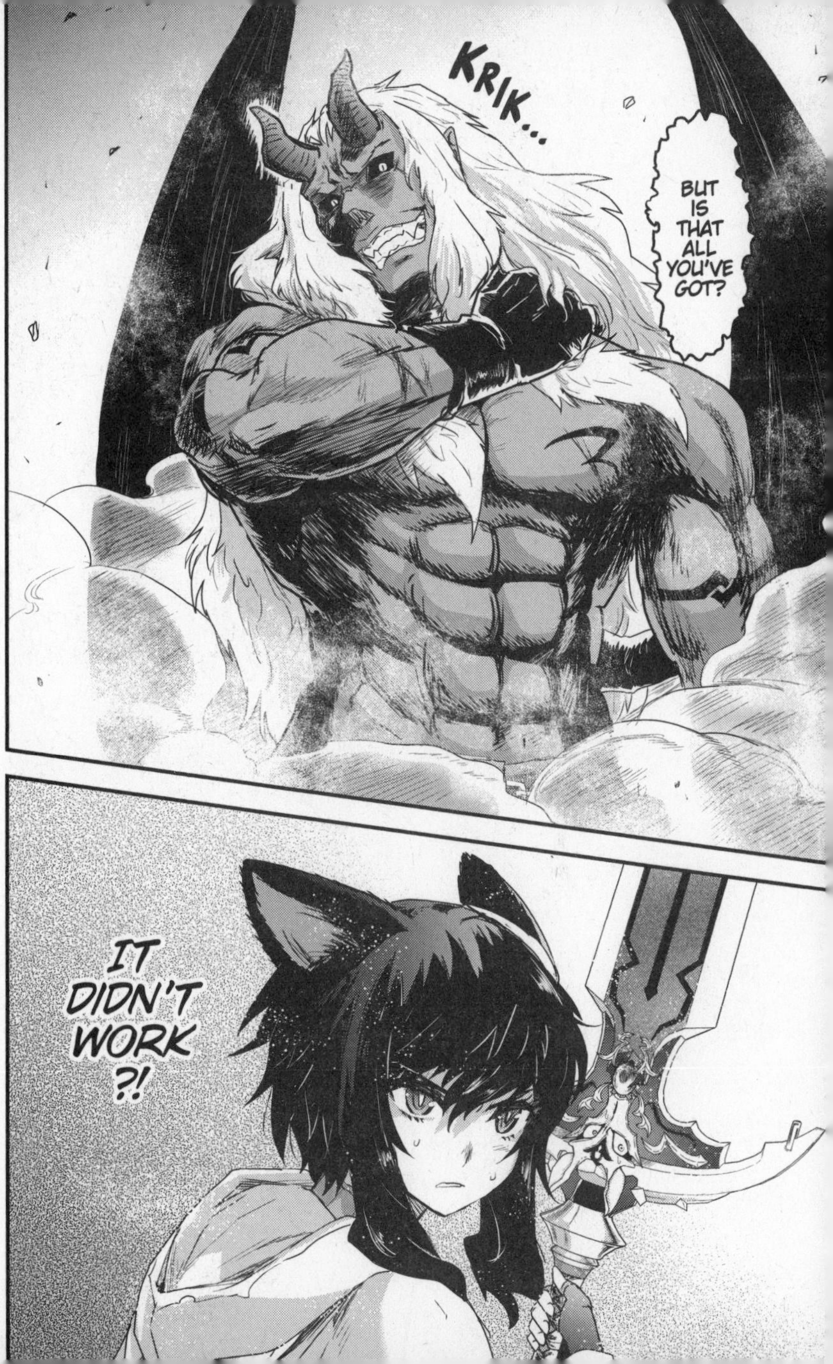
KRIK...
BUT IS THAT ALL YOU'VE GOT?
IT DIDN'T WORK ?!

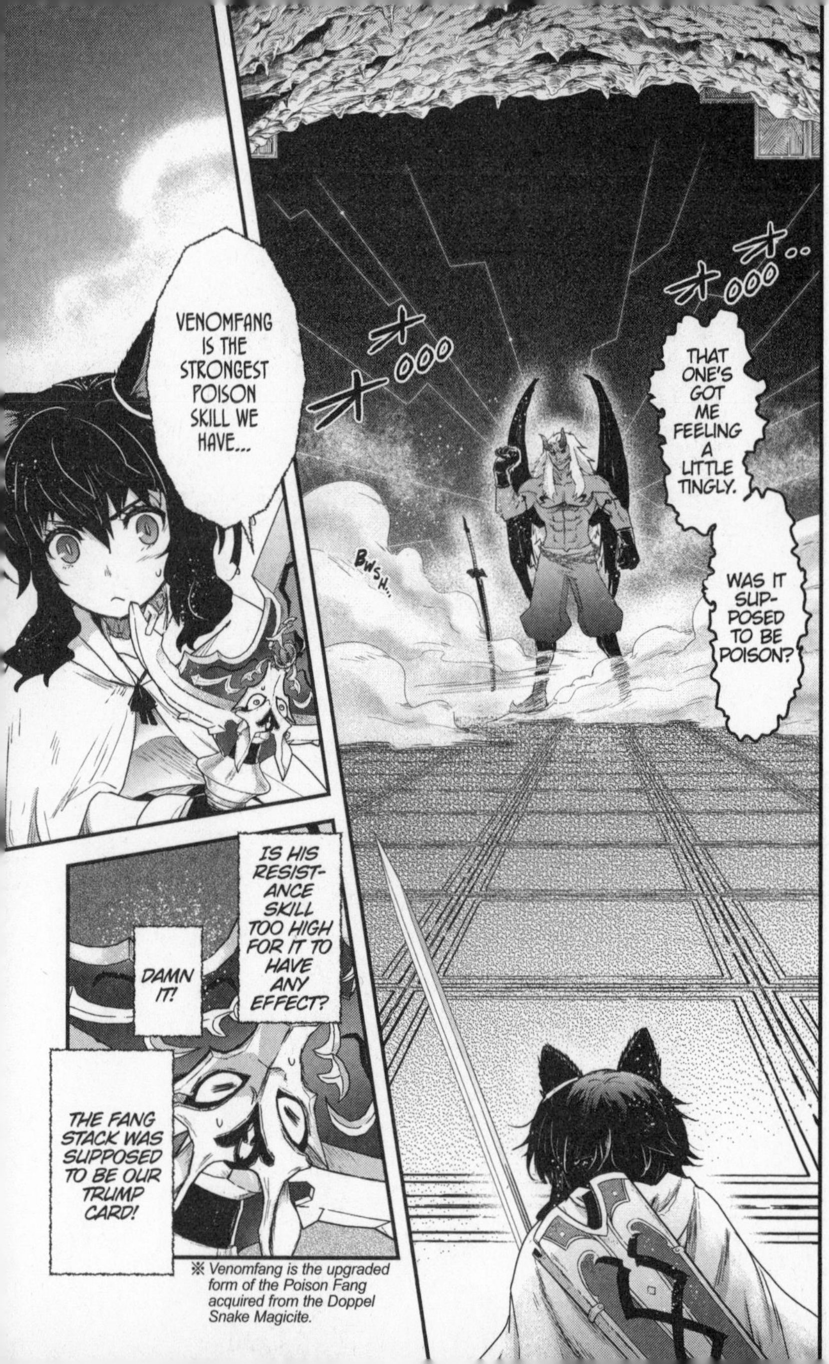
オOOO..
オOOO
THAT ONE'S GOT ME FEELING A LITTLE TINGLY.
WAS IT SUP-POSED TO BE POISON?
オOOO
オ
BWSH..
VENOMFANG IS THE STRONGEST POISON SKILL WE HAVE...
IS HIS RESIST-ANCE SKILL TOO HIGH FOR IT TO HAVE ANY EFFECT?
DAMN IT!
THE FANG STACK WAS SUPPOSED TO BE OUR TRUMP CARD!
※ *Venomfang is the upgraded form of the Poison Fang acquired from the Doppel Snake Magicite.*

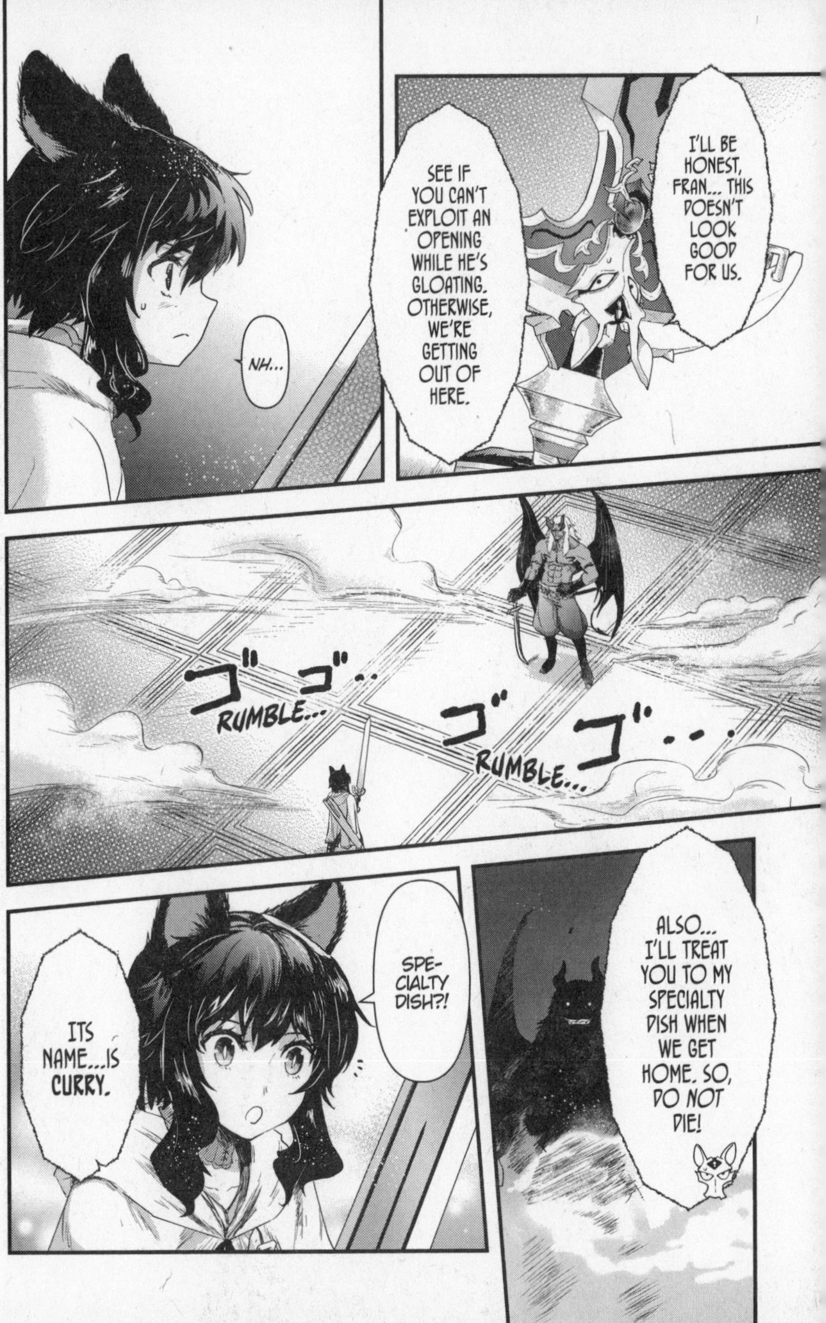
I'LL BE HONEST, FRAN... THIS DOESN'T LOOK GOOD FOR US.
SEE IF YOU CAN'T EXPLOIT AN OPENING WHILE HE'S GLOATING. OTHERWISE, WE'RE GETTING OUT OF HERE.
NH...
ゴゴ..
RUMBLE...
ゴゴ...
RUMBLE...
ALSO... I'LL TREAT YOU TO MY SPECIALTY DISH WHEN WE GET HOME. SO, DO *NOT* DIE!
SPE-CIALTY DISH?!
ITS NAME...IS CURRY.

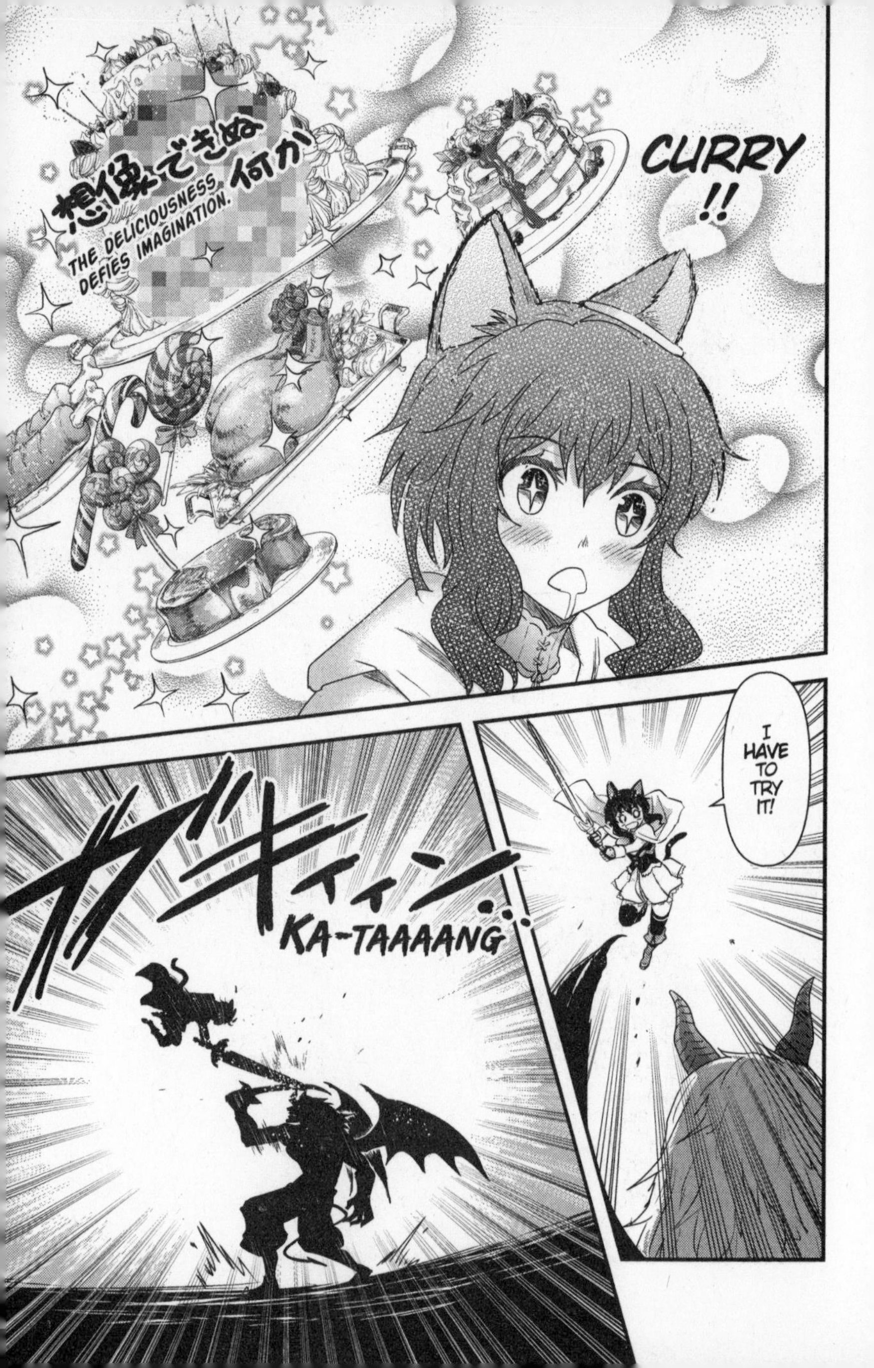
CURRY !!
想像できぬ何か
THE DELICIOUSNESS DEFIES IMAGINATION.
I HAVE TO TRY IT!
KA-TAAAANG

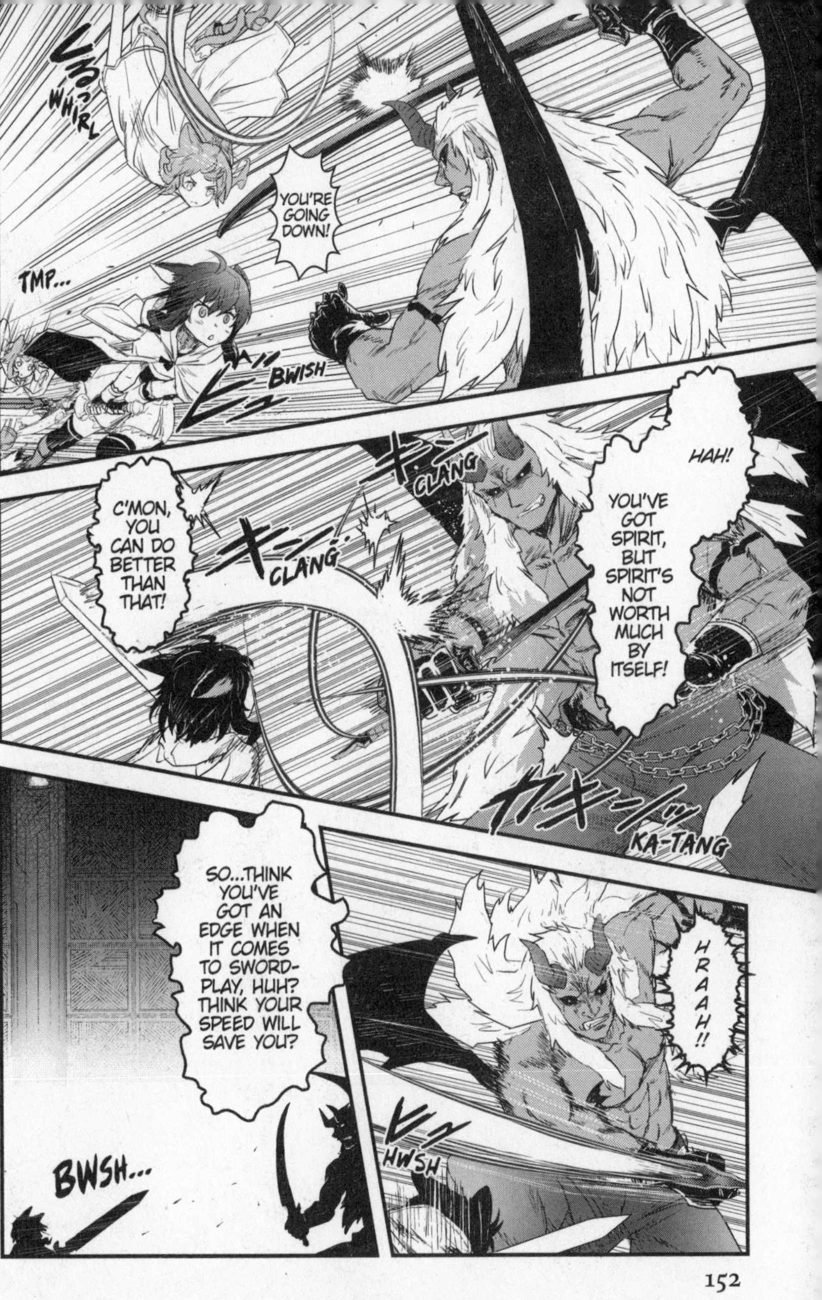

YOU'RE GOING DOWN!
WHIRL
TMP...
BWISH
HAH!
YOU'VE GOT SPIRIT, BUT SPIRIT'S NOT WORTH MUCH BY ITSELF!
CLANG
CLANG
C'MON, YOU CAN DO BETTER THAN THAT!
KA-TANG
HRAAAH!!
HWSH
SO...THINK YOU'VE GOT AN EDGE WHEN IT COMES TO SWORD-PLAY, HUH? THINK YOUR SPEED WILL SAVE YOU?
BWSH...

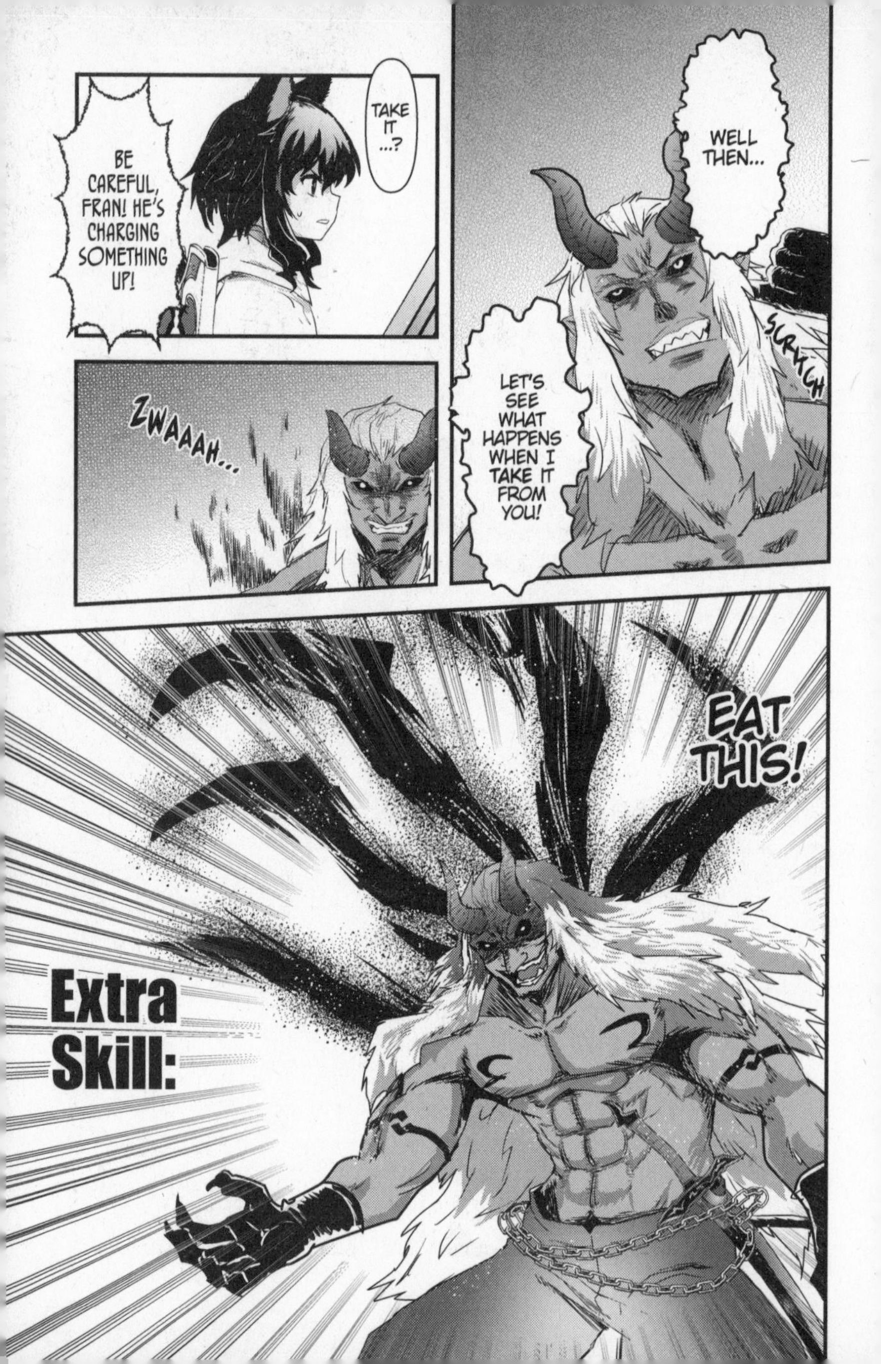
WELL THEN...
SCRKKCH
LET'S SEE WHAT HAPPENS WHEN I TAKE IT FROM YOU!
TAKE IT ...?
BE CAREFUL, FRAN! HE'S CHARGING SOMETHING UP!
ZWAAAH...
EAT THIS!
Extra Skill:

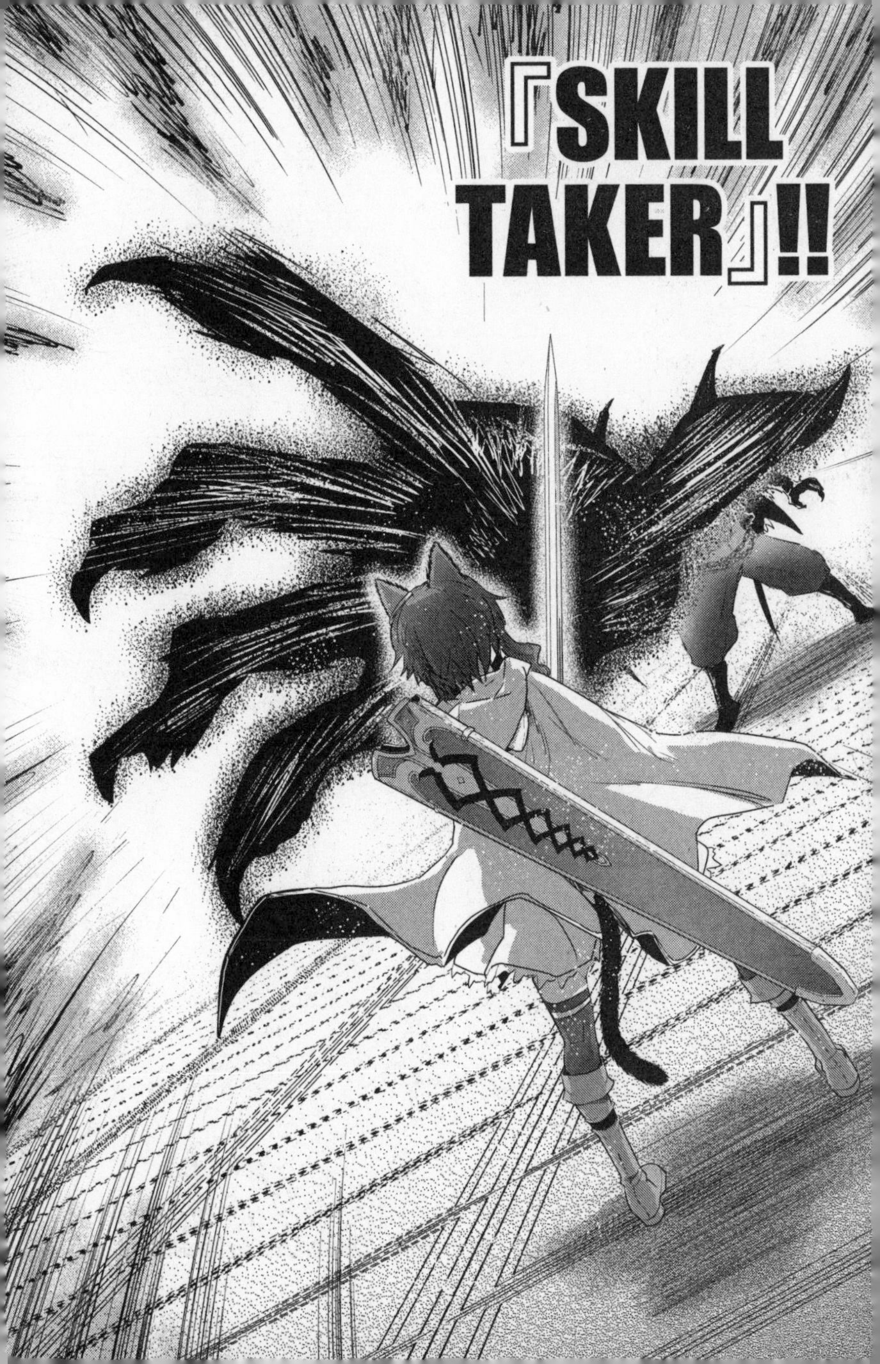
『SKILL TAKER』!!

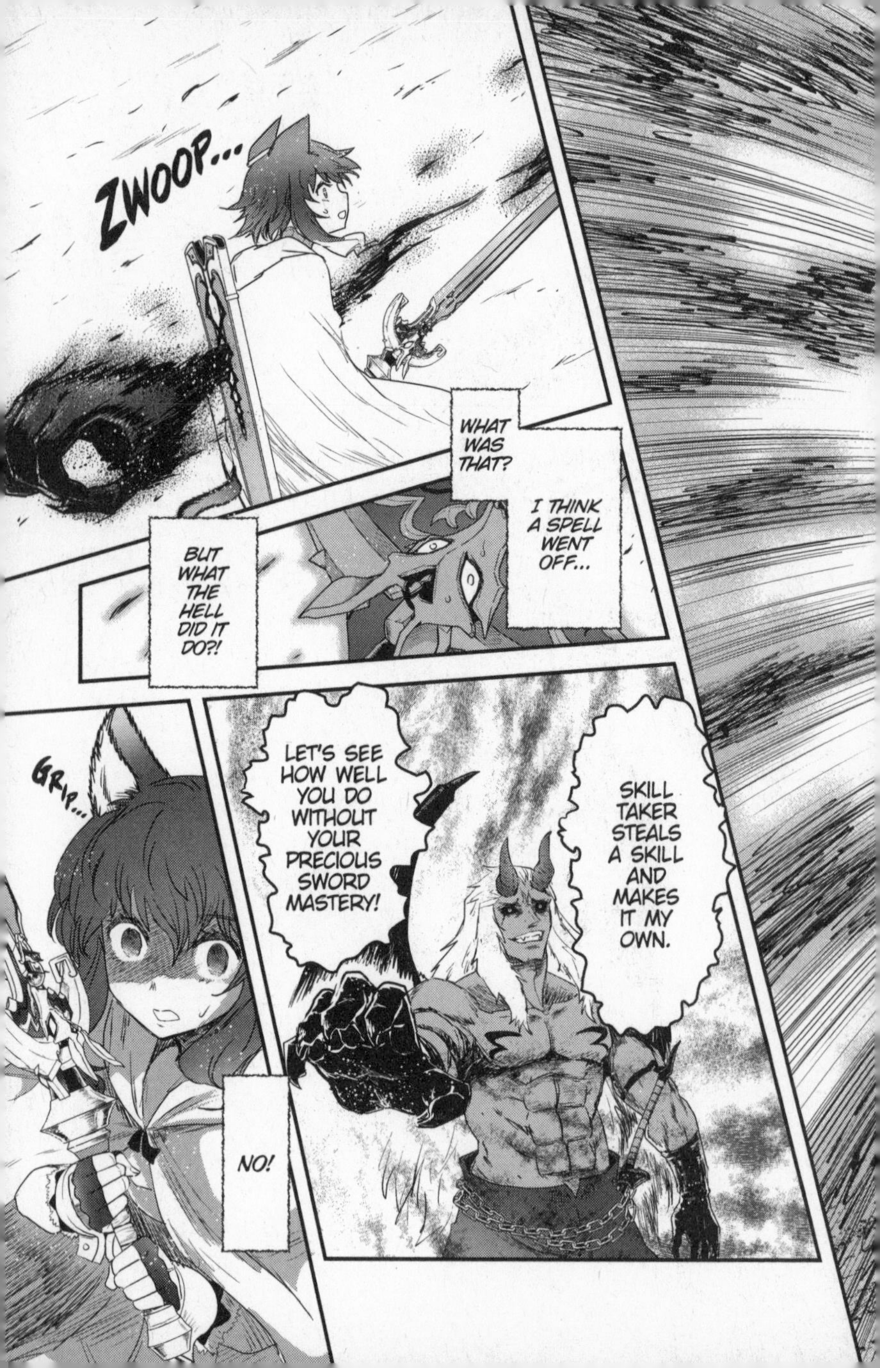
ZWOOP...
WHAT WAS THAT?
I THINK A SPELL WENT OFF...
BUT WHAT THE HELL DID IT DO?!
SKILL TAKER STEALS A SKILL AND MAKES IT MY OWN.
LET'S SEE HOW WELL YOU DO WITHOUT YOUR PRECIOUS SWORD MASTERY!
NO!
GRIP...

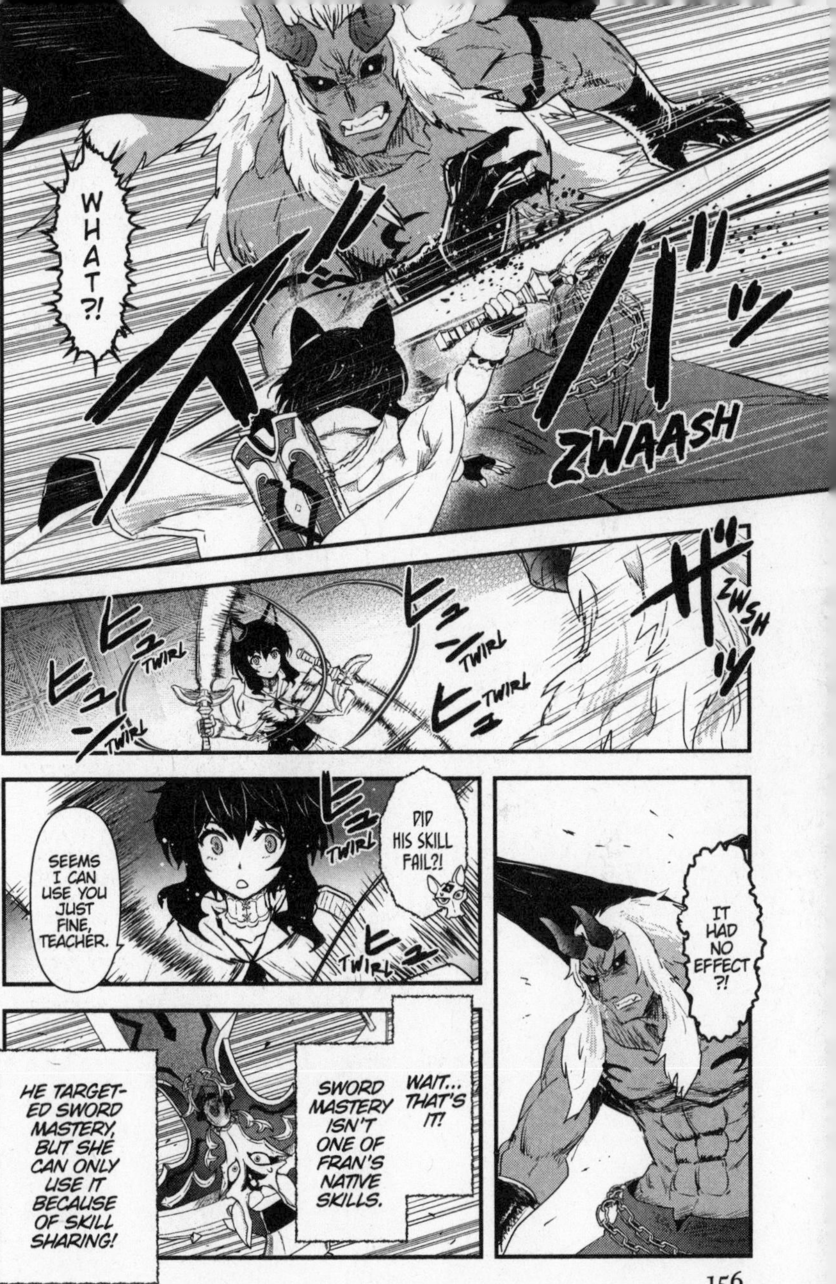
WHAT?!
ZWAASH
ZWSH
TWIRL
TWIRL
TWIRL
TWIRL
IT HAD NO EFFECT?!
DID HIS SKILL FAIL?!
TWIRL
SEEMS I CAN USE YOU JUST FINE, TEACHER.
TWIRL
WAIT... THAT'S IT!
SWORD MASTERY ISN'T ONE OF FRAN'S NATIVE SKILLS.
HE TARGETED SWORD MASTERY, BUT SHE CAN ONLY USE IT BECAUSE OF SKILL SHARING!

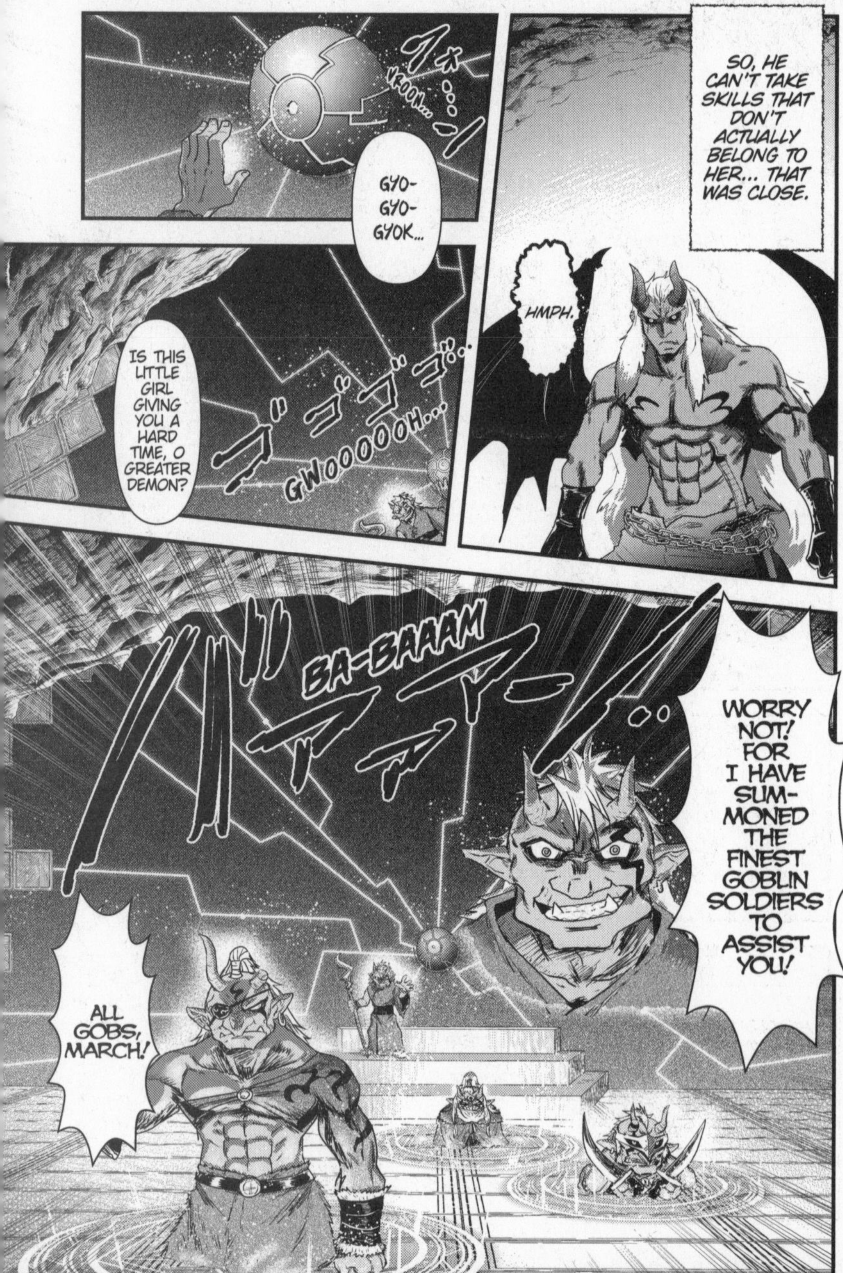
SO, HE CAN'T TAKE SKILLS THAT DON'T ACTUALLY BELONG TO HER... THAT WAS CLOSE.
HMPH.
VROOM...
GYO-GYO-GYOK...
GWOOOOOOH...
IS THIS LITTLE GIRL GIVING YOU A HARD TIME, O GREATER DEMON?
BA-BAAAM
WORRY NOT! FOR I HAVE SUM-MONED THE FINEST GOBLIN SOLDIERS TO ASSIST YOU!
ALL GOBS, MARCH!

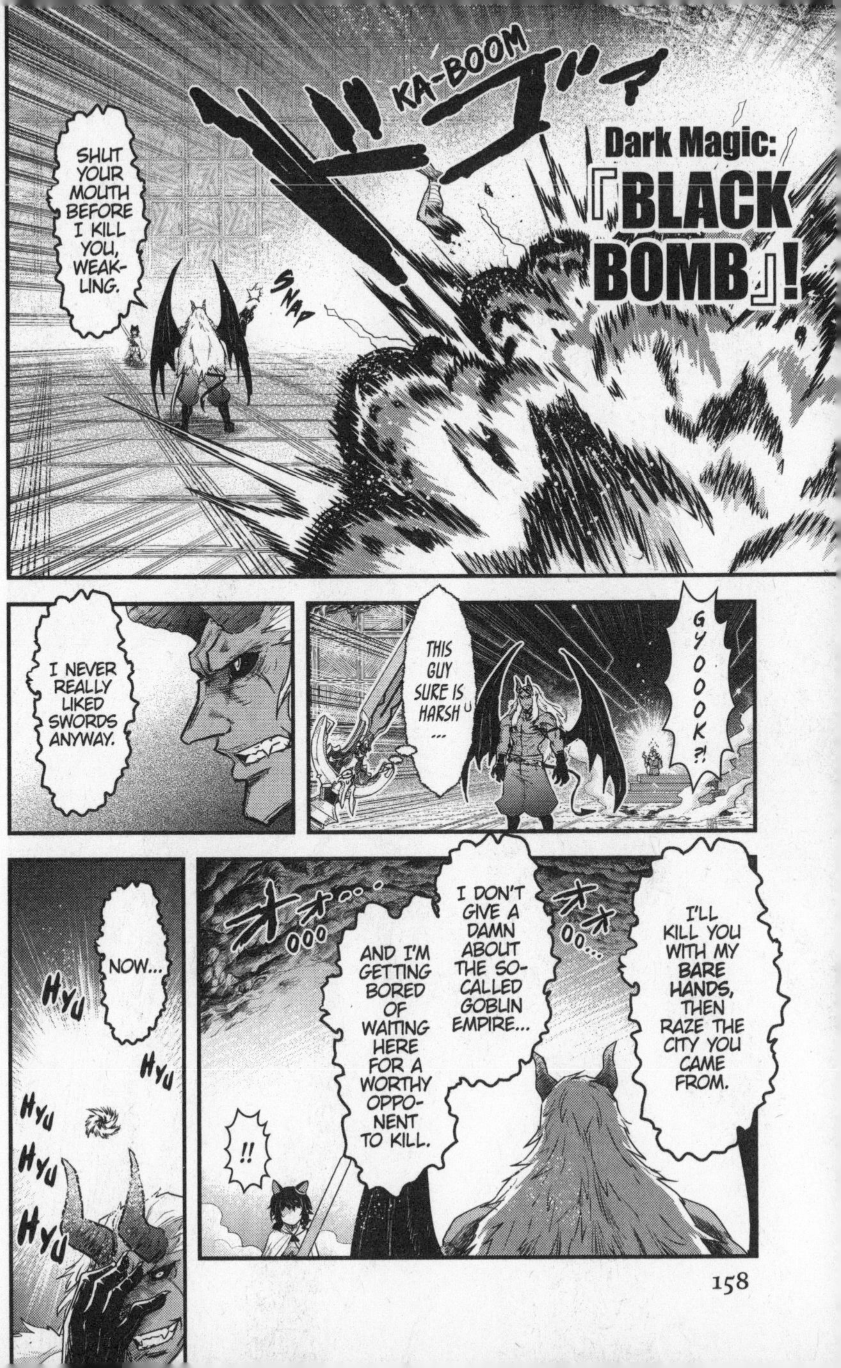
KA-BOOM
Dark Magic: 『BLACK BOMB』!
SNAP
SHUT YOUR MOUTH BEFORE I KILL YOU, WEAK-LING.
GYOOOOK?!
THIS GUY SURE IS HARSH...
I NEVER REALLY LIKED SWORDS ANYWAY.
I'LL KILL YOU WITH MY BARE HANDS, THEN RAZE THE CITY YOU CAME FROM.
OO...
I DON'T GIVE A DAMN ABOUT THE SO-CALLED GOBLIN EMPIRE...
AND I'M GETTING BORED OF WAITING HERE FOR A WORTHY OPPO-NENT TO KILL.
OOO
!!
NOW...
HYU
HYU
HYU
HYU
HYU
HYU

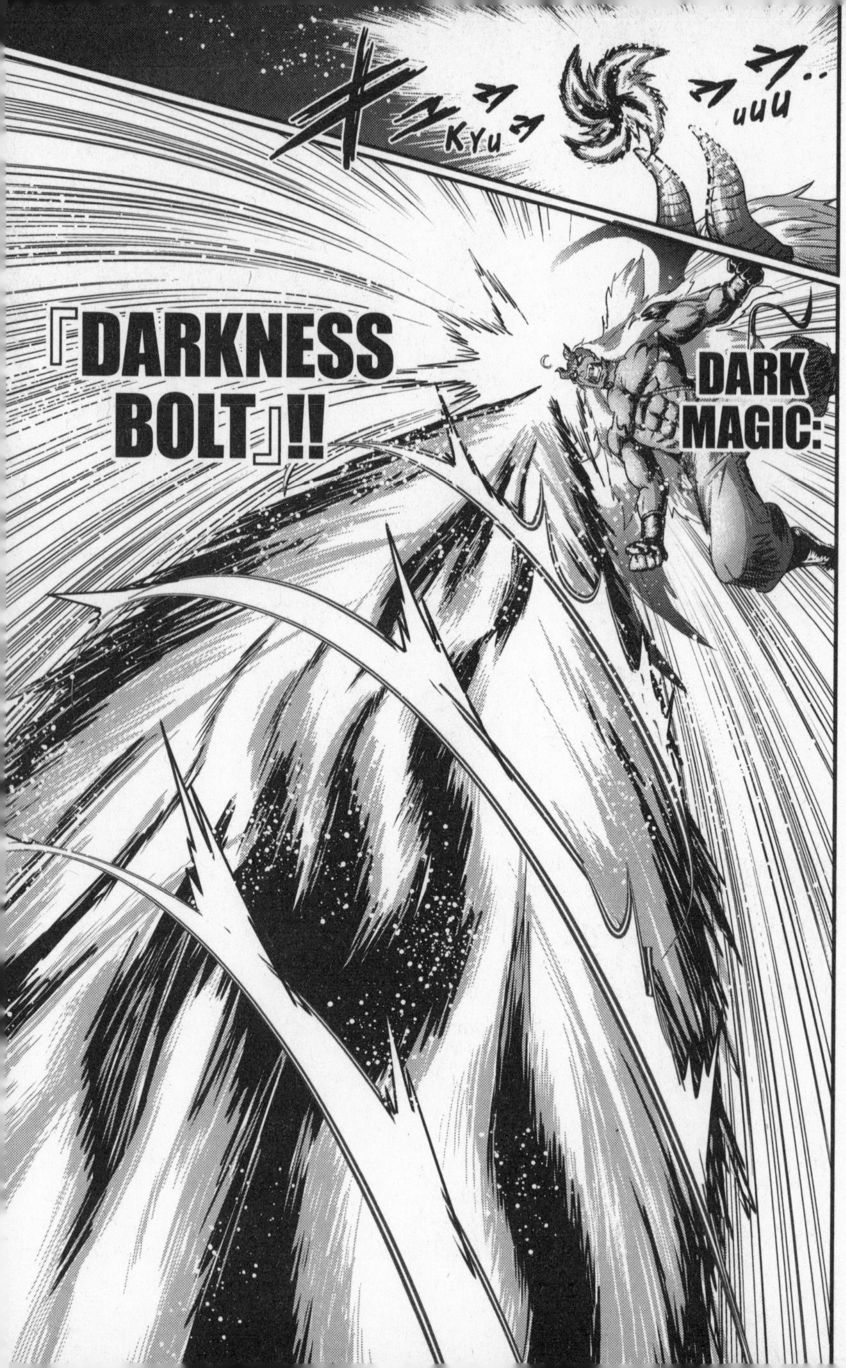
KYU
UUU
DARK MAGIC:
『DARKNESS BOLT』!!

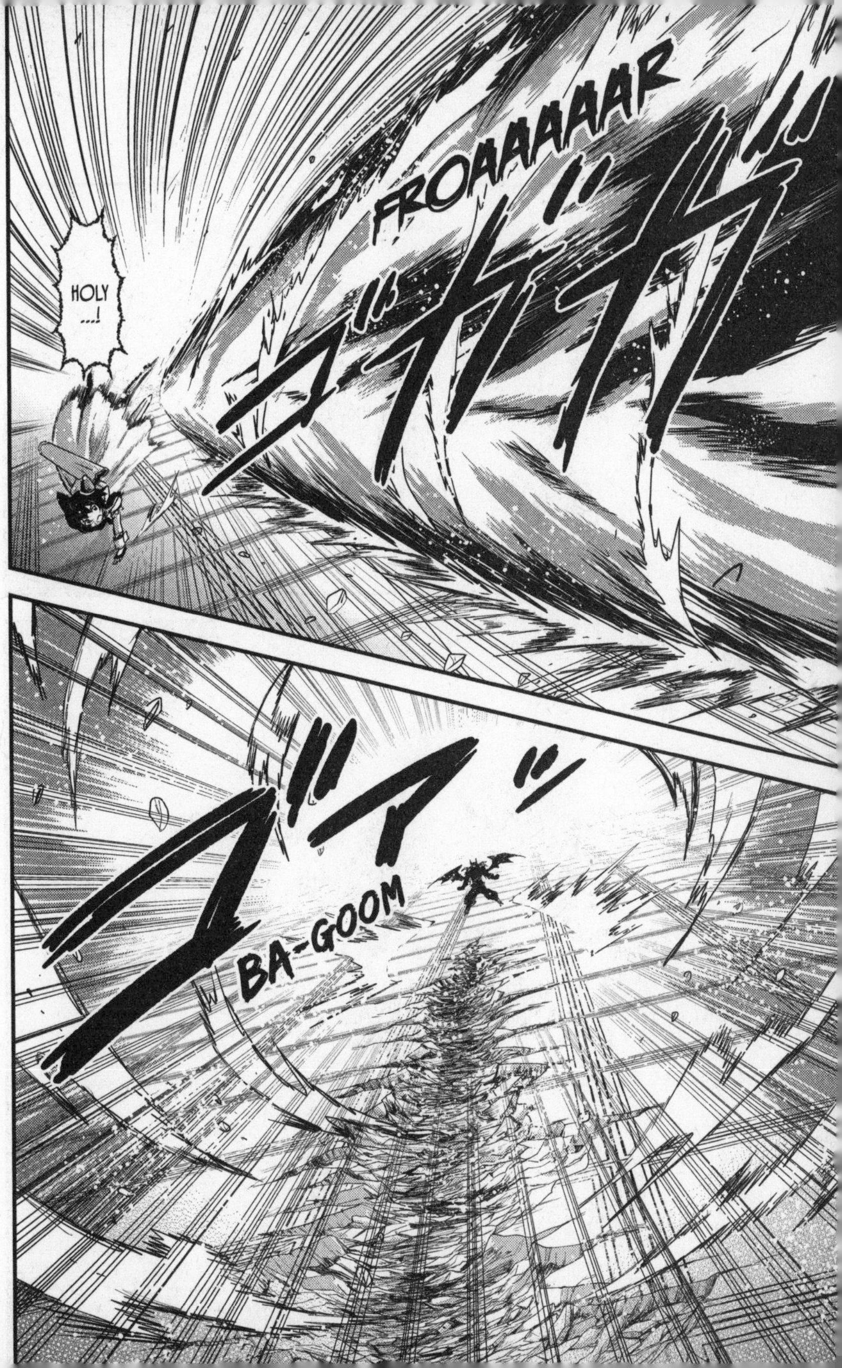
FROAAAAAR
HOLY ...!
BA-GOOM

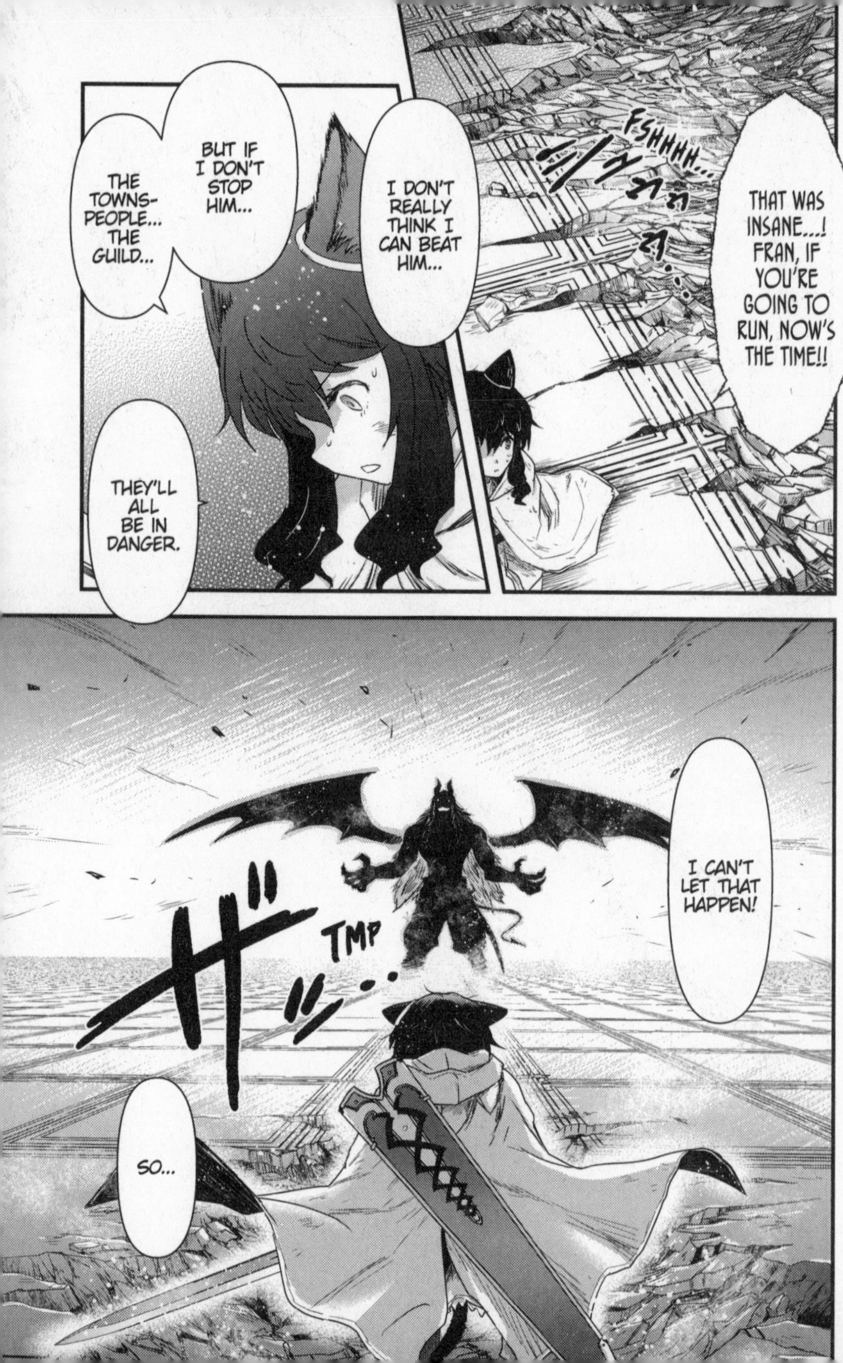
FSHHHH...
THAT WAS INSANE...! FRAN, IF YOU'RE GOING TO RUN, NOW'S THE TIME!!
I DON'T REALLY THINK I CAN BEAT HIM...
BUT IF I DON'T STOP HIM...
THE TOWNSPEOPLE... THE GUILD...
THEY'LL ALL BE IN DANGER.
I CAN'T LET THAT HAPPEN!
TMP
SO...

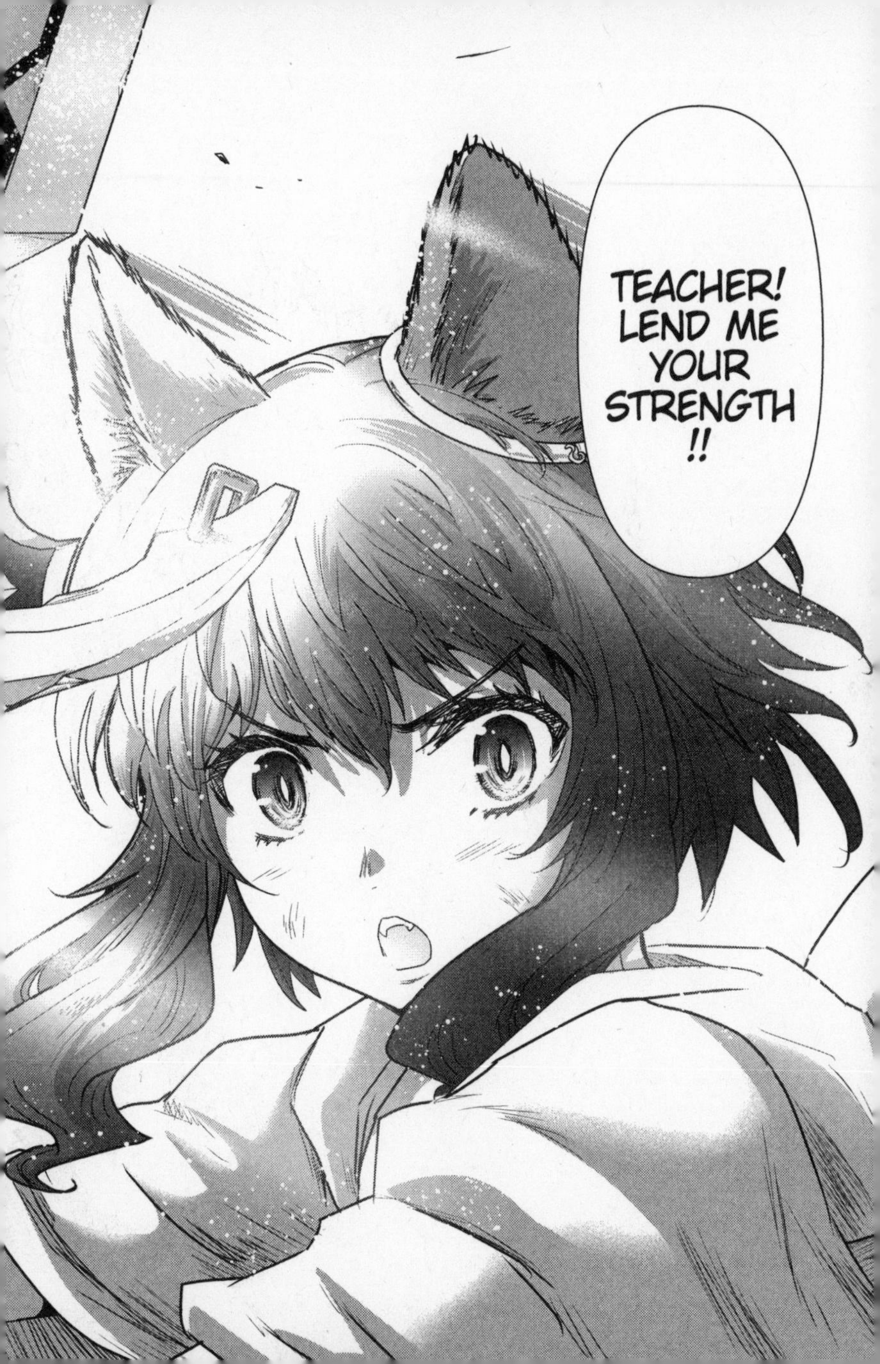
TEACHER! LEND ME YOUR STRENGTH !!

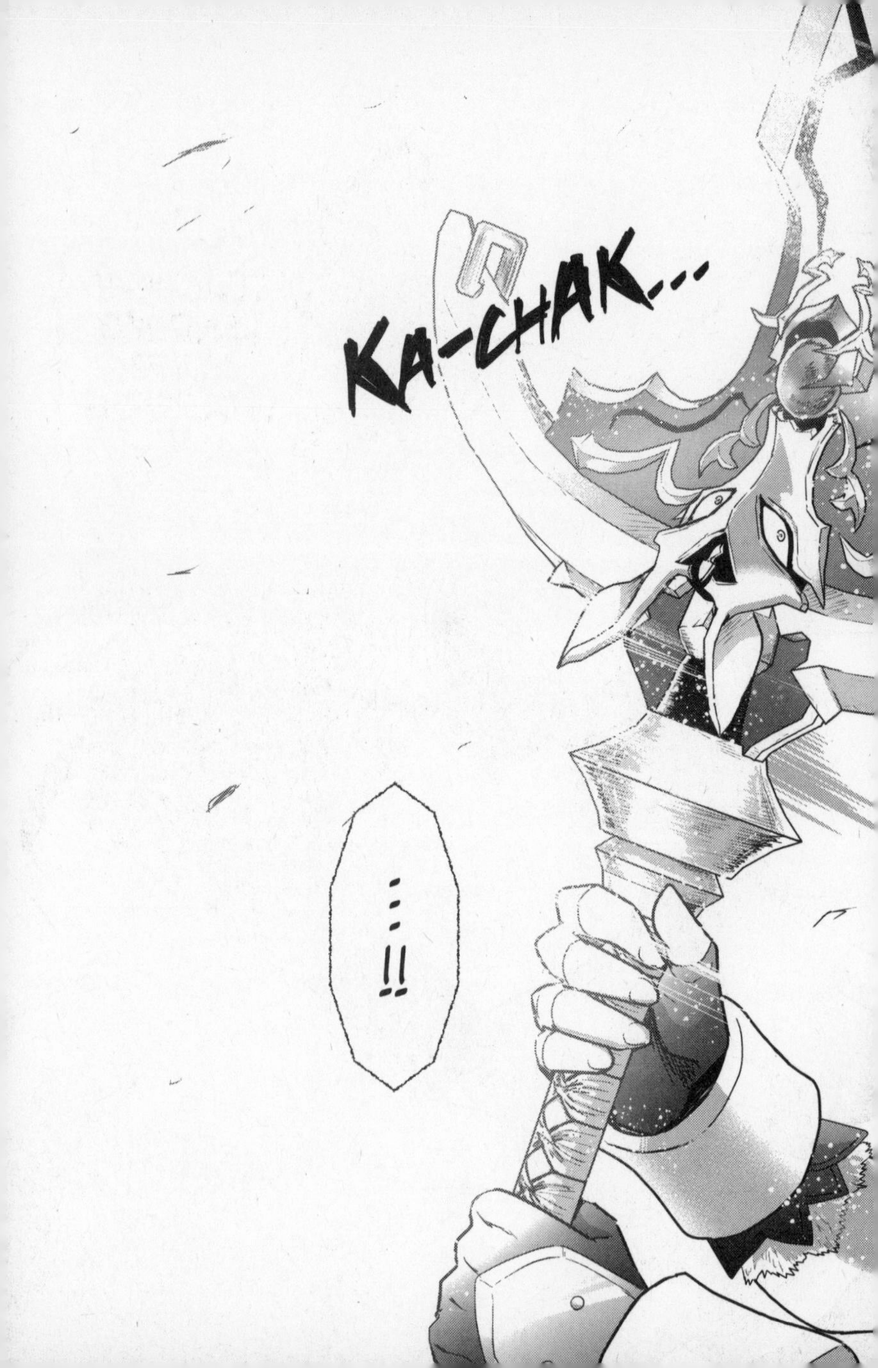
KA-CHAK...
...!!

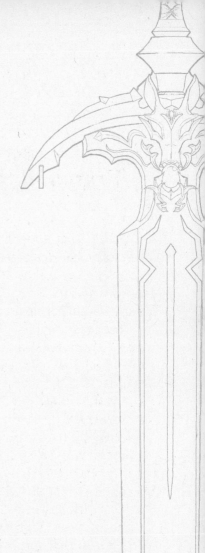

Reincarnated
as a sword

Reincarnated as a Sword

Bonus Story

Fran and the Hot Springs

"Wow! What is this place, Teacher?"

Fran's eyes gleamed as she gazed at the scenery before her. Despite the cold air, her thin cheeks were flushed with excitement. I'd never seen her so excited for anything other than food.

"Teacher?"

This is a natural hot spring. Steaming water gushes from the rocks, making a pool right here in the wilderness.

"A hot spring! I've heard of those. They're like outdoor baths!"

That's one way of putting it.

Fran didn't seem interested in listening to the benefits of a natural hot spring, but that was all right as long as she knew what it was for.

"It's really cramped, though."

The pool was quite small, per Fran's observation. Even Fran, a little girl, would be hard pressed to stretch her legs out in it. It reminded me of the shoddy bathtub I had in my university days.

"Is it for kids only or something?"

It sure is, compared to the bigger indoor baths

you've seen.

The civilization of this world was comparable to Europe in the middle ages, except for some advancements in magic and magic-related technologies. A less obvious exception was its bathing culture. The upper-middle class had baths inside of their homes, while the lower classes visited bathhouses for their washing. Those bathhouses were much larger than the average Japanese bathhouse, while being much cleaner and coming equipped with amenities such as shampoo.

Fran had been born the daughter of an adventurer, wound up sold into slavery, and now she was travelling with me. She'd used indoor baths all her life, and was unprepared for the size of this natural hot spring.

Looking at the small bath in front of her, she clearly thought that it had been prepared especially for children.

Would you like to get warmed up here?

"Of course!"

She nodded enthusiastically and began testing the temperature of the water.

How is it?

"Perfect," Fran declared with a smile. "Just right."

We'd come across other hot springs in our travels, but she'd been nowhere near this enthusiastic. It was a matter of time and place, I supposed.

We were currently high up in the mountains. If I had to guess, I'd say that the highest peak was as tall as Mt. Fuji itself. It was on this mountain that we'd found the solitary hot springs.

Owing to her Black Cat heritage, Fran wasn't particularly fond of colder climates. I could feel her malaise growing as we ascended the snowy mountain

slopes. Her levels had given her the strength to tolerate the cold, but it didn't change her preferences. At least she didn't get altitude sickness.

At the height of her exhaustion, the hot springs appeared before us. The sight alone was enough to make her heart soar.

That's not all. The hot springs were decorated with a layer of freshly fallen snow; it couldn't have been more than a day old. No one had come before us, either, so it lay pristine and undisturbed. The perfect contrast of cold snow and hot springs made me feel like reaching for a drink to complete the picturesque nature of it. But even without alcohol, the sight alone was enough to intrigue.

Adding to the beauty were thickets of white flowers in bloom. These flowers were called Frostblooms, and they grew only at high altitudes. They were also the object of our current quest.

The night sky was so clear that it looked like the stars themselves might join the snow in falling to the earth. The mountain summit made the cosmos seem all the closer, and Fran's arms seemed long enough to pluck them out of the sky. But the stars were only a frame for the full moon at the center of it all.

Snow and flower. Star and moon. Hot springs.

It wasn't every day that nature put on her best attire. Even Fran, the queen of living in the moment, was struck with awe.

We can put off the gathering until later.

"Mm!"

Fran started taking off her gear in frantic excitement. I wished she had the decency to arrange them all in the same stack.

She then proceeded to jump right into the cramped pool. Her sudden entrance caused the springs to overflow, depleting the already scarce amount of water within. Manners, Fran! No one else was here to complain, at least.

Oh, crap!

I had decided to put off our gathering quest for later, but seeing as the Frostblooms were in danger of being drowned in Fran's deluge, I had to move fast. The flowers were notoriously fragile, wilting at even the slightest bump. I wasn't going to let our trek up these snowy peaks be wasted because of a hot spring!

Phew... We're in the clear for now.

As Fran relaxed in her bath, I gathered up twenty of the flowers to finish our mission.

"Teacher," Fran called to me.

What is it, Fran?

"I want some juice. Something cold."

Fran knew from instinct that a cold drink contrasted the hot springs perfectly. Very good!

Which one do you want?

A myriad of food and drinks were stocked away in my Pocket Dimension. Things stored there weren't affected by the passage of time, so it perfectly preserved foods in temperature and freshness.

You want sour or sweet?

"I want the fizzy red one!"

The drink in question was pomegranate juice mixed with carbonated water. I took a pitcher of it out of storage and set it next to the hot springs, remembering to stick a straw in it for easy consumption. The straws of this world were made of literal straw. I quite liked them.

Here you go.

"Thanks."

Fran dipped herself all the way to her chest and leaned against a rock. She wore the expression of a middle-aged man in a massage chair. Her arms rested on top of some rocks while the lower half of her folded legs stuck out of the pool. She seemed to enjoy the heat of the hot springs around her body while her limbs remained cool outside.

Munch!

Pomegranate soda was insufficient to sate her appetite. Fran pulled some skewered dumplings out of her personal Pocket Dimension and stuffed them in her cheeks. She ate while bathing and gazing at the moon. A little rude, but I gave it a pass.

"Perfect circle!"

Fran held her dumpling skewer up to the full moon with a satisfied grin. She hummed as she rummaged through her inventory, taking out some ice cream this time. Ice cream in a bathtub. She was living every kid's dream.

Good?

"Delicious!"

The pomegranate soda, dumplings, and ice cream would usually constitute an entire meal for her...

But tonight, they were mere appetizers. Urged on by her appetite, Fran pulled out the main dish. Something I didn't think was appropriate for the bath.

Are you seriously going to eat curry here?

I'd seen pictures of hot sake floated on top of a wooden plate before, but never curry.

"The best spot deserves the best food."

She had a point.

If you say so. Just don't spill it, all right?

"I won't do something so wasteful," Fran boasted, a touch of curry at the corner of her mouth.

"Munch, munch."

Come on, you need to be more careful.

"Hm?"

I wiped the curry off her lips with a handkerchief.

"Hey, Teacher."

Yeah?

"This is amazing." Fran admired the stars that lit up the snowy terrain around her.

She had never seen such beautiful scenery before, and it reminded me of the suffering she had endured during her time as a slave. I wanted to show her more of this beautiful world.

It is. But I'm willing to bet that there are even prettier places than this mountain all around the world.

"Really?"

Yeah. I'm sure there are places so beautiful we can't even begin to imagine them.

"I wanna see what they're like! I bet they'll be great places to eat curry."

It was just like her to prioritize curry over scenery.

"We'll go together."

Fran pointed her hands and feet to the sky to show her resolve.

Hey, you'll spill your curry that way! Your spoon's about to tip over...

"We can go anywhere on the planet together."

I won't fight you there.

"Mm!"

Reincarnated
as a Sword

to be continued

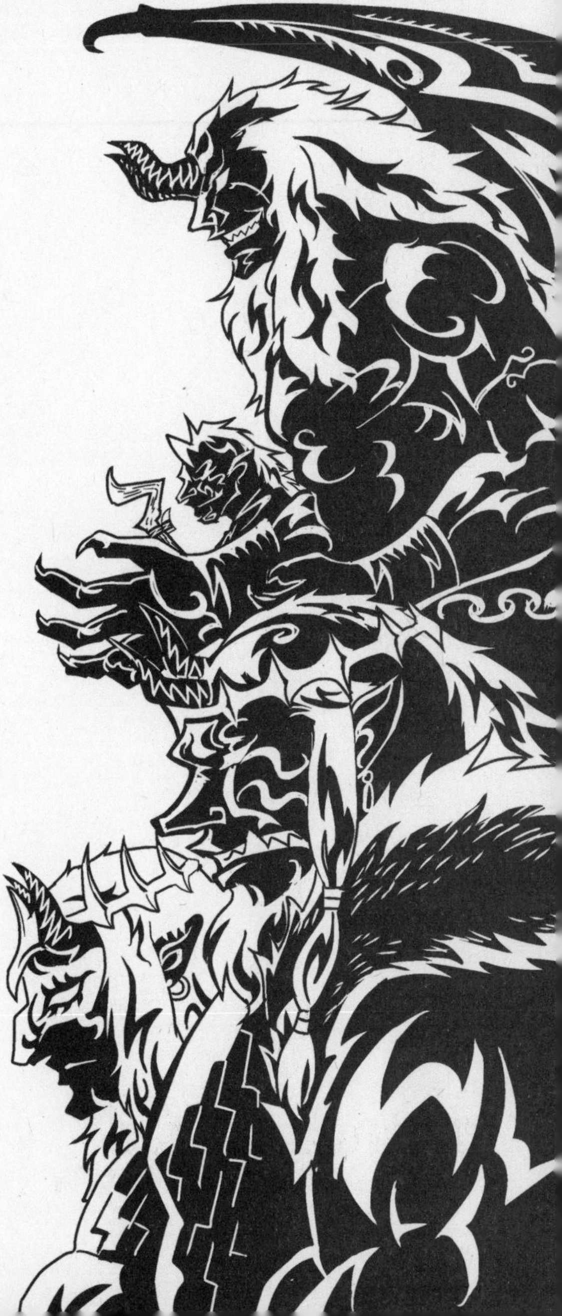

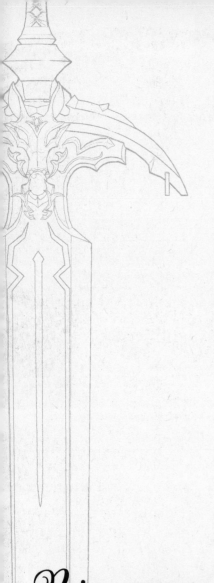

Reincarnated
as a sword

Reincarnated
as a sword